THE PROMISE AND PERIL OF THINGS

The Promise and Peril of Things

Literature and Material Culture in Late Imperial China

Wai-yee Li

Columbia University Press   New York

 This publication was made possible in part by an award from the James P. Geiss and Margaret Y. Hsu Foundation.

Columbia University Press wishes to express its appreciation for assistance given by the Chiang Ching-kuo Foundation for International Scholarly Exchange and Council for Cultural Affairs in the publication of this book.

Columbia University Press
Publishers Since 1893
New York   Chichester, West Sussex
cup.columbia.edu
Copyright © 2022 Columbia University Press
All rights reserved

Library of Congress Cataloging-in-Publication Data
Names: Li, Wai-yee, author.
Title: The promise and peril of things : literature and material culture in late imperial China / Wai-yee Li.
Description: New York : Columbia University Press, 2022. | Includes bibliographical references and index.
Identifiers: LCCN 2021041824 (print) | LCCN 2021041825 (ebook) | ISBN 9780231201025 (hardback) | ISBN 9780231201032 (trade paperback) | ISBN 9780231553896 (ebook)
Subjects: LCSH: Chinese literature—Ming dynasty, 1368–1644—History and criticism. | Chinese literature—Qing dynasty, 1644–1912—History and criticism. | Material culture in literature.
Classification: LCC PL229v6 .L465 2022 (print) | LCC PL2296 (ebook) | DDC 895.109/004—dc23/eng/20211122
LC record available at https://lccn.loc.gov/2021041824
LC ebook record available at https://lccn.loc.gov/2021041825

Cover image: *Antiques and Flowers: A Composition*, eighteenth century, Qing dynasty (Qianlong reign). Hanging scroll, double-sided *kesi* embroidery. Open Data, Palace Museum, Taipei, Taiwan.

Contents

Acknowledgments — vii
Abbreviations — ix

Introduction — 1

CHAPTER ONE
People and Things — 13

CHAPTER TWO
Elegance and Vulgarity — 81

CHAPTER THREE
The Real and the Fake — 158

CHAPTER FOUR
Lost and Found — 212

Epilogue — 278

Notes — 283
Bibliography — 331
Index — 353

Acknowledgments

Sabbatical leave from Harvard University and grants from the Guggenheim Foundation and the American Council of Learned Societies (2018–2019) facilitated the research and writing of this book. I gratefully acknowledge their generous support. The first half of chapter 4 is developed from an article I first wrote in Chinese, "Shibian yu wanwu," which was published in the *Journal of the Institute of Literature and Philosophy*, Academia Sinica (2008). Versions of the first two chapters were given as part of the Wang Meng-ou Lectures at the National Chengchi University (2019), the Ch'ien Mu Memorial Lectures at the Chinese University of Hong Kong (2019), and the Yip So Man Wat Lectures at the University of British Columbia (2021). I incorporated portions of chapter 3 in talks given at the Baptist University of Hong Kong, Academia Sinica (Taiwan), Rutgers University, and Stanford University. I thank colleagues in these institutions for their suggestions and questions, and for providing forums for stimulating intellectual exchange. Ellen Widmer read an earlier draft and offered encouragement and advice. Reviewers of the book for Columbia University Press gave helpful suggestions. I thank Christine Dunbar, Christian Pizzaro Winting, and Leslie Kriesel for steering the book through production, and Kangni Huang for compiling the index. The image on the cover is based on a piece of embroidery from the Qianlong era. I am grateful to the Palace Museum of Taipei for permitting its use. My family provides love and support, as always.

Abbreviations

CX	*Zhongguo gudai chaxue quanshu* 中國古代茶學全書, comp. Yang Dongfu 楊東甫. Guilin: Guangxi shifan daxue chubanshe, 2011.
CYL	Li Yu 李漁. "Cuiya lou" 萃雅樓. *Shi'er lou* 十二樓. In *Li Yu quanji* 李漁全集, 5:128–50. Hangzhou: Zhejiang guji chubanshe, 1998 (1992).
DQC	Dong Qichang 董其昌. *Dong Qichang quanji* 董其昌全集, ed. Li Shanqiang 李善強. 8 vols. Shanghai: Shanghai shuhua chubanshe, 2013.
HLM	Cao Xueqin 曹雪芹 and Gao E 高鶚. *Honglou meng bashi hui jiaoben* 紅樓夢八十回校本, ed. Yu Pingbo 俞平伯 and Wang Xishi 王惜時. 4 vols. Hong Kong: Zhonghua shuju, 1985.
JPM	Lanling xiaoxiaosheng 蘭陵笑笑生. *Jin Ping Mei cihua (Mengmei guan jiaoben)* 金瓶梅詞話（夢梅館校本）, ed. Mei Jie 梅節. 3 vols. Taipei: Liren shuju, 2007.
LDMHJ	Zhang Yanyuan 張彥遠. *Lidia minghua ji* 歷代名畫記, ed. Qin Zhongwen 秦仲文 and Huang Miaozi 黃苗子. Beijing: Renmin meishu chubanshe, 1983 (1963).

MLC	*Moling chun* 秣陵春. Wu Weiye 吳偉業. *Wu Meicun quanji* 吳梅村全集, ed. Li Xueying 李學穎, 3:1235–1387. Shanghai: Shanghai guji chubanshe, 1990.
QMC	Zhang Yingwen 張應文. *Qing mi cang* 清秘藏. In *Qing mi cang wai liu zhong* 清秘藏外六種. Shanghai: Shanghai guji chubanshe, 1993.
QMZ	Qian Qianyi 錢謙益. *Qian Muzhai quanji* 錢牧齋全集, annot. Qian Zeng 錢曾, ed. Qian Zhonglian 錢仲聯. 8 vols. Shanghai: Shanghai guji chubanshe, 2003.
QTS	Peng Dingqiu 彭定求 et al., comps. *Quan Tang shi* 全唐詩. 25 vols. Beijing: Zhonghua shuju, 1960.
Roy	David Tod Roy, trans. *The Plum in the Golden Vase, or Chin P'ing Mei*. 5 vols. Princeton, N.J.: Princeton University Press, 1993–2013.
SKQS	*Yingyin wenyuan ge Siku quanshu* 景印文淵閣四庫全書. Taipei: Shangwu yinshuguan, 1986.
TPGJ	Li Fang 李昉 et al., comps. *Taiping guangji* 太平廣記. Taipei: Shangwu yinshu guan, 1975.
WL	Shen Defu 沈德符. *Wanli yehuo bian* 萬曆野獲編. 3 vols. Beijing: Zhonghua shuju, 1997 (1959).
WMC	Wu Weiye. *Wu Meicun quanji*.
XQOJ	Li Yu. *Xianqing ouji* 閒情偶寄. In *Li Yu quanji*, vol. 11.
YHD	Yuan Hongdao 袁宏道. *Yuan Hongdao ji jianjiao* 袁宏道集箋校, ed. Qian Bocheng 錢伯城. 2 vols. Shanghai: Shanghai guji chubanshe, 1981.
YPX	Li Yù 李玉. *Yi peng xue* 一捧雪. In *Li Yù xiqu ji* 李玉戲曲集, ed. Chen Guyu 陳鼓虞, Chen Duo 陳多, and Ma Shenggui 馬聖貴, 1:1–103. Shanghai: Shanghai guji chubanshe, 2004.
YSZ	Jiang Shaoshu 姜紹書. *Yunshi zhai bitan* 韻石齋筆談. In *Zhibuzhu zhai congshu* 知不足齋叢書, first series, comp. Bao Tingbo 鮑廷博. 1872.

YZY	Li Yu. *Yizhong yuan* 意中緣. In *Li Yu quanji*, 2:317–418.
ZGSHQS	Lu Fusheng 盧輔聖, Cui Erping 崔爾平, and Jiang Hong 江宏, eds. *Zhongguo shuhua quanshu* 中國書畫全書. 14 vols. Shanghai: Shanghai shuhua chubanshe, 1993–2000.
ZSBJ	Gao Lian 高濂. *Zunsheng bajian* 遵生八箋. Chengdu: Ba Shu shushe, 1988.
ZWZ	Wen Zhenheng 文震亨. *Zhangwu zhi* 長物志, annot. Chen Zhi 陳植, ed. Yang Chaobo 楊超伯. Nanjing: Jiangsu kexue jishu chubanshe, 1984.
ZYZ	Chen Qinghao 陳慶浩, ed. *Xinbian Shitou ji Zhiyan zhai pingyu jijiao* 新編石頭記脂硯齋評語輯校. Taipei: Lianjing chuban gongsi, 1986.

THE PROMISE AND PERIL OF THINGS

Introduction

The ways we assign value to things define us. Arguably universal, this aspect of human experience is also rooted in cultural-historical contexts, once we start asking the question of how things become meaningful. The following anecdotes from a mid-seventeenth-century miscellany, *Speaking of the Past at Flower Village* (*Huacun tan wang*) by The Messenger Watching What Passes By at Flower Village (Huacun kan xing shizhe), give us glimpses into some extreme possibilities.[1]

CALAMITIES BROUGHT ON BY ANTIQUES

In the final years of the Wanli reign (1563–1620), there was a white Dingware censer in Loudong [in Jiangsu]. An old village woman used it to worship the Buddha—who knows how many generations had used it that way. One of its feet had a slight blemish. It so happened that a hunter of antiques bought it from her for a tael of silver. The old woman was overjoyed: this became the means to provide for her final years and funeral. The hunter of antiques cleaned the censer, polished the blemish, wrapped it in brocade, and sold it to the great Yunjian [in Jiangsu; it overlaps with present-day Shanghai] collector Gu Tinglin. Fulfilling his wildest hopes when he received 40 taels for it, he was even more elated than the old woman: this became the means to provide for an enjoyable life to the end of his days. Tinglin sold the censer to the minister Dong Qichang. As its value was properly judged, its price had soared to 120 taels. The minister was not too enamored of it, and after about a year of appreciative viewing he sold it to Xiang Yuanbian of Zuili [in Zhejiang] for 250 taels. Dong paid 100 taels to the middleman, whose entire family thrived because of it. When Cheng Jibai, an expansive gallant from Xin'an [in Anhui] proud of his connoisseurship, heard about it, he requested to see it. Xiang chose among several auspicious dates, put up curtains and brocade covers, and set forth superior wine and a magnificent feast, spending almost 100 taels. Jibai was entranced. Later he offered 800 taels for the censer. Xiang dawdled for quite a while before agreeing, and even then only sold it as a reluctant concession. Jibai took the censer to Suzhou and made its case with gems and jade, which he then wrapped in layers of Sichuan brocade. He brought it to the capital, taking great pride in the marvelous item. Jibai was an imperial secretary in the Wenhua Palace. When he entertained guests for appreciative viewing sessions, he always set up a table separately for the censer with layers of brocade cushion and embroidered screens, marking it as an object to be honored with supreme respect. He would not burn in it anything but famous incense from beyond the seas or extraordinary incense made inside the palace. Jibai gained the reputation of lofty spirit and refined sensibility because of the white Dingware censer. Only those in the most exalted circles or his closest kinsmen and friends gained glimpses of it. At that time the eunuch Wei Zhongxian and his ally Cui Chengxiu were at the height of their power. Wei Zhongxian wanted to see the censer. Jibai had always been on close terms with those in the Donglin league and proudly refused to come close to Wei.[2] Being also afraid that the censer, once sent in, would not come out again, he jealously guarded it. The eunuch was furious, implicated him in involvement with what the Eastern Depot branded as the treasonous faction, and imposed on him a prison sentence.[3] When guards on horseback came to arrest Jibai, he was just then facing the white censer, brushing the table and burning incense. Blows from cudgels and truncheons pelted down. The censer was dashed to smithereens at the steps. Jibai did not know that everything happened because of this thing. When Wei Zhongxian knew what came to pass, he ordered that the broken pieces be picked up. Looking at them carefully, he laughed out loud. Later Jibai was detained for a long time in prison and died there.[4]

A "hunter of antiques" could spot a broken censer used by a village woman to burn incense in front of Buddha's statue and identify it as valuable ceramic from the famed Ding kiln of Song dynasty (960–1279). Its worth could then exponentially increase as it changed hands. Its buyers became its history: their fame as collector and connoisseur affirmed its heightening value. Dong Qichang (1555–1636) was a scholar-official famous for his calligraphy and painting. Dong Qichang, Gu Tinglin (not to be confused with the great thinker and scholar Gu Yanwu [1613–1682], who had the sobriquet Tinglin), Xiang Yuanbian (1525–1590), and Cheng Jibai (d. 1626) were scholar-officials and literati acclaimed for their taste, connoisseurship, and impressive collections. Xiang Yuanbian died in 1590, before the temporal setting of the account in "the final years of the Wanli reign" (1610s) and Tianqi reign (1620–1627, when Wei Zhongxian [1568–1627] rose to power), so there is good reason to question the authenticity of this anecdote. However, Cheng Jibai's ownership of a rare white Dingware censer is confirmed in other reliable sources,[5] and stories of how the corrupt and powerful eunuch Wei Zhongxian brought about Cheng's downfall because Cheng refused to give up a prized possession were told elsewhere.[6]

Irrespective of whether its details are all historically verifiable, this story draws on recurrent tropes on the folly of the obsessive collector and the rapacity of powerful men.[7] One may infer from it the existence of a thriving and lucrative late Ming market for art and antiques, trace a web of transactions spanning Jiangsu, Zhejiang, and Anhui, consider the tenuous boundary between the art dealer and the literati connoisseur, or speculate on the relationship between literati identity and rising mercantile power. (Both Xiang and Cheng came from rich merchant families.) Beyond the sociocultural history of owning and appreciating art and antiques, we see a deeper concern with the arbitrariness of value and the dangers of attachment to things. The value of the Dingware censer seems to have risen because of its gem-studded case, brocade covers, the manner of transaction, and the elaborately staged settings for "appreciation sessions." While those who treat it as a commodity profit by it, the "expansive gallant" (literally, "the great knight-errant")—here defined as an unconventional person famed for his liberality or disdain for money—who believes in its worth and ostentatiously displays his aesthetic enjoyment and pride of possession dies because of it. Its cultural prestige promised a self-contained world of aesthetic absorption, yet it could not escape the destructive fury unleashed by those abusing power.

The story of the white Dingware censer is followed by an account of three jade cups that belonged to Emperor Huizong of Song (r. 1100–1126), whose artistic talent and passion for collecting and connoisseurship were enmeshed with misgovernment that led to the Jurchen conquest of North China.[8] "The first one was called 'Teaching the Son to Ascend to Heaven.' The second, 'Valor and Power on Eight Sides.' Both were pure white with a warm glow and carved with entwining dragons. The third one had a single dragon as handle. Finely carved flowers adorned its outside. Its twirling patterns and radiant whiteness exceeded the other two cups, although its numinous aura paled slightly in comparison." The scholar-official Zhu Dashao (1547 *jinshi*), a famous Yunjian collector, received them from his disciple. They were sold and redeemed and ended up in the possession of his cousin's adopted son, a student in the imperial academy. A prominent man from the clan of the student's adoptive mother coveted these jade cups, framed him in a lawsuit, and had him detained, implicitly demanding the cups as the price for his release. The student's wife, née Hu, was so angry that she wanted to destroy the cups but ultimately refrained from doing so. She addressed the cups: "I heard that when you were in front of the emperor, you were placed on a golden basin held high by kneeling attendants, filled with sweet dew and ambrosia, and presented with the accompaniment of songs and dance. Now I will use four coins to buy the cheapest wine, have slaves and maidservants sit on the floor and fill you to the brim with that, and let them make a show of drinking without permission. This is to diminish you." Forty years later, Hu's two sons had both attained the *jinshi* degree as top candidates in the capital examination. The prominent man's grandson was implicated in a case of treason. He returned the jade cups and was released through the intercession of Hu's two sons. "The senior lady [Hu] received the three cups and tearfully told her two sons: 'Forty years ago I already wanted to destroy them. Now they have come back to our family, but I will not let them bring calamity to our descendants.' By then her husband had long been dead. She brought out family-brewed wine, personally offered libation, wept as she told all to her husband's spirit tablet, and used each cup to again present offerings. With a loud clang, she smashed them beneath the steps."[9]

The usual plot of such stories would pit rightful ownership against lawless misappropriation and would end with the restoration of the lost treasure. Here ownership seems accidental, and destruction unexpectedly follows the restoration. These jade cups with proper names (likely based on words carved on them) are almost anthropomorphized. Hu vents her anger by creating a humiliating context to diminish the cups' exalted value. The drama she stages for their devaluation is almost a mockery of the extraordinary value they have accrued as imperial possession and as the objects whose transferal would determine the fate of her entire family. She addresses them as if they were human foes, reversing the usual association of anthropomorphization with intense attachment. The final smashing of the cups may seem like a wanton act of destruction, but it is also the logical conclusion of Hu's reasoning that rare and exquisite things become harbingers of calamity by inviting jealousy.

In the third and final story under this entry, Yan Shi, the son-in-law of the late Ming minister Wen Zhenmeng (1574–1636), the great grandson of the painter and calligrapher Wen Zhengming (1470–1559), discovered a Three Dynasties ritual vessel in a shop for tinware in the Wu area (Jiangsu) in the early years of the Qing dynasty (1644–1911). It was part of the loot that a military man, Cao Hu, obtained as he raided the Songjiang area (present-day Shanghai) during the Ming-Qing dynastic transition. Yan paid two taels for it and hid it in a secret chamber, planning to pass it on as "the hidden treasure for a hundred generations." But Yan was impoverished by a lawsuit three years later and sought to offer his antique vessel to the suing party, only to have it misappropriated by the middleman claiming to intercede on his behalf. In less than a year both the suing party and the middleman got into legal troubles, and the middleman's wife pawned the vessel, treating it as being no different from other tinware. Yan's discovery of the antique vessel could have been a "rescue mission," an act of recognition that restores meaning to a historical vessel and reaffirms ties with the past in the midst of political turmoil, and that is indeed a recurrent trope in writings about objects during the Ming-Qing dynastic transition.[10] Instead value seems subjective and arbitrary, and ownership is again presented as contingent and dangerous.

How do things become meaningful? How should their value be adjudicated? The rich and growing scholarship on Ming and Qing material culture has tried to answer the question in different ways. Historians and art historians have studied the production and consumption of things, the mechanisms of the market, and the relationship between taste and social distinctions.[11] Some scholars have focused on the experience of the materiality of things, their role as agents of pleasure, knowledge, or power.[12] Our understanding of literary texts has been augmented by precise and captivating descriptions of the things found in them,[13] which add new dimensions to the study of the representation of things as a literary choice of tropes and styles. Focusing on the perceptual horizons opened up by things and concrete sensory experience has led to new modes of defining meaning in a text.[14] The anecdotes related here can be meaningfully read in the light of these perspectives, but they may also pose questions beyond their purview by reminding us of the cultural and philosophical roots of the discourses on things: How do the worlds of aesthetic value and political power intersect? What does it mean to anthropomorphize a thing? How subjective or objective is value? What determines authenticity and aesthetic appeal? What does it mean to write such stories at specific historical moments, say in the wake of the fall of the Ming dynasty (1368–1644)?

These anecdotes are relatively reticent on the mindset of the owners—aside from the possessive pride and jealous enjoyment that motivate Cheng Jibai and Yan Shi—but there is no lack of contemporaneous writings on notions of taste, ownership, subjectivity, and memory in the discourses on things. Indeed, the period spanning the late sixteenth to mid-eighteenth centuries in China (i.e., late Ming to high Qing dynasty) is a particularly fruitful period for considering these questions because of its rich sources on material culture and its interest in recording the perception and experience of things. The fall of the Ming dynasty (1644) transformed the debates on the value of things. The political turmoil of the Ming-Qing dynastic transition heightened the appeal of an aesthetic existence bound up with the appreciation of things even as it stoked suspicion of its presumed connection with self-indulgence and irresponsibility, especially in historical retrospection on the final decades of the Ming dynasty. The late Ming commercial boom and the political disorder of dynastic transition thus bring into sharp focus the paradoxical concerns underlying the discourses on things. The boundaries between people and things can seem both self-evident and elusive. How can things be both external and internal? Elegance and vulgarity are apparently determined by both normative social codes and arbitrary flights of fancy. How can the meanings of things be both social and idiosyncratic? "The real thing" beckons as ideal even as the fascination with forgeries grows. Why is the real thing a seductive ideal even as it remains elusive or becomes expendable? The things that survive cataclysmic historical changes become both the confirmation of loss and its negation. How can one own what is irrevocably lost? How can the world of things be transformed into the space of refuge or resistance? These questions continue to reverberate in the eighteenth-century masterpiece, Cao Xueqin's (1715?–ca. 1763) *Honglou meng* (*The Dream of the Red Chamber* or *The Story of the Stone*), which is heir to not only late Ming sensibility but also its continuation and transformation in the crucible of cataclysmic collapse.

I begin by canvassing, in chapter 1, the recurrent terms defining the relationship between people and things (*wu* 物) in the Chinese tradition. Scholarship on late imperial material culture often focuses on contemporaneous materiality, consumption, and their implications for social distinctions. However, the richness and complexity of the Ming-Qing discourses on things can be properly understood only if we explore their historical roots and frame them in the context of long-standing debates about subjectivity and aesthetic value. By examining issues in philology, early thought, and intellectual history relevant for thinking about late imperial material culture, I hope to add another perspective to the prevailing emphasis on social consumption, mercantile trends, and status markers in the current discussion of the subject.

Talking about things reaches back to a cultural vocabulary with deep roots in the Chinese tradition. Further, the emergence and history of these terms clarify the issues at stake with their late imperial iterations.

For example, references to "things" multiply as the vocabulary of inwardness develops during mid- to late Warring States (ca. 4th–3rd c. BCE): the internalization of "myriad things" (*wànwu* 萬物) recurs as an image for conceptualizing interiority. The flowering of aesthetic thought in the Six Dynasties (3rd–6th c. CE) is marked by a new interest in "being moved by things" (*ganwu* 感物) and "giving form to things" (*tiwu* 體物). Moral self-examination relies on "the investigation of things" (*gewu* 格物). Agency and self-sufficiency are threatened by "taking pleasure in things" (*wánwu* 玩物) and superfluous things (*zhangwu* 長物).

Ruminations on things and the discourses on subjectivity and moral agency are thus intertwined in important moments in the history of Chinese thought. Chapter 1 takes stock of the philosophical reflections on the promise of mastery and transcendence through things, the specter of the dangerous pleasures of things, and the negotiation of boundaries between these two poles. It then turns to the late Ming discourse on obsessions and shows how it embraces a wide spectrum of attitudes that implicitly respond to the philosophical positions discussed in the first half of the chapter. This late Ming discourse in turn prepares us for exploring the idea of objectifying people and humanizing things in two masterworks of vernacular fiction, *Jin Ping Mei* (*The Plum in the Golden Vase*) and *Honglou meng*. Recalcitrant things resist sentimentalization and function in an economic system of transactions in *Jin Ping Mei*. Overwhelming materiality seems to be divorced from the workings of inner life: things can arouse envy or possessive desire but are rarely endowed with emotional, moral, or spiritual meanings. People are appraised in terms of market value and the potential for instrumentalization. At the same time there is fascination with, even compassion for, the frenetic energy driven by the appetite for things. A comparably close attention to things obtains in *Honglou meng*, but the sympathetic characters in the book, especially Baoyu and Daiyu, subscribe to the notion that the mind animates things and invests them with value. The vision of sentient and affective things responding to human will and desire promises freedom and power, yet it is often associated with alienation, death, and destruction. The fluid boundary between human beings and things may signal empathy and generosity of spirit, yet it can also erect new barriers and breed delusions.

The relationship between people and things takes us to the question of assigning value to things, the focus of chapter 2. The flourishing literature of connoisseurship (pertaining not just to art but to all aspects of literati existence) is often normative, even prescriptive, in tone. At the same time, taste can be expressed in whimsical or perverse ways. Notions of normative elegance and self-conscious elegance both have deep cultural roots. The tension and balance between normative system and individual difference unfold in manuals of taste, miscellanies, as well as accounts of the personal appreciation of things. Of all the terms of judgment, perhaps the pair most enmeshed in such considerations is elegance (*ya* 雅) and vulgarity (*su* 俗). Ruminations over their meanings and cultural boundaries raise new questions: What is the line between the refinement of good taste and the force of obsession? Is elegance compromised by self-consciousness? How can an object of appreciation be both commodity and anticommodity (inasmuch as true appreciation and the greatest worth are not measurable in economic terms)? Are elegance or vulgarity determined by affirming social consensus or challenging it? How do the fellowship and competition among connoisseurs drive the definition of elegance? Why are "elegant things" associated with nature and reclusion but also embedded in social relations among the rich and the powerful? Can good taste become bad taste, and vice versa?

Explored in manuals, miscellanies, and essays, these questions also take us to the fascination with vulgarity in *Jin Ping Mei*, the contradictions of elegance in "The House of Elegant Ensemble" (Cuiya lou), a story by Li Yu (1611–1680), and the implications of redefining elegance and vulgarity in *Honglou meng*. Literary instantiations like the vulgar connoisseur Ying Bojue in *Jin Ping Mei*, the self-conscious aesthetes of "The House of Elegant Ensemble," or the disdainful arbiter of taste, the nun Miaoyu in *Honglou meng*, turn the ideal of elegance into something desirable yet elusive, irrelevant, solipsistic, or dangerous by exploring its contextualization. In these examples, the social, economic, and political pressure as well as the moral conundrums that the discourse of elegance sets out to displace or repress often come back with a vengeance, even as the ideal of elegance retains its aura and elastic definition.

The discourse of elegance and vulgarity is inseparable from deliberations of authenticity, since a person's genuineness (or lack thereof) can problematize the elegance-vulgarity polarity, and good taste presumes the power to distinguish between the real and the fake, the focus of chapter 3. While mythologizing the aura of the authentic, the Ming-Qing cultural milieu also granted cultural authority to the forger, the copier, and the authorized delegate. Both the moralization of the distinction between the real and the fake and the refusal to moralize it raise questions on the meaning of artistic creation, connoisseurship as social practice, and the vagaries of the art market. Anecdotes, stories, and plays about authenticity and forgery proliferate during this period. What do they tell us about late Ming aesthetic and literary sensibility and their continuation or transformation in the Qing? Do forgeries, copies, and imitations lead to more general anxieties about the "fakeness" of people, social practices, or conventional morality? How does one establish the authority to distinguish the real from the counterfeit? What exactly is the aura of "the real thing"? What are the distinctions separating the forger from the copier or the authorized delegate? Do economic calculations compromise or justify aesthetic judgment? How do aesthetic judgment and moral judgment intersect and diverge in accounts that glorify the connoisseur's discernment or decry his perfidy and rapacity?

To consider these questions, I turn to anecdotes from miscellanies and two plays: Li Yù's (ca. 1610–after 1667) *An Offering of Snow* (*Yi peng xue*, ca. early 1640s, hereafter *Snow*), whose plot develops around a priceless jade cup and its counterfeit, and Li Yu's *Ideal Matches* (*Yi zhong yuan*, 1650s), which turns forgery into the medium for self-expression and romance.[15] In *Snow*, obsession over the nonpareil jade cup stokes errors of judgment and the abuse of power on a grand scale. The price of a fake cup is a substitute head: the real cup's owner, offering a counterfeit to a powerful minister, would have paid for the deception with his life but for a loyal servant willing to die in his place. Rightful ownership of the real thing is moralized through the discourse of absolute loyalty and self-sacrifice. By contrast, *Ideal Matches* celebrates the unstable boundaries between the real and the counterfeit, affirming economic calculations and transactional romance. In some ways, this economic model answers some of the ambiguities and contradictions in late Ming sensibility and social reality: the valorization of genuine self-expression coexists with a keen interest in expediency, compromise, and liminal solutions. The concern with the real and the fake, with genuineness and its contradictions, will gain new metaphysical dimensions with the dialectics of reality and illusion in *Honglou meng*.

Ruminations on the real and the fake are often premised on the inevitability of loss, thus Li Yu proposes the ideal match between the artist and the forger, the authentic work and the counterfeit in the aftermath of Ming collapse, when the historical counterparts of his protagonists are dead and the quest for the authentic seems in historical retrospection to be mired in late Ming self-indulgence. Chronicles of what is lost (i.e., things, and by implication time past) and what remains are common in the early Qing cultural landscape. There is a new pathos linking objects (even quotidian ones) to historical memory and moral or aesthetic meanings after the fall of the Ming dynasty. Both public and private symbolism gains new dimensions in this context. In the aftermath of Ming collapse, some objects from the Ming imperial palace resurfaced, inspiring lament and nostalgia and becoming emblems of Ming history or its final years of decline and fall. Writing about such objects became a way to articulate one's convictions or to defend one's political choices, and sometimes poetic exchanges on objects charted relationships in evolving socio-literary communities. Numerous early Qing poems, essays, and anecdotes develop these themes.

How do political upheaval and changing economic circumstances affect notions of ownership? How does the fall of the Ming discredit or bolster the figure of the collector and the connoisseur? How is the symbolic quotient of Ming imperial objects determined by the moral and political self-definition of their new owners? Summing up some of these issues, Wu Weiye's (1609–1672) play *Spring in Moling* (*Moling chun*, ca. 1650) articulates perspectives on historical memory and political accommodation through objects from a fallen dynasty. Set during the dynastic transition from Southern Tang (937–975) to Song (960–1279), it uses four objects from the Southern Tang court to tell a love story between scions of families with deep connections to the fallen dynasty. The historical memory embodied by objects dignifies or justifies their romantic-aesthetic associations, even as romantic love promises to save objects from the weight of history by introducing fantasy and elevating private life.

The trajectory of things, being lost or found, takes us to the economic, political, moral, and aesthetic meanings of ownership. Writing about a place or a thing and giving it a literary life may amount to a stamp of ownership. What is lost can be repossessed through memory, imagination, and the act of writing. Indeed, the beauty and allure of lost things can be heightened this way. The early Qing literature of remembrance often pays tribute to this idea. Invariably nostalgic and elegiac, it often seeks solace in recalling the particularities of things and their experience. Sometimes loss can also bolster the claim of critical retrospection. This duality of distance and immediacy in retracing personal and mediated memory and summoning a lost world through writing is reprised in *Honglou meng*.

The promise and peril of the world of things thus shape the trajectory of late imperial Chinese literature. The crisis of Ming collapse is a useful inflection point because the implicit counterpoint of an aesthetic existence—and in many cases the things we examined are beautiful and sensuous things that can be turned into constituents of an aesthetic existence—is often defined by the dangers and frustrations of political life. Intersections of the worlds of aesthetic appeal and political power help us rethink what determines authenticity, beauty, and value. The discourses of things define the claims of aesthetic existence in relation to its material basis, and the question is how such claims encode or resist social change, political crisis, and personal loss.

CHAPTER ONE

People and Things

The graph *wu* 物 appears as 𝕐 and 𝕎 in oracle bones and is used in relation to sacrificial creatures and objects.¹ According to Wang Guowei (1877–1927), it has etymological roots in the mixed-color bovine and by extension means mixed-color silks and "myriad different things."² Wang's attention to difference echoes the focus on multiplicity and inclusiveness in earlier discussions of the word by thinkers and exegetes through the ages. Our sensory perception confirms the multifariousness of things in *Zhuangzi* (ca. 4th–3rd c. BCE): "That which has form, shape, sounds, and colors are all things" (*Zhuangzi* 19.634). For *Xunzi* (3rd c. BCE), *wu* answers the need for categorical naming: "That is why although the myriad things are numerous, there are times when one wants to refer to all of them, hence we call it *wu*. *Wu* is the great common name" (*Xunzi* 22.315).

The Han lexicographer Xu Shen (d. ca. 147) glosses *wu* (物 in seal script, the script Xu was using) as "myriad things" or "myriad kinds of things": "The bovine is a great thing [in sacrifice]. The numbering of heaven and earth starts with the Cowherd Asterism; that is why it has 'bovine' as the constituent component. *Wu* 勿 [on the right] is the phonetic component."³ Xu Shen's reasoning may be historically inaccurate, but his conclusion summarizes the semantic range of *wu* in early texts. Qiu Xigui argues that *wu* on the right (𝕨 in seal script, 𝕩 in oracle bones, 𝕫 in bronze inscriptions) has etymological roots in and associations with notions of cutting, separating, and categorizing.[4] A word that can mean "anything" or "all things" needs a constituent component meaning "distinctions." In a later lexicographical text, Gu Yewang (518–581) simply states: "Everything that comes into existence between heaven and earth is called *wu*."[5] "Definition" may be a futile exercise for a word or concept with such elastic boundaries: it can refer to things, objects, categories, affairs, pursuits, matter, situation, scene, materials, creatures, human beings, nature, spirits, and even abstract entities like ideas, *yin*, *yang*, or the Way. While the discussion of the discourses on *wu* in this book pertains mostly to things and objects, it is important to remember the polyvalence of that word as it generates a rich and varied vocabulary defining human existence in relational terms. That lexicon is devoted to charting the relationship between people and things: it promises mastery and transcendence, warns of dangers, and negotiates the possibilities between these two poles.

MASTERY AND TRANSCENDENCE

Conceptions of human existence inevitably turn to the relationship between humans and the world of things. As one may expect, the word *wu* appears frequently in early Chinese texts, notably *Zuo Tradition* (*Zuozhuan*, ca. 4th c. BCE) and *Zhou Rituals* (*Zhouli*, ca. 3rd c. BCE), in discussions of ritual, encompassing specific prescriptions (e.g., things to be used as sacrificial offerings or diplomatic gifts, objects defining ranks and prerogatives) as well as categorical judgments of what constitutes ritually proper relations with the world. Somewhat more surprisingly, the metaphysical turn in Chinese thought also dwells on "things." The phrase "myriad things" began to appear from about fourth century BCE onward; it pertains to a widening and deepening conception of the multifariousness and mystery of existence, notably in *Laozi* (ca. 5th–3rd c. BCE) and the Xici commentary (5th–2nd c. BCE) in the *Classic of Changes* (*Yijing*, ca. 9th–2nd c. BCE).[6] At the same time, it also generates a discourse on ordering or transcending "myriad things" that is sometimes linked to conceptualizing interiority. References to *wu* multiply as the vocabulary of perception, understanding, and inwardness develops. Discussions of things and the discourses on agency, morality, and mental powers are thus intertwined.

The word *wu* appears proportionately more frequently in *Zhuangzi* than in any other pre-Qin texts, with the exception of *Laozi*.[7] It also offers more descriptions of the sensory perception of and affective connection with things than other texts, even as it contains numerous injunctions to transcend sensory reality. Things are declared to be inferior to the Way ("The Way has no beginnings and endings; things have lives and deaths") (*Zhuangzi jishi* 17.584), yet the Way is perceivable only through things ("it does not escape from things") (22.750).[8] "Knack stories" (A. C. Graham's term) present mastery of mundane tasks and crafts, such as Cook Ding's perfection of butchering skills (3.117–24), the hunchback's effortless success in catching cicadas (19.639–41), or the woodworker Qing's creation of a bell stand (19.658–59), as attainment of the Way. The world of things becomes instrumental for imagining mental and spiritual powers, and expanding interiority challenges the boundaries between the subject and his world. Mastering the oneness, difference, and transformations of myriad things is the path to transcendence in *Zhuangzi*: the Daoist sage "merges the myriad things to create oneness."[9]

This transformative power over myriad things is imagined as the "emptying out" of preconceptions and sensory perception. One of its most important metaphors is the "fasting of the mind" (*xinzhai* 心齋): "Do not listen with the ears but listen with the mind. Do not listen with the mind but listen with the vital energy. Listening stops with the ears; workings of the mind stop at correspondences. The vital energy is that which is empty and wait upon things. The Way alone gathers at emptiness. Emptiness is the fasting of the mind" (4.147–50). In *Zhuangzi*, "fasting of the mind" banishes the senses and mental processes and appeals to *qi* (vital energy), a force that seems both spiritual and material, to promise transcendence of the divide between inward power and external things: "When one follows ears and eyes to reach inward being while relegating to externality the workings of mind and knowledge, gods and spirits could come and find their resting place, how much more so human beings! This is the [fulcrum of the] transformation of myriad things" (4.150).

The mutual implication of emptiness and plenitude in "fasting of the mind" is a recurrent paradox in *Zhuangzi*. "Discourse on Making Things Equal" (Qiwu lun) in *Zhuangzi* begins with a master described by his disciple as having the appearance of "withered wood and dead ashes" (2.43–50). He declares that he has "lost himself" but proceeds to give the most vivid and compelling description of the sound of wind blowing through multifarious crevices in early Chinese literature. He calls this sound "the piping of earth" (*dilai* 地籟), analogous with "the piping of humans" (*renlai* 人籟) (music from instruments) and pointing to the "piping of heaven" (*tianlai* 天籟), the force that allows the other two kinds of "piping" to come into their own. The holes in a wind instrument, the supposed apertures in the heart, the crevices through which wind howls, the facilitating force that "lets each comes into its own" (2.45–50): all these are images of generation based on negation. To have "lost oneself" seems to be the precondition for heightened awareness of things and the disquisition of its meaning.

Being able to shift perspectives and see the myriad things as big and small, valuable and lowly, existent and nonexistent defines freedom of the spirit (17.577). In *Zhuangzi*, the discourse on "making things equal" (*qiwu* 齊物) turns "things" into components in a reasoning process that strives to overcome distinctions. We find, for example, declarative moments like this: "Heaven and earth are born with me; the myriad things are one with me" (2.79). Sometimes such rhetorical confidence yields to the celebration of fluid boundaries. Transcendence veers between dismissing the question of "what is there to wait for" (1.17) and embracing "[the state of] being empty and waiting upon things" (4.147). Things are instrumental for imagining the reversibility of subject and object. In one anecdote, a tree deemed useless by a carpenter appears to the latter in a dream: "Moreover, you and I are both things. Why indeed should we regard each other as mere things? You are but an aimless person approaching death, how can you know about the aimless tree!" (4.172). *Wu* as verb (to objectify, to regard as a thing) is both mastery and self-negation.[10] As the former, it is associated with metaphors of power and rulership: "He who is in possession of the land possesses a great thing. He who possesses a great thing cannot be regarded as a thing. To have a thing and not be regarded as a thing: that is why he can treat all things as [mere] things" (11.394).[11] But mastery is built on self-negation. "The one who regards things as things has no boundaries with things. And yet things do have boundaries, the so-called boundaries of things. This means that which has no boundaries moves to that which has boundaries; and that which has boundaries moves to that which has no boundaries" (22.752). As in many other passages in *Zhuangzi*, affirmation and negation, instrumentality and obstruction are intertwined.

Zhuangzi offers the idea of *you* 遊 (to roam, to wander, to play), a word suggesting movement and mediation, as the possible answer to this contradiction. The goal is to "ride things and let the mind roam, find a place in what cannot be avoided in order to nourish what is within" (4.160). To roam is to be grandly receptive and forgetful, to both embrace the multifariousness of things and to transcend attachment to them. The transcendent sage "roams in the realm where things cannot escape and coexists with all of them" (6.244); "roams where the myriad things begin and end" (19.634); "lets his heart roam at the beginning of things" (21.712). The most famous parable in *Zhuangzi* implicitly appeals to such notions of play, mediation, and movement: "Zhuang Zhou once dreamed he was a butterfly—joyous and carefree in being a butterfly. His heart's desires were fulfilled, and he did not know about Zhuang Zhou. All of a sudden he woke up; there he was, palpably and irrevocably Zhuang Zhou. He did not know whether he was Zhuang Zhou dreaming of being a butterfly, or a butterfly dreaming of being Zhuang Zhou. Between being Zhuang Zhou and being a butterfly there must be a difference. This is called the Transformation of Things" (2.111–12). Elsewhere in *Zhuangzi* the phrase "transformation of things" (*wuhua* 物化) is used to lament inexorable death and destruction (3.115, 13.462). But as the conclusion of the butterfly dream it is medial, aspiring not to the stasis of sameness (i.e., equating life and death, dreaming and waking states) but to the flux of encompassing opposites, thus linking it to the affirmation of "myriad transformations that know no limits" (6.244) and "the merging of myriad things to create oneness" (1.28).[12] It is the naming of a process that affirms continuity behind rupture and forgetfulness, bringing celebration of freedom for the spirit to the anguish of skepticism and mortality.[13]

The idea of roaming informs both subjective projection and "selfless" receptivity in later literary and aesthetic thought.[14] Thus Lu Ji (261–303) conjoins the Daoist vocabulary of spiritual purification with the image of roaming of the mind as the genesis of creation in "Poetic Exposition on Literature" (Wen fu):

其始也	Thus it begins:
皆收視反聽	Retraction of vision, reversion of listening,
耽思旁訊	Absorbed in thought, seeking all around,
精騖八極	My essence galloping to the world's eight bounds,
心遊萬仞	My mind roaming ten thousand yards, up and down.[15]

"Retraction of vision" and "reversion of listening" echo the abovementioned notion of "following ears and eyes to reach inward being" from *Zhuangzi*. In *Literary Mind and the Carvings of Dragons* (*Wenxin diaolong*, hereafter *Literary Mind*), Liu Xie (ca. 465–521) delineates the workings of imagination thus: "When thought takes form in wondrous ways, the spirit roams with things. The spirit abides in inner recesses, as intent and vital energy controls its workings; things follow the eyes and ears, as words and phrases manage their meanings."[16] The idea of "roaming" here suggests balance and mediation. The cadence of parallel prose posits two interlocking processes: moral purpose motivating the spirit and words giving form to the sensory perception of things.

Articulating the process and meaning of literary creation means taking stock of the world of things. Poetry is said to "articulate intent" (*yanzhi* 言志) in the *Documents* (*Shangshu*) and *Zuozhuan*.[17] The Mao Preface posits feelings stirred within and taking form in words. A closely related text, "Record of Music" (Yueji), a chapter in *Records of Rituals* (*Liji*, ca. 3rd c. BCE), adds the component of sensory reality in the process of affective response: music comes into being when human beings are "moved by things and stirred (literally, set in motion)." Being moved by things and giving form to them are juxtaposed with the articulation of intent in Six Dynasties literary thought.[18] Zhong Rong's (ca. 468–518) preface to his *Classification of Poetry* (*Shipin*) builds on the Mao Preface by incorporating the emphasis on external things in the "Record of Music": "The vital energy stirs things, and things move people. That is how innate nature and feelings are swayed and take form through dancing and chanting."[19]

The notion of responsive movement (to stir, to sway) and the potential loss of control it implies exist in balance or tension with the imperative of concentration and mastery. Thus in Lu Ji's "Poetic Exposition on Literature," the poet "looks upon myriad things and dwells on their multifariousness," lamenting falling leaves in autumn and being gladdened by soft branches in spring, but with inward clarity he seeks to "control myriad things with the tip of the brush."[20] Liu Xie in *Literary Mind* writes about "the heart being swayed" by "changes in the sensual reality of things": the act of literary creation is a response to "being summoned by the sensual reality of things"; to capture the spirit and delineate the form is to "follow things and turn with them."[21] At the same time, he emphasizes being rooted in the Way and the classics and uses the vocabulary of inner purification reminiscent of *Zhuangzi*.[22] The impetus of literary creation is thus not simply "responding to things"—it is a mutual engagement of mind and things that confirms meaningful patterns underlying both: "Emotions arise because of [the order of] things, that is why meanings have to be clear and proper"; "[the order of] things become observable because of emotions, that is why verbal expressions have to be clever and beautiful."[23] Both things and emotions are embedded in a system of affective correspondences: "Poets are moved by things and summon endless categorical correspondences."[24] Beyond individual control, correlative thinking, the notion that emotions correspond to patterns of temporal and spatial changes, adds implicit regulation to the potential instability of being "swayed" and "stirred" by external things.[25]

Whereas transcendence in *Zhuangzi* and the aesthetic thought it inspires are premised on overcoming the boundaries between the self and the world of things or celebrating their interaction, there is in the tradition a persistent discourse on things that emphasizes control. Among Warring States texts, *Xunzi* stands out in developing a vocabulary emphasizing mastery of things with verbs about fruition, instrumentalization, subjugation, regulation, rightful response, observation, order, knowledge, assessment, and distinctions, as suggested by terms such as *cai wanwu* 財(裁)萬物,[26] *jia yu wu* 假於物, *shengwu* 勝物, *yiwu* 役物, *guiwu* 規物, *dingwu* 定物, *wu zhi er ying* 物至而應, *liwu* 理物, *jiwu* 稽物, *quanwu* 權物, *guanwu* 觀物, and *bianwu* 辨物: all these formulations combine *wu* with a verb indicating control or active intervention.²⁷

In "Disquisition on Heaven" (Tianlun) in *Xunzi*, to fulfill human potential to its fullest is to regard heaven itself as a mere thing:

> To magnify heaven and to yearn for its meaning: how can that compare to treating heaven as a thing and controlling it!... To follow the nature of things and thereby multiplying them: how can that compare to giving full rein to one's mental powers to transform them! To yearn for things and regard them as things: how can that compare to ordering things and thereby not losing them! To pin one's hopes on that which generates things: how can that compare to possessing that which brings things to fruition! That is why to neglect human concerns and to yearn for heaven's meaning is to miss the truth of myriad things.
> (*Xunzi jianshi* 17.233–34)

The emphasis on human agency may be an implicit response to the preoccupation with omens, anomalies, and cosmic correspondences among contemporary political leaders and "petty Confucian scholars" who thrive by harping on such concerns (*Shiji* 74.2348).²⁸ Human resolve and success in creating ritual order depend on understanding, using, regulating, and mastering things. The phrase "myriad things" recurs in discussions of the expansive powers of the noble man or the ideal ruler to establish ritual order in *Xunzi*.²⁹ This ordering impetus in *Xunzi* is echoed in *Liji*, in which ritual is defined as "the standard of things" (*wu zhi* 物之致) (*Liji* 24.469) and that which "brings order to (*li* 理) myriad things" (23.449). The moral reasoning in *Xunzi* becomes the basis for the ritual ordering of things in *Liji*.

To conceptualize expanding dimensions of interiority, one needs recourse to the internalization of "myriad things" as metaphor. We see this already in *Zhuangzi*, but there is also ample evidence from the Confucian tradition. Thus *Mengzi* (4th c. BCE): "The myriad things are all encompassed within me. There is no greater joy than turning to oneself and finding one's sincerity fulfilled" (*Mengzi* 7A.4). Zhao Qi (d. 201) glosses "things" as "affairs" (*shi* 事) and "sincerity" (*cheng* 誠) as "truth" or "actuality" (*shi* 實): joy comes when one examines one's conduct and finds moral goals actually fulfilled.[30] Zhu Xi (1130–1200) explains "myriad things" as "the fundamentals of reason"—that means to look inward is to find reason already embedded there.[31] Both commentators (especially Zhu Xi) are trying to moralize the internalized "myriad things" as the kernel of inner moral nature. Mengzi, however, may be merely claiming that the perception and consciousness of myriad things provide the basis for self-reflection and the fulfillment of moral nature.

In *Xunzi*, the predominant concern with ordering and managing the world of things is also linked to inner truth and inner illumination: "Without sincerity, one cannot transform the myriad things" (*Xunzi jianshi* 3.28). The revelation, assessment, and regulation of myriad things depend on the proper, deliberate, and sustained cultivation of impartial understanding and concentration: "To be void of preconceptions, focused on oneness, and achieve quietude is called 'the great clear brightness,' whereby there is none among the myriad things that has form but is not revealed, none that is revealed but not ordered, none that is ordered but not find its proper place" (21.298). The image of emptiness may suggest an affinity with the "fasting of the mind" in *Zhuangzi*, but the reasoning cannot be more different. While the "fasting of the mind" banishes or transcends sensory perception and mental effort, in *Xunzi* mental focus builds discriminatory powers in processing sensory data and culminates in illumination ("the great clear brightness") that facilitates moral action.

In developing the moral reasoning behind the creation of ritual order, *Liji* also takes up the role of things in the process of self-cultivation, especially in the chapters "Great Learning" (Daxue) and "Doctrine of the Mean" (Zhongyong).[32] "Investigation of things" is the beginning of knowledge and the first of the famous eight steps in the programmatic striving toward moral perfection.[33] Moral self-cultivation posits continuities and analogies between the understanding of things and the fulfillment of moral nature in oneself and others. "Doctrine of the Mean" envisions full engagement with all things as self-completion and participation in a cosmic, generative process:

> One who is able to fully realize his inborn nature can thereby bring to full realization the nature of other people; one who is able to bring to full realization the nature of others is thereby able to bring to full realization the nature of all existing things; and

one who is able to bring to full realization the nature of all existing things can partake thereby in the transformative and generative process of Heaven and Earth. He who can partake in the transformative and generative processes of Heaven and Earth can stand, by virtue of this capacity, as a third term between them in the cosmic continuum.[34]

Neo-Confucianism takes up the oneness of things and the Way and emphasizes moral agency in "the investigation of things" as the cornerstone of self-cultivation. Zhu Xi's exegesis of "the investigation of things" as an act of understanding that "extends one's knowledge," "makes one's thoughts sincere," and "rectifies one's mind" emphasizes "coming to things and fathoming their reason for being" (*jiwu qiongli* 即物窮理): the moment of illumination comes when persistent effort results in "a sudden breakthrough to integral comprehension,"[35] whereby the infinite capacity of heart and mind seamlessly matches the infinite reasons for being of all things under heaven. Zhu Xi claims to be paraphrasing Cheng Hao (1032–1085), who indeed speaks of "sharing the same being with things, erasing distinctions."[36] In a similar vein, Zhang Zai (1020–1077) proclaims: "Enlarge one's mind and one can empathize with all things under heaven."[37]

The project of understanding and ordering things is inseparable from the elevation of moral and intellectual agency, the capacity of the heart and mind to overcome the boundaries of self and "become one with things." In discussing the ideal "observation of thing" (*guanwu* 觀物), Shao Yong (1011–1077) stipulates: "It means to not observe with the eyes but observe with the mind, to not observe with the mind but observe with reason." The highest kind of seeing, however, is that of the sage: he "reverses observation" (*fanguan* 反觀) and "can unify the truth of myriad things" by "observing things with things" (*yi wu guan wu* 以物觀物).[38] Again the point is ultimately to seek transcendence through overcoming the boundaries of self and things. The discourse on things thus becomes a discourse on the mind. There were manifestations of this development in Song thought, but it became especially prominent in the Ming. According to Wang Yangming (1472–1529), affective, intuitive interactions and correspondences bind the mind and the world of things. "Things" are but the objects of mental and emotional activities. "To investigate things is to investigate things in one's mind, to investigate things in one's thoughts, to investigate things as objects of one's knowledge. To rectify one's mind is to rectify the mind of things. To make one's thoughts sincere is to make the thoughts of things sincere. To extend knowledge is to extend the knowledge of things. How can there be any distinction of inside and outside, self and other in this!"[39] We come to the point when the mind animates all things. This idea is perhaps best encapsulated in one of Wang Yangming's poems, where he turns sentient nature, a common trope in poetry, into a philosophical statement. Birds and fish privy to the truths of the Way in the second couplet— "Hidden fish under water transmit the mind's secrets, / Roosting birds on the branch tell of the Way's truth" 潛魚水底傳心訣，棲鳥枝頭說道真— are followed by two lines affirming the continuity between the self and myriad things, between the experiences of the self and the highest truth: "Do not say that the secrets of Heaven are different from desires, / Let it be known that the myriad things are my body" 莫謂天機非嗜欲，須知萬物是吾身.[40]

PLEASURES AND DANGERS

The language of mastery, receptivity, internalization, and transcendence in references to things in the previous section strives toward the triumph of mind over matter. But there is also a plethora of references to the dangers of things. Things beckon as sensual reality, and ungoverned responses signify loss of control. Thus *Mengzi*: "The organs of eyes and ears do not think but are deceived by things. When things [like eyes and ears] entangle with things, they can only be pulled along [and become lost]" (*Mengzi* 6A.15). Xunzi declares (perhaps quoting an older saying): "The noble man drives things. The petty man is driven by things" (*Xunzi* 2.15). A similar logic obtains in *Guanzi* (ca. 4th–1st c. BCE): "The sage regulates things and is not driven by things" (*Guanzi* 37.647); "The noble man uses things and is not used by things" (49.777). *Zhuangzi* warns of "the burden of things" (*wulei* 物累), reiterates the imperative to "not let things wear down one's will" and "not let things harm oneself," and draws a contrast between the power to "treat things as things" (*wu wu* 物物) and "being turned into a (mere) thing by things" (*wu yu wu* 物於物) (*Zhuangzi jishi* 13.462, 12.407, 17.588, 20.668).

The dangers of things arise when the calmness of innate moral nature is disturbed by the stirring of desire as one is "moved by things" (*gan yu wu* 感於物). This vision is powerfully articulated in the "Record of Music":

> Humans are born calm: this is their heaven-endowed nature. They are stirred when being moved by things: these are the desires of nature. Things come and the conscious mind becomes aware of them, and inclinations and aversions take shape. When inclinations and aversions are not regulated within, when consciousness is enticed by external things, and when self-examination fails, heavenly principles are extinguished. For things can move human beings in countless ways, and if the likes and dislikes of humans are not regulated, then things draw nigh and humans are transformed by things. To have humans being transformed by things means that heavenly principles are extinguished as human desires are pushed to their limits."
> (*Liji zhushu* 19.666)

This idea—summarized as "consciousness being enticed and transformed by things" (*zhiyou wuhua* 知誘物化)—is to become important in the writings of Song Confucian scholars.[41]

"To seek pleasure in things is to lose one's will" (*wanwu sangzhi* 玩物喪志). Such is the dire warning from one of the later strata in *Shangshu*.[42] The occasion is a Zhou minister's remonstrance with King Wu of Zhou (r. ca. 1122–1115 BCE) regarding the potentially baleful effects of a hound sent as a tributary gift from the western domain of Lü. In the context of the chapter, the tributary gift comes in the wake of the Zhou conquest of Shang and hints at dangerous hubris.[43] Classified as an "exotic thing" and "a thing from afar," held up in contrast to "useful things," the hound from Lü belongs to a discourse disparaging extravagance, curiosity, and sensual indulgence in early China. Pleasure always invites suspicions, and opprobrium extends to the connoisseurs. Thus Yiya, said to have masterful discernment of taste in *Mengzi* (6A.7) and *Xunzi* (*Xunzi* 27.387), morphs into a sinister figure willing to kill his son and serve him as a choice dish to his ruler, Lord Huan of Qi, to curry favor in various Warring States and Han texts, including *Han Feizi* (3rd c. BCE), *Guanzi*,

Huainanzi (139 BCE), *Lüshi chunqiu* (ca. 239 BCE), and *Shiji* (2nd–1st c. BCE), where he is blamed for Lord Huan's inglorious end.[44]

An object does not have to be exotic to threaten political order. The issue is the attitude toward the object in question. The words for inclination, passion, or obsession (*shi* 嗜, *hao* 好) are often associated with negative consequences and the need for regulation in early texts. In *Zuozhuan* (ca. 4th c. BCE), for example, one ruler's obsession with cranes leads to disaster: "In winter, in the twelfth month, the men of Di attacked Wei. Lord Yi of Wei was obsessed with cranes, and there were cranes that rode in the dignitary's carriage. When they were about to do battle, those from among the inhabitants of the capital who had been issued armor said, 'Send the cranes! If it is the cranes who hold salary and rank, then how can the likes of us go to fight?'"[45] Wei predictably suffers a crushing defeat. Chinese history offers memorable examples of the disastrous consequences of mixing power and obsessions. One of the most notorious cases is the miscreant minister Jia Sidao (1213–1275), who authored the *Classic on Crickets* (*Cuzhi jing*) and is said to have been crouching on the ground with his concubines absorbed in cricket fights as the Song dynasty was crumbling (*Songshi* 474.13784).

Jia Sidao's wayward passion echoes the Tang emperor Xuanzong's (r. 712–756) interest in cockfights (remembered as one of the omens of Tang decline)[46] and will be repeated by the Ming emperor Xuanzong (r. 1425–1435), whose obsession with crickets caused national furor as officials vied to submit superior specimens.[47] But Jia Sidao was more than a master of trivial pursuits. He was also a collector and connoisseur of calligraphy, paintings, ancient vessels, curios, and artifacts. Do objects replete with the aura of aesthetic significance, cultural authority, and historical continuity legitimize mental preoccupation? Apparently not, since the literature of connoisseurship contains many cautionary tales against the accumulation of such treasures: power enables the creation of great collections, but they can also mark moral failure or presage destruction.

In a section on "The Fortunes of Paintings" in his *Record of Famous Paintings Through the Ages* (*Lidai minghua ji*, hereafter *Famous Paintings*), the scholar and painter Zhang Yanyuan (ca. 815–after 875) describes how fatuous attachment to art collection is often part of a narrative of the downfall of the powerful. Huan Xuan (369–404), a powerful minister briefly ascendant and poised to seize power in the waning years of the Jin dynasty (265–420), was an avid and rapacious collector and at one point obtained the finest specimens from the Jin imperial collection. He traveled with his treasures and artworks in a light boat, being prepared to escape with them in case he suffered reversals in battle: "What with the dangers of warfare, if anything untoward happens, one should make transportation easy on a light vessel" (*Jinshu* 99.2592). This very arrangement might have undermined morale and contributed to his defeat. After Huan Xuan's downfall, his collection was carted away by Liu Yu, who became Emperor Gaozu of Song (r. 420–422).

Huan Xuan is remembered in official historiography as a usurper, and jealous possessiveness conjoined with tenuous ownership may be some sort of analogy for political illegitimacy. Zhang Yanyuan gives other examples of how immersion in the creation and collection of art becomes the marker of dynastic decline. Emperor Wu (r. 502–549) and Emperor Yuan (r. 552–555) of Liang built an impressive collection, which went up in flames during Hou Jing's (503–552) rebellion. Whatever remained of the collection was taken to Jiangling, which fell to the siege by the Western Wei general Yu Jin (493–568).

> When Emperor Yuan was about to surrender, he collected two hundred and forty thousand scrolls of famous paintings, calligraphy, and books and sent the palace official Gao Shanbao to burn them. The emperor wanted to throw himself into the conflagration and perish with them, and he was only spared because his consorts grabbed him by his clothes. He broke two precious swords from Wu and Yue by hacking the pillars with them and sighed, "That I, Xiao Shicheng, should have come to this! The way of learning and refinement comes to an end tonight!"[48]

The tragic pathos behind this wanton destruction and would-be martyrdom points to collapsing boundaries separating personal, political, and aesthetic categories. The emperor's impulse to perish with his collection seems to unveil in the most dramatic fashion one of the reasons behind the doom looming over himself, his collection, and the dynasty. Zhang Yanyuan also describes how Emperor Yang of Sui (r. 605–618), often represented as a stereotypical pleasure-loving last emperor, brought his collection along during his pleasure tour to Yangzhou in 616. When the boat containing his prize possessions capsized, we are given to understand that the disaster presages Sui downfall and might have been a providential warning against excessive attachment to things (*LDMHJ* 7).

The Liang emperor's tragic fate is repeated by the last ruler of the Southern Tang, Li Houzhu (Li Yu 937–978, r. 961–975), who is also said to have given orders to burn his collection of artworks, books, and treasures when Southern Tang fell to the siege of Song troops.[49] As a regional power holding out against Song unification, the Southern Tang never had much chance of survival, but in historical memory and popular imagination, the fall of the Southern Tang came to be intertwined with Li Houzhu's poetic talent, aesthetic sensibility, and pride in his collection. Li Houzhu's treasures became part of the Song palace collection, which was vastly expanded under the aegis of the Song emperor Huizong (r. 1101–1126).[50] The catalogs of calligraphy, painting, and antiquities in Huizong's collection (*Xuanhe shu pu*, *Xuanhe hua pu*, *Xuanhe bogu tu*), chronicling works that are mostly no longer extant, yield insights into its richness.[51] Patricia Ebrey argued that Huizong amassed his collection "to revive the image of the emperor as a patron of culture" and possibly to improve emperor-literati relations.[52] Perception of Huizong in historiography and literature, however, harks back to warnings about the disastrous conjunction of aesthetics and politics. The negative appraisal of his activities as collector and connoisseur is also tied up with the construction of the Genyue Garden (1117–1127).[53] Huizong's reign ended with the Jurchen conquest of Song territories north of the Huai River and the captivity of Huizong, his son the emperor Qinzong, imperial clansmen, consorts, and palace ladies. *History of the Song* (*Songshi*) ties "seeking pleasure in things" with political disaster and concludes categorically: "Ever since ancient times, when rulers seek pleasure in things and lose their will, indulge their desires and subvert proper standards, their downfall is inevitable. Huizong was an extreme example of this, [and] that is why we have emphasized it as a warning" (22.418).

Daoist and Buddhist teachings urge nonattachment to things as the prerequisite of freedom or enlightenment. The injunctions against indulging in the "pleasures of things" become ever broader in application in the Song Confucian discourse of moral self-cultivation, so much so that literary composition, mastery of historical details, or even exegesis of canonical classics can come under its rubric. The reasoning is that mental fixation easily detracts from greater moral and metaphysical goals. Thus Cheng Yi (1033–1107) opines: "In all cases of literary endeavors, one cannot excel without focusing one's mind. Yet to focus one's mind is to limit one's goal to this—how then can one be as great as heaven and earth?. . . To engage in literary endeavors is to 'seek pleasure in things.'"[54] By the same logic, his brother Cheng Hao chided Xie Liangzuo (1050–1103), who took pride in committing historical texts to memory, with the same phrase.[55] Even compiling a volume of quotations from the Five Classics earned Xie the same reproach from Cheng Hao.[56] Such statements should not be taken as proof that Cheng Hao disparaged learning culled from dynastic histories and canonical classics or that Cheng Yi categorically negated literature.[57] Rather the reasoning is that no matter how exalted the "thing" in question, a mental attitude linked to "seeking pleasure" (*wan* 玩) can potentially descend to frivolity, vanity, and self-absorption. The exchange between Cheng Hao and Xie Liangzuo came up frequently in sixteenth- and seventeenth-century writings, when stern moralists set broad definitions for "seeking pleasure in things."[58] The unforgiving stringency of Cheng Hao's judgment made it an interesting limit case for weighing the expectations for self-cultivation and the place of pleasure in an age when ever-finer attention to mental processes in moral self-examination was matched by contemporary extravagance in material culture and heightening attention to the perception and experience of things.

NEGOTIATING BOUNDARIES

By now it should be obvious that the positive and negative appraisals of the relationship between people and things sometimes draw from the same conceptual categories. Thus experiencing and contemplating "the transformation of things" (*wuhua*) in *Zhuangzi* celebrate the freedom of the spirit, but the idea of erasing boundaries between self and other is seen in the "Record of Music" as the collapse of inner moral balance as the self is "transformed by things."[59] That dire outcome originates in how things stir human beings, but "being moved by things" (*ganwu*) is also the beginning of music and poetry, a point elaborated in the "Record of Music" and later literary thought, as we have seen.

The matrix of "being moved by things" spans positive meanings of cosmic generation and moral transformation and negative implications of temptation and deviance. Hexagram 31, Reciprocity (Xian 咸), in the *Classic of Changes* exemplifies the positive pole of this semantic range.[60] It is explained as the mutual stimulation and generation of the forces or vital energy embodying hardness and softness: "Heaven and earth move each other and the myriad things come into being; sages move human hearts and there is peace all under heaven. Observe what is being moved, and the truth of heaven, earth, and the myriad things can be revealed."[61] Literary and aesthetic thought drawing on the stimuli-response model often implicitly appeals to these associations with cosmic generation and moral transformation as defense and justification. On the negative side, being moved by things is related to being overwhelmed by external stimuli and the loss of moral focus. "What undermines one's ability to firmly hold on to the principle of oneness is the state of being moved by things": as explanation of this line from *Lüshi chunqiu* (25.1652), Gao You (early 3rd c.) glosses *gan* 感 as *huo* 惑 (to be confused).

The semantic range of *ganwu* is by no means an isolated example. The term *wanwu* ("to savor things" or "to seek pleasure in things"), whose negative implications were explained earlier, also has a positive dimension. The word *wan* ("to play with," "to toy with," "to appreciate," "to concentrate on") can be used affirmatively in accounts of moral self-cultivation. According to Cheng Yi, "one has to fully savor (*wanwei* 玩味) the sage's aura" to learn the sage's way.[62] Cheng Hao eulogized Shao Yong's moral self-cultivation as "letting his heart savor what is highest and brightest (*wan xin gaoming* 玩心高明)."[63] Cheng Hao's approach to the *Classic of Poetry* (*Shijing*) is described as "leisurely savoring"; he disregarded philological details and emphasized chanting and intuitive understanding.[64] Zhu Xi introduces the valence of pleasure to his exegesis of the *Analects* (7.6): "Set your goal on the Way, steadfastly hold on to virtue, adhere to humaneness, and roam freely in the arts." About this last phrase, Zhu Xi explains:

> To "roam freely" means to "seek pleasure in things to accommodate one's feelings" (*wanwu shiqing* 玩物適情). As for "the arts," the refinement of ritual and music, the rules of archery, horsemanship, writing, and mathematics are all repositories of ultimate principles

indispensable for daily use. To roam freely therein morning and evening is to broaden the pleasure of reason and principles—one can then have more than enough wherewithal to deal with all affairs and one's heart will have no reason to be let loose and to go astray.[65]

The path to sagehood is presented as natural and pleasurable through the image of "roaming" and "serene immersion" (*hanyong congrong* 涵泳從容).[66] The doubleness of the word *wan* is rooted in the ambivalence about pleasure, which is perceived as distracting and dangerous but also essential to moral self-cultivation. Confucius may complain about the dearth of people that "love virtue" in comparison with the hordes that "love sensual beauty" (*Analects* 9.18), but the comparable mental act of focus also promises a kind of continuity: "To know something [the Way] is not as good as to love it, to love it is not as good as to find joy in it" (6.20). The idea that virtues have sensual appeal is implicit in the canonical classics, where "bright virtue" is said to move the spirits by its "fragrance."[67]

Different interpretations of terms like *wuhua*, *ganwu*, and *wanwu* suggest that there is room for negotiation, equivocation, and rhetorical maneuver in presenting the relationship between people and things. Of course, the object of attention also makes a difference. The scholar-official and poet Ouyang Xiu (1007–1072) was unapologetic about collecting the rubbings of stone inscriptions, describing them as "the most bizarre and extraordinary, majestic and striking, skillfully crafted, and delightful of material things"[68] and declaring his intention to "grow old seeking pleasure in them."[69] Aesthetic pleasure in antique calligraphy is justified as the preservation of traces from the past.[70] Ancient vessels easily rank high by holding out the promise of a tangible connection with the foundations of ritual order. Song antiquarian interest led to a systematic study of Shang-Zhou bronze vessels, whose appreciation links sensual appeal to moral suasion. The painter and scholar-official Li Gonglin (1049–1106) made that justification in his *Illustrated Investigation of Antiquity* (*Kaogu tu*, 1086–1092), which is no longer extant but whose argument is summarized in Zhai Qinian's (mid-12th c.) *History of Ancient Scripts* (*Zhou shi*):

> Sages created vessels and elevated images, using them as a vehicle for the Way and handing down warnings. They lodged

untransmitted marvels in the midst of vessels as a gift to posterity, so that those of broad understanding can seek the images by coming to the vessels and seek the meanings by coming to the images, grasping in their hearts and seeing with their eyes the principles behind investing meanings in things.... day and night they can contemplate unspoken mysteries.... How can these be merely vessels for pleasing the eyes of those dazzled by beauty and covetous of pleasure![71]

Li's *Illustrated Investigation of Antiquity* has a tangible influence on later works, including Lü Dalin's (1046–1092) eponymous text (1092). Lü was Cheng Yi's disciple and made a conscious effort to link his study of bronzes to his interest in ritual.[72] Refuting the argument in *Zhuangzi* that the classics are but "the dregs of the ancients," Lü defends "old traces" as the tangible means for seeking the moral principles whereby those traces took form. He disclaimed any intention of "using the vessels for sensual appreciation"; instead they would become the medium whereby "his understanding meets the intent of the ancients, perhaps reaching back to the original context of their creation, supplementing what is missing or lost in the classics and their commentaries, and correcting the errors of various scholars."[73] There were numerous Ming and Qing reprints of Lü's work as well as Wang Fu's comprehensive catalog of the bronze vessels in Emperor Huizong's collection (1123). Versions of the arguments by Li Gonglin and Lü Dalin appear in the writings of Yuan Haowen (1190–1257), Jiao Hong (1540–1620), Gu Yanwu (1613–1682), Tang Zhen (1630–1704), and Yao Jiheng (1647–ca. 1715), among others.[74]

The moral and political meanings of ancient ritual vessels set them apart as a category of things whose appreciation is easy to justify. In most cases, to counter the critique of excessive attachment, one needs to claim to maintain a balance between attachment and detachment. In "The Ling Stream Rock" (Ling xi shi ji, 1046), Ouyang Xiu wrote about moving a gigantic and curiously shaped rock, a remnant from the estate of the late ninth-century military commander Liu Jin, to the side of the Abundant Joy Pavilion (Fengle ting), which he built when he was exiled to Xuzhou in 1045.[75] "When it comes to the wondrous among things, it is a pity to have it abandoned in hidden wilderness. But if it is placed where it can be seen, those who love it cannot help but take it away." Ouyang Xiu places the rock by the pavilion next to the city wall, a favorite site of excursion for the town's inhabitants. By moving the rock, he commemorates the bygone strivings of Liu Jin, offers a warning against excesses and the fatuous belief in permanence, and celebrates communal pleasures. Ouyang Xiu concludes: "When lovers of wonders hear about this rock, they can be content with one act of appreciation. Why would it be necessary to take it away?" Optimal appreciation of things requires the purging of possessiveness.

Su Shi articulates a similar reasoning in "Account of the Hall of Treasured Paintings" (Baohui tang ji, 1077), which he wrote at the behest of his friend, the artist, collector, scholar-official, and imperial son-in-law Wang Shen (ca. 1048–ca. 1104): "A gentleman can let his mind linger awhile on things, but he cannot let his mind fixate on things. If the mind lingers awhile on things, then even the tiniest thing is enough to bring pleasure and even the most bewitching thing is not enough to cause harm. If the mind fixates on things, then even the smallest thing is enough to cause harm and even the most bewitching thing is not enough to bring pleasure."[76] Attitudes of mind, rather than the object in question, determine our relationship with the world of things. Laozi disparages sensual pleasures, but the sage does not negate them, so as to "have the wherewithal to let their minds linger awhile." Su Shi then substantiates this idea with examples of heroic and defiant characters apparently absorbed in trivial pursuits: Liu Bei (161–223) braiding horse hair, Ji Kang (223–262) forging iron, and Ruan Fu (ca. 278–ca. 326) waxing clogs. To linger (as distinct from staying) is not merely a matter of shorter temporal duration; it implies a higher purpose and ultimate control.

In the scheme of things, calligraphy and paintings are supposed to afford pleasures that edify. "When it comes to delightful things that are enough to please people but not to divert them from the right way, none compares to calligraphy and painting" ("Baohui tang ji"). But even calligraphy and painting can become the harbinger of disasters for those obsessed with mastery or possession. Su Shi offers well-known examples of follies stemming from such obsessions: Zhong Yao (151–230), who robbed a grave to obtain a masterpiece of calligraphy; Emperor Xiaowu of Song (r. 453–464), whose petty competition with Wang Sengqian (425–485) over specimens of calligraphy overshadowed affairs of state; the military commander Huan Xuan, who loaded his war-boat with prized possessions and suffered shameful defeat (an example mentioned earlier); the Tang minister Wang Ya (764–835), who hid masterpieces of calligraphy and painting inside thick walls only to witness their inevitable plunder. Su Shi then tells of his own path toward an optimal relationship with calligraphy and painting. He started out being possessive, but, recognizing jealous and acquisitive ownership as deviant and irrational, he reasons his way to a more detached attitude. "When I see delightful examples, even though I still often keep them, I no longer feel regret when they are taken away by others. It is just like mist and clouds passing in front of my eyes or numerous birds pleasing my ears: how can I not receive them gladly? But once they are gone, I no longer hanker after them. Thus these two things constantly bring me pleasure but cannot cause me harm" ("Baohui tang ji"). What does it mean to offer dire warnings about possessiveness in response to an implicit appeal to write a celebratory essay? Wang Shen was reportedly not pleased with references to historical examples of fatuous owners, but Su refused to make changes. Does the remonstrance about paintings and calligraphy mask graver admonitions? Su Shi claimed that art collecting was Wang's only weakness, describing him as an otherwise abstemious person who banished sensual pleasures, but various sources indicate otherwise.[77] Was he delivering a subtle criticism of Wang's taste, inasmuch as acquisitiveness has no necessary connection with discernment?[78] Was Su Shi consistent about sublime detachment to things? The calligrapher, painter, and collector Mi Fu (1051–1107) claimed that Su Shi borrowed an inkstone from him and liked it so much that he wanted to be buried with it.[79] In 1090, when Wang Shen asked to borrow Su Shi's "Qiu Pool Rock," Su wrote a playful poem to preemptively forestall Wang's design to "seize" rather than merely borrowed the treasured rock, suggesting an improbable exchange of the rock for Wang's prized paintings. Other friends chimed in with their poems; one suggested the fantastic solution of destroying both the rock and the paintings to overcome vain attachment.[80] Does the self-dramatizing mood of mock-heroic jocularity in these poetic exchanges belie the supposed competition for ownership?

The Qiu Pool Rock remained in Su Shi's possession. When he saw a rock at Hukou in 1094, he called it "Nine Blossoms in a Gourd" and wanted to buy it for a hundred taels so that it could be "a companion to the Qiu Pool Rock."[81] The purchase did not materialize. In 1101, when he passed by Hukou again, someone had bought that rock. The mournful poem he wrote about this links the missed connection to the vicissitudes of his life: "The extraordinary thing is already gone, along with the vain dream" 尤物已隨清夢斷. (The phrase "extraordinary thing" [*youwu* 尤物] is also used to describe a woman of bewitching beauty.) What is the difference between Su Shi's attachment to the rock and Wang Shen's pride in his art collection? Su might have said in self-defense that, unlike Wang Shen, who seems to have been led by conventional judgments, his fondness for the rock is defiantly idiosyncratic; like the eccentric pursuits of Ji Kang and Ruan Fu, it is but a way to express his higher purpose and uncompromising spirit.[82] The issue here is not so much whether Su Shi's philosophy of simultaneous enjoyment and detachment can be consistently sustained but rather that it is inherently unstable: detachment as stasis would mean attachment to the idea of detachment; meaning-making in notions of control and purpose behind "letting the mind linger" easily becomes empathetic identification that erodes detachment.

Su Shi's "Account of the Hall of Treasured Paintings" is a recurrent reference point in later periods. The idea that an optimal balance of appreciation and detachment vis-à-vis aesthetic objects encourages rather than undermines moral self-cultivation recurs in the Ming-Qing literature of connoisseurship. *Thirteen Points About Antiques and Objets d'art* (*Gudong shisan shuo*, 1621), a treatise attributed to Dong Qichang (1555–1636),[83] claims that connoisseurship is the privilege of "worthy men": "Antiques and objets d'art are the playthings of our time. Only worthy men can love them without pitfalls."[84] Cautious and abstemious men regard these as "useless things" and dismiss them because of their own vulgar limitations, while greedy ones vie for them and guard them jealously as commodities. By contrast, the author depicts the true connoisseur's temperament and mode of operation: "If a person can put himself in the space of ease and leisure, keep his mind on learning, and understand the beginnings and endings of things, then in responding to things he would not lose the balance between big and small, trivial and important, nor would he miss the functional application of constancy and expediency. He can thus see the Way by drawing close to things (*ji wu jian dao* 即物見道), consolidate the Way through learning, and distinguish its aspects through questions. His progress cannot be fathomed!"[85]

There are Song authors who elevated the moral significance of connoisseurship (e.g., Zhao Xigu [*jinshi* 1190], *Dongtian qinglu ji*), but the theme became much more prevalent in Ming writings. Seeking pleasures in things is said to manifest, illuminate, elevate, or nourish one's will (*jianzhi* 見志, *mingzhi* 明志, *shangzhi* 尚志, *yangzhi* 養志). In addition, there are frequent references to how connoisseurship contributes to good health and physical well-being. In his preface to Cao Zhao's (14th c.) *Essentials for Investigating Antiquity* (*Gegu yaolun*, 1388), Shu Min (14th c.) argues that collecting antiques "can be said to help with investigating things and bringing about knowledge."[86] He further links connoisseurship to discernment in judging people. Cao explains his method as patient study: "Whenever I see a vessel, I will not stop until I have gone through all available pictures and templates to examine its origins, evaluate its quality, and distinguish what is true and false in the accounts."[87] In a colophon to his friend's art collection, the scholar-official Xu Youzhen (1407–1472) opines: "There are those who seek pleasure in things and lose their will, and those who seek pleasure in things and find true meaning. Thus those who excel at seeking pleasure in things seek pleasure in the principles of things; those who fail to do so seek pleasure in the form of things. Those who seek pleasure in principles nourish their minds; those who seek pleasure in form lose control over their minds."[88] "Principles" in this case refer to the edifying potential of the subject matter of the paintings—Xu explains, for example, how flora and fauna can encourage meditation on "generation and transformation," mountains and rivers can be linked to contemplation on the virtues of nobility and wisdom, and portraits of exemplary figures can inspire imitation. It does mean, however, that the sensuous and affective response to artistic form is edited out of this version of tasteful appreciation.

There are more explicit appeals to pleasure in writings that defend the appreciation of things with Daoist echoes. In *Unworldly Routine of the Morning Pickings House* (*Zhaocai guan qingke*, 1604 prefaces), which details the leisured refinement of a semireclusive existence, Fei Yuanlu wrote: "There are three ways of wandering in the Way: that of heaven, that of the spirits, that of humans. Wandering in the heavenly way, both form and spirit are transformed. Wandering in the spiritual way, the idea takes off while the form remains. Wandering in the human way, one merely braces one's will to cut loose from conventions and seeks pleasure in things to pick the truth (*wanwu caizhen* 玩物采真)."⁸⁹ The phrase "wandering for truth-picking" (*caizhen zhi you* 采真之遊) is from *Zhuangzi*; it evokes the image of picking flowers or herbs and portrays not the deliberate quest for truth but its free and easy "picking" in the course of joyous wanderings. This harks back to one of the central paradoxes in *Zhuangzi*: while there are ample warnings against attachment to external things, it also celebrates playfulness and the pleasures of sensual reality.

The mental attitude toward things determines the moral meanings of possession and connoisseurship. If subjective projection or appropriation can trivialize its object (no matter how august), it can also, by the same logic, dignify what may otherwise be considered insignificant. Qian Qianyi (1582–1664) summarizes this position in his preface (1640) to a treatise on the zither by his late friend Yan Tiaoyu:

> In ancient times there were men who pursued their passions and obsessions to the extent that they broke open graves and dug up coffins, held on to the boat's bow and threatened to jump into the water.⁹⁰ To plumb the depths of these feelings is, in all cases, to yield the decision over life and death, and to make light of one's moral nature and very existence. Those who seek pleasures in their passions and inclinations seek pleasure in things, those who investigate them investigate things, and those who regard them as equal equalize things. Between things and the will, manifestation and the Way, how can there be any difference!⁹¹

The object of the various mental dispositions can be just "things" or "passions" (*shi* 嗜) and "inclinations" (*hao* 好): I opt for the latter to obviate tautology and also because there seems to be a built-in self-reflexivity about this proposition—that is why Qian concludes by equating "things" and "the will" (or rather the mental attitude toward things). Qian seems to suggest that the line between the pleasure of immersion in the experience, moral quest, and Daoist transcendence is fluid because of the self-conscious choice and ultimate agency controlling these transitions. Yan, famous for his mastery and connoisseurship of the zither, was also known for his moral probity and political engagement. Qian implies that he moves easily between these different aspects of his character and sees the continuity between them.

Inner distance in one's apparent devotion to things is a persistent theme. Having completed *History of the Vase* (*Ping shi*, 1599), a treatise on flower arrangement, Yuan Hongdao (1568–1610) nevertheless takes pains to distinguish himself from the truly obsessed. Those with a true passion for flowers brave dangers and hardships to acquire rare specimens, observe every phase of blooming with intensity, and gain vast and intuitive knowledge about flowers. Yuan considers these "true connoisseurs" (*zhen haoshi* 真好事) whom he does not presume to emulate: "As for the way I keep flowers, I just use them to dispel the affliction of withdrawal and solitude. It is not that I can be truly passionate about it. If I could, I would have been the one by the entrance to the Peach Blossom Cave!⁹² How could I be still an official in the dust and grime of the human realm!" (*YHD* 1:826). Yuan's treatise details necessary choices and rules of taste with the methodical meticulousness typical of obsession, yet he is also claiming the cultural space of shared taste and eschewing the radical subjectivity of the truly obsessed. Indeed, the assertion of ultimate control and the fear of real disequilibrium underline the discourse on passions, extreme emotions, and obsessions during the late Ming.

THE DISCOURSE ON OBSESSIONS

Yuan Hongdao's disclaimer is typical. One may expect the discourse on obsessions to focus on excesses and imbalance, but in fact it is just as concerned with imposing control and boundaries. In that sense it encompasses the spectrum of reflections on the relationship between people and things outlined earlier, ranging from intimations of transcendence, dire warnings of dangers, assertions of moral and intellectual justifications, and negotiations of limits and ambiguities. The Chinese words commonly used to translate obsession include *shi* 嗜, *hao* 好, *ai* 愛, *chi* 癡, and *pi* 癖: they all imply excess or imbalance caused by extreme attachment. At the same time, there is room for equivocation or even redemption, especially in moments of heightened interest in affective states and the parameters of consciousness in Chinese cultural history.

Whereas *shi*, *hao*, and *ai* signify desire without necessarily implying pathology—since negative implications arise from improper objects of desire or excessive desire rather than in the act of desiring—*chi* and *pi*, words of later provenance, have the "sickness" (*chuang* 疒) radical. Xu Shen defines *chi* as "mental deficiency." When the word first appears in late Warring States and Han texts, its semantic range includes lunacy, idiocy, folly, and confusion (in compounds such as *kuangchi* 狂癡, *yuchi* 愚癡, and *chiwan* 癡頑). Likewise, the word *pi* was first used in Ge Hong's (284–364) *Master Embracing Simplicity* (*Baopu zi*) to refer to the accumulation of phlegm because of excessive drinking.[93] Medical texts describe *pi* as the accumulation of adverse energy or bloating inside the rib cage arising from the clash of hot and cold, yin and yang forces.[94] Both *chi* and *pi* come to mean intense attachment or obsession by the fourth or fifth century. In *New Accounts of Tales of the World* (*Shishuo xinyu*, 5th c.), for example, the words command a new range of associations, including idiosyncrasy, deep feelings, and the gulf between self and society. It is not uncommon to find proud declarations of obsessions with poetry, books, the beauty of nature, wine, tea, or flowers in poetry from the Tang onward. The context is sometimes a sense of alienation from worldly expectations, as in these lines by Lu Tong (d. 835): "No true friends in the world beyond things, / a king of obsessions in the human realm" 物外無知己，人間一癖王 (*QTS* 387.4370).

Obsession became part of a more general discourse celebrating subjectivity and eccentricity only in the sixteenth and the seventeenth centuries. Miscellanies and collections of earlier and contemporary anecdotes about fixation flourished, notably the chapter "Obsessions and Passions" (Pishi) in Feng Menglong's (1574–1646) *Past and Present Aids to Conversation* (*Gujin tangai*) and Hua Shu's (1589–1643) *Short History of Obsessions and Lunacies* (*Pi dian xiaoshi*). Affirmations of obsessions seem ubiquitous. In a letter to Pan Zhiheng (1556–1622), Yuan Hongdao describes obsession as the necessary marker of superior sensibility: "I would say that for people of this world, so long as they have an extraordinary obsession and do not give it up their whole life, they count as notable gentlemen, just like Lin Bu with plum blossoms and Mi Fu with rocks. If their objects of obsession can be replaced with other things, then they cannot claim a distinct style. Even if their obsessions can be changed, it would not necessarily do much to augment their moral character" (*YHD* 2:1597).[95] Here Yuan implicitly juxtaposes moral and aesthetic categories of judgment: obsession is deemed necessary for aesthetic sensibility, and its removal, which the moralist may recommend, may not result in moral improvement. Wu Congxian (17th c.) quotes Tang Binyin (b. 1568): "A person cannot be without obsessions," and Yuan Hongdao: "A person cannot be without fixations." Wu Congxian concludes: "Thus there is actually no need to be rid of fixations or to be cured of obsessions."[96]

Writing about his friend Qi Zhixiang's homosexual passion, Zhang Dai (1597–ca. 1680s) declares: "One cannot befriend a person without obsessions, for he would lack deep feelings; one cannot befriend a person without flaws, for he would lack the spirit of genuineness."[97] Obsessions, like flaws, confirm a person's genuine emotions and individual spirit because individuation is conceived of as deviation, the correction of cold perfection. Paradoxically, this reasoning implies that obsessions can be cultivated as a mark of "deep feelings," and apparent loss of control can confirm agency on another level. Zhang Chao (17th c.) opines in *Secret Dream Shadows* (*Youmeng ying*): "Flowers cannot do without butterflies, mountains cannot do without springs, rocks cannot do without moss, water cannot do without aquatic plants, evergreen trees cannot do without vines, a person cannot do without obsessions."[98] Obsession is no longer something one succumbs to; rather, it almost becomes an adornment. The person immersed in his fixation self-consciously becomes an aesthetic spectacle—this is especially true of conventionalized accounts of obsessions with "refined things" (such as flowers, poetry, or art). When the importance of obsession is presented as "aesthetic necessity," it becomes a self-conscious choice implying the subject's control.

Yuan Hongdao conflates connoisseurship with excessive devotion in the chapter "Connoisseurship" in the aforementioned *History of the Vase*, citing antecedent models in a tone of approbation. Even in such apparently straightforward praise of obsessions, however, the quest for a deeper intention implies an ultimately moral justification and a kind of self-division, whereby obsession is but the expression of a lofty spirit that cannot find accommodation in the mundane realm. Yuan Hongdao explains:

> The way Ji Kang was with forging iron, Wang Ji with horses, Lu Yu with tea, the Mad Mi (Mi Fu) with rocks, or Ni Zan with cleanliness—in all these cases they were using their obsessions to lodge their distinct, soaring, uncompromising spirit. From what I have

seen, the ones whose words are insipid and whose countenances are unappealing are all people without obsessions. If one is truly obsessed with something, then one would immerse and indulge in it, one would put life and soul into it, how could one have time to spare for things such as money, servants, officialdom, or trade? (*YHD* 1:826)

The evaluation of obsessions reminds us of its social function: it is a way to establish individuality, claim superior sensibility, and define an oppositional stance vis-à-vis the powers that be. Yuan Hongdao's first example of obsession is the famous poet Ji Kang.[99] A well-known anecdote from *Shishuo xinyu* describes the encounter of Ji Kang, as he is absorbed in "forging iron," with the aristocrat Zhong Hui (225–264) along with his distinguished retinue. "Ji Kang hammered away without stopping as if there were no one around him. Moments passed and they did not exchange any word. Zhong Hui rose to leave, and Ji Kang said, 'What have you heard that made you come? What have you seen that made you leave?' Zhong Hui replied, 'By coming, I have heard what I heard. Upon leaving, I have seen what I saw'" (*Shishuo xinyu* 24.3). The exchange points to the competition between the "performer" of obsession and its "audience." Ji Kang, defiantly absorbed in his fixation, challenges Zhong Hui to respond to his refusal to communicate. Zhong has enough wit to bolster his dignity with an evasive and noncommittal reply. Ji and Zhong, identified respectively with "Daoist naturalness" and Confucian "moral teachings," also belonged to opposing political factions. Zhong Hui eventually stoked the calumny that brought about Ji Kang's downfall.

Yuan Hongdao's second example, Wang Ji, also appears in *Shishuo xinyu*: Wang Ji excelled in understanding horses. He once rode a horse decked out with patterned leg-shields. Coming to a river, the horse refused to cross it for the longest time. Wang said, "This must be because it cherishes the shields." He had someone remove them, and they crossed right away (20.4). Wang Ji's love for the horse transcends the connoisseur's judgment—he humanizes it as it becomes the object of empathy and communion. The *Zuozhuan* scholar Du Yu (222–284) compares Wang's "obsession with horses" to He Qiao's "obsession with money" and his own "obsession with *Zuozhuan*."[100]

Yuan Hongdao's other examples are about specialized knowledge and artistic powers. Lu Yu (733–804) is famous for his *Classic of Tea* (*Cha jing*). The great painter and calligrapher Mi Fu was obsessed with strangely shaped rocks; so much so that he would don official robes and bow to an interesting rock, calling it "older brother."[101] Another great artist, Ni Zan (1301–1374), is featured in a number of anecdotes detailing his obsessive fear of contamination. Yuan Hongdao is thus linking obsession to a range of attributes, including political defiance (Ji Kang), empathetic understanding (Wang Ji), connoisseurship (Lu Yu), and artistic powers (Mi Fu and Ni Zan). Their common denominator is the idea that the self invents its own order, one that displaces the vulgar concerns shared by the common run of humanity.

Single-minded focus on an external object seems to purge the self of contingencies, yet this is ultimately about the vagaries of the self. In a marginal comment on an entry about Mi Fu's love of rocks in Feng Menglong's *Past and Present Aids to Conversation*, Yuan Hongdao opines: "Chrysanthemums for Tao Yuanming, plum blossoms for Lin Bu, rocks for Mi Fu are not about loving chrysanthemums, plum blossoms, or rocks—in all these cases it is the self loving the self."[102] "The self loving the self" can be taken simply as loving attention to one's own preferences, but it can also mean an insistent search for the self's objective correlative and appreciation for that search: as such it suggests potential self-distancing or even self-division. Yuan Hongdao uses the word *ji* 寄 (to lodge, to entrust oneself to something) to describe the ways whereby restless discontent and proud defiance seek solace and recompense in obsessions. The word *ji* suggests a temporary abode, a choice to come and go as one pleases—quite the contrary of the idea of a person succumbing to obsessions. In other words, with *ji* the obsessing self regains a measure of control. Like the idea of "letting the mind linger" (*yuyi* 寓意) in Su Shi's "Account of the Hall of Treasured Paintings," to "lodge" one's spirit suggests a higher concern and deliberation rather than compulsion. In other words, as with the notion of moderation discussed above, obsession also plays with ideas of self-observation and self-division in negotiating the boundaries of the positive and negative implications of engagement with the world of things.

In tandem with the celebration of individual difference, we find from the sixteenth century on more and more examples of writers who dramatize their unique appreciation for or identification with objects that others deem worthless. Lu Shusheng (1509–1605), for instance, affirms his affinities with his collection of inkstones by naming his studio after them and adopting the sobriquet "Master of Ten Inkstones." A connoisseur tells him that his specimens are all inferior. Lu defends his obsession by alluding to varying judgments of inkstones among Song literati. He modestly claims to lack the reputation to confer value on his possessions. "However, as for my attachment to inkstones, it cannot be transferred to other precious, exquisite things. The inkstones thus depend on me for being the object of obsession. Who knows whether they may not acquire value that way? That is why my obsession has not been reasoned away."[103]

Lu Shusheng describes how he would sit "facing the inkstones, proud and rapt." By far more common in writings from this period is a dramatic demonstration of empathic understanding. In "Postscript to Poems from Half-Stone Studio" (Banshi zhai shi ba), Li Weizhen (1547–1626) relates a dialogue in which he asks Fang Ziqian, who requests the postscript on behalf of a poet whose sobriquet is Half-Stone Studio, about the meaning of the latter's name.[104] Fang replies, "Shaowen (Half-Stone Studio) is talented but luckless, for long an unsuccessful candidate, he acquired half a slab of stone and considers it extraordinary." (The character for "luckless" and "extraordinary" is the same, though pronounced differently as *ji* 奇 and *qi* 奇.) Shaowen and the half-stone become inseparable. "When inspiration seizes him, he would grind ink and put brush to stone, writing in a rapid and flowing manner, as if aided by it. When he finishes, he would hit and slap the stone and sing, as if it were issuing echoes in response." Enumerating stone lore that links the stone to foundational myths, history, artistic creation, and moral probity, Shaowen concludes: "My talent is but half of that of the stone. I entrust my sense of being at ease with the stone, and in my poetry also I come only halfway to what poetry can be." The halved state of the stone makes it the perfect objective correlative for the poet as well as his metaphorical complement.

In a similar vein, Xu Wei (1521–1593) writes in the preface to his "Inscription on the Broken Pear-Shaped Vase Chime Stone" (Podan qing ming bing xu): "My family kept an ancient white porcelain vase. I once gathered plum branches and steeped them therein. Spring and summer passed, and the plum branches bloomed and bore fruit. Later it broke because the water inside it froze. I pondered its sound: it was like the excellent chime stones on the banks of River Si. Taking half of it and hanging it in my studio, I inscribed its name as 'the Broken Vase Chime Stone.'"[105] The inscription reads:

膽之成	When the vase was intact,
水入空	Water entered the empty space
出以養其莖	And left by nourishing the stem.
目觀其色之榮	Our eyes observed its color's glory.
膽之冰	When the vase was frozen,
水出空	Water left the empty space,
人以縣其傾	And people hung its slanting form.
耳聞其聲之鏗	Our ears listened to its sound's sonority.
一出一入	Coming and leaving,
為聲為色	Becoming sight and sound.
見聞別差	What we see and hear may be different,
妙性不忒	But its wondrous nature does not vary.

The inscription compares the visual pleasure afforded by the intact vase with the auditory pleasure yielded by the broken vase. *Shangshu* mentions "floating chime stones by the Banks of River Si,"[106] and River Si is also associated with the area where Confucius taught his disciples. Water makes the vase a life-generating object but breaks it when it turns into ice; yet in its broken state it becomes a chime stone linked to the ritual and music defining the beginnings of culture. Perhaps the sound of its breaking is itself also a kind of music. The inscription cannot be dated with certainty, but it is tempting to link the notion of creation through destruction to an oppositional stance that pits the self against an uncomprehending world. Madness, self-mutilation, attempted suicide, the verdict of murder, and incarceration dogged Xu Wei's tragic life.

Distinct from such idiosyncratic perspectives that often seem to attribute sentience to things are the numerous voices assimilating things to a vision of order and optimal enjoyment even while humanizing them, especially in the genre of epigrammatic adages called "exquisite sayings" (*qingyan* 清言). For example, Lu Shaohang (early 17th c.) writes: "Strangely shaped rocks are honest friends, famous zithers are harmonious friends, good books are beneficial friends, marvelous paintings are discerning friends, calligraphic models are exemplary friends, superior inkstones are polishing friends, precious mirrors are illuminating friends, immaculate low tables are unstinting friends, ancient porcelain vessels are accommodating friends, old censers are refining friends, paper curtains are pure friends, dusters are friends in quietude."[107] The nature of each object is translated into a human attribute—e.g., the word for "honest" also means "substantial" and refers to the rocks' concreteness; inkstones are made through chiseling and polishing and are used to grind ink, and chiseling and polishing are metaphors for self-cultivation and for friends who offer advice and correction;[108] what I translate as "accommodating" is literally "empty" or "accepting (of criticism)" and describes the function of the vase to hold things, and so on. The emotional investment in anthropomorphizing things is tempered by the rhetoric of moral improvement.

There are ubiquitous comparisons of flowers with women. Yuan Hongdao pairs different flowers with historical beauties in *History of the Vase* (*YHD* 1:825). In an essay on the peach blossoms of Six Bridges, he indulges in an extended panegyric comparing the flowers in different states and contexts with the varying moods, poses, and gestures of beautiful women.[109] For Tian Yiheng (late 16th c.–early 17th c.), even exalted literary figures like Ouyang Xiu and Su Shi were guilty of wanton destruction when they hosted parties that called for the cutting of too many flowers. On a day when his own flowers bloomed, he wrote a warning for the friends he invited:

> Famed flowers are just like beauties: they can be appreciated but not trifled with, loved but not broken. To break off a leaf is to rip the beauty's skirt, to leave a trace on the blossom is to scratch her skin, to break a branch is to tear off her limb, to spray the flowers with wine is to spit at her, to let incense touch the flowers is to smoke her eyes, to take off your clothes in shameless abandon is to chase her around in your gross nakedness. Those who look too closely can be called blind; those who bend the stem to smell the flowers can be said to have olfactory impairment. As the saying goes, "One would rather run into a fierce hound than risk having a beautiful scene ruined." I vow to never again invite those who fail to learn even after receiving instruction.[110]

Beneath the tone of facetious jest is an earnest plea for cherishing things as humans.

The standard conceit in this kind of writings anthropomorphizes the object and sometimes uses the rhetoric of friendship and romantic love, replete with references to fated encounters, mysterious attraction, and solemn recognition. In the painter Jin Junming's (1602–1675) four short accounts of orchids, for instance, he describes how, during a boat ride in a lake in 1639, he spots a friend's boat in the distance and "sensed something extraordinary."[111] It turns out to be a pot of white orchids: "I have seen many orchids over the years, at the most one speaks of fragrance or luxuriance, never have I seen one which captivates at first sight, almost eliciting a reverent bow, like these blossoms." His friend gives the orchids to him, and he affirms his bond with the plant: "Voice and spirit, in affective affinities, call out to each other: this is of course the way it should be." He writes in the third account: "I was surprised by joy and giddy, somewhat like Li Jing when he first received Hongfu's regard." In a famous ninth-century tale, Hongfu, a singing girl in the household of the minister Yang Su, proposes elopement to Li Jing, who would later play a pivotal role in the founding of the Tang dynasty.[112] But another friend who also becomes enamored of the orchids sends Jin a dramatic letter: "If you do not let me have it, I would for sure splash my neck's blood on the flowers, following the example of the mad Mi Fu in bygone days. If my neck's blood is splashed on the flowers, what would remain of my five fingers? Who would then make records of your paintings? You have to make haste to rescue me! Make haste!" In this faintly ridiculous missive, the friend invokes the example of Mi Fu, who, as mentioned earlier, threatened to jump into the river if he does not get a coveted piece of calligraphy from its owner. The friend also alludes to some prior promise to carve seals for Jin—if he were to die, who would fulfill that promise? Jin gives up his orchids in return for a pair of carved seals from his friend and adopts the pose of the unworthy, regretful lover: he does not dare to see the flowers in its new owner's abode, "for the orchids are going to mock me for not measuring up to Shi Chong." The historical Shi Chong (249–300) did not betray his beloved concubine Lüzhu, who in turn died to vindicate her devotion to Shi Chong. The friend gives his own orchids to Jin in exchange, and the final account ends with Jin's contemplation of the new flowers and his desire to paint them. Here the histrionic gestures and the

People and Things 45

self-conscious dramatization of perception and experience stand in sharp contrast to the actual transaction and the relative ease with which Jin Junming gives up his prized possession. This is a group of men who complacently celebrate their fine taste and feel the need to dramatize it. The author seems to be winking at the reader, gesturing toward his interactions with his friends as a kind of inspired joke.

Even when the obsession seems genuine and compelling and is described with sympathy, a hint of irony is often discernible. Zhang Dai wrote about his friend Fan Yulan, who was obsessed with his potted miniature tree and called it his "concubine." When Zhang Dai forced him to lend it to him for a few months and it withered under his care, he remorsefully brought it back to Fan. Horrified, Fan made soup from ginseng and used it to water the plant, stroking it day and night. A month later the withered plant came back to life.[113] Qian Qianyi used even more dramatic language when he had to sell his prized possessions, the Song printings of the *History of the Han* (*Hanshu*) and *History of the Later Han* (*Hou Hanshu*). They were from the collection of the famous painter and calligrapher Zhao Mengfu (1254–1322), and Wang Shizhen (1526–1590) owned them closer to Qian's time. Qian "redeemed" (*shu* 贖) them with 1,200 taels from a Huizhou collector and kept them for twenty years, but sold them for 1,000 taels in 1643 to Xie Sanbin.[114] "When these books left me, it was really difficult to make peace with their loss. The mournful scene when Li Houzhu, the last ruler of Southern Tang, left his kingdom and listened to the songs from the Music Registry and 'waved away tears as he faced the palace ladies' is somewhat comparable to this."[115] Qian also feels that his devotion to these rare books pales beside that of other collectors such as Li Weizhu (younger brother of the aforementioned Li Weizhen): "He [Li Weizhu] once said to me: If I obtained the *History of the Han* from Zhao Mengfu's collection, I would burn incense and bow to it every day, and when I die I would use it to accompany me in burial. His words put me in deep shame" (*QMZ* 3:1781). Qian wrote these postscripts half a year before the fall of the Ming. There is grim irony in lamenting the loss of a rare book as the loss of a kingdom, when unbeknownst to Qian real political disaster is around the corner. When Qian reencounters these volumes in the possession of another collector (we do not know when Xie Sanbin sold them) in the aftermath of the fall of the Ming, he marvels at their survival, for not only was the dynastic transition "a great calamity for books and texts past and present," most of his own collection had perished in a fire in 1650 (6:1529–30). The pathos of this later postscript ponders the meanings of ownership in the midst of devastation; the 1643 lament, by contrast, is slightly tongue-in-cheek, mixing genuine attachment with practical economic considerations.

The urge to humanize things capitalizes on the affective power of subjective projection. As these examples show, it usually brings attention back to the voice professing identification or empathy, and it is sometimes playful and ironic. Stories about how things respond to human attachment often describe their transformation into friends and lovers. Such stories also sometimes come with ironic or melancholy echoes that remind us of the slippery boundaries and inherent paradoxes in the discourses on things (i.e., "the good" and "the bad" often share a similar vocabulary, which leads to ruminations on "the negotiable"). Take, for example, some stories about obsession in Pu Songling's (1640–1715) *Strange Stories from the Liaozhai Studio* (*Liaozhai zhiyi*), such as "Yellow Blossoms" (Huangying), "Hemp Scarf" (Gejin), "The Bibliophile" (Shu chi), and "Shi Qingxu."[116] Unlike most other *Liaozhai* stories, in which foxes, spirits, and ghosts often come unbidden, in these stories the objects of obsessive devotion (chrysanthemums, peonies, books, a strangely shaped rock) respond to the intense attachment of the protagonist by taking human form and becoming his friend or lover. In "Yellow Blossoms" and "The Bibliophile," the incarnation of the object of obsession ironically questions the meanings and justifications of that obsession. These stories are also untypical of the collection in incorporating death and destruction—although death may also be seen as a kind of muted apotheosis that emphasizes the empathetic identification of a character with the object of his desire.[117]

PEOPLE AS THINGS IN *JIN PING MEI*

If the accounts of obsession with things that emphasize the tenuous balance between subjective projection and self-control form one end of the spectrum, then on the other we find insistent materiality resisting emotional association. When we consider such recalcitrant things and the related discourse about the dangers of things and warnings against "being transformed by things," perhaps no example is more compelling than the late Ming novel *Jin Ping Mei* (*The Plum in the Golden Vase*). First mentioned in the 1590s, *Jin Ping Mei* was probably written in the late sixteenth century. The earliest edition (*Jin Ping Mei cihua*) carries a 1617 preface; another recension, also called the Xiuxiang edition, dates from the Chongzhen reign (1628–1644).[118] The identity of the author, whose pseudonym is "The Laughing Scholar of Lanling" (Lanling xiaoxiao sheng), remains unknown. The sprawling hundred-chapter narrative depicts the world of the rich merchant Ximen Qing, his wife, five concubines, and various lovers, as well as his sycophants, underlings, business associates, and official connections. We see Ximen's steady ascendancy until his death from sexual excesses. The book ends with the disintegration of his household, the fall of the Song dynasty to invading Jurchens, and some version of Buddhist salvation (his son, who is his reincarnation, becomes a monk). Although set in the early twelfth century, the world the novel evokes is unmistakably that of the sixteenth century. Unlike all previous works of Chinese fiction, *Jin Ping Mei* takes us to a world without heroes: this is a suffocating and all-too-human world dominated by the greed for power, money, and sexual gratification.

Jin Ping Mei is chock-full of things. It lingers insistently on the surface. A character's appearance is usually accompanied by a detailed description of her (or his) articles of clothing, jewelry, and shoes—not only when we first meet her (or him), but on nearly every occasion. No repast seems insignificant enough to not merit a listing of all the dishes. Indeed, there are ubiquitous lists of things, and description often consists of enumeration of attributes. Almost all the gifts and bribes are carefully itemized, sometimes with details about their market value. We know the exact cost of almost everything. There is often close attention to the décor of certain kinds of interior or enclosed space (e.g., rooms, halls, gardens), with occasional excursus on the particulars of furniture (notably the bed). What does this relentless attention to the world of things signify? On the most obvious level, it confirms what historians tell us about the abiding concerns with consumption, extravagance, and the material markers of status and power in late Ming Chinese society. In symbolic terms, *Jin Ping Mei* stands alone in the literary tradition in its insistence on depicting characters defined by their material desires. In the process they are not only "transformed by things"; they are dehumanized and transformed into things.

Almost everything has a price tag in *Jin Ping Mei*. No maid is bought or sold without mention of the price. (Interestingly, the price of male servants is rarely mentioned. However, Ximen Qing's page boys and catamites, Shutong and Wang Jing, come to him via a network of favors sought and bestowed, a process akin to "pricing" [*JPM* chaps. 31, 55].) Chunmei, an orphan (29.416) who starts out as the maid of Ximen's principal wife Wu Yueniang but becomes his concubine Pan Jinlian's maid and confidante as well as Ximen Qing's unofficial concubine (9.116, 10.135), is bought and sold for sixteen taels (85.1468). Some comparisons in prices are in order here. Ximen pays five taels for Xiaoyu, the maid who replaces Chunmei in Yueniang's rooms. Qiuju, bought to serve Jinlian, costs more (six taels), perhaps on account of her presumed culinary skills, or more probably because Ximen has a greater passion for Jinlian (9.116). (It is ironic that Qiuju, the constant object of Jinlian's sadistic ire, should cost more than Xiaoyu, who, by marrying Dai'an, Ximen's trusted servant and eventual inheritor of what remains of his wealth [100.1695], rises in the world by default.) Gratified by the sexual proclivities of his new paramour Wang Liu'er, the wife of his underling Han Daoguo, Ximen uses four taels to buy a maid, Jin'er, to serve her (37.549). After leaving the Ximen household, Chunmei's fortunes soar through her marriage with the commandant Zhou Xiu, and she buys the cheapest maid in the book, paying 3.5 taels for Jinqian'er, one tael less than the asking price (97.1647). What does it mean for Chunmei to cost about three or four times as much as an average maid? She has a higher market value because of her beauty, wit, and cleverness (10.135). For all that, she can still be bought and sold. Wu Yueniang makes a point of adhering to the price of purchase when she puts her up for sale to indicate that Chunmei's years in the Ximen household do not matter—they have done nothing to enhance or diminish her value (85.1468).[119]

Pan Jinlian was sold at age nine for an unspecified amount to the household of Imperial Commissioner Wang, where she acquired various accomplishments and musical skills that enabled her mother to resell her at age fifteen to a rich man, Zhang, for thirty taels. Under pressure from his jealous wife, Zhang sends Jinlian away, but he marries her to an impoverished and ugly dependent, Wu Da, so that he can continue his liaison with her. The adultery of Ximen Qing and Pan Jinlian and their murder of Wu Da is of course the story from *Water Margin* (*Shuihu zhuan*) that becomes the opening act of *Jin Ping Mei*. Wu Song's almost immediate vengeance is delayed for almost eighty chapters in *Jin Ping Mei*. One of the reminders that we are in a different fictional universe is Jinlian's price, which draws attention to her fate of commodification. Wu Da gets her for free but continues to "pay" by acquiescing to Zhang's continued access to his wife, which turns Wu Da into a complicit partner in a sordid arrangement. (In *Water Margin*, Jinlian has no prior history in Commissioner Wang's house. She enters the story as a maid in the Zhang household. Zhang marries her to Wu Da out of vindictiveness after she resists his predatory advances. The concern of the novel is to bring together the mismatched Jinlian and Wu Da and set the scene for Jinlian's adultery and murder of Wu Da; it is not interested in Jinlian's victimhood.)

In the aftermath of Wu Da's murder, Ximen Qing delays the marriage with Jinlian, being distracted by the prospect of marrying a concubine, Meng Yulou, who brings a handsome dowry, and by the expensive arrangement for the deflowering of the courtesan Li Gujie. Jinlian is no longer linked to the thrill of acquisition and can wait. His wedding with Jinlian has minimal pomp, paling in comparison with analogous ceremonies for his union with Meng Yulou and Li Ping'er.[120] After Ximen Qing's death and the exposure of Jinlian's affair with her son-in-law Chen Jingji, Yueniang sends Jinlian away with some veneer of respectability (she leaves in a sedan chair, taking with her some trunks) but in effect puts her up for sale, through the go-between Dame Wang, for a hundred taels. Yueniang is not willing to settle for less because Ximen Qing expended more than enough money on her "to cast a silver figurine to match her dimensions" (*JPM* 86.1480, Roy 5:111).[121] Jinlian and Chunmei become close allies because of their shared fate of being bought and sold as things. Modern interpretations taking a more sympathetic view of these characters see Chunmei's pride, Jinlian's jealousy, and their temper, ruthlessness, and vindictiveness as resistance against that fate.

Women who command financial resources are no less caught in the web of buying and selling. Ximen Qing decides to marry Meng Yulou before setting eyes on her. He is easily swayed by the matchmaker's account of Yulou's dowry and her late husband's wealth. We know the exact value of Ximen's bribe for Auntie Yang (the paternal aunt of Yulou's late husband)—an initial offering of a bolt of cloth and four baskets of food, followed by two more bolts and a hundred taels. It is good investment: with Auntie Yang's support, Yulou's beds, curtains, and trunks were carted off with whirlwind efficiency to Ximen's house, foiling the self-serving designs of the maternal uncle of Yulou's late husband. The farcical scene depicting the competing claims over these possessions shows that legal or poetic justice about property rights is at best elusive or irrelevant.

In Li Ping'er's case, the things she owns are connected to the highest echelons of political power. She was the concubine of the privy councilor Liang Shijie, and when Liang's household was ravaged by the avenging fury of Li Kui (another character and plot detail from *Water Margin*), she escaped the carnage and took with her "a hundred large Western Ocean pearls and a pair of sapphires weighing two taels" (10.133). Eunuch Hua then arranges her marriage with his nephew Hua Zixu. There are broad hints that the eunuch had illicit relations with Ping'er: this would explain why his trunks of valuables, which include objects from the imperial palace as well as insignia of office such as python robes and jade belts, end up in her keeping. (Ping'er claims that Hua Zixu does not know about their existence, but he alludes to them.) The sex toy (the Burmese bell) and the pornographic album that Ping'er enjoys with Ximen Qing—objects that he then uses with Jinlian—retain the aura of things originating from the imperial palace. One may question Ping'er's rights to these things, but their original owners also have but dubious claims to them. We are in a fictional universe where the frenetic quest for things moves the plot, but no rightful ownership can be established to restore equilibrium. The transference of Ping'er's possessions to Ximen Qing's household—first clandestinely transported over the garden wall and then endlessly paraded through the streets—engages as much narrative attention as her own move into it. Ping'er tries to buy favors and acceptance with her possessions, but she is diminished rather than empowered by them. Her very entry into the Ximen household fulfills this logic. After the transference of her things is complete, he humiliates her and drives her to despair. The issue is not Ximen Qing's greed per se—he is quite generous with his sycophants—rather it is the identification of desire with inner vacuity and the obsessive need for acquisition.

Ximen Qing pays fifty taels and four sets of clothing for the privilege of deflowering the courtesan Li Guijie (chap. 11). In that sense, marriage shares the transactional logic of the "licensed quarter," with the difference that the former sometimes brings financial gain for Ximen Qing, while the latter involves expenditure. Ximen's household and the licensed quarter frequently intersect. Courtesans socialize with Ximen Qing's wives; two of them adopt Wu Yueniang and Li Ping'er as "mothers" (chaps. 32, 42). Ximen Qing claims to be visiting courtesans when he is in fact having a clandestine rendezvous with Ping'er, prompting Jinlian to mock him: "So it turns out that her house is the licensed quarter!" (13.181). During Ping'er's liaison with Ximen Qing, one of his sycophants refers to her as "a tart outside, not inside, the quarter" (15.207). Pan Jinlian comments on different styles of shoes favored by "denizens of the quarter" and "outsiders" (58.895), but "outsiders" also try to emulate the style of "insiders of the quarter" (e.g., Wang Liu'er in chap. 42, Pan Jinlian in chap. 52). Ximen complacently exclaims when he sees Pan Jinlian and Meng Yulou dressed in finery: "They look just like a pair of courtesans, and they'd cost a good amount of silver too" (11.138). Value is enhanced through the thrill of purchase; perhaps that is why Pan Jinlian dresses up as a maidservant newly bought for sixteen taels to "market her favor" (*shi'ai* 市愛)[122] and counter the ascendancy of Li Ping'er (chap. 40). Value is also perceived as the pleasure of appropriating what belongs to others; that is why Ximen Qing can be as excited by his liaison with a social superior like Madame Lin, the widow of a commissioner, as by his affair with Ruyi'er, the former nurse of his dead son, so long as she cries out about being another man's wife during intercourse (78.1352).

The transactional nature of sex is fully on display in the numerous scenes of intimacy or intercourse when the woman asks for things. The maidservant Song Huilian, who agrees to a rendezvous after Ximen Qing sends her a bolt of blue silk, plies him with requests, from tea to a fret for her hair. Pan Jinlian interrupts the fellatio she is performing on Ximen Qing to ask for the fur coat that belonged to Li Ping'er, which, according to Ximen Qing, is worth sixty taels (74.1227–28). Sexual acts associated with pain, violence, and perversion are sometimes accompanied by the most specific requests. While enduring bloody sodomization, Jinlian asks for "a drawnwork silk skirt of glossy gosling-yellow with silver stripes, and an inset of gold-spangled sheepskin, trimmed with varicolored thread" sported by Li Guijie and "purchased in the licensed quarter" (*JPM* 52.780, Roy 3:257). After burning moxa on Ruyi'er's body, Ximen Qing offers her "a patterned vest of jet color satin" (*JPM* 78.1352, Roy 4:604). A tryst that begins with Ruyi'er's wish for a gold "tiger-shaped tiara" ends with Ximen urinating in her mouth (*JPM* 75.1252), an indignity she is induced to bear because he boasts about Jinlian's similar act as a mark of her abject devotion and also because, in the interval, Ximen additionally offers a bolt of red chiffon and promises to promote Ruyi'er to the status of concubine should she bear a child.

As if to underline the connection between sex and economic calculations, Ximen Qing, while having intercourse with Li Ping'er, discusses business with his servant Dai'an (who is standing outside the window) and explains his calculations to Ping'er (16.216). Among Ximen Qing's sexual partners, Wang Liu'er, the wife of his underling Han Daoguo, is the most businesslike. They go over details of business arrangement in coitus (50.986–87). While burning moxa on Wang's body, they reach an agreement that her husband should become Ximen's buyer and manager down south (61.746). Enumerating her gains through the liaison, Wang explains to her husband: "It's all owing to my willingness to surrender my body to him. We might as well take advantage of the opportunity to get what we can out of him and improve our life-style." Han heartily agrees and urges his wife to "cater to his every whim" (*JPM* 38.561, Roy 2:392). After Ximen's death, Wang suggests to Han that they abscond with the thousand taels of silver in his keeping, arguing that the loot would only be belated payment for her sexual service: "Given the way he has taken advantage of me in the past, for us to make use of these few taels of his silver is hardly wrong" (*JPM* 81.1415, Roy 5:7). Unlike Song Huilian and Pan Jinlian, whose desire for things is bound up with pride, self-worth (or lack thereof), and (in Jinlian's case) jealousy and insatiable sexual needs, Wang Liu'er sells her body with purposeful and methodical calculation.[123] Her acquisitiveness is unburdened by compulsion or obsession. Ironically, she ends up the winner, enjoying a measure of financial security by inheriting the property of her last paramour, Magnate He, even as Song rule collapses and chaos ensues in the final chapter.

The measure of a man lies in the things he consumes.[124] Li Ping'er considers Ximen Qing vastly superior to Jiang Zhushan, the quack doctor to whom she was briefly married after the death of Hua Zixu, because of Ximen's fine clothes and attendants. She says to Ximen Qing, "Even the delicacies that constitute your daily fare are such things as he would never see, were he to live for hundreds of years. How can he be compared to you?" (19.268). Ximen Qing claims that even divine clemency can be bought with "good works" after sexual transgression against goddesses because the Buddhist heaven and hell depend on economic contributions from humans: "I've heard it said of the Buddha's heavenly realm that it was no more than a matter of paving the ground with gold; and that even in the Ten Courts of the underworld, one needs paper money to get things done. As long as I use what I own to do a lot of good works, even if I were to rape Chang E, fornicate with the Weaving Maid, abduct Xu Feiqiong, or steal the daughter of the Queen Mother of the West, it would do nothing to diminish the Heaven-splashing wealth and distinction that I now possess" (*JPM* 57.882, Roy 3:399).[125] Divine mercy, lives, sexual favors, affection, position, and apparently everything else that defines being human can be bought and sold. In that sense, people are no different from things. A person is often referred to as "a thing" (*huo* 貨 or *hanghuo* 行貨, literally, merchandise), a term conveying disdain or jocularity.[126]

The logic of "objectification" extends beyond the women: Ximen Qing himself is strangely objectified. His obsession with sexual prowess reduces him to an instrument of sexual gratification—his penis is described in greater detail than any other part of his body. Dependent on, and almost enslaved by, aphrodisiac and his bag of "sexual implements," he is strangely pathetic even as he revels in his power. It is fitting that the Indian monk who gives him aphrodisiac at the midpoint of the novel should appear as the personification of the male sexual organ (*JPM* 49.735–36),[127] and that Ximen's death should be followed by an absurd eulogy from his sycophants filled with puns and terms with double entendre depicting the phallus (80.1398–99). Phallic potency is matched by the loss of agency;[128] this is most evident in the lurid scene of Ximen's death when Jinlian administers an overdose of the Indian monk's aphrodisiac and straddles over the unconscious Ximen Qing (79.1377–78).

Love tokens (*biaoji* 表記) belong to a wonted convention in Chinese fiction and drama. In *Jin Ping Mei*, such exchanges are either perfunctory (as when Ximen Qing and Jinlian exchange a hairpin and a handkerchief through the urging of Dame Wang [4.55]) or merely provocative (as when Jinlian gives Chen Jingji a handkerchief in return for her red shoe, which Jingji picked up in the garden [28.401]). In any case, no love token is described with as much interest and detail as sex toys like the Burmese bell (16.218) and the satin bands that precipitate Ximen Qing's death: "[Jinlian] got out her sewing box, selected a strip of white satin, and employed backstitching in order to crimp it. She then reached into the porcelain container in her cabinet with her slender fingers, poured out some of the aphrodisiac called 'The Quavery Voices of Amorous Beauties,' and backstitched it securely inside the band with her deft technique" (*JPM* 73.1203, Roy 4:385). Jinlian's white satin band is matched by Wang Liu'er's final gift to Ximen Qing: it was "a lock of her dark-black glossy hair, bound into a circlet with variegated satin displaying the motif of 'joined hearts,' and with two brocade straps attached to it, so that it could be fastened around the root of his chowrie handle. It was a work of exquisite craftsmanship" (*JPM* 79.1371, Roy 4:630). (In both cases, the description is less detailed in the Chongzhen edition.) Both objects are supposed to enhance Ximen Qing's sexual performance, and both are linked to the image of bondage, perhaps echoing the footbinding cloth with which Ximen Qing ties up both women in earlier sexual games. Paradoxically, self-aggrandizement ends in objectification. Ximen Qing becomes a mere thing, summed up as a sexual organ subjected to manipulation.

RECALCITRANT THINGS IN *JIN PING MEI*

Does the prevalent objectification of humans leave room for symbolic, affective connections between people and things? Meng Yulou has a hairpin engraved with lines that encode her name (which means "jade tower"): "The golden-bridled horse neighs among fragrant grass, / The one on the jade tower is drunk in apricot blossom season" 金勒馬嘶芳草地，玉樓人醉杏花天. Contrary to expectation, no symbolic connection between the character and her hairpin develops. We first hear of it when Pan Jinlian finds it in Ximen Qing's topknot, but the scene of Yulou giving the hairpin to Ximen Qing is elided (*JPM* 8.108). In the throes of a passionate affair with Jinlian that led to Wu Da's murder, Ximen Qing has nevertheless stopped visiting Jinlian while arranging a financially advantageous marriage with Yulou. Unaware of this development, Jinlian mistakes the hairpin as a gift from a courtesan. Indeed, the lines evoke the image of a romantic encounter and recur in fiction, drama, song lyrics, and vernacular songs from Song through Qing dynasty, sometimes in the context of a courtesan-literati romance.[129] The hairpin is mentioned again when, after Ximen's death, Jinlian consummates her adulterous affair with her erstwhile son-in-law Chen Jingji and finds Yulou's hairpin in his sleeve (82.1431). Chen has merely picked it up in the garden, but his possession of it later allows him to threaten Yulou with false accusations after she remarries. In other words, the hairpin functions to move the plot rather than give us insights into Yulou's character. One may argue that her eventual second marriage (90–91) fulfills the romantic promise of the hairpin, but even there the connection seems tenuous.

In the same episode that Jinlian discovers Yulou's hairpin in Ximen Qing's possession, she gives him a hairpin in the shape of a double lotus, one among several birthday gifts. It is engraved with a quatrain professing love and devotion: "I have a twain-bloom lotus, / A gift for holding your topknot. / In all things be twain and one: / Do not easily cast me aside" 奴有並頭蓮，贈與君關髻。凡事同頭上，切勿輕相棄 (8.109). Ximen Qing is delighted by this display of cleverness (the quatrain is presumably composed by Jinlian); they rekindle their passion, and shortly thereafter Jinlian enters Ximen's household. But for him this mark of enhanced value—very much like Yulou's skill with the round lute—does not preclude pursuit of other objects of desire. The chapter is preceded by his marriage with Meng Yulou and followed by his liaison with the courtesan Li Gujie and his prolonged absence, which in turn leads to Jinlian's abortive affair with a young male servant. The hairpin with the quatrain is a would-be symbol of love in a world that negates such symbols.

If Yulou's hairpin merely moves the plot and that of Jinlian becomes a flawed symbol, the hairpins Li Ping'er gives to Ximen Qing show how power negotiations overtake sentimental value. At the beginning of their affair (when Ping'er is still married to Hua Zixu), Ping'er takes two gold hairpins from her chignon and puts them in Ximen Qing's hair, saying to him: "If you go to the licensed quarter, don't let Hua Zixu see it" (13.179). She wants this token of their secret bond to be hidden from her husband but also more generally from the prying eyes of others. When Jinlian finds out about the affair, however, Ximen Qing does not hesitate to offer the hairpins to placate her, pretending that Li Ping'er intended them as a gift to Jinlian. In fact, we get their description first through Jinlian's eyes: "Taking them into her hand and looking them over, Jinlian saw that they were a pair of gold, openwork pins, in the shape of the character for long life, which had been deeply chased in intaglio and inset with azurite. It was obvious from the extraordinary intricacy of the craftsmanship that they had been manufactured for imperial use and came from the palace" (*JPM* 13.182, Roy 1:270). Jinlian then happily acquiesces to the clandestine affair and even promises to assist Ximen Qing. It is fitting that we should see the hairpins through Jinlian's eyes: she appreciates their material value (enhanced through imperial associations) as well as symbolic value as the facilitator of triangular desire. Powerless to stop Ximen Qing, Jinlian reclaims lost ground through information and repetition—she demands to be told the details of his intimacy with Ping'er and reenacts Ping'er's sexual acts with Ximen Qing, down to the use of the aforementioned pornographic album and Burmese bell. When Ximen's wife Wu Yueniang remarks on the hairpins and seems to regard them as Ping'er's gift to Jinlian at Jinlian's birthday party, Ping'er betrays no unease (has she just found out that Ximen Qing transferred her gift to Jinlian?) and offers to give Yueniang and the other concubines each the same set of hairpins (*JPM* 14.196, 199). A private love token becomes a tool for preparing her entry into, and management of the power balance within, Ximen's polygamous household. Later Ximen Qing is to offer a set of these hairpins to his new paramour Wang Liu'er for her birthday (51.743). A love token is used to facilitate other dalliances.

The hairpins of Jinlian and Ping'er demonstrate how sentimental objects become embroiled in rivalries and power negotiations. Although there are also examples—admittedly rare—of objects that become symbols of unalloyed emotional attachment, they are exceptions that prove the rule. Further, even in those cases, affective value can seem nebulous or easily sidetracked. After Ping'er marries Ximen Qing, she gives birth to a son, Guan'ge, who dies not long after his first birthday through the machinations of Jinlian. Unable to part with Guan'ge's coffin, Ping'er is overcome with grief when she sees the clapper-drum that he used to play with (59.932). The toy is first mentioned as one item in a list of congratulatory gifts that Eunuch Xue presented to Ximen Qing when Guan'ge was born. In "a pair of square lacquer gift boxes decorated with inlaid gilt designs," we find "a bolt of red government-quality shot silk, four gold-plated silver coins bearing the characters for 'good fortune,' 'long life,' 'health,' and 'tranquility,' a toy clapper-drum decorated with a varicolored, gold-flecked portrait of the God of Longevity, and two taels worth of silver trinkets in the shape of 'eight treasures'" (JPM 32.456, Roy 2:244). Tactfully checking whether his close associate Eunuch Liu had sent his gift, Eunuch Xue is mainly concerned with how he would compare with his potential rival. In that context, the clapper-drum belongs to a list as a mere marker of social transactions and obligations, just like most other gifts in the book. For a fleeting moment, however, Li Ping'er endows a social object with emotional meaning as it triggers mournful remembrance of Guan'ge.

Scenes with sentimental objects evoking longing for the dead or absent beloved are quite rare in the book. Ximen Qing commissions the painter Han to paint portraits (one half-length and one full-length) of Li Ping'er after her death. Han has to create the likenesses based on the corpse and on his memory of a past encounter. Instead of dwelling on the pathos of tenuous connection between the person and the image, the narrative quickly shifts attention to its social significance. The countenance in the half-portrait is said to be "pale and fragrant." If that seems vague, it may be because the hair ornaments and gown of figured scarlet material are described in all their particularity (JPM 63.1014). The half-length portrait invites the comments of Ximen's other wives and is admired by the guests at the funeral. Ximen Qing asks Han to "lavish even greater attention" on the full-length portrait; in an earlier comment Ximen stipulates the style for both portraits: "She must be depicted in both cases in bright blue and green style, with pearls and trinkets adorning her chignon, wearing a scarlet full-sleeved variegated brocade robe over a flower-sprigged skirt. And it should be mounted on patterned damask, with ivory knobs on the ends of the roller" (JPM 63.1010, Roy 3:88).[130] Again, the external paraphernalia seems to matter more than verisimilitude or expression. It is as if surface details resist access to affective meanings. We have a detailed description of the garb of the Daoist presiding over the ceremony of displaying and dedicating Li Ping'er's full-length portrait, and, in a faintly ridiculous scene, Chen Jingji, Ximen's son-in-law, in the role of the "filial son," intones an elaborate but scarcely heartfelt eulogy of Li Ping'er in front of the portrait (*JPM* 65.1039–40).

For a moment, Ximen is overwhelmed with emotions as he watches a funereal drama performance that mentions a character bequeathing her self-portrait (63.1019). There is also a scene of Ximen Qing looking at the portrait as he spends the night in front of Li Ping'er's spirit tablet in her room. The narrator inserts a conventional poem describing the sadness of bereavement (65.1042). However, mourning soon becomes another sexual orgy as Ximen Qing starts an affair with Ruyi'er, Guan'ge's erstwhile wet nurse who stays on in Ping'er's room (67.1081–82). The social and ritual functions of Li Ping'er's portraits are fully delineated, but their affective meaning for Ximen Qing is easily superseded by another sexual adventure. Li Ping'er's lavish funeral takes up four chapters in the book. We know all the details of the ceremony, the amount Han is paid for the portraits, the mourners' gifts, and the gifts given in return. Ximen Qing's grief is extravagantly displayed, but somehow the reader feels a lack of access to his inner life. He has no deep communion with Li Ping'er's portraits, the objects most likely to arouse sentimental associations. After Ximen Qing's death, Wu Yueniang has the portraits unceremoniously burnt.

If Li Ping'er's portraits seem enmeshed in social display and make-believe ritual functions even as they may claim to have sentimental value for Ximen Qing, Jinlian's bed, which Chunmei tries to recover as a memento after Jinlian's death, shows the pressure of economic transactions. The bed is featured in the rivalry between Ping'er and Jinlian. Jinlian "induced Ximen Qing to spend sixty taels of silver in order to buy a balustraded bedstead of inlaid mother-of-pearl for her" because Li had a similar bed (*JPM* 29.418, Roy 2:187).[131] The bed is described in great detail: the narrative lingers over the side panels with mother-of-pearl designs depicting "towers and terraces, halls and chambers, flowers and foliage, birds and animals" (*JPM* 29.418, Roy 2:187), motif of pines, bamboos, and plum blossoms on the three comb-back-shaped backrests, and the purple gauze bed curtains with brocade sashes and silver hooks.[132] The bed is the setting for a seduction scene: clad in nothing but a bodice of red chiffon and red slippers, Pan Jinlian "had secretly mixed the stamens of jasmine blossoms with butterfat and face powder and rubbed the mixture over her entire body" until it was "white and glossy, shiny and smooth" (*JPM* 29.419, Roy 2:188) in the hope of besting her rival Li Ping'er, whose fair skin entranced Ximen Qing (*JPM* 27.385). The bed is but the symbolic extension of the body; both belong to the same scheme of sexual competition and voracious desire.

As Jinlian's loyal ally and the conspicuous third party in her sexual exploits,[133] Chunmei replicates her desires and aversions, especially after her death. It is fitting, therefore, that Chunmei should seek to recover Pan Jinlian's bed after she was eviscerated by her nemesis Wu Song—in some ways she is recovering part of herself. In the wake of a reversal of fortune, Chunmei, now the wife of the commandant Zhou Xiu, visits the declining Ximen household after Ximen's death, finds general dilapidation, and asks about Jinlian's missing bed. Ximen Qing had taken the "gilt lacquer Nanking bed with retractable steps" that Meng Yulou had brought with her as part of her dowry and had given it to his daughter, Ximen Dajie, as part of her trousseau when she married into the Chen family (8.101). When Meng Yulou remarries Li Gongbi after Ximen Qing dies, Wu Yueniang turns over Pan's bed to Meng to make up for the Nanking bed (91.1551). A potential sentimental object turns out to be a link in a chain of substitution. Objects are replaceable because of consensual monetary value. Chunmei accepts this inexorable economic logic and asks about the fate of the other beds. Yueniang reclaims Ximen Dajie's bed (the reason for the loss of Jinlian's bed) after Dajie's suicide and sells it for a mere eight taels of silver. Li Ping'er's bed, which had inspired the competition, was sold for thirty-five taels of silver. Chunmei remembers its original cost (sixty taels) and regrets the cheap resale: "If I had known that you were getting rid of it, I would have been willing to pay you thirty or forty taels of silver for it. I would have really liked to have it" (96.1627, Roy 5:316). In other words, her mind is quickly diverted from the sentimental value of Jinlian's bed to the monetary value of the beds related by substitution and association. She would not have minded paying for Li's bed the amount that Yueniang sold it for. It would have been a bargain.

If things usually do not command sentimental or emotional value and if the logic of the marketplace reigns supreme, what are we left with? Do we see the objectification of people as the index to moral collapse?[134] Is oppressive materiality a self-subverting proposition—does it necessarily imply its own vacuity and meaninglessness? Things in *Jin Ping Mei* resist the imposition of emotional, moral, and spiritual meanings. They even resist their own negation. Interpretations of the book based on a stringent moral or religious vision presume revulsion against the venality and futility of its material surface, yet the implied author has an undeniable fascination with all its details. Recalcitrant things can nevertheless have momentum that drives the narrative. Think of Pan Jinlian's shoes and how they function in numerous scenes of flirtation, sexual orgy, jealousy, and rivalry. It may be precisely because they do not have "deeper meanings" that they are so evocative of desires and fears as lived experience. The characters may be defined by their material existence and sometimes reduced to mere "things," but they are not thereby dehumanized. On some level the author still seems to empathize with their fatuous desire for or reliance on things as the basic struggles of the human condition—in other words, the desire for things can dehumanize, but it also stems from the life force seeking affirmation and resisting the fate of being reduced to a "mere thing." The paradox of *Jin Ping Mei* lies in how it entrances with its plethora of things even while denying their connections with interiority, and how the human condition of being defined by things still stirs sympathy without any consistently convincing appeal to a moral or religious system.[135]

AFFECTIVE THINGS IN *HONGLOU MENG*

No other works of Chinese fiction before *Jin Ping Mei* show the same obsession with material reality. Of all Chinese genres, *fu* (variously translated as "rhapsody," "prose poem," or "poetic exposition") displays the most sustained focus on exhaustive description. Some of its most famous examples, such as Sima Xiangru's (d. 117 BCE) "*Fu* on Shanglin Park" (Shanglin fu) and "*Fu* on the Great One" (Daren fu), Ban Gu's (32–92) "*Fu* on the Two Capitals" (Liangdu fu), and Zuo Si's (250–305) "*Fu* on the Three Capitals" (Sandu fu), also encompass a grand inclusiveness and aspire to evoke a sense of plenitude. Numerous *fu* on objects tirelessly list their attributes and history. It could be that Chinese fiction, in trying to summon the illusion of totality, draws from the penchant for descriptive details endemic to *fu*. Indeed, in *Jin Ping Mei* there are numerous passages of parallel prose, often announced by the phrase *danjian* 但見 (behold), devoted to topics as various as a person's appearance, the décor of a room, gardens, natural scenery, storms, temples, a matchmaker's wiles, religious ceremonies, sexual intercourse, aphrodisiac, the lantern festival, feasts, and funerals, that are in effect mini-*fu*. Couched in somewhat categorical and formulaic language, descriptive passages like these, though less impressive in range, are also found in earlier works of vernacular fiction. Where *Jin Ping Mei* diverges from precedents is the enumeration of less tidy lists of attributes built into the narrative and attention to contemporary particularities that engross the implied author.

The aesthetic ideal of *fu*, according to the poet Lu Ji, is to "give form to (or embody) things" (*tiwu* 體物). Even this implied principle of externalization, however, comes to presume "a true understanding of the meaning of things" or "communion with things." Poetry taking things as its objects of attention (*yongwu shi* 詠物詩, *yongwu ci* 詠物詞) also upholds the primacy of their affective meanings and blurs the boundaries between the poet and his or her object. This takes us back to notions of mastery and transcendence in people's relationship with things discussed earlier. There are countless literary examples of attributing affective meanings to things and imagining communion between the poet and the external focus of the poet's attention. Poetic ideals of the comingling of feelings and scenes, the merging of the mind and its object (*qing jing jiaorong* 情景交融, *xin wu jiaorong* 心物交融) seem to answer the hope that the mind animates all things. In other words, despite some affinities in the principle of exhaustive description, there are significant differences between the underlying aesthetics of *fu* and that of the sixteenth-century novel.

Jin Ping Mei stands alone in frequently rejecting the notion that things should command affective and symbolic associations—a staple of the tradition manifested in the examples of obsession and anthropomorphized things discussed earlier. That idea reaches its most complex realization in the eighteenth-century masterpiece, Cao Xueqin's *Honglou meng*. Cao might have started to write *Honglou meng* in the 1740s. By 1754 manuscripts of the book, with comments by Red Inkstone Studio (Zhiyan zhai), and more sporadically by Odd Tablet (Jihu) and others, began to be circulated among the author's friends and family. We do not know the identity of these commentators, but they were privy to the author's family history and knew of his aesthetic design. Cao did not live to finish *Honglou meng*. The eighty or more chapters he wrote circulated as hand-copied manuscripts for more than three decades before the novel's publication in a 120-chapter version in 1791 and 1792. Another author, possibly Gao E (1763–1815), wrote the final forty chapters.

The paradoxical implications of humanizing things constitute perhaps the most intriguing aspect of the discourse on things in *Honglou meng*, although what typically invites scrutiny is the delineation of specific objects contributing to the reader's visualization and experience of the novel's texture. Exotic objects or unusual things, such as the European pendulum clock (*HLM* 6.65); the silk flowers from the palace (7.72–75); the *qiang* wood for Qin Keqing's coffin (13.129); the plate glass mirror (17/18.171–72,[136] 26.266, 41.441, 51.553, 56.621); the European spotted pug dog (37.392); the walnut-sized gold watch (45.485); the snuffbox with the enamel image of a blond, winged, naked European girl, the *wangqia* tobacco inside, the European medicinal patch applied at the temple for curing headaches (52.562); the Russian peacock feather cloak (52.566, 570–71); and the golden model of a Western ship (57.627, 63.700), are bound to arrest the reader's attention and have indeed invited assiduous research.[137] As is well known, Cao Xueqin's forbears won the trust and favor of the Kangxi emperor (r. 1661–1722), and his bannermen family was rich and powerful before going into steep decline during Cao's early years. Cao Xueqin drew on personal reminiscences and family history in writing the novel, although the extent of correspondence between Cao and the protagonist Jia Baoyu is open to debate. Despite (or perhaps because of) its autobiographical dimension, the book is deliberately evasive about its setting: "but the precise details of dynasty, period, region, and locality were unexpectedly missing" (1.3). Many readers feel that objects, especially exotic and valuable things, provide glimpses into that repressed history, offering a sense of the novel's contemporary setting and Cao Xueqin's background or even clues to Qing court culture.[138]

Some objects in the novel have an obvious symbolic quotient. The jade Baoyu holds in his mouth at birth and subsequently wears around his neck is the earthly incarnation of the stone deemed unfit to repair heaven. Its dual function as being both the essence of Baoyu and the narrator dispassionately commenting on Baoyu holds the key to our understanding of desire and irony in the novel.[139] The mirror (both the European style glass one mentioned above and the traditional bronze ones) has multifaceted Daoist and Buddhist associations with the dialectics of reality and illusion.[140] The improbably ancient objects with romantic and erotic associations in Qin Keqing's room, where Baoyu dreams of visiting the Illusory Realm of Great Void, obviously straddles the boundary of dreaming and waking, illusion and reality (5.46–47). But it is the particular conceit of *Honglou meng* that even ordinary things can be invested with singular significance beyond standard cultural meanings. The novel inherits the fascination with material and mundane details in *Jin Ping Mei*, but in contrast to *Jin Ping Mei*, things invite subjective illumination, symbolic construction, and sentimental association in *Honglou meng*.[141] In another kind of symmetric inversion, scenes affirming such meanings often come with echoes of unease and intimations of destruction in *Honglou meng*, even as things with recalcitrant materiality inured to affective associations supposedly undermine the humanity of characters in *Jin Ping Mei* but can still stir sympathy for them.

Baoyu lives by the creed that myriad things are sentient and respond to human emotions. In chapter 23, Baoyu and the girls he admires and loves move into Grand View Garden. The garden has been built for the visit of the Imperial Consort Yuanchun, Baoyu's eldest sister. That visit takes place during winter, when artificial flowers and bright lanterns disguise the austerity of nature. But when Baoyu and the girls move into the garden, we see spring in all its glory. For all that, fallen blossoms capture the sense of the relentless passage of time. The first significant act in the garden is the attempt of Baoyu and Daiyu to protect the purity of fallen petals. That memorable scene begins with Baoyu reading *The Western Wing* (*Xixiang ji* or *Huizhen ji*) under a peach tree. "He opened *The Western Wing* and savored it from the beginning. Just as he came to the line 'petals falling in hosts of red,' a gust of wind brought down a rain of peach blossoms, and petals fell all over him, his book, and the ground. Baoyu was about to shake them off but was afraid he would step on them, so he had no choice but to collect them in his skirt, come to the pond's edge, and shake them off at the pond." It is at this juncture that Daiyu enters the scene, bearing on her shoulder a hoe with a silken bag attached to its end and holding a flower broom in her hand. She reminds Baoyu that this will not do: the water in the garden looks clean, but once it flows to the grimy world outside, the fallen blossoms will not escape defilement. She proposes to bury them in a bag in a "flower grave": "as time passes, naught will happen but that it will be one with the earth. Isn't that a clean solution?" (23.234).

Baoyu first becomes aware of the rain of petals because he has come to a line describing just such a scene in *The Western Wing*, one of the most famous romantic plays in the Chinese tradition. Things seem to become sentient because of the easy transition between the text and the world, between imagined reality and perception. A northern play in five acts and twenty scenes, *The Western Wing* is based on a Tang tale, Yuan Zhen's (770–831) "Yingying's Story" (Yingying zhuan), also called "Encountering the Goddess" (Huizhen ji). It is a story of forbidden love and betrayal: Zhang pursues the initially reluctant Yingying and has a clandestine affair with her but subsequently abandons her. Wang changes the tragic ending of the story and reunites the lovers. *The Western Wing* was extremely popular; there are about 140 extant editions from the Ming and Qing dynasties. The most prevalent edition for reading during the Qing dynasty was the version with commentaries by Jin Shengtan (1610–1661). According to Jin, Wang Shifu's play ends at scene 16, when Zhang, after leaving Yingying and heading toward the capital, dreams of Yingying coming to him, only to be almost taken away by pursuing officers. Jin characterizes the fifth act (scenes 17 to 20), which enacts the happy ending, as the "sequel" by Guan Hanqing (13th c.). Cao Xueqin notes that *The Western Wing* Baoyu and Daiyu are reading has sixteen scenes: "Before the duration of a meal elapsed, she [Daiyu] had already finished all sixteen scenes" (23.234). One version of the play that includes only the first sixteen scenes is the *Yuan Dynasty Northern Western Wing* (*Yuan ben bei Xixiang*, printed 1680), with commentaries by the Ming loyalist Pan Tingzhang (b. 1612), who emphasizes a Buddhist interpretation. The fact that Baoyu refers to the play by the name *Encountering the Goddess* and as "a set" (*yitao Huizhen ji* 一套會真記) suggests that the version may be Min Qiji's (1580–after 1661) *Six Illusions of Encountering the Goddess* (*Huizhen liuhuan*), especially since it lists the first sixteen scenes and the last four as two separate plays.[142] Min's set includes *The Cause of Illusion* (*Huanyin*, Yuan Zhen's "Yingying's Story"); *Music of the Illusion* (*Chouhuan*, Dong Jieyuan's [12th c.] *The Western Wing in All Keys and Modes*); *Play as Illusion* (*Juhuan*, the first sixteen scenes of *The Western Wing* by Wang Shifu); *Continuing the Illusion* (*Genghuan*, the last four scenes of *The Western Wing*, attributed to Guan Hanqing); *Another illusion* (*Geng huan*, *The Western Wing in the Southern Style* by Li Rihua [15th c.]); and *The Illusion Leaves* (*Huanwang*, *The Western Wing in the Southern Style* by Lu Cai [1497–1537]).[143] The twenty-one color print illustrations bearing Min's name might have been part of the set—they emphasize themes of mediation, illusion, and self-reflexivity by framing scenes from the play through other media.[144] Whether Cao Xueqin is referring to Min Qiji's set or another Jin Shengtan edition, the idea of "all sixteen scenes" precludes the happy ending and highlights the mutual implication of love and dreams, desire and illusion.

Daiyu objects to throwing the petals in the water because they will inevitably be contaminated by the filth in the outside world. Her implicit belief is that the garden is an enclave of innocence and purity and that it is possible to keep external reality at bay. Yet the origins of the waterways in the garden remind us that the illusion of purity is precarious. The Grand View Garden incorporates the Converging Scents Garden in the Eastern Ning Mansion—indeed, it is built by extending the Converging Scents Garden in the northwestern direction, so that it directly links up with the eastern courtyard of the Western Rong Mansion (16.157–58). The Tower of Heavenly Fragrance in Converging Scents Garden is where, in an earlier draft, a maid surprises Qin Keqing in her tryst with her father-in-law Jia Zhen and where she later hangs herself. In the present version there is no explicit reference to this lurid story, but Qin Keqing's mysterious death and her excessively lavish funeral hint at dark secrets. It is also the place where Jia Rui pursues an adulterous liaison with his cousin's wife Wang Xifeng, an ill-fated venture that costs him his life. The Converging Scents Garden is watered by a stream led in by a culvert that runs under the corner of a northern wall (16.158). In other words, the water in the garden is integrated with a stream from another garden marked by sexual transgression, crime, and punishment, and whose stream is in turn fed by water from the outside: the boundaries between being "inside" and "outside" the garden seem both self-evident and elusive.¹⁴⁵

Converging Scents Garden is also where Baoyu visits the Illusory Realm of Great Void in a dream while sleeping in the room of Qin Keqing, who is a few years older despite being the wife of Baoyu's nephew (5.46–47). During that dream visit, Baoyu experiences the epitome of sensual pleasures that culminate in sexual initiation with the goddess Disenchantment's sister Jianmei (combining beauties), who looks like Daiyu and Baochai and also has a mysterious connection with Qin Keqing. Pursued by demons at the end of the dream, Baoyu wakes up calling: "Keqing, save me!" The figural connections of Jianmei with Keqing, Daiyu, and Baochai suggest that it is impossible to disentangle spiritual longing and carnal desire, and that both are impermanent and dangerous. When Baoyu tours the garden for the first time, he is forcibly struck by a sense of having visited the place before, pointing to the symbolic connection between the garden and the Illusory Realm (17/18.170). This means that the garden will repeat the paradox and warning of the Illusory Realm: it promises earthly delights but also portends their inevitable destruction. The attempt to preserve the purity of fallen blossoms, and by extension the purity of the garden world, is doomed to failure.

Fallen blossoms are insentient things, yet Baoyu and Daiyu cherish them and worry about their fate of being "defiled" by the outside world. Such powers of empathy or self-projection give credence to their final evaluative epithets. According to Red Inkstone, the book should end with a "Final Listing" that ranks all the characters according to their relationship with love, and each will be described with an epithet that include the word *qing*. Cao Xueqin did not live to finish that chapter, or it was lost if it had been written, but Red Inkstone tells us that Baoyu's epithet is *qing bu qing* 情不情, which can mean, among other things, "love for what is loveless or insentient" or "love that turns into its negation" (*ZYZ* 8.199, 19.354, 19.367, 31.551).¹⁴⁶ His concern for the fallen blossoms would belong to the first definition—he attributes feelings to insentient things, believing that by the power of imagination and empathy he can animate them. Indeed, next to the line that Baoyu "was afraid that he would step on them," Red Inkstone comments: *qing bu qing* (23.455). Daiyu's epithet is *qing qing* 情情, "loving love" or "redoubled love" (19.367). Hers is the self-consuming love whose intensity is based on focus on her feelings, including her empathetic identification with things.

In chapter 27, Daiyu composes and chants a poem in which she dwells on her death even as she mourns and buries fallen blossoms. It shows clear filiation with earlier poems on fallen blossoms, including some that feature the idea of their burial. Daiyu's poem departs from its antecedents through its focus on the person burying flowers and her poetic creation: "Last night, beyond the courtyard, a mournful song rises: / Is this the spirits of the flowers or of the birds?" 作宵庭外悲歌發，知是花魂與鳥魂 (*HLM* 27.283). Close empathetic identification with the fallen blossoms is thus also the beginning of self-observation and self-reflection. Overhearing Daiyu's chanting on the other side of the hill, Baoyu is overwhelmed by imagined loss.

> Just think, there will be a time when Lin Dai-yu's beauty would be no more.... And would he still exist? If he could not even know where he would be or where he would go, then this place, this garden, these flowers, these willows—to whom would they belong? And thus from one thing to another, his thoughts went back and forth in circles. Truly he did not know at that very moment what sort of an obtuse thing he had to become,[147] or how he could be completely divested of all sentience and knowledge, so that he could escape the Great Creation, leave the net of dust and grime called life, and find some relief from this deep sadness.
> (*HLM* 28:285)

Baoyu's thought process shows how the different meanings of *qing bu qing* mentioned above can be connected: from investing all things with affective significance, he moves to negating emotion as the path to freedom. Elsewhere Red Inkstone describes this inevitable negation and self-distancing, stoked by disappointments and frustrations, as the "poison of excessive emotions" (*qing ji zhi du* 情極之毒, *ZYZ* 21.416). Red Inkstone calls Daiyu's poem "a gatha for the destinies of all the beauties" and "the prelude to all the beauties in Grand View Garden returning to their origins" (27.516, 532)—i.e., their inevitable tragic end. In that sense, Baoyu's reaction is justified. The poem based on affinities with fallen blossoms becomes an elegy for an entire world. Glorying in the power of subjective projection inevitably leads to an awareness of its limits.

The empathetic imagination animating all things also facilitates the communication of emotions. Burying fallen blossoms deflects the momentary tension caused by the language of love from *The Western Wing* (*HLM* 23.234–35):

> Baoyu smiled, "Coz, what do you say? Isn't it wonderful?" "It is indeed appealing." "I am that 'body plagued by too many sorrows and ailments,' and you are that 'beauty that topples kingdoms and cities.'" When Daiyu heard this, a vivid flush rose to her cheeks and reached all the way to her ears, and right away up went those eyebrows that seemed to be frowning yet not quite, glowering were those eyes that seemed to be staring yet not quite, and anger overspread her delicate face. She pointed at Baoyu and said, "How dare you spew such nonsense! You brought in these lewd songs for no good reason, and you learnt drivel from them to insult me. I am going to tell uncle and aunt." Even as she was coming to the word "insult," her eyes reddened from prickling tears, and she turned and left. All rattled, Baoyu blocked her way: "Good coz, please do forgive me this once. Indeed I misspoke. If I meant to insult you, may the day come that I tumble straight into the pond, get swallowed by a scabby-headed turtle, and turn into a huge turtle myself, so that when you become in due time a Lady of the First Rank, and move on to Western Heaven upon dying of old age, I will be carrying the stele at your grave for eternity."
>
> Daiyu could not suppress a giggle, rubbed her eyes and said, "So that's how scared you can be. And still you will not let go of your nonsense. 'Pschaw! You turned out to be the sprouting shoot that would not shoot straight—you are just the solder spear that looks like silver!'" Baoyu heard her out and said, "And now it's your turn! I too am going to tell on you." Lin Daiyu smiled, "You think that you can remember lines from a cursory reading, so why wouldn't you credit me with the same quickness?" Baoyu said with a smile as he put the book away, "Let's get serious and bury the flowers, don't say anything more about that."

Just like *Honglou meng*, *The Western Wing* uses the idea of illusion to capture the ineffability and pathos of desire: "He has become the lover in the reflection, I have become the beloved in the painting" (act 2, scene 4).[148] But the play also includes explicit sexual description, as in this aria about the rendezvous of Zhang and Yingying: "I will loosen your buttons, untie your silken sash, as fragrance wafts through the quiet studio.... The warm scent of her jade-like body in my embrace ... her willow waist sways. Gently opening the flower's pistil, as dewdrops make the peony bloom.... Half resisting, half drawing close, both surprised and rapturous" (act 4, scene 1).[149] How does the frank sensuality of the play affect Baoyu and Daiyu? "I am the one plagued by many sorrows and ailments, how can I withstand your beauty that topples kingdoms and cities?" (act 1, scene 4)—when Zhang sings these lines, carnal desire and romantic longing are intertwined.[150] The sexual innuendoes explain why Daiyu feels insulted when Baoyu quotes them.

The relationship between romantic longing and carnal desire is usually not presented as a problem in the Chinese literary tradition. Both *The Western Wing* and *The Peony Pavilion* (*Mudan ting*) by Tang Xianzu (1550–1616), the other play that plays a key role in chapter 23, embrace their apparently seamless transition, a scenario unthinkable in *Honglou meng*. Many critics assert the contrast between the innocent and playful romantic relationships between Baoyu and his female companions in the garden and the predatory sexuality of other men in the novel, such as Jia Zhen, Jia Lian, and Xue Pan. Baoyu has his first earthly sexual experience with the maid Xiren (*HLM* 6.59–60), and there are strong hints of a homosexual romance with Qin Zhong (15.148) and with the actor Jiang Yuhan (28.297), but his relationship with the girls in the garden seems decidedly chaste, despite hints of physical intimacy. Yet the author also rejects a convenient dichotomy. During Baoyu's dream visit to the Illusory Realm, Disenchantment dismisses as sheer hypocrisy those who claim "appreciation of beauty free from lust" (*haose bu yin* 好色不淫) and "spiritual affinity different from lust" (*qing er bu yin* 情而不淫): "To appreciate beauty is already lust, to know love and longing even more so." Baoyu's "Lust of the Mind" (*yiyin* 意淫) is so dangerous precisely because it eludes conventional distinctions (5.57). As mentioned earlier, Disenchantment's sister has figural ties with Daiyu, Baochai, and Qin Keqing and seems to encompass multiple dimensions of desire. If romantic longing and carnal desire, despite being intertwined, also seem to exist in tension in the novel, it may be because the latter brings love down to earth, and the author seems to want to posit a love that has infinite reach because it is embedded in the primal lack of one's being and cannot be accommodated by mundane arrangements (e.g., liaisons, marriage, or its most frequent form in traditional fiction, polygamy).

In Dante's (1265–1321) *Divine Comedy* (Canto V), Francesca tells of the forbidden love between her and Paolo, her brother-in-law. It all begins when they are reading together the story of another forbidden love, that between Lancelot and Guinevere, the wife of King Arthur. Perhaps this kind of self-reflexivity is to be expected. What can be more fitting for a love story than the choice to elevate the power of love stories? It is tempting to see *The Western Wing* as a similar conduit for mimetic desire. If, as Tang Xianzu wrote in *The Peony Pavilion*, "Love is of all things in the world the hardest to tell" 世間只有情難訴, at least one may be able to communicate it through the language of romantic drama. Indeed, there will be more examples of Baoyu and Daiyu intimating longing by using lines from *The Western Wing* (*HLM* 26.268–69). Yet unlike Paolo and Francesca, Baoyu and Daiyu will not reenact the romance they have read: there will not be any secret rendezvous or sexual transgression. Baoyu placates the offended Daiyu by jokes about their karmic connection in death, Daiyu mocks him for being useless by quoting another line from the play, and the scene begins and ends with the burying of fallen blossoms. The preferred "lesson" from *The Western Wing* is the inevitable connection between love and illusion, desire and evanescence. Yet the melancholy is tempered with playfulness. There is, as yet, no deep sense of inadequacy when Baoyu and Daiyu try to overcome loss. Daiyu insists, and Baoyu agrees, that the fallen blossoms preserve their purity by becoming one with the earth in the garden. The only problem is that the term "pure" or "clean" (*ganjing* 乾淨) is associated with death, dispersal, and final renunciation in the symbolic scheme of the book (5.56, 22.223). Cherishing the fallen petals is a paean to the lyrical worldview; it is also a futile gesture of resistance against the passage of time and the inevitable loss of innocence. Ultimate purity is also a negation of existence.

For Baoyu and Daiyu to bury fallen blossoms together in the context of reading *The Western Wing* is to seal their bond and resolve the contradictions of desire through an elegiac gesture. At the end of chapter 23, Daiyu overhears arias from scene 10 of *The Peony Pavilion*. In that scene, the protagonist Du Liniang dreams of making love with a man who claims to have been searching for her. She is to die pining for the love in her dream and will be brought back to life by the lover she dreams up. As with *The Western Wing*, the erotic undertone is marked. But Daiyu's mind registers only the profound melancholy of these arias about love. Other lines on the falling and fading of flowers crowd into her mind, bringing associations with the impermanence of all things, the indifference of the natural world, and the inevitable end of youth, innocence, beauty, and love, and she is profoundly affected: "Thinking over all that carefully, she could not help being seized with pain and shaken in spirit, and tears filled her eyes" (23.236). Affective things desexualize longing by bringing love and death together, hence the elegiac, though still playful, pathos of burying fallen blossoms in chapter 23.

THE SECRET MESSAGES OF THINGS IN *HONGLOU MENG*

Love and its articulation are bound up with death and destruction: this becomes an intermittent refrain in the book. Love cannot be told—again and again we see the frustrations of miscommunication and inadequate expression and the deleterious consequences of articulating one's feelings. In chapter 32, Baoyu struggles to put his feelings for Daiyu into words, and by the time he manages to speak, Daiyu has walked away, and it is Xiren who listens to the avowal of his feelings (32.338–39). Xiren will tell Baoyu's mother her suspicion of "scandal," and that will eventually lead to the search of the garden and its end (34.355–56). The standard tropes of romantic fiction and drama, such as love poems, the material markers of predestined unions, and the exchange of love tokens, are either conspicuously absent or deliberately reframed when it comes to the idealized characters in the book. (An unworthy character like Jia Lian has no trouble employing his nine-dragon jade pendant as a "love token" in the game of seduction [64.722].)

Baoyu's dazed confession in chapter 32 comes on the wake of a misunderstanding about love tokens. Earlier he found a golden kylin among the gifts Daoist Zhang presented to Grandmother Jia when the family attended a religious service at Pure Void Temple. He kept it when he heard that his cousin Shi Xiangyun has a similar kylin. "He saw that nobody paid much attention: Daiyu alone looked at him and nodded, as if in tacit admiration" (29.307–8). Daiyu is jealous but perhaps also takes pride in being the only one who understands his inchoate desires. Baoyu later loses the kylin in the garden, and Xiangyun and her maid come upon it in the middle of a discussion of yin and yang that brings them to the kylin Xiangyun is wearing (31.332–33). Fictional conventions point to a match between Baoyu and Xiangyun, especially since the second line of the titular couplet of chapter 31 seems to hint at it: "The kylin is the omen of twin stars in their twilight years." The received text of the novel contains no such match, but several nineteenth-century readers mentioned another version of the ending whereby Baoyu and Xiangyun, after the death of Baochai and Xiangyun's husband, are reunited in the end.[151]

However, if "twin stars" refer to the Cowherd and Weaver Maid, then the kylins portend brief union and lasting separation. According to Red Inkstone, Baoyu's kylin is what Wei Ruolan, possibly Xiangyun's future husband, wears in an archery scene (*ZYZ* 31.551). The present version of the text has no such scene and mentions only Wei Ruolan in passing (*HLM* 14.141), but in all likelihood in the original design of the book Baoyu acts as the mediator through whom the tokens of karmic ties are exchanged, reprising the role he assumes with his maid Xiren and the actor Jiang Yuhan, whereby they exchange sashes through Baoyu (28.297–98). (In that case, the sashes marking homoerotic longing turn out to presage the eventual union between two objects of Baoyu's desire.) "Twin stars" may suggest that the marriage of Shi Xiangyun and Wei Ruolan ends in separation. Irrespective of the merit of these various theories, the immediate consequence of the kylin is to bring Baoyu and Daiyu closer. Daiyu, uneasy that the pair of kylins may become love tokens as in romantic novels, comes to Baoyu's quarters to allay her suspicions, only to overhear Baoyu ardently defending her unique sympathy with his sensibility in front of Xiangyun and Xiren. Instead of simply feeling reassured, Daiyu's gladness is mixed with apprehension about the future and sadness over her own sickness (32.337). As she walks away, Baoyu catches up with her and tells her: "Do not worry" (32.338), three words that come closest to conveying his feelings. But when he tries a fuller articulation, it is the wrong person who hears it, as mentioned earlier.

In other words, love tokens have unexpected lives in the novel. They give false signals and bring unintended consequences. Objects charting other relationships pass through Baoyu because it is the mantra of the novel that "cases of emotional entanglement throughout the book have to be registered through Brother Stone [Baoyu]" (*ZYZ* 46.627). The most prominent objects promising predestined connection are Baoyu's jade and Baochai's golden locket, and the reciprocal gaze of each on the other's symbolic object brings us their first examination up close (*HLM* 8.83–85). Yet this will be a union wherein "the heart is ultimately not at peace" (5.54), and when Baoyu cries out about the "love karma of gold and jade" in his dream, it is to refute its claim by elevating "the love karma of wood and stone" (36.378), the bond between Baoyu and Daiyu sealed by their previous incarnations, when Divine Jade Attendant (the stone) gives the gift of life and love by watering Crimson Pearl Herb, who thereby incurs "a debt of tears."

"The love karma of wood and stone," the deepest karmic bond carried over from a former existence, has no concretized token and eludes articulation. Perhaps that is why gestures of private symbolism investing ordinary things with deep meanings take hold. We have a moment of perfect nonverbal communication, when Baoyu sends his maid Qingwen to deliver two old handkerchiefs to Daiyu. When Qingwen questions the appropriateness of this "gift," Baoyu says confidently, "Don't worry. She will naturally understand." A maid is drying handkerchiefs as Qingwen enters Daiyu's quarters, a reminder of their connection with Daiyu's tears. Initially puzzled by the old handkerchiefs, Daiyu "took pains to ruminate over them. Only after pondering a good while did she fully grasp their meaning" (34.357). Qingwen remains befuddled, and her incomprehension as unwitting messenger highlights the mystery of private symbolism.

> For her part Lin Daiyu, having divined the meaning of the handkerchiefs, could not help being entranced; her feelings were tumultuous: That Bao-yu should take such care to understand my tortuous thoughts makes me happy. But what will the future hold for these thoughts? That makes me sad. That he should send me two old handkerchiefs out of the blue—suppose he were to miss my meaning, I would have found it laughable just looking at these

handkerchiefs. Just think—for him to send me secret messages like that—it makes me fearful. Ever so often I cry, and come to think of it, it seems so pointless that it makes me ashamed.

The description reprises Daiyu's contradictory reactions when she overheard Baoyu's ardent defense of their shared sensibility (32.337). The symbol of unspoken understanding deserves an interior monologue and indirect free style because it arouses conflicting emotions. Daiyu responds by writing three poems about her own tears of longing and lamentation on these handkerchiefs. Unlike the furtive exchange of handkerchiefs between Jia Yun and the maid Xiaohong that hints at a vaguely illicit liaison (24.248–49, 26.267, 27.275–76), here the circuit of exchange is broken. Daiyu does not return the handkerchiefs with her poems. Their meaning is fulfilled with her tacit acceptance and inscription. But the context is ominous: this moment of confirming their bond is preceded by the aforementioned meeting of Xiren with Madame Wang, when Xiren recommends that Baoyu moves out of the garden to obviate the possibility of scandal. It is also immediately followed by intimations of death. Daiyu looks into the mirror, and the flush she sees is the sign of consumptive feverishness (34.357–58). As with the burying of fallen blossoms, private symbolism invests things with special meanings and communicates what eludes language, but it cannot become a bulwark against loss: again, love and death seem intertwined.

Perhaps it is fitting that the drama of the secret messages of things should be repeated with Qingwen, who shares Daiyu's character traits and looks like her. Commentators refer to her as Daiyu's "shadow" or "reflection" (*yingzi* 影子). After a tiff about Qingwen's carelessness when she breaks the ribs of a fan, Baoyu and Qingwen finally make peace and he asks her to bring fruit on a plate. Qingwen protests that she should not be trusted with the task because she may break the plate as well. Baoyu replies: "If you want to break them, break them. These things are only meant for our use—you want them this way, and I that way: each can follow his or her own feelings. Just like that fan—it's originally for fanning, but you can tear it for fun—just don't do it to vent your anger. Or like cups and plates—they are meant to hold things, but if you enjoy the sound of their breaking and smash them deliberately, that too would be acceptable. Just don't use them to vent your spleen when you fly into a passion. That is what's meant by appreciating things." Qingwen laughs and replies: "In that case, bring me fans for tearing. I love to listen to the sound when they are torn" (31.227–28). What is the difference between tearing a fan in anger and tearing it for fun? Or between breaking plates in anger and breaking them because one enjoys the sound of their breaking? By Baoyu's logic, "appreciating things" (*aiwu* 愛物) means that one's relationship with things would always be optimal so long as one's attitude toward them is deliberate, focused on one's pleasure and sensibility, and unencumbered by other motives. Yet there are unmistakable echoes of heedlessness and selfishness (after all, one of the fans belongs to another maid, Sheyue), death and destruction. The legendary femme fatale Moxi, consort of the tyrant Jie, last king of Xia, is said to have enjoyed the sound of tearing silk, and Jie ordered the tearing of silk to try to win her smile.[152] The wanton destruction became a portent of the decline and fall of Xia. The torn fan seems to be a symbol of Qingwen's eventual fate. Calumny leads to her expulsion from the garden and early death (chaps. 77, 78).

The subtext for the argument between Baoyu and Qingwen is perhaps also the ambiguities in their relationship. When Baoyu chides Qingwen for her carelessness and she retorts with sarcasm, Xiren tries to mollify her by saying "it was our fault to begin with." Her use of the pronoun "our" fans Qingwen's jealousy: "You cannot fool me even with that thing you do in stealth and secrecy—is that enough for you to say 'we' and 'our?'" (31.325). Early on in the novel, Baoyu repeats the sexual initiation in his dream visit to the Illusory Realm of Great Void with Xiren (6.59–60). Thereafter there is no reference to their sexual relationship, but Qingwen alludes to its implication for the power dynamics in Baoyu's quarters as Xiren positions herself as Baoyu's future concubine. As Baoyu and Qingwen make peace, she declines his offer to "wash together" and laughingly hints at impropriety and intimacy between Baoyu and another maid Bihen—on an earlier occasion she attended to his bath for two or three hours and the water swamped the feet of the bed and soaked the mat. Qingwen implies that she does not want to be like Bihen. What is Qingwen asking of Baoyu? Is it a more genuine commitment or a truer love? Is it a plea to be treated differently from other maids? In the context of that society, does it mean the status as Baoyu's future concubine? These are all practical questions that the book displaces by keeping the characters in an undefined prepubescent state and resorting to the discourse instrumentalizing things to create a space for emotions hard to define and articulate. Red Inkstone uses the episode to explain Baoyu's epithet in the "Final Listing": "'tearing fans' is about using insentient things to earn the smile of one who is beautifully contrary, one who cannot understand worldly ways. This is so-called 'feeling for the non-feeling'" (ZYZ 31.551). Baoyu's speech seals his bond with Qingwen through a code of understanding things shared only by them and offers the illusion of comfort by imagining a world of things that gain meanings through one's desires. His reasoning promises freedom yet bodes destruction. Private symbolism may keep encroaching reality at bay, but all too briefly.

The discourse of mastery over things and of transcending the boundary between self and things humanizes things, but it also justifies fashioning the meaning of things according to one's whims and desires. Perhaps that is why the scenes that celebrate Baoyu's affective ties with his world and the powers of his empathy and imagination sometimes carry unmistakable ironic overtones. After a severe beating by his father, the convalescent Baoyu needs to be fed. The maid Yuchuan tries to help him eat hot soup but ends up spilling it on Baoyu's hand. Oblivious to his own burn, Baoyu is solicitous only about Yuchuan, being overwhelmed by the fear that she might have burnt herself. Two old women servants leaving the room see this as further evidence of Baoyu's foolishness (*daiqi* 獃氣). One of them comments:

> "When I last came, I heard the way he talked. Many in the family complain about him: truly he is a bit of a fool. In the middle of a downpour when he was soaked, all he could do was tell another person, 'It's raining! Hurry away from the rain!' Wouldn't you say it's ridiculous? Often, when there's no one by his side, he would cry and laugh for no reason. When he sees the swallows, he talks to them. When he comes upon fish in the stream, he talks to them. He sees the moon and the stars and would either heave sighs or mutter nonsense."
> (*HLM* 35.369)

At first glance this seems to be a simple affirmation of Baoyu's superior sensibility. He can commune with birds, fish, or the moon and the stars by imagining them as sentient and responsive. Further, this ability to humanize things is linked to his empathy with his social inferiors: in this case Yuchuan and the actress Lingguan. The old women's account of the obliviously rain-soaked Baoyu refers to an earlier episode when from behind an arbor he espies Lingguan obsessively scratching a character on the ground (30.319–20). Entranced by this spectacle of a girl obviously burdened by intense but inexpressible longing, Baoyu calls out to her when the rainstorm comes, oblivious to the fact that he himself is getting soaked.

Yet empathy is also inseparable from selfishness. Baoyu can empathize with Lingguan's emotional conundrum to the point of self-forgetfulness, but when the drama of Lingguan's relationship with his kinsman Jia Qiang unfolds in front of him, the realization of his own insignificance in Lingguan's eyes leaves him deeply disconsolate. He is fascinated by the spectacle of emotional entanglement and misunderstanding between Lingguan and Jia Qiang, which in some ways mirrors his own relationship with Daiyu, but self-pity leaves no room for real concern for the fate of the young actress (36.380–81). His solicitousness toward Yuchuan also has a troubling backstory. Yuchuan's sister Jinchuan committed suicide three chapters earlier after Baoyu's mother, Madame Wang, caught her flirting with Baoyu and expelled her from the household (32.341–42). She blamed Jinchuan for seducing Baoyu, when in fact Baoyu is at least as culpable, if not more so. By the time Madame Wang erupted in anger, Baoyu "had already vanished like a puff of smoke" (30.318–29). He was not there to defend Jinchuan. Yuchuan's initial sulkiness is rooted in her anger with Baoyu for being the cause of her sister's suicide. Baoyu's attentiveness in turn springs from feelings of guilt and the desire to mollify Yuchuan. Expansive empathy erasing the boundary between self and other turns out to be both altruistic and self-centered.

Subjective illumination is also delusion. The garden world ends when Madame Wang leads a group of older female servants to search the garden for evidence of illicit relationships after a purse embroidered with an explicit sexual image is found in the garden. Baoyu's maid Qingwen is targeted because of her beauty and unspecified slander aimed at her. Despite the absence of any incriminatory evidence, Madam Wang expels her from the garden. As her illness worsens, Baoyu construes a correspondence between her fate and the crabapple tree in front of his rooms.

The latter's mysterious withering in spring is retrospectively interpreted as an omen for the calamity that befalls Qingwen. Baoyu opines: "Not only plants and trees, but all things that have a reason for being are just like humans: when they find someone who truly understands them, they become absolutely numinous" (77.877).

There is a direct continuity between this declaration and Baoyu's belief that Qingwen has become a goddess of the hibiscus after her death. His "Elegy to the Hibiscus Spirit" (Furong nü'er lei) is a defiant answer to the collapse of the garden world (78.898–903). Appropriating the conventions of the *Verses of Chu* (*Chuci*, ca. 3rd–2nd c. BCE) and using the figure of the loyal but maligned minister from that corpus to mourn the victimization of Qingwen, Baoyu implicitly reverses the allegorical formula of using sensual beauty and romantic longing to articulate political and moral convictions (*meiren xiangcao* 美人香草)—here political analogies serve to mourn a maid and to justify longing for the lost beloved. He eulogizes Qingwen as the spirit of hibiscus, an ultimate celebration of the power of the mind to animate and consecrate things. At the same time the reader knows the compelling myth is based on a lie. Earlier Baoyu questioned a young maid about Qingwen's final moments; she obliges him by inventing a story about Qingwen's celestial appointment as the goddess of hibiscus. The myth-making power that defies destruction is also rooted in delusion. The narrator intervenes to comment on the preposterousness of Baoyu's composition, as if eager to introduce ironic distance to the intense pathos of lyrical projection.[153]

Just as Daiyu's poem on burying fallen blossoms is overheard by Baoyu, here Daiyu overhears Baoyu's elegy. Whereas the earlier scene, already discussed, takes us from empathetic identification with things and self-pity to intimations of the need for transcendence, Daiyu as the hidden audience of Baoyu's elegy introduces new contradictions. When she comes out of the shadows, they discuss the revision of the four lines that directly describe the ties between the mourner and the dead maid. Daiyu suggests that "scarlet gauze window" should replace the more clichéd "red silk bed curtains," perhaps seeking to diminish the sensual innuendoes of the original composition. Baoyu goes along and suggests that the mourner should be female and the elegy can be Daiyu's lamentation for Qingwen. Daiyu dismisses this "inelegant" (*bu dianya* 不典雅) formulation, and Baoyu finally settles on these lines: "Under the scarlet

People and Things 79

gauze window, / my love was destined not to be. / In the tumulus of brown earth: / how star-crossed you were!" 茜紗窗下，我本無緣；黃土壟中，卿何薄命. "When Daiyu heard this, she was troubled and changed color. Although there were boundless doubts and questions in her heart, she refused to show anything, and instead immediately nodded and smiled, praising the excellence of the lines" (79.905). Not only does the discussion of rhetoric, revision, and transferability introduce a slightly jarring distance to an intense lamentation, it reminds us of contradictions unaccommodated by elevated rhetoric. Many critics, starting with Red Inkstone, believe that the elegy is an omen for Daiyu's demise (*ZYZ* 79.723). This makes sense symbolically, inasmuch as figural repetition ties Daiyu and Qingwen. Yet on a more mundane level we are left with Daiyu's jealousy and emotional pain. (To imagine a world in which Daiyu and Qingwen would become principal wife and concubine seems a downright affront to both.) "Eloquence is heard, poetry is overheard.... Poetry is feeling confessing itself to itself in moments of solitude."[154] Staging how poetry is overheard is a reminder of how performance and self-reflexivity are built into the lyrical act. Indeed, both Daiyu's poem and Baoyu's elegy contain references to the act of composition. Much more marked in Baoyu's case, such self-reflexivity imbues mythmaking with dark echoes of futility. We come back to the ambiguities in the discourse of things. Even as the cynicism of treating "people as things" in *Jin Ping Mei* leaves room for empathy, the lyricism of regarding "things as human" is weighed down by disquiet and intimations of destruction.

CHAPTER TWO

Elegance and Vulgarity

The evaluation and appreciation of things take us to a complex vocabulary parsing perceptions and experience. Before we enter that world, we should first reflect on the notion of superfluous things (*zhangwu* 長物), which implicitly negates the notion that mere things should be worthy of attachment or attention. The locus classicus of that term is found in the first chapter ("Virtuous Conduct") of *Shishuo xinyu*.

> Wang Gong (d. 398) returned from Kuaiji. Wang Chen (d. 392) visited him and, upon seeing him sitting on a six-foot long bamboo mat, said to him, "You came back from the east—it is fitting that you should have this thing. You can let me have one." Gong said nothing. After Wang Chen left, Wang Gong then took what he was sitting on and sent it to him. Having no other mat, he thus sat on the floor. Later Wang Chen heard about this and was greatly shocked: "I had thought you owned many of these, that is why I asked for it." Wang Gong replied, "You, sir, do not know me well. My way of being is such that I have no superfluous things."
> (*Shishuo xinyu* 1.44)

What does the anecdote say about Wang Gong? The apparent message is that he has a sublime indifference to worldly possessions. He has no "superfluous things"—not only does he own only one bamboo mat, he is willing to give it up upon his clansman Wang Chen's request. That is, even the object he is using can be given up as superfluous, for he accepts ownership as itself contingent. *Jin History* (*Jinshu*) quotes this passage as evidence of Wang Gong's "simple directness" (*jianshuai* 簡率).[1]

The image of Daoist detachment is confirmed in another anecdote about Wang Gong's ethereal grace. One observer sees him perched on a high carriage wearing a cloak made of crane feathers and exclaims in admiration: "This is truly one of the immortals!" (*Shishuo xinyu* 16.6). Wang Gong is an Eastern Jin aristocrat known for his lofty mien and bons mots. He is praised for "the distinction of his romantic élan" (5.64) and described as "soaring upward with masterful grace" (8.154), "pure and cleansed like a willow under a spring moon" (14.39). He is remembered for his famous quip: "So long as one does nothing in particular, drinks with abandon, and reads *Encountering Sorrow* (*Lisao*) countless times, one can be called a gentleman of distinction" (23.53).

Laozi compares vainglorious self-assertion to "leftover food and unnecessary acts" (*yushi zhuixing* 餘食贅行);[2] disdain for superfluous things is the first step toward Daoist transcendence. Yet accounts of Wang Gong's life tell of his self-righteousness and relentless attacks against his political enemies. As the son and the grandson of powerful Jin ministers and the brother and the nephew of two empresses, Wang Gong was also deeply involved in the court intrigues of his times. He died in the aftermath of an abortive campaign against the dominant faction at court. Does Wang Gong's readiness to give his mat to Wang Chen indicate a deep friendship? His cavalier attitude toward his possession may be taken as a mark of his regard for Wang Chen, remembered in anecdotal literature and historical writings as an unconventional character that indulged in excessive drinking. There are clues suggesting that the two were indeed kindred spirits, but eventually they ended up on opposite sides of factional struggles. Some accounts show their open hostilities; others tell of their plots to bring down each other.[3] An anecdote about friendship and disdain for superfluous things might have concealed or suppressed violent power struggles. By the same token, the discourse on the perception, experience, and evaluation of things leads us not only to aesthetic arguments but also to the contradictory crosscurrents that such arguments may be addressing. Also, an aristocrat known for his grace and refinement claims to be indifferent to the material basis of that refined existence. The simultaneous dependence on and suspicion of economic resources is one of the paradoxes of good taste or elegance.

THE TASTE OF WATER

Extant sixteenth-century editions of *Shishuo xinyu* (1535, 1580, 1586), including one two-color commentary edition, as well as numerous sixteenth- and seventeenth-century imitations, testified to an abiding interest in the text during the late Ming and early Qing. Its interest in parsing perception, experience, and sensibility resonates with the late imperial literature on taste and connoisseurship. By the late Ming, there were manuals, treatises, miscellanies, formal and informal prose, poetry, and fiction on virtually every object, ranging from the quotidian to the exalted, that call for evaluation, appreciation, and categorization. There were Tang and Song antecedents, but their ubiquity from the sixteenth century on was unprecedented. From food, clothing, and furniture to the ornaments of literati culture (e.g., musical instruments, fans, paper, ink-stones, ink-sticks, brushes, seals, incense, flowers, vases, swords, rocks, gardens), from humble utensils to conventionally elevated items such as calligraphy, paintings, or ancient bronze vessels—nothing seems to escape scrutiny and commentary. How objective or subjective is value? How does one claim the right to chart these discourses? What do such discussions tell us about social mores and economic forces? I will begin to explore these issues with a case study: the taste of water.

The scholar and connoisseur Li Rihua (1565–1634) named his studio "Savoring Water" (Weishui 味水). The appraisal of water has a distinguished pedigree. In his *Classic on Tea* (*Cha jing*), Lu Yu (733–804) rated water thus: mountain water comes first, then river water, and last of all water from wells. Of mountain water, one should choose spring water or water flowing slowly over stone pools and avoid water from swift currents. Among the lower ranks, he recommends river water far from human habitation and water from wells frequently used.[4] These relatively straightforward prescriptions are amplified, modified, and mythologized in later writings about water and tea. The Tang official Zhang Youxin (9th c.), citing an older friend Liu Bochu, begins by listing and grading seven locales with superior water in "An Account of

Boiling Water for Tea" (Jian chashui ji), also called "Classic on Water" (Shui jing, 825).[5] Zhang collects specimens from these places, confirms Liu's evaluation, and adds two more based on personal investigation.

Zhang Youxin then relates an encounter with a monk from Chu in a temple in 814, the year he came first in the civil service examination. The monk had with him "An Account of Boiling Tea" (Zhucha ji), which tells of a meeting about fifty years earlier between the official Li Jiqing and Lu Yu. In this story within a story, Li Jiqing, eager to show the tea master the fine water in the area under his jurisdiction, sends an officer to go upstream and fetch water from the Nanling tributary of the Yangzi River to make tea. (Nanling water is supposed to rank first according to Liu Bochu.) When Lu Yu tastes the water, he identifies its provenance as "being close to the bank." After pouring out half of the bucket, he tastes it again and declares, "From here on it is Nanling." The stunned officer confesses: having spilled half of the bucket he was hauling from Nanling, he has filled it with water by the bank.[6] Faced with such proof of Lu Yu's supernatural powers of discrimination, Li Jiqing asks Lu Yu to provide a comprehensive evaluation of water from different locales. Lu Yu declares laconically, "Chu water ranks first, Jin water last."[7] Li Jiqing then records Lu Yu's oral delivery of a graded list of water from twenty places, whereby Nanling water ranks seventh.[8]

The two lists in Zhang Youxin's account (the list attributed to Lu Yu and Zhang's own list) include water from wells, rivers, and waterfalls, which Lu Yu disparages in his *Classic on Tea*. This discrepancy, the device of a story within a story, as well as the sensational nature of the Nanling water anecdote prompt Ouyang Xiu to question Zhang, whom he decries as devious and deceitful in any case because of his role in Tang factional politics, in "Account of the Water from Great Brightness Temple" (Daming shui ji, 1048).[9] In another essay, "Account of the Water from Floating Raft Mountain" (Fucha shan shui ji, 1058), Ouyang Xiu dilates on his appreciation of the spring water from Floating Raft Mountain, which is not mentioned in Zhang Youxin's account; the omission confirms Ouyang Xiu's suspicion of Zhang's judgment. Zhang chooses instead to promote the neighboring Dragon Pond Water, which Ouyang Xiu deems far inferior.[10] The water from Floating Raft Mountain is a gift from Ouyang's friend, the official Li Duanyuan, who discovered it. Ouyang praises Li for combining the privilege of power and wealth and attention to his political responsibilities with the recluse's taste for the joys of nature. He concludes with ruminations on the idea of recognizing worth: "There are cases when an object cannot reveal itself but must wait for someone to be glorified. There are also cases when an object may not be valued but must rely on someone to be prized."[11] The water from Floating Raft Mountain acquires value because of Li Duanyuan's commendation and Ouyang Xiu's essay, which also brings moral and political meanings to its worth and recognition.

The discourse on water is integral to the appreciation of tea. Water is called "the Controller of Fate for tea" (*cha zhi siming* 茶之司命).[12] As the Ming writer Zhang Dafu (1554–1630) observes: "The nature of tea has to be manifested through water."[13] Tea that is less than perfect becomes excellent when conjoined with good water, while perfect tea is proportionately diminished by mediocre water. There are numerous precursors to the discourse on water that proliferated from late Ming on, but the Tang and Song examples recounted earlier are the most frequently invoked and also raise questions that continue to reverberate in later writings. How does an apparently ordinary thing like water become a valuable commodity exchanged as gifts among high officials? Why is an object associated with nature and reclusion also embedded in social relations with the rich and powerful? What builds up consensus in judgment? How does a connoisseur articulate his divergence from the consensus?

Discussions of water greatly increased in number from mid-sixteenth century on.[14] The connoisseurship of water is sometimes described with a vocabulary as elaborate as that reserved for judging wine in our times. At the same time, the niceties of appreciating water invite suspicions that intangible merit may be like the emperor's new clothes, validated only through pretension. In a postscript (1596) on a friend's poem on the Hui Spring (famous for its water), Yuan recalls how his friend Qiu Tan (sobriquet Changru) transported thirty jars of Hui Mountain spring water from the Wu area to his native Tuanfeng (Hubei). Qiu left the water in his servants' charge while returning first. Unhappy with transporting such heavy items, the servants dumped the water into the river and refilled the jars with local spring water upon arrival. Qiu Tan invited "the various aficionados in the city" to taste the prized water. There was much discussion of the water during the gathering. "Only after prolonged inhaling and savoring did they swallow slowly, with an audible gurgle down their throats. They then looked at each other and sighed, 'Marvelous indeed is this water! If not for Changru's lofty interest, how can the likes of us have the wherewithal to taste such water in our lifetime?' They all expressed effusive praise and envy before leaving" (*YHD* 1:194–95). The servants' ploy eventually leaked, much to the chagrin and embarrassment of Qiu Tan and the aficionados. They fail to live up to the model of the fabled water connoisseur like Lu Yu in Zhang Youxin's account. There are other examples. In one tenth-century anecdote, the Tang prime minister, Li Deyu (787–850), asks a friend to bring back a jug of water from the Zhongling tributary of the Yangzi River. The friend gets drunk and forgets the request, only to remember it when his boat passes by Jinling, where he fills the jug and presents the water to Li Deyu in Chang'an. Li, of course, can tell the difference right away (*TPGJ* 399.3201). The inspiration for water discrimination stories may be a saying attributed to Confucius in various early texts: "The Zi and Mian Rivers might have merged, but upon tasting Yiya knew it (i.e., could tell them apart)."[15] Such powers of discrimination are compared to the ability to discern "subtle words" (*weiyan* 微言). Sensory fastidiousness comes to be detached from its original metaphorical context of heightened powers of moral and intellectual judgment and either is celebrated on its own terms or invites suspicion of pretension or criticism of indulgence.

The mockery in Yuan Hongdao's postscript is gentler when it comes to his younger brother Yuan Zhongdao (1570–1623), who had brought back two jars each of water from Hui Mountain Spring and Central Cold Spring, all carefully labeled. After a monthlong journey, however, the writing on the label had faded away. Yuan Hongdao asked his brother to identify them, and Zhongdao could not tell the difference even with careful tasting: "We looked at each other and laughed out loud." Unmasking pretentious connoisseurs, however, does not rule out the viability of judgment. Yuan Hongdao hastens to add: Hui Mountain Spring is definitely superior to Central Cold Spring and, after having served as an official in the Wu (Suzhou) region and having tasted fine water, he "could already tell the difference." Appreciating Hui spring water became de rigueur. In the vernacular story "Graduate Tang's Love Karma Sealed by One Smile" (Tang jieyuan yixiao yinyuan, *Jingshi tongyan* 26, 1624), the poet and artist Tang Yin moors his boat to fetch Hui spring water while in hot pursuit of the beautiful maid servant Qiuxiang. The smiling maid on the grand boat of an official family bewitches him, but the water demands a stop: "Now that I am here, if I don't fetch water from the Hui Mountain spring, that would be vulgar."[16] Tang's image as a free spirit of sensibility and fine taste depends as much on adhering to a fastidious preference for Hui Spring water as on succumbing to a romantic impulse.

Once water is graded according to locales, the means and modes of transportation turn it into a potential luxury item. The aforementioned Li Deyu is said to have transported Hui Mountain Spring water from Changzhou (in Jiangsu) to the Tang capital Chang'an through a network of "water post stations" (*shuidi* 水遞).[17] Zhang Dafu relates an anecdote illustrating how transportation places prized water beyond the reach of the poor: a friend of Ouyang Xiu gave him Central Cold Spring water as gift. Ouyang Xiu expressed surprise that a poor scholar could send such a "marvelous benefaction" (*qikuang* 奇貺). Looking at the vessel for the gift, however, he said slowly, "But the taste of the water is all gone." "For the spring water is cold and has a fast-moving nature. Unless it is locked within gold and silver vessels, one cannot be certain whether the taste has broken through the vessel and vanished." Zhang Dafu adds that, in any case, Central Cold Spring water, obtained from a crevice above swift currents, is highly inaccessible and thus beyond the reach of the poor. The matter of vessel just confirms the "class divide." Zhang Dafu concludes with a disclaimer: "My nature is foolish and uncouth, and I am not picky with either tea or water. The reason I mentioned all these is simply to make 'tea talk' as I taste tea today."[18]

The discourse on water and tea celebrates the pleasures of nature and detachment, yet it seems also inextricably tied to power and privilege, as Li Deyu's water transportation system and Zhang Dafu's story remind us. Li Rihua forges economic considerations with the rhetoric of lofty reclusion, mixing stylistic registrars of the sublime and the mundane in his "Contract on Transporting Spring Water from the Pine Rain Studio" (Songyu zhai yun quan yue):[19]

> For the likes of us, our spirit looks to the snow on bamboo, and our senses, to the wind among pines.[20] For now we just go along with

others, eating and drinking in the human realm, but ultimately, we intend to wander freely beyond the boundaries of things. Not having yet reached the famous mountain, how can we take leave of the sea of dust? But then, as we search for the marvelous and refine our lines, the creative juices easily dry up; and for cleansing torpor or clearing mental obstacles, the spring for making tea cannot be abandoned. I gladly open the missive that comes with a hundred pieces of "moon rounds,"[21] as the bonfire fueled by locust wood makes the water roil with bubbles like so many "crab eyes."[22] Lu Yu's writings on tea have already been honored as canonical, how can Zhang Youxin's compilation fail to further spread its fame? In the past, Li Deyu reached the rank of imperial secretary and took inordinate pains to transport water. Du Fu lived in seclusion among the Gorges of Kui and called out to the perilous landscape under clouds heavy with rain. Now we are situated at the rim of Mount Hui, with a distance a little over 200 *li*. If we cross the River at Songling, it will take no more than three of four days. Rise to the level of the new water and give up the old water: the transportation can work as wondrously as a pulley. Take what is convenient at a modest price: the effort expended is less than that of a well-sweep. We gentlemen of pure spirit should all enter into this fine covenant. Inscribed by the Recluse of Lazy Bamboo.

The ornate, allusive parallel prose of the "contract" is followed by instructions regarding the cost for transporting water (relatively cheap at three *fen*), the gradation of jars, the procedure for collecting the water, and the payment schedule. The tone here is both playful and practical. Li Rihua combines the standard images for ethereal pleasures (snow on bamboo, wind among pines) and for the intensity of literary composition. He avows the wish to transcend mundane cares and to find peace as a recluse, though the historical exemplars he evokes are Tang poets and scholar-officials deeply engaged with contemporary politics (Li Deyu, Du Fu). These apparent paradoxes are typical—the more obvious incongruity is that between the elevated description of the function and historical genealogy of tea drinking and the pragmatic excursus on convenience and payment. Being after all not very far from Hui Mountain Spring means that Li Rihua can mimic Li Deyu's water transportation at a relatively low cost without incurring suspicion of abusing power or indulging in wasteful extravagance.[23] This is above all a playful exercise that showcases that connoisseur's pleasure in conjoining the refined and the mundane to create his own brand of elegance.

Li Rihua and his coterie of paying friends exemplify the social dimension of connoisseurship in literati circles. The most famous anecdote about the friendship among water and tea connoisseurs, however, crosses social boundaries. Included in Zhang Dai's *Dream Memories of Tao'an* (*Tao'an mengyi*), it describes Zhang Dai's encounter with the tea vendor Min Wenshui:[24]

> Zhou Monong could not stop talking to me about Min Wenshui's tea. In the ninth month of the *wuyin* year (1638), I came to the Southern Capital (Nanjing). Having reached the shore, I immediately visited Min Wenshui at Peach Leaf Crossing. It was mid-afternoon, and Wenshui had gone out. Returning late, he turned out to be an old man of free and easy mien. Just as we were talking, he rose suddenly and said, "I forgot my staff at someone's house." He then left again. I said, "How can I return today empty-handed?" Wenshui delayed his return for quite a while. By the time he came back, it was the evening. He looked steadily at me: "Is the guest still here? Why is the guest still here?" I said, "I have admired the honored Old Min for a long time. If I cannot have a hearty drink of Old Min's tea, I will certainly not leave."
>
> Wenshui was pleased and rose to personally work at the stove. He was swift as wind and rain, and the tea was soon ready. He led me to a room with bright windows and clean low tables. Jingxi teapots[25] and porcelain cups from the Chenghua (1464–1487) and Xuande (1425–1435) reigns, all of the finest make, numbered about a dozen. The color of the tea, when observed under lamplight, was no different from that of the porcelain cup, but its fragrance was irresistible, and I marveled at its excellence. I asked Wenshui: "What variety of tea is this?" Wenshui said, "This is Fairy Land Tea." I took another sip and said, "Don't fool me. This is produced with the Fairy Land method, but the taste is different." Wenshui hid his smile and said, "Do you know what variety this is?" I took another sip and said, "How come this is so very similar to Luojie Tea?"[26] Wenshui stuck

his tongue out and said, "Amazing, amazing." I asked, "What water is this?" He said, "Hui Spring." I said, "Don't fool me. How can Hui Spring water, after having been transported over a thousand *li*, preserve its distinctive character despite the tumult?" Wenshui said, "I no longer dare to hide the truth. This is the way I take Hui Spring water—I have to dig a well and wait for the new spring water to arrive in the quiet of the night, and then I draw the water right away. I use mountain pebbles to line the bottom of the jar. My boat would not sail unless there is wind, that's why the water acquires this roundness and depth. Even ordinary Hui Spring water pales in comparison, let alone water from other places." He stuck his tongue out again and said, "Amazing, amazing." Before he finished talking, Wenshui was gone. Sometime later, he brought a pot and filled my cup, saying: "Taste this." I said, "The scent is overwhelming, and the taste is very modulated and deep. Is this spring tea? The tea you brewed earlier was made with tea leaves picked in autumn." Wenshui laughed out loud and said, "I am seventy—when it comes to discerning connoisseurs, there's none like you." We thus established our friendship.[27]

In the way he initially tries Zhang Dai's patience, Min Wenshui behaves like masters of esoteric knowledge, such as the mysterious old man (Master Yellow Stone) in the biography of Zhang Liang (d. 187 BCE) in *Shiji*. In that account, the old man drops his shoe and asks Zhang Liang to pick it up and put it on for him, then makes an appointment to meet Zhang but twice dismisses him for being tardy. Zhang Liang has to prove his humility and sincerity before Master Yellow Stone would impart his knowledge of the art of war to him (*Shiji* 55.2034–35). Here Zhang Dai turns out to be no acolyte, however—his quest is less for knowledge than for recognition. All the same, he has to prove his sincerity and powers of discrimination to gain Min Wenshui's trust and approval. According to Zhang's "Preface to the *History of Tea*" (Cha shi xu), when Min Wenshui visited Zhang's friend Zhou Youxin (i.e., the "Zhou Monong" mentioned at the beginning of the account) in Shaoxing, he also tried to meet Zhang Dai and was disappointed at missing him. His deliberate elusiveness in this account may thus be an attempt (on his part or Zhang's part) to dramatize the encounter. Their eventual meeting reminds us of accounts of "tea competition" (*doucha* 鬥茶), whereby tea connoisseurs try to best each other with ever more exquisite specimens.[28] The test of taste can also be one way to assert general intellectual superiority, as in the episode from the vernacular story "Wang Anshi Thrice Posed Hard Questions for Academician Su" (Wang Anshi san nan Su xueshi, *Jingshi tongyan* 3), where Wang Anshi puts Su Shi in his place by correctly identifying Su Shi's gift, the water supposedly from the Middle Gorges of the Yangzi River, as being actually taken from the Lower Gorges. Water connoisseurship in this case is dignified as "broad knowledge about things" (*bowu* 博物), which also allows Wang to best Su in other tests of poetic wit and textual knowledge.[29]

The agonistic momentum of Zhang's encounter with Min is different, however; it feeds the test of friendship, and the account ends with the two of them becoming good friends.[30] Connoisseurship depends on social consensus (e.g., the merit of Hui Mountain Spring water), but it is always a game about pushing boundaries—the individual's discoveries and refinement or redefinition of the consensus. Thus many late Ming connoisseurs of water write about their own discoveries of hitherto unknown springs (e.g., Zhang Dafu, Zhang Dai). At the same time, individual preferences need confirmation from the like-minded chosen few. The groups that emerge may or may not correspond to our notions of social distinctions or literati identity. Min Wenshui made his own brand of tea, sold tea at a shop by Peach Leaf Crossing at Nanjing, and became a celebrated cultural figure.[31] He was a good friend of Wang Yuesheng, a courtesan and fellow tea lover who sometimes met her friends (including Zhang Dai) and favored clients at Min's teashop. Zhang Dai describes Wang Yuesheng as proud and reticent, "lofty and detached like the lone plum blossom and the cold moon."[32] The unlikely trio of the literatus, the tea vendor, and the courtesan shows how the regime of taste defies social boundaries and celebrates an aristocracy of sensibility. It is not clear whether Zhang Dai wrote his account about Min Wenshui before or after the fall of the Ming, but it is included in a book that purports to collect "dream memories" of fine things and exquisite experiences in the waning years of the Ming dynasty. As such it is colored by deep nostalgia for a lost world. In this case, after the fall of the Ming, Min Wenshui and his sons continued to sell tea at Peach Leaf Crossing, patronized by Qing scholars and officials. The anecdote thus does not share the pathos of destruction that characterizes accounts of how treasured possessions were lost or how great collections of art works and books suffered ruin and dispersal.

What does water connoisseurship have in common with evaluation in other spheres (e.g., utensils, antique vessels, or objects of art)? There are notable differences. Literati self-definition is commensurate with ignorance about water (e.g., both Yuan Zhongdao and Zhang Dafu confess to it, although Yuan claims to eventually learn discrimination and Zhang shows his knowledge elsewhere), but indifference to calligraphy or painting would be more unusual.[33] There are obvious continuities as well: quasi-fantastic elaborations of powers of discrimination, the tension between consensus and individual preference, the competition and fellowship among connoisseurs, the unmasking of "fake connoisseurship" and social pretension, and the uneasy balance between commodifying the object of appreciation and elevating its value as absolute and being beyond economic exchange. Li Rihua's "Contract" that mixes price lists and cost distribution with elevated rhetoric and erudite allusions, as well as Zhang Dai's friendship with Min Wenshui that breaks down social barriers while erecting new ones between the select few and everyone else, also draw attention to the need to break and redefine boundaries in the discourse of connoisseurship. All these are salient for considering ideas about elegance and vulgarity.

NORMATIVE ELEGANCE

The word "elegant" in English is related to the Latin verb for "elect" (*eligere*), and if one plausible translation of *ya* 雅 is "elegant," it may be because an activity, a person, or a thing designated as *ya* often implies exclusion. Its opposite, *su* 俗, often translated as "vulgar," also means "common" and "customary." Xu Shen, for examples, defines *su* as "common practice (*xi* 習)."[34] Chen Jiru (1558–1639) opines about tea appreciation: "One person would get the spirit; two, the élan; three, the taste; but for seven or eight persons this can only be called offering tea like Buddhist alms."[35] This is perhaps less a matter of social distinction or vigilant defense of literati identity than the pride of individual difference, or individual difference as confirmed through fellowship with a select few.

We are reminded of Zhang Dai's tea stories and the unlikely trio of the literatus, the tea-vendor, and the courtesan.

Elegance, however, is also supposed to be normative, even as the select few hold the secret that others aspire to. Indeed, the word *ya* in early texts is sometimes interchangeable with *xia* 夏 (Zhou, the central domains),[36] and among its early associations are *yayan* 雅言, "the standard way of speaking" or the speech of the noble man, and *yayue* 雅樂 or *yasheng* 雅聲, music linked to the foundational Zhou ritual and political order. Zheng Xuan (127–200) explains the term *yayan* in the *Analects* as correct enunciation: "In reading the rules and standards of the former kings, it is necessary to correctly enunciate the sounds. For it is only thus that the meaning is complete."[37] *Ya* comes to be understood as proper or correct (*zheng* 正), as when Xunzi states: "that which is rooted in ritual propriety is correct (*ya*)" (*Xunzi jianshi* 2.13), "rules that deviate from those of the later kings are called incorrect (*bu ya*)" (8.95).[38] The Mao Preface to the *Classic of Poetry* links *zheng* (proper or correct) to its homophone *zheng* 政 (government) in defining *Ya* (sometimes translated as Odes), one of the three sections in the *Classic of Poetry*: "To speak of the affairs of all under heaven and to give form to the mores of all places is called *Ya*. *Ya* means 'proper.' This means speaking of the reason for the rise or decline of royal government."[39] According to this, poems in the *Ya* section are deeply concerned with the political destiny of the entire realm (as distinct from the more local "airs" [*feng*] or songs of individual domains) and its roots in moral authority or lack thereof. *Ya* is universally and perennially applicable, as distinct from *su* (linked to *feng*), that which applies to the mores of a specific time and place. This understanding of the *ya-su* polarity as universal principle versus local application is almost the opposite of its articulation as exclusion versus common practice outlined earlier, although the exclusionary principle also implies normative validity.

The word *ya* expresses approbation in the evaluation of character from about the third century on—it is associated with high principles, learning, and cultivation. The moral valence of *ya* runs through literary and aesthetic thought as notions of order, balance, restraint, and filiation with the canonical classics. These ideas form a neat contrast with the association of *su* with "common desires." Liu Xi (2nd–3rd c.) in *Shiming* (Elucidation of Names), using a mode of phonetic exegesis, glosses *su* as *yu* 欲 (desire): "*Su* means 'desire'—what the common people desire."⁴⁰ Sima Qian (ca. 145–ca. 86 BCE) rejects extravagant and fantastic stories about the Yellow Emperor as injudicious, inelegant, or "lacking in propriety and decorum" (*bu yaxun* 不雅馴). Yang Xiong (53 BCE–8 CE) contrasts elevated music with its opposite in *Model Sayings* (*Fayan*): "What is proper and correct is elegant music. What involves the sounds of excessive emotions is the Zheng style."⁴¹ In his *Classification of Poetry*, Zhong Rong praises Cao Zhi (192–232) for "combining elegant order with rancor," implying the balance and productive tension between control and excess. He criticizes Ji Kang for impairing "the elegance of all-encompassing order" (*yuanya* 淵雅) by being too sharp and forthright, and faults Bao Zhao (407–466) for being too clever and too fond of unusual turns of phrases, thereby diminishing "the resonance of pure elegance" (*qingya zhi diao* 清雅之調).

Liu Xie in *Literary Mind* defines "classical elegance" (*dianya* 典雅) as the style that "incorporates the model of canonical texts and proclamations and follows the tracks of Confucian teachings."⁴² Wang Shizhen, one of the major sixteenth-century champions of classical revival in poetry and prose, links elegance to "gentle moderation" (*wenhou heping* 溫厚和平), "a noble man's sense of proper measure" (*junzi zhi du* 君子之度), and emotions kept "within the parameters of moral nature" (*zhi yu xing* 止於性).⁴³ The definition of "elegance" as propriety or something rooted in tradition is also evident in Wang Shizhen's discussion of how customs and rituals changed in the course of Ming history. He regards these changes as the corruption of standards that should have been immutable.⁴⁴ Many late Ming writers noted rising tides of extravagance, and some of them linked the erosion of sumptuary laws to the rising wealth and power of merchants. Modern scholars often interpret elite writings on this phenomenon in terms of their resentment of and sense of being threatened by the nouveau riche.⁴⁵ Wang Shizhen's observations, however, pertain to sartorial changes observable before the late Ming and indicate a political (rather than economic) anxiety: for him these infractions have been committed by Ming scholar-officials from mid-Ming—he did not mention merchants—and are signs of moral corruption and political instability.

However, the most common associations of elegance are not moral and political but aesthetic. In the celebrations of aestheticized existence that became ubiquitous from the late sixteenth century on, we often find appeals to ideals of purity (*qing* 清), removal from the mundane (*yuan* 遠), and calm leisure (*xian* 閑) in definitions of elegance. A useful reference point is the imagistic delineation of "classical elegance" in the *Twenty-four Categories of Poetic Styles* (*Ershisi shipin*) attributed to Sikong Tu (837–908) but more likely dated to the late sixteenth or early seventeenth century:[46]

玉壺買春	Buy spring with a jade flask,
賞雨茆屋	Savor the rain in a thatched hut.
坐中佳士	Fine men are seated,
左右修竹	Flanked by slender bamboo.
白雲初晴	Under white clouds freshly sunlit,
幽鳥相逐	Distant birds chase one another.
眠琴綠陰	Sleep by the *qin* in the green shade,
上有飛瀑	Where above the waterfall flies.
落花無言	The falling blossoms are wordless;
人淡如菊	The person is muted like chrysanthemums.
書之歲華	Write this as the year's splendor:
其曰可讀	May one say that it's worth the reading.[47]

In solitude or with select company (the "fine men" among bamboo recalls the famous fourth-century literary gathering at Orchid Pavilion), simple pleasures gain the aura of Daoist transcendence. We have here the aesthetics of reticence and indirectness; sights and sounds are subtly registered through soft light and quietude.

In a similar vein, Xu Shangying (ca. 1580s–ca. 1660s) in *Moods of the Zither by Streams and Mountains* (*Xi shan qin kuang*, ca. 1641) links elegance in *qin* (zither) music to being "quiet, distant, muted, unworldly" (*jing* 靜, *yuan* 遠, *dan* 淡, *yi* 逸).[48] He further defines elegance by elaborating its opposite, vulgarity, variously identified with "the eagerness to please through cleverness," "heavy and impure fingering," "love of furor and bustle," "fingers limited by constraints," "the choice of coarse and harsh sounds," "the overly quick plucking of strings," "unregulated methods of playing," and "a shallow, impatient temperament." The vocabulary of Xu's treatise often carries echoes of *Laozi* and *Zhuangzi*, but it also harks back to the notion of elegance as balance, harmony, and equanimity achieved through moral self-cultivation. This merging of perspectives is not uncommon. In a letter (dated 1605) refuting the Daoist understanding of elegance and vulgarity, the Ming scholar-official Xu Guangqi (1562–1633) elaborates his moral definitions of those terms and concludes: "For what is elegant must be difficult, what is vulgar must be easy; what is elegant must be muted, what is vulgar must be sensually overpowering; what is elegant must be restrained, what is vulgar must be freewheeling; what is elegant must be bitter, what is vulgar must be sweet."[49] Moral rectitude and aesthetic fastidiousness meet in the conception of "elegance" as the embodiment of normative standards hard to attain and a shared disdain for mere sensual pleasures. Both emphasize balance, order, and restraint.

The core emphasis on "elegance" persists in the extant literature on connoisseurship from Tang to Qing despite divergences or reformulations. The valence of the term "elegance" ranges from classical and normative to a self-consciously superior aesthetic sensibility that can be idiosyncratic. Objects described as elegant reject ostentatious display; they tend to be understated and subtle, embodying the aura of the ancients (*guyi* 古意) or evocative of nature (*tianqu* 天趣, *ziran* 自然), as attested by compounds such as *danya* 淡雅 (muted elegance), *qingya* 清雅 (lofty elegance), *guya* 古雅 (wonted elegance), *yachun* 雅醇 (gentle elegance), *ruya* 儒雅 (learned elegance), *yunya* (韻雅 resonant elegance), *fengya* 風雅 (elegant cultivation). Balanced with what is original or unexpected, the result is *qiya* 奇雅 (surprising and elegant). (This is an uncommon formulation, however. The embodiment of *ya* usually implies norms and decorum, while that of *qi* tends to flout them. Thus, Liu Xie in *Literary Mind* pairs the two as opposites: "Elegance is the opposite of the strange or unexpected."[50]) This does not mean, of course, that the discourse on taste remains static through the centuries. Indeed, it is the continuities and changes in the discourse that show how the authority of judgment is fashioned.

The authors of manuals, treatises, and essays on the art of living and rules of style and taste offer precise, meticulous descriptions, and these texts sometimes read like practical guides to the choice and arrangements of the details of daily living. The mood is normative, as evinced by the recurrence of words like *jing* 經 (canon, classic), *shi* 史 (history), *pu* 譜 (catalog, genealogy, classification), *lu* 錄 (record, account), *shuo* 說 (excursus, treatise) or *zhi* 志 (record, treatise) in the titles. These words indicate authority: they buttress the claims of these works to define the essential attributes and cultural (and sometimes even moral and metaphysical) meanings of the thing in question. There is a surprising degree of overlap and mutual copying. In some cases, duplication is the result of publishers putting the names of famous literati and connoisseurs on works with contents pilfered from existing texts.[51] Their terse and impersonal tone contributes to the sense of consensus, as if the authors were proclaiming universally applicable rules of taste. The keywords are *ya*, *yi* 宜 (suitable), *xu* 須 (necessary), *ke* 可 (acceptable), *yu* 欲 (desirable), and their opposites, *su*, *ji* 忌 (tabooed) or *buke* 不可 (avoid, not acceptable). These injunctions are sometimes meticulous in the extreme. For example, exact (and overlapping) descriptions of measurements and styles for various kinds of beds and tables appear in Gao Lian's (16th c.) *Eight Treatises on the Art of Living* (*Zunsheng bajian*, hereafter *Eight Treatises*, 1591 preface), *Remaining Concerns of the Recluse* (*Kaopan yushi*, hereafter *Remaining Concerns*) attributed to Tu Long (1542–1605), and Wen Zhenheng's (1585–1645) *Superfluous Things* (*Zhangwu zhi*).[52]

Noting the degree of convergence among texts on connoisseurship, Clunas suggests that it may be helpful to "think of Ming connoisseurship literature in its entirety as constituting a single 'text,' repeated and reaffirmed by a number of separate individual authors."[53] The chronological boundaries of this "text" have to go beyond the Ming, however, since some of the common assertions are easily traceable to earlier sources, although their dissemination was made possible by late Ming print culture. The academicians of the *Four Treasuries* project observe that both Zhang Yingwen's (16th c.) *Pure and Secret Collection* (*Qing mi cang*) and Wen Zhenheng's *Superfluous Things* show clear filiation with the Song scholar Zhao Xigu's (1170–1242) *Pure Rewards of the Cavern Heaven* (*Dongtian qinglu*).[54] Zhao Xigu's *Pure Rewards* seems to be the earliest extant progenitor of a wide-ranging discourse on art and aesthetic objects, although his judgment of paintings and calligraphy echoes remarks by Su Shi, Huang Tingjian (1045–1105), and Mi Fu, and his comments on zithers, inkstones, bronze cauldrons, and rocks echo Tang and Song treatises on those subjects.[55] Zhao Xigu in his preface distinguishes his *Pure Rewards* from Zhang Yanyuan's *The Enjoyment of Leisurely Living* (*Xianju shouyong*), which discusses, among other things, furniture and utensils for living quarters and ways of preparing and preserving food. This work, which Zhao implicitly criticizes as trivial, is no longer extant, and Zhang is now remembered chiefly as the author of *Famous Paintings*, a masterful treatise on the history and connoisseurship of paintings. Zhao's contemporary Lin Hong (13th c.), however, extends the compass of connoisseurship to include culinary art and other quotidian pleasures.[56] Writing in the early Ming, Cao Zhao's *Essential Criteria in the Investigation of Antiquity* (*Gegu yaolun*) is more self-consciously scholastic; the word "investigate" (*ge* 格) in its title evokes the neo-Confucian principle of "the investigation of things" (*gewu*). In fact, the language of knowledge in *Essential Criteria* borrows the vocabulary of appreciation from Zhao's *Pure Rewards*. Both deliberately delimit the objects deserving of aesthetic attention and are in that sense distinct from Lin Hong's corpus as well as late Ming works such as *Remaining Concerns*, Gao Lian's *Eight Treatises*, or Wen Zhenheng's *Superfluous Things*: those texts try to aestheticize daily life by encompassing mundane subjects such as clothing, utensils, and furniture (and in Gao Lian's case also diet and medicine). The quest for elegance is expanded to include the quotidian.

Many ideas in the Ming literature on connoisseurship are derived from Song and Yuan precedents. For example, Mi Fu's *History of Inkstones* (*Yanshi*) and Ouyang Xiu's *Catalog of Inkstones* (*Yanpu*) are echoed in almost all subsequent treatises on the subject (from Southern Song to Qing), and Mi Fu's warning in *History of Paintings* (*Huashi*) about the adverse effects of remounting calligraphy and paintings also recurs in many later texts.[57] The description of how to adjudicate superior and inferior paintings in Zhao Xigu's *Pure Rewards* is paraphrased or repeated verbatim in many Ming and Qing accounts.[58] Similarly enduring genealogies are traceable in Zhao's discussion of how to tell the real from the fake when it comes to antique paintings on silk, bronze vessels, or crack patterns on ancient zither.[59] In general, technical knowledge (e.g., the locales for the best inkstones, the dating of bronzes) is most likely to be repeated.[60] Advice on the practice of connoisseurship is also often replicated. For example, the injunction against looking at paintings by lamplight or in an inebriated state, first articulated in Yuan writings, including Tang Hou's (fl. 1320s) *Mirror for Paintings* (*Huajian*) and Xia Wenyan's *Precious Mirrors for Pictures* (*Tuhui baojian*, 1365), reappears frequently in Ming and Qing connoisseurship literature.[61]

But taste did shift in some cases. Thus Mi Fu decries the decorative use of precious materials for the axis in scrolls as vulgar, but some Ming writers consider it elegant to adorn axis with jade, ivory, or rhinoceros horn, thus returning to Zhang Yanyuan's recommendation on the subject in *Famous Paintings*. Rationalization of tradition builds consensus. For example, the Song painter Li Gonglin is said to eschew composition of paired scrolls (*duizhou* 對軸).[62] Mi Fu, however, supports the practice of hanging scrolls in pairs, noting the need to match size and quality.[63] Zhao Xigu claims in *Pure Rewards* that the spontaneous self-expression of the literati painter does not generate paired composition. Zhao's reasoning must be appealing. He Liangjun (1506–1573) repeats it,[64] and the idea that a scroll should be hung alone and that hanging them in pairs is vulgar is reprised in Cao Zhao's *Essential Criteria*, with additions by Wang Zuo, Gao Lian's *Eight Treatises*, Tu Long's *Remaining Concerns*, as well as Wen Zhenheng's *Superfluous Things*.[65] Sometimes we see subtle shifts in emphasis. The Yuan collector Tang Hou writes in *Mirror for Paintings*: "Looking at a painting is like looking at a beautiful woman—her aura, spirit, and bone structure are beyond mere form" (*ZGSHQS* 2:902).[66] This saying reverberates in the writings of Ming and Qing artists and connoisseurs.[67] Wen Zhenheng repeats the rule with a twist: "Looking at calligraphy and paintings is like facing a beautiful woman—one must banish even the merest hint of shallowness and coarseness" (*ZWZ* 5.147). The same image supports an argument, not about grasping the meaning beyond form, but about reverence and attentiveness.

Clunas argued that changes in the discourse on aesthetic judgment reflect the elite's anxiety about the rising wealth and influence of the merchant class and their attempt to invent new distinctions to reinforce cultural and social hierarchy: "Once a society has been fully penetrated by commodity exchange and a mechanism of fashion and emulation set up, it is a constant and self-sustaining system, in which those who are constantly encouraged to catch up with the makers of taste can never do so, as the desirable acts of consumption are constantly shifted."[68] While there is little doubt that the discourse on the appraisal and enjoyment of things are social acts, inasmuch as they define a way of being in the world that presumes relevance for like-minded readers and may become a venue for asserting cultural authority, it is not clear how their circulation and popularity in the form of published books can be reconciled with the dynamics of exclusion. To be sure, there is criticism of ostentation, pretension, and fake connoisseurship, but this sense of "us versus them" is shifting and not based on a clear sense of "group identity."

Theories of social distinction imply a well-defined group identity that can be challenged or has to be constantly redefined. Scholars of the late Ming have often painted a picture of literati anxieties about fluid social boundaries and the encroaching pretensions of wealthy merchants. Rich merchants are indeed often typecast as tasteless collectors. Qian Qianyi, for example, is disdainful in his "Postscript to Dong Qichang's Letter to Feng Mengzhen" (Ba Dong Xuanzai yu Feng Kaizhi chidu): "After Feng died, this scroll was bought by a rich man from Xin'an (Huizhou). The mist and clouds of brush and ink have fallen and ended up in copper mountains and coin storehouses for more than thirty years. Only when I traveled in the Yellow Mountains did I redeem it and bring it back. This is like the divine swords of Fengcheng emerging overnight from the depths of a prison.[69] If the two venerable men (Dong and Feng) have a numinous presence, they would surely clap for this scroll" (QMZ 3:1788–89). Qian depicts his acquisition of Dong Qichang's calligraphy from a rich Huizhou collector (presumably a merchant) as the rightful restoration of literati solidarity. Hearing of the acquisition of a famous piece of calligraphy by a rich man from Huizhou, Shen Defu (1578–1642) laments: "This is like the Tang minister Xu Jingzong's daughter being sold in marriage to the barbarian chief. It's worse than using Zhaojun to make peace with the barbarians!" (WL 2:657). While the Han dynasty palace lady Zhaojun's marriage with the Xiongnu ruler may be dignified as diplomacy, Xu married his daughter to the rich man ("the barbarian chief") in Guangdong for purely mercenary reasons.

However, this may be but one facet of a complex picture. Wang Hungtai described a fluid social landscape wherein the "worldly turn" (shisu hua 世俗化) of literati culture created a productive dialectical relationship between elegance and vulgarity.[70] Yu Ying-shih discussed the rise of "literati-merchants" (shishang 士商) in the late Ming.[71] Disparaging references to ostentatious and predatory Huizhou merchants or to rich but undiscerning would-be aficionados abound in literary and historical writings, but we also have notable connoisseurs, artists, and scholar-officials, such as Zhan Jingfeng (1519–1602), Wang Daokun (1525–1593), or Wang Ruqian (Wang Ranming, 1577–1655), coming from merchant families (all three hailed from Huizhou). Wang Daokun defines the "Confucian merchant" (*rugu* 儒賈) as one "merchant in name and Confucian in action."[72] Indeed, the trend started well before the late Ming. We have mid-Ming examples from the Wu area: the painter and scholar-official Wu Kuan's (1435–1504) father was a merchant, as were the poet and painter Tang Yin's (1470–1524) father and the scholar-official Wang Ao's (1450–1524) father and grandfather.

Even anecdotes supposedly highlighting literati suspicions of the rising merchant class indicate an undeniable symbiosis. Wang Shizhen, who hailed from Taicang (near Suzhou) in Jiangsu, reportedly said to Zhan Jingfeng, "When Xin'an merchants see Suzhou literati, they gather like flies over mutton." Zhan Jingfeng is said to have retorted: "When Suzhou literati see Xin'an merchants, they also gather like flies over mutton." In response Wang "smiled and said nothing."[73] The fact that Wang wrote 59 laudatory epitaphs for merchants (out of a total of 360 in his collection) also confirms the ties between merchants and literati.[74] Sometimes a mercantile background is indeed linked to the spirit of acquisitiveness and possessiveness, as when Jiang Shaoshu (mid-17th c.) mocked the indiscriminate stamping of seals by the wealthy collector Xiang Yuanbian: "Having used pearls and gems to pledge troth with the beauty, he still fears that she would marry someone else. He thus tattoos her face to leave his mark. In extreme cases, the whole body is tattooed so that there is no unblemished skin left. This is even more cruel and horrifying than 'the beauty Xi Shi covered with filth'" (*YSZ* B.17b).[75] At the same time, there is ample evidence that Xiang was comfortably embedded in elite society and that his collection and connoisseurship were treated with respect.[76] He also has his defenders: Chen Yidian (1554–1638) commended him for his broad knowledge and love of antiquity and praised his calligraphy.[77] Yao Yuanzhi (1773–1852) claimed that Xiang's seals "did not impair elegance and propriety,"[78] perhaps because the famous calligrapher Wen Peng (1498–1573), Wen Zhengming's son, carved many of the seals.

Merchants and artisans also produced treatises on connoisseurship that were prized by their literati contemporaries. Notable examples include the ink-stick makers Fang Yulu (active 1570–1619), who wrote the popular *Fang Treatise on Ink* (*Fangshi mopu*), and his rival Cheng Dayue (1541–ca. 1616), whose *Cheng Garden of Ink* (*Chengshi moyuan*) also had wide circulation.[79] Literati comments on their rivalry point to the web of connections linking the endeavors of Fang and Lu to their readers and sponsors.[80] The lacquer maker Huang Cheng's (ca. mid- to late 16th c.) *Record of Lacquering* (*Xiushi lu*), with annotations by another lacquer maker, Yang Ming (1625 preface), suggests contemporary interest in alternative voices, although the extent of its circulation cannot be ascertained.[81] The text survived in Japan and did not gain attention in China until the 1920s. It could be that some forms of skills and knowledge (e.g., ink making, bamboo carving, seal carving, designing rockery in gardens) elevated the artisans more than others (e.g., metal work, jade polishing, lacquering).

The impetus for defining normative elegance may thus not be anxieties about social boundaries. Personal and regional rivalries as well as assertion of individual difference can play a role. The most famous literati and scholar-officials sometimes questioned one another's taste, even when social hierarchy was an irrelevant issue. For example, Zhan Jingfeng gleefully narrates how he exposes Wang Shizhen's error of judgment, Shen Defu questions Chen Jiru's connoisseurship,[82] and Wen Zhenheng and Tang Zhiqi (1579–after 1652) tacitly criticize Dong Qichang's (1555–1636) use of shiny white silk for his paintings as "smacking of officialdom" (*jinxian qi* 進賢氣).[83] In his entry on "Famous masters" (*mingjia* 名家), Wen lists Dong Qichang among the calligraphers but does not include him among the painters, indicating his reservations (*ZWZ* 152–53). The exchange between Wang Shizhen and Zhan Jingfeng on the mutual dependence of Suzhou literati and Huizhou merchants cited earlier points perhaps more to regional rivalry between Suzhou and Huizhou than to competition between literati and merchants. Wang Shixing (1546–1598), who hailed from Zhejiang, observes how Suzhou people controlled the discourse of taste and implicitly critiqued how others blindly followed their lead since the Jiajing reign (1521–1567).[84] Shen Defu, another Zhejiang (Jiaxing) native, disparaged Suzhou literati for their frivolity and deceit.[85] Zhang Dai also lamented how his compatriots from Zhejiang slavishly imitated ever-changing Suzhou fashions.[86]

UPHOLDING AND CHALLENGING NORMS

Beyond personal and regional rivalries, some imply that the true spirit of elegance lies in defying norms. As mentioned earlier, Yuan connoisseurs like Tang Hou warn against viewing paintings under a lamp. After repeating the rules about when *not* to look at paintings in *Superfluous Things*, Wen Zhenheng adds: "But in striving to avoid taboos in everything, there is the danger of straining to strike a pose of elegance" (ZWZ 5.147). Wu Qizhen (1607–ca. 1678) records how he and his friend Ji Yuyong (1622 *jinshi*) viewed paintings under lamplight in 1656. Ji wonders whether they should break the taboo, and Wu replies, "How can anything that suits one's mood so well be inadmissible?... The romantic élan is such that it matches the spirit of the Golden Valley Garden."[87] Literati who hail performers and artisans as "people like us" (*wobei zhong ren* 我輩中人) and befriend them (as in Zhang Dai's case) seem to delight in flouting social boundaries, implying that true elegance encompasses the freedom to redefine the boundaries between the elegant and the vulgar or the mundane; the same may be said of Li Rihua's "Contract" mentioned earlier. Literati interest in vernacular genres appeals to the same logic. In claiming that popular songs and dramatic language embody genuineness or that vernacular fiction upholds the standards of canonical classics, these literati champions of "the voice of the people" and new genres in effect argue for redrawing the line between elegance and vulgarity.[88] In such cases, there is often implicit appeal to the definition of *ya* as normative moral principles and disregard for its association with aesthetic restraint.

The balance between upholding and challenging norms under the rubric of elegance is most interesting when it comes to two intertwined issues: fashion and money. Scholars have tended to focus on the negative comments linking fashion with its excess and arbitrariness to mercantile wealth and extravagance. Indeed, the quest for novelty, sensory pleasures, and the appropriation of the ornaments of literati culture or their imitation by anyone who can afford it (and this seems to be an ever expanding category) seems to threaten any notion of normative elegance.[89] Wu Qizhen noted in 1639 how fashion determined "elegance" in Huizhou: "Formerly, when it came to splendor in my native Huizhou, none could compare to the Xiuning and She counties. And the distinction between elegance and vulgarity hinged on whether one owned antiques. That was why people did not begrudge high prices when acquiring them."[90] Here "elegance" seems to be no more than social consensus driven by imitation.

Fashion, however, can also point to fundamental shifts in taste and new aesthetic trends. Wang Shizhen disparages contemporary fashions that usurp the rightful place of "antiquity" (*gu* 古) in aesthetic judgment:

> Among paintings Song works should be valued. But in the last thirty years Yuan works were suddenly prized, so much so that for works from Ni Zan (1301–1374) to Shen Zhou (1427–1509) of the Ming dynasty, the price rose steeply tenfold. Among pottery, Ge and Ru vessels [from the Song dynasty] should be valued. But in the last fifteen years people suddenly prize pottery from the Xuande, Yongle (1403–1425) and Chenghua reigns; their price also rose steeply tenfold. These trends were likely started by Wu people and channeled by Huizhou people. Both cases are passing strange.[91]

Wang Shizhen lumps together the rise in value of Yuan paintings and early Ming pottery. But while the latter might have been explained in part by supply and demand, the former signals change in taste with the rise of the so-called Wu School in painting.[92] Upholding Northern Song masters as the ultimate ideal, Wang Shizhen implicitly disparages the less representational and more emphatically expressive style of Ni Zan.[93] Wang seems to be taking up but also tacitly criticizing the equation of the elegance-vulgarity axis with that spanning abstraction and verisimilitude: "The painters before Wu Daozi [8th c.] and Li Sixun [651–716] are realistic but come close to being vulgar (*shi er jin su* 實而近俗); the painters after Jing Hao [ca. 855–915] and Guan Tong [ca. 906–960] are elegant but too abstract (*ya er tai xu* 雅而太虛). Now the way of elegance still exists, but the virtue of verisimilitude is ailing."[94] For Wang, contemporary fashion elevating the Wu School embraced a version of elegance unmoored from attention to substantive details.

Beyond implicit debates on aesthetic judgment, there is general unease about how novelty and market demands threaten stable criteria of evaluation. Shen Defu observes that early and mid-Ming bronze vessels, porcelain, and lacquerware were valued as highly as antique vessels by the late sixteenth century and explains this as a market necessity: tenth- and eleventh-century porcelain and lacquerware or ritual vessels from the Three Dynasties should be the best, but such items are simply too rare or fragile; "that is why more recent creations are used to meet the demand." Who adjudicates the value of these things? Shen Defu imagines the ripple effect that starts with "one or two persons of refined taste," whose appreciation is extended to "Jiangnan gentlemen of rank and means who are also aficionados" and is finally picked up through hearsay by Huizhou merchants and becomes pervasive fashions. The greater the sums involved, the more judgments become arbitrary. "We have come to the point that paintings of Shen Zhou and Tang Yin are elevated to the same level as the works of Jing Hao and Guan Tong, that calligraphy of Wen Zhenming and Zhu Yunming are promoted to the ranks of Su Shi and Mi Fu. The perversity of such judgments knows no bounds" (*WL* 2:653).

Rich merchants may be blamed for blind conformism and surging prices, but the trendsetters were the literati and scholar-officials who could also have profited from price fluctuations. Having elevated Ni Zan as the preeminent literati painter, Dong Qichang, repeating a similar comment by Shen Zhou, declares with a hint of self-congratulation: "As for Ni Zan's paintings, people in the Lower Yangzi area use their possession or lack thereof as the criterion for judging loftiness (*qing* 清) or vulgarity."[95] He played a decisive role in enhancing Ni Zan's reputation by naming him one of the "four Yuan Masters."[96] His immensely influential definition of the Southern School (*nanzong* 南宗) and of "literati painting" (*wenren zhi hua* 文人之畫) as expression that prizes intuitive immediacy elevates Yuan masters like Ni Zan and Ming artists like Shen Zhou and Wen Zhengming.[97] Dong thus invents a genealogy to which he is heir as he advocates the eradication of "cloying vulgarity" (*tiansu* 甜俗) by employing calligraphic brushwork in painting and by claiming to seek self-expression and self-contained joy in painting (*yi hua wei ji* 以畫為寄, *yi hua wei le* 以畫為樂).[98] This definition of elegance implies a more abstract, uncompromising expressiveness and lofty unconcern for what pleases the multitude, although the price of his calligraphy and painting rose steeply in his lifetime.

Shen Defu's observation on the market demand for recent and contemporary art points to the idea that antiquity may not be the decisive criterion of worth, which recurs in treatises on connoisseurship from late sixteenth century onward. Zhang Yingwen notes, for example, that only in calligraphy are the ancient masters unsurpassable: no such standards apply to paintings (*QMC* A.7b). Zhang also considers bronze censors from the Xuande reign superior to Tang and Yuan antecedents (*QMC* A.4b–5a). Li Yu goes one step further and considers contemporary pottery superior to specimens from the Chenghua and Xuande reigns (*XQOJ* 223). Yuan Hongdao mocks the use of ancient vessels as vases: "How is that different from burning incense in the ancestral hall? Even if the vessel is ancient, it would still be vulgar" (*YHD* 1:821). As recent or even contemporary vessels and artifacts became fashionable and expensive, certain artisans consorted with the literati as social equals.[99] Li Rihua, for example, commissioned the potter Hao Shijiu to make a "Flowing Clouds Cup" in shimmering colors and praised his creation with a poem. He also commended Hao's poetry and calligraphy and described him as "a recluse among the potter's wheels."[100] Shi Dabin (1573–1648), famous for his teapots, befriended Chen Jiru; he initially carved from the calligraphy of others but eventually mastered calligraphy and carved his own. Among the bamboo carver Pu Zhongqian's friends were Qian Qianyi (*QMZ* 4:36) and Zhang Dai.[101] Writings addressed to and about Zhang Nanyuan, who specialized in garden rockery, appear in the collections of well-known literati and scholar-officials, among them Wu Weiye and Huang Zongxi (1610–1695).[102]

But the phenomenon of fashionable artifacts and the consequent blurring of social boundaries between literati and artisans also aroused unease. Wang Shixing describes the artifacts that stoke fashionable demand as "anomalous things" (*wuyao* 物妖; the word *yao* means baleful spirits or anomalies).[103] Shen Defu calls the superlative ink produced by the aforementioned Fang and Cheng families of Huizhou "anomalous ink" (*moyao* 墨妖) and describes their rivalry as "the war of ink" (*mobing* 墨兵). Shen also observes that it is the famous artisans who set the fashion for using animal bones as fan ribs that made the price of fans soar—Shen indicates his disapproval by calling these "anomalous fans" (*shanyao* 扇妖).[104] Yuan Hongdao, commenting on the idea of fashion, expresses ambivalence at how "trivial skills and minor artifacts" gained great fame. He cites Song and Yuan precedents and acknowledged the superb skills of some artisans, but he also holds Suzhou "madcaps" (*juanzi* 獧子)

106 *Elegance and Vulgarity*

responsible for spreading the fame of artisans, thereby inflating prices through branding to fool the rich and creating fashions taken up by the literati (*YHD* 1:730–31).[105] Yuan Hongdao's attitude is ambiguous. He admires some of these artifacts, saying, for example, of Gong Chun's wares: "The yellowish hue is plain yet supple, its radiance glows like jade." Yet he is also suspicious of fads that would give mere artisans greater fame than the literati. But this apparent threat is also a confirmation: it is precisely the literati who had the power to turn names into brands and make celebrities of artisans. The elite could, through their appreciation, turn artifacts into something as valuable as painting and calligraphy. By recognizing the literary and cultural sensibility of the artisan, the literati could elevate their craft as the Way, a promise already held out in *Zhuangzi*.[106] In other words, fashion seems to threaten normative elegance but can also expand its authority and flexibility.

The opposite of elegance is excessive decoration and vulgar display of wealth. Zhao Xigu emphasizes, for example, that the studs of the zither must not be decorated with gold, jade, ivory, or rhinoceros horn.[107] While many treatises on connoisseurship include sections on gemstones, precious metals are often sidelined. Shen Defu claims that only fans made from palm fiber or bamboo are deemed "elegant things to be taken into one's sleeves" (*huaixiu yawu* 懷袖雅物); fans made with more expensive materials like purple sandalwood, ivory, and black wood are all regarded as vulgar (*suzhi* 俗製).[108] While the critique of the vulgar rich is a constant refrain through the ages, the paradoxical double role of wealth as both the agent and the potential enemy of taste seems to have become a common topic only from the late sixteenth century onward. Qian Yong, who lived in the eighteenth century but expressed views also applicable to earlier periods, observed: "Wealth and position are close to vulgarity. Poverty and lowliness are close to elegance. Those who enjoy wealth and honor while being vulgar are legion, but hard it is to find the poor and lowly who are also elegant."[109] Poverty (or at least simplicity) is closer to elegance if we understand it as the precondition for some sense of spiritual superiority, yet the ornaments of culture—the usual paraphernalia of supposed refinement—depend on material well-being.

There is wariness about acknowledging how artwork and aesthetic objects are embedded in economic transactions; at the same time there are frank discussions of prices. The ambivalence is nothing new.

Writing in the ninth century, Zhang Yanyuan claims that ancient masterpieces are "all timeless treasures whose price cannot be discussed," but he ends up weaving a frank discussion of prices into his ranking of famous painters, thus confirming the double lives of artwork as commodity and anticommodity (*LDMHJ* 2.29–32). According to Mi Fu, "One cannot discuss the price of calligraphy and paintings, and it is difficult for scholars to have to obtain them like goods. To understand how calligraphy and paintings can be exchanged is certainly elegant."[110] Mi Fu recorded the prices of various paintings in his *History of Paintings*, however, and he frequented the art market in Xiangguo Temple in Kaifeng to look for bargains. He also referred to his collection as being worth ten thousand taels of silver. Among late Ming collectors, Xiang Yuanbian was famous for recording the prices and details of transactions on scrolls and albums. His critics averred that his mercantile background accounted for this predilection. Thus Jiang Shaoshu: "This was no different from the account books of merchants. He did so only because he wanted his descendants to keep the scrolls and albums. Even if they were to sell them, he hoped they would do so, based on the original value, by asking for a higher price. His planning was careful indeed" (*YSZ* B.17b).[111] The early Qing collector and scholar-official Gao Shiqi (1645–1704) often recorded prices in his colophons also but was not criticized for the practice.[112]

By the late Ming, the language of emotional intensity adds new complexities to the question of value. Li Rihua observes in his dairy: "With all flowers one can speak of buying and selling, the only exception are plum trees. One can only speak of pledging troth to a plum tree or marrying it."[113] As a symbol of lofty detachment, the plum blossoms should rise above transactions. Li is taking issue in jest with the self-characterization of the Song recluse, poet, and plum lover Lin Bu (967–1028), who claimed that he "sold a plum tree every day."[114] Although romance (or at least its semblance in courtesan quarters and the purchase of concubines) and marriage could hardly escape economic considerations, deep emotional commitment is still supposed to take us beyond the world of transactions. Aesthetic appreciation is translatable into economic value but also rebels against the very idea of the market. The more everything can be bought and sold, the more intense is the yearning for defining value beyond the marketplace.

In *Subtle Words on Painting* (*Huishi weiyan*), Tang Zhiqi tells this story to illustrate how "ancient paintings are priceless": Wang Guxiang (1501–1568) obtained four exquisite Shen Zhou scrolls. A "vulgar official" from the Wu area offered to buy them with two hundred taels of silver, but Wang finally refused. "Later, when Wang Xiyuan caught sight of them, he sat and slept by the scrolls for two days.[115] Wang Guxiang said that for the paintings to meet such a person is like having a real soul mate. He thus told the story about the two hundred taels. Xiyuan offered an estate, worth a thousand taels, in exchange for the scrolls."[116] The conclusion is somewhat unexpected. Shouldn't the difference between a "vulgar official" and a "real soul mate" warrant a discount or perhaps even the offering of these scrolls as a gift? Wang Guxiang's fastidiousness (in refusing to sell to the first official) and his telling of it almost seem like shrewd bargaining. But perhaps Wang Xiyuan needs such a grand gesture to dramatize his special bond with these Shen Zhou scrolls.

The exchange of property for paintings, though it puts the question of value front and center, obviates the need to handle money. Both aversion to the talk of prices and keen interest in recording transactions coexist in late Ming writings. Tang Zhiqi finds especially distasteful the discussion of prices among the undiscerning: "Using their ears as eyes, their hands clutching the scroll, their mouths expounding on high or low worth: this is truly the deviant way."[117] The same lines appear in Wen Zhenheng's *Superfluous Things* (*ZWZ* 5.135), although Wen, in a passage also found in Zhang Yingwen's *Pure and Secret Collection*,[118] proceeds to expound on the adjudication of value: in calligraphy works in the standard script are most valuable (*ZWZ* 5.139–40; *QMC* A.6a–6b). Barring masterpieces whose worth cannot be calculated through the number of characters, one hundred characters in cursive script equal one column in semicursive script, while three columns in semicursive script equal one column of standard script.[119] He extends the equivalences to painting. Mountains, waters, bamboo, and rocks are classed with standard script; small figures, flowers, and birds are the equivalent of semicursive script. Figures of gods and Buddha as well as palaces and pavilions count as much as cursive script.[120] Note that in speaking of equivalences, Wen and Zhang manage to avoid mentioning prices and to stay within the parameters of elegant exchanges (of calligraphy and paintings) as lauded by Mi Fu. All the same, such mechanical calculations seem almost unworthy of a connoisseur. Instead of being taken literally, the passage should perhaps be read as a rueful admission that the value of most paintings and calligraphy (especially by contemporaries) is too enmeshed in social ties or determined by social occasions (i.e., the reason why the artwork was given as a gift [*renshi* 人事]) to be discussed in monetary terms.[121] In that sense the arbitrary equivalences amount almost to a kind of dismissal—a way to talk about monetary value while staying above the fray.

SELF-CONSCIOUS ELEGANCE

This heightened ambivalence on how to address the question of value is echoed in the sharpened self-consciousness on what it means to be or to appear as an "elegant person." This becomes evident when we compare his image in Zhao Xigu's thirteenth-century text with its late Ming iterations. Zhao lists the right ways of burning incense and facing flowers, the moon, and water when one plays the zither—one needs incense with pure scent and minimal smoke, flowers with gentle fragrance and muted colors, the right timing (after the first watch and before the third), a pellucid pond by a window or a bamboo grove. He dismisses the idea of cranes dancing to zither music: "It's not certain that the cranes will dance. The onlookers would be in a furor, and the zither player would not be able to concentrate. How is this different from watching entertainers? This is truly not the noble man's proper concern."[122] What Zhao is cultivating is the image of the elegant zither player inspired by properly subtle sensual stimuli, being in perfect harmony with the world and rising above clichés such as "playing the zither as the crane dances."

Zhao's injunctions are quoted or paraphrased in late Ming writings about the zither, including *Remaining Concerns* and Gao Lian's *Eight Treatises*. The former develops the imagistic associations of zither music: "The zither should be played in the midst of pine wind and rustling streams, for all three are sounds of nature. It is fitting that they should be grouped together."[123] Gao Lian offers practical instructions on how to train a crane to dance: "Wait till it's hungry. Leave food out in the open space, have a lad clap and sway in joy, wave his arms, and lift his feet to lure it. It will flap its wings and cry, raise its feet, and dance. Having practiced this enough, it will start dancing once it hears clapping. This is called transformation through feeding. For a residence in the empty wood, how can one do without such a lofty friend oblivious to mundane cares even for a day?" (*ZSBJ* 567).[124] There seems to be an even keener sense in the late Ming examples that the image of elegance has to be managed and cultivated. The deliberate training for a supposedly spontaneous crane dance is discussed with no hint of irony.

Refined pleasures underlie harmony and moral self-cultivation: this implicit assumption in Zhao's text becomes a constant refrain. In late Ming writings that broaden the application of elegance to daily life, however, harmony is both integration with mundane rhythms and idiosyncratic self-expression. The most notable example is Gao Lian's *Eight Treatises*, an amalgam of moral homily, historical examples, personal reflections, and practical (including medical and culinary) advice. In the "Treatise on Living in Harmony with the Four Seasons" (Sishi tiaoshe jian), Gao maps the correspondences between the seasons, the months, and the various organs and provides a detailed guide to exercises, breathing discipline, and meditation techniques appropriate to each phase of the year. At the end of each seasonal section, however, he also dwells on historical examples of "whimsical anecdotes" (*yishi* 逸事) and highly idiosyncratic instances of "what Master Gao secretly appreciates" (*Gaozi youshang* 高子幽賞) for each season. The prevailing emphasis on taxonomy, correspondences, and regularity also accommodates moments of self-consciously intense emotion. Gao Lian describes his reaction as he watches the splendid autumnal sunrise from the highest level of the Baochu Pagoda: "After gazing at it for a long while, my eyes were confused and my spirit was shaken. I suddenly let out a wild shout and my voice shook the heavens" (*ZSBJ* 213). Ecstatic shouts are ubiquitous in travel writings from this period.

Gao Lian is also typical of his contemporaries in combining earnest self-cultivation with a focus on self-aestheticizing display. "Nourishing life" involves not only aesthetic pleasure but also the enjoyment of perceiving oneself as an aesthetic image. In the entry "Riding a donkey in search of plum blossoms after the snow clears," Gao Lian asks why paintings on this subject always feature a figure dressed in red: "How can this be for no reason? It is as if the painter wants to decorate a scene to match with the season, so that it will have the interesting mood of soaring above the mundane." Shih Shou-chien suggests that "paintings" here refer specifically to the paintings of pleasure excursions by Wen Zhengming and the Wu School, where indeed one finds elegant gentlemen clad in red.[125] Accordingly, Gao Lian wears a red cape and rides a black donkey on his winter excursions, followed by a lad carrying his wine flask. "I step on the snow among streams and mountains and seek plum blossoms in the woods and valleys. All of a sudden I come upon a few blooming plum trees. I then want to sit on the ground next to the plum and drink with abandon. Reveling in inebriation as the scent of plum blossoms flutters on my sleeves, I no longer know that I am the body among the flowers and have also forgotten that the flowers belong to the vision before my eyes" (*ZSBJ* 244). Gao Lian imagines the rapture of a self-forgetful encounter, but it is also a carefully curated scene.

The supposed self-forgetfulness that overcomes the boundary of self and other is actually a mode of self-observation and self-aestheticization. We see this implicit reasoning in another entry, "Sweeping snow to make tea and enjoying paintings" (Saoxue pengcha wanhua): to make tea with snow and to contemplate ancient paintings of snow scenes is to "approach the illusory and face the real in order to observe the ancients' masterful brushwork of imitation." "For one must know that all painterly scenes in the world belong to the schemes of Transformation. Approach the self that holds onto the painting, and one has a person appreciating a scene. If one faces the scene and observes the self, can one say that the self is not in the scene? The karmic entanglements of a thousand years: What is reality? What is illusion? One should seek enlightenment from paintings" (*ZSBJ* 246–47).

There is often an implicit mentality of "us versus them" in such ruminations. Gao Lian writes in "Listening to the Snow Hitting the Bamboo at the Mountain Window" (Shanchuang duixue qiaozhu):

> Drifting snow has a sound, whose elegance peaks only among bamboos. On cold nights by the mountain window, I often listen to the snow falling on the bamboo grove. An unmistakable murmur, a continuous rustle: the drawn-out music purifies my hearing. Suddenly the wind turns and urgently blows, breaking a bamboo branch with a sound that heightens the chill as I wrap myself in a blanket. I secretly think of the people enjoying themselves in golden

chambers in the midst of intoxicating music from jade pipes—I fear this is not what would please them.
(*ZSBJ* 248)

The gentle rustle of snow falling on bamboo becomes something more austere and uncomfortable when the wind snaps a bamboo branch, but what ensues is a sense of self-conscious superiority as Gao Lian reflects on the meaninglessness of what enthralls him for vulgar people ensconced in their luxurious pleasures. On the thrill of breaking the ice as his boat drifts on West Lake when its surface is barely frozen, he notes: "Others may not share it" (*ZSBJ* 243–44).

Self-observation is paradoxically both about purveying images as cultural identity or self-conscious superiority as well as a playful and pseudo-religious exercise in self-distancing. Psychological distance seems to determine the difference between elegance and vulgarity. Thus Lu Shaoheng: "Living in the mountains is an excellent thing. But once it verges on attachment, one may as well be at court and the marketplace. Appreciating calligraphy and paintings is an elegant affair. But once it verges on greed and obsessive possessiveness, one may as well be a merchant or a trader."[126] Distancing facilitates aesthetic contemplation. Yuan Hongdao mentioned several times that he is not a drinker and is more interested in tea, but he wrote *Rules on Drinking* (*Shangzheng*), presumably because he enjoyed the idea of drinking as aesthetic image: "There are rules of decorum in intoxication. Intoxication among flowers is appropriate for the day, so that one can receive their light; intoxication in snow is appropriate for the night, so that one can merge with its purity; intoxicated in joy, one should sing to bring about harmonious tranquility; intoxicated at parting, one should hit the brass plate to elevate one's spirit" (*YHD* 2:1416). Wu Congxian (17th c.) describes "rules for reading" as if he were framing and ordering elements in a painting:

> One should read history in the reflection of snow to bring brightness to the dark mirror [history is compared to a mirror]; one should read philosophy with the moon as companion to send one's spirit soaring; one should read Buddhist books facing a beautiful woman to avoid falling into emptiness; one should read

> *Classic of Mountains and Rivers, Classic of Waterways,* miscellanies, and stories leaning against sparse blossoms and slender bamboos, cold rocks and chilly moss, so as to bring one back from boundless wanderings and to restrain the discourse of fantasy; one should read the biographies of the loyal and the heroic while playing reed pipes and plucking a zither to spread their fragrant names; one should read the discussions of miscreants and flatterers while striking with a sword or clasping wine to vent one's spleen; one should read *Encountering Sorrow* while wailing in lamentation in an empty mountain so as to shock the ravines; one should read rhapsodies with wild shouts by the water so as to make the wind turn back; one should read poems and song lyrics with singers keeping the beats; one should read miscellaneous accounts of gods and spirits while burning candles so as to pierce the darkness.[127]

With the repeated use of the word *yi* ("should," "suitable"), the passage recalls the normative bent of treatises and manuals on connoisseurship. Here, however, the self-observation is more deliberate: acts of reading become an integral part of their meaningful frames or unfold in paradoxical tension with them. Inner life finds its objective correlative, be it complementary or corrective, and is itself the object of aesthetic contemplation.

Nature imitates art in this world where the mood of aesthetic contemplation is pervasive. Travel writings and landscape descriptions are filled with observations on how a certain scene recalls a famous painting. Thus Yuan Hongdao: "I once observed that West Lake is like a Song painting, and the landscape of Shanyin is like a Yuan painting. Flowers, birds, and human figures—the finest details of everything, be they overpowering or faint, are all wondrously delineated. Such is the landscape of West Lake. Human figures that may not have eyes, trees that may not have branches, mountains that may not have vegetation, water that may not have waves—hidden and evanescent, a faraway aura that yet seems vivid. Such is the landscape of Shanyin" (*YHD* 1:441). Dong Qichang describes the shape-shifting morning clouds at Dongting Lake as "veritably Mi Fu's ink play."[128] In an essay on a friend's garden built for reclusion, he compares the paintings he owns to his friend's garden, since both can be venues for the mind's wandering: "For your garden can be a painting, and the paintings in my house can be a garden."[129] This predilection translates into deliberate attempts to re-create nature as art. A passage about training miniature trees in pots to look like famous paintings appears (with slight variations) in both *Remaining Concerns* and Wen Zhenheng's *Superfluous Things*: "Most ancient and elegant of all are trees like the pines of Tianmu. They are about one foot in height and an arm's size in girth, the needles are short and dense. They may be knotted and trained to embody the slanting bent and tortuous curves of Ma Yuan [active 1190–after 1225], the bare tops and forceful reach of Guo Xi [after 1000–ca. 1090], the repose and layering of Liu Songnian [Southern Song], the sweeping, soaring openness of Sheng Zizhao [Yuan] and so on."[130]

Heightened interest in perception accounts for the numerous references to observing and evaluating how others are looking at the world around them. Enjoyment of travels seems to be enhanced by disparagement of how others are merely following the undiscerning crowd. Many express exasperation at how beauty in nature is defaced by vulgar poetic inscriptions carved on stone or plastered over pillars and beams of pavilions.[131] Writing about his excursion to the Brimming Well (Manjing), a popular site in the suburb of Beijing, Wang Siren (1542–1605) describes only the visitors. He drinks with his friend under a reed awning, "returning only after having seen our fill of the visitors' antics."[132] Zhang Dai famously declares that the only thing worth seeing on the night of the full moon in the seventh month at West Lake are the people looking at the moon. He divides them into five categories: "those looking at the moon in name but who actually do not see the moon"; "those who are under the moon but who do not actually look at the moon"; "those also under the moon, also looking at the moon and hoping that others look at them looking at the moon"; "those who look at the moon and also the people looking at the moon as well as those who don't, but who actually do not see a thing"; and "those looking at the moon, but others do not see them making a show of looking at the moon and also do not make a point of looking at the moon." For all five categories, Zhang Dai repeats with the authority of the ultimate spectator: "We look at them."[133] It is only when almost all the visitors are gone that the hitherto hidden ones (perhaps including the fifth category) come out and enjoy the sublime beauty of West Lake on a moonlit night with

Zhang Dai and his friends. They mock the self-consciously elegant as vulgar, but their self-congratulatory sense of superiority and the idea of implicit competition are also supremely self-conscious.

The aristocracy of sensibility delights in—perhaps even depends on—the bafflement of the vulgar majority. Zhang Dai recounts how he staged a theatrical performance at Jinshan temple in 1629 in the middle of the night to the utter bewilderment of the resident monks, who "could not tell whether we were humans, ghosts, or evil spirits."[134] In another entry, Zhang Dai describes how he encounters two fellow lovers of snowy scenes when, in the early hours of the dawn after a snowstorm, he makes his way to the Heart of the Lake Pavilion at West Lake. The two men already in the pavilion, travelers from Jinling, are surprised by joy: "How can there be another person in the Lake!" The boatman mutters, "One shouldn't say that your honor is obsessive; there are those more obsessive than your honor!"[135] In this momentary communion based on shared appreciation of a snowy scene, there is deliberate whimsicality as well as celebration of an accidental connection that excludes the multitude.

Self-observation is nowhere more evident and multifaceted than in the discussions of the meanings of connoisseurship. A notable antecedent is the Song painter Mi Fu's definition of the reality and pretension of connoisseurship: the connoisseur (*shangjian jia* 賞鑒家) of paintings collects excellent specimens because he has "steadfast interest," has read widely and kept records, has real insights, and is himself a painter. The would-be aficionado (*haoshi zhe* 好事者) boasts of the material means of acquisition, has no real passion but "wants to advertise his refinement, so much so that he relies on the eyes and ears of others for his judgment."[136] Ming writers who repeat, paraphrase, or indirectly allude to Mi Fu's distinction include, among others, Hu Yinglin (1551–1602), He Liangjun (1506–1573), Gao Lian, Xie Zhaozhi (1567–1624), Shen Defu, and Zhang Yingwen, as well as his son Zhang Chou (1577–1643).[137] "Connoisseurs by hearsay" (or those who "eat with their ears" [*ershi* 耳食]) also come up for frequent criticism and dismissal. Although the meanings of the terms *shangjian* and *haoshi* differ in various contexts and their hierarchy is by no means stable, there is no question that evaluating or adjudicating the level of aesthetic judgment is the criterion for determining elegance and vulgarity and thus a favorite exercise among the literati.[138]

The defense or demarcation of "true appreciation" (*zhenshang* 真賞) is especially common in prefaces. Shen Chunze's (d. 1629) preface to Wen Zhenheng's *Superfluous Things* is a case in point (*ZWZ* 10–11):

> To extol and draw attention to the beauties of nature, to discriminate and write on wine and tea, to collect and arrange things such as paintings, books, drinking vessels, or cauldrons—for the world these are idle activities; for the body, superfluous things. And yet those who rank and appraise people use these things to measure taste, talent, and sensibility. Why should this be so? To gather the pure and wondrous air of past and present in front of my eyes and ears so that I can breathe it; to spread the small and trivial things of heaven and earth on mat and table so that they await my direction; to hold the vessel which in my daily existence provides neither warmth against the cold nor sustenance in hunger, and yet revere it more than precious jade and a thousand pieces of gold—to do all these is to find a proper home for my ardent, restless spirit. Unless one has true taste, true talent, and true sensibility to live up to this role, the manner of appreciation is quite different. In recent times, some wealthy people, together with their vulgar and ignorant associates, congratulate themselves on their connoisseurship. Whenever they exercise appreciation and discrimination, they issue only commonplaces, and whatever enters their hands is roughly handled. Indulging in exaggerated display of gleeful rubbing or protective fondling, the affront and defilement they bring about is indeed extreme. As a result, the gentlemen of true taste, true talent, and true sensibility warn each other not to speak of elegance and culture. Alas, this avoidance too is excessive.

Here metaphors of internalization (breathing, inhaling) and mastery ("await my direction") suggest that it is precisely idle activities and superfluous things that best define the freedom of the spirit, insofar as apparently unimportant things are whimsically invested with the greatest value, although, as mentioned in chapter 1, the word *ji* (to find proper abode for, to lodge temporarily) implies merely provisional absorption. Self-definition is attained through the process of assembling and ordering things. Yet the expectation of being appraised and ranked according to one's taste and sensibility validates the authoritative guidelines the book offers. The book thus enjoins conformity to rules of taste supposedly embodying both individual sensibility and objective standards. Avoiding the subject of "elegance and culture" because of its appropriation by vulgar people suggests that the aristocracy of sensibility is keenly aware of how its image must be managed (and can be degraded), even as it glories in the rhetoric of spontaneous and intense emotions.

Toward the end of the preface, Shen Chunze constructs or records a dialogue in which he asks the author why he bothers to write, considering how the latter's distinguished lineage (Wen Zhenheng was the great grandson of the famous fifteenth-century artist and poet Wen Zhenming) should make the family's authoritative aesthetic judgment self-evident. Besides, since he already inhabits the world of objects and the rules of taste he sets forth, why bother to write about them? To this Wen Zhenheng replies, "What I fear is that as the minds and the hands of the people of Wu change from one day to the next, the beginning foundation of what you call trivial, idle activities or superfluous things can perhaps no longer be known in the future. This work is just meant to prevent this." Shen continues, "This is true! It is enough to preface the book with one line: 'prune the excessive and eliminate the extravagant.'"

As mentioned earlier, the regime of simplicity and restraint is a constant refrain in the discourse on taste. In the first chapter, "Living Quarters" (Shilu), Wen writes: "The best is to live among mountains and waters; next to that is to live in a village; next to that is to live in the outskirts of a city." City dwellers, deprived of the preconditions of harmonious integration with nature, should nevertheless enjoy elegant simplicity in a manner reminiscent of the sensibility of the recluse (*youren* 幽人) and the free-spirited gentleman (*kuangshi* 曠士). This claim of reclusive intent is typical. Devotion to objects without apparent sociopolitical meaning implies withdrawal from the public realm; at the same time the discourse on objects and ownership is also an implicit statement of solidarity in the tastes and sensibilities of the cultural elite, which partly overlaps with the groups wielding economic and/or political power.

This double-edged function is perhaps best captured in Yuan Hongdao's preface to *History of Vases*, where he describes his interest in the subject as an index to his liminal mode of existence in the world. A proper recluse would have banished worldly ties and enjoyed his freedom in nature: "This is the proper province of the recluse, and what a man of heroic determination can do. I have always aspired to that state without insisting on it. Fortunately, I remain between being hidden and being seen. Staying out of what can potentially become the ground of competition and contention, I would have liked to slant my cap on high cliffs and wash my cap-tassels in running streams, yet I am tied down by a lowly official position. Only in cultivating flowers and bamboo can I enjoy myself" (YHD 1:817). Even that modest pleasure, however, is thwarted by constant changes of residence and a damp, narrow courtyard. Yuan Hongdao thus turns to a more convenient enjoyment of flowers in vases, but he is aware of this position as a compromise, falling short of the true connoisseur's obsession, as we have seen in chapter 1. Although Yuan Hongdao modestly disclaims "true connoisseurship" (zhen jianshang 真鑑賞), he obviously harbors little doubt that his pleasure is as genuine as his judgment is authoritative. His keen yet disinterested appreciation is thus the counterpart of his mode of being between engagement in and withdrawal from the public realm.

This mode of self-definition is common, as evinced by the frequency with which late Ming literati and scholar-officials adopted sobriquets that include epithets like "mountain person" (shanren 山人), "Daoist" (daoshi 道士), or "recluse" (jushi 居士).[139] By the late Ming, the term "mountain person" is also applied specifically to a group of literati who held no office and often made their living as dependents or secretaries of officials or by capitalizing on their reputation as writers, artists, and connoisseurs. Inasmuch as their survival and prosperity despite nonparticipation in officialdom depended on social connections and social recognition of their literary or artistic skills, one may dub them "social recluses." Among the most famous in this category are Chen Jiru (Eyebrow Daoist) and Wang Zhideng (Mountain Person of Jade Shade, 1535–1612). Social recluses have sometimes been charged with hypocrisy and pretension,[140] perhaps because they traversed social boundaries and their cultural capital, based on aesthetic sensibility and judgment, is judged to be amorphous enough to leave room for fakery. Their social liminality was what aroused suspicion. As noted earlier, however, many self-consciously cultivated the image of liminality as the basis of capacious understanding and aesthetic judgment. Connoisseurs write about cherishing tranquility and detachment while being absorbed in worldly affairs. Things and activities described as "elegant" gesture toward the ideal of reclusion, but the optimal balance between engagement and detachment can also seem elusive. True elegance supposedly stems from unself-conscious genuineness, yet evidence of self-consciousness is ubiquitous. The aesthetics of restraint and reticence is implicit in the discourse on elegance, yet there is unmistakable fascination with sensual details, excesses, and intensity. Normative elegance calls for rules, but self-consciously flouting rules and redefining norms can also feed the claim to elegance.

DEMOTIC ELEGANCE

In many ways, Li Yu's *Leisure Notes* (*Xianqing ouji*, 1671 preface by Yu Huai [1616–1696]) responds to these paradoxes.[141] Among early Qing works on the art of living, it stands out for its originality. As noted earlier, there are significant overlaps in the late Ming literature of connoisseurship. Li Yu, by contrast, repeatedly avows his aversion to any degree of borrowing. Indeed, a good portion of the sections on "Living Quarters" (Jushi) and "Furnishings and Artifacts" (Qiwan) consists of Li Yu's gleeful accounts of his many inventions, ranging from a chair that keeps warm in winter (*XQOJ* 204–7), mosquito nets with button-like closures (208–11), to a receptacle for the ashes of an incense burner (217).[142]

What remains in the realm of suggestion or perceptual organization in late Ming writings is concretized as techniques and inventions in *Leisure Notes*. The idea of fusing nature and art or artifice, for instance, is prevalent in late Ming writings, and one of its corresponding expressions in Li Yu's work is a special window frame design for boats, by which both the view from within and the view from without mimic the effect of a painting (ever-changing when the boat is in motion). Its effect is to both "entertain oneself" and "entertain others." Li Yu calls this "taking the view by borrowing" (*qujing zai jie* 取景在借, 170–71).[143] Unable to afford a boat, he adapts the design to a window at his house, creating a "small painting window" (*chifu chuang* 尺幅窗) or "accidental painting" (*wuxin hua* 無心畫). By putting framing materials for a scroll around his window, he turns the rockery in his courtyard into a painting of a mountain (171–72). Flowers on a hidden stand, possibly fashioned from gnarled branches or interesting rocks, shrouded between layers of a gauze bed net, perhaps also painted or embroidered with flowers, turn sleep into a reenactment of Zhuangzi's butterfly dream (209). The enjoyment of illusions as a palpably sensuous experience is evident in the celebration of trompe l'oeil in Li Yu.

He delights in visual tricks and unexpected combinations. He proposes to "transform the study into a ceramic vessel," so much so that being inside his study creates the illusion of being inside a ceramic vessel. He first papers the walls with reddish black paper and then paste pieces of pale green paper over it, leaving cracks in between to mimic the "cracked ice" (*binglie* 冰裂) pattern on Ge- and Ru-type glazes on ceramics. On the bigger pieces one can also write poems or paint—the conception would be analogous to inscriptions on bronzes (186). With this elision of different imagined surfaces, he also transforms the exalted ritual function of bronze inscriptions into quotidian pleasures. Li Yu is also interested in effacing the boundaries of indoor and outdoor space. For the main hall in his abode, he has trees and clouds painted on the four walls and attaches stands for parrots to painted branches. The real birds bring the painted scenes to life: the goal is to savor the fluidity between reality and illusion (184–85).

More generally, Li Yu celebrates the intellectual and psychological resources that allow him to defamiliarize or elevate the mundane, manipulate optical illusions, prolong or optimize pleasure, debunk conventions, or potentially set trends in innovation. His avowed goal is to inspire others to become similarly innovative (188). Although he sometimes announces "universal principles," these often turn out upon closer inspection to be no more than glorified personal preferences. Instead of setting forth rules of taste, Li Yu prefers to explore and sometimes challenge the assumptions behind such rules. Departing from the normative rigor of late Ming treatises and manuals, he offers general guidelines instead of precise instructions. Queried for his failure to offer specific instructions in the section on food, he counters: "If I do that, I would be no more than a cook. How can that be worth valuing!" He dismisses works like Gao Lian's *Eight Treatises* as being no more than "cook's manuals" (309). The chapter "Creating Pleasure" (Xingle) in the section "Nourishment and Cultivation" (Yiyang) thus begins not with to-do lists but instructions for psychological self-manipulation.

Above all Li Yu delights in testing or inverting the boundaries of elegance and vulgarity. Hanan contrasts his "demotic attitudes" with the "aesthetic exclusivism" that characterizes some late Ming writings: Li Yu "consciously takes on the role of the plain man's guide in aesthetic as well as practical matters, as a kind of demotic connoisseur," in the process demystifying the aura surrounding "the conventionally aestheticized aspects of daily life."[144] Despite his protestations of poverty, Li Yu did support a household of about fifty, keep a family theatrical troupe, and build gardens, so he was a "plain man" with resources. By advertising how he extends his resources to "create the appearance of magnificence" (*zhuangdian haohua* 妝點豪華), he reframes elegance to include the contrivance of its pleasures.[145] His targets extend beyond what is "conventionally aestheticized" to include idiosyncratic definitions of elegance. Li Yu seems to be implicitly taking aim not only at the rigid rules of taste in manuals and treatises but also at the preciosity of the self-conscious aesthete.

The primacy of pleasure equalizes different categories of experience. Li Yu declares: "For example, sleeping has its pleasure, sitting has its pleasure, walking has its pleasure. . . . Even disrobing and being naked, going to the toilet and defecating or urinating: for all kinds of dirty and demeaning things, so long as one deals with it properly, each would afford its own pleasure" (321). By the same logic, even "the coarsest and most vulgar language (*yu* 語)" can with minor judicious changes become "the most original and elegant composition (*wen* 文)" in drama (22). Note that in thus "creating elegance from vulgarity," Li Yu is departing from the usual justification of vernacular literature through reference to its moral purpose, as in the moral definition of *ya* discussed at the beginning of this chapter. Instead, he focuses on the technique of using well-chosen words to delight the reader and audience with the unexpected chemistry of mixed stylistic registers.

The discourse of elegance is associated with disinterested aesthetic absorption and thus tends to bypass functional considerations. The implications of this notion find a visual metaphor in *Zhong Kui in a Cold Forest* (*Hanlin Zhong Kui*, 1535), painted by Wen Zhengming (probably in collaboration with Qiu Ying [1494–1552]). It shows a quizzical and smiling Zhong Kui standing alone in a wintry forest, hugging the official's tablet with his hands folded inside his sleeves. The conventional presentation of Zhong Kui the demon catcher emphasizes his fearsome mien and his power to drive away demonic spirits and bring blessings.

According to Shih Shou-ch'ien, a nonfunctional Zhong Kui, transposed to a context more typically featuring a recluse or lonely traveler, focuses attention on the boundary between elegance and vulgarity, elite culture and popular culture.[146] Reimagining or recontextualizing the functional thus has the effect of defamiliarizing the conventionally elegant. Perhaps that is why Li Yu emphasizes a dual focus on the aesthetic and the practical. "For pathways (in gardens), nothing is more efficient than convenience, and yet nothing is more wondrous than winding detours. For all those who deliberately create winding paths to achieve interesting effects, it is necessary to open up another side door to allow servants to move swiftly. Open it in urgent situations and close it in leisurely ones. In this way both elegant and common concerns can benefit, and practical reasoning as well as interesting effect are encompassed" (158). An "elegant gathering" (*yaji* 雅集) in the garden needs the labor of servants; to dwell on its enabling mechanism is to claim a more capacious understanding of elegance.

Aesthetic transformation can be all-inclusive. Li Yu writes of his invention, the fan-shaped window that frames all observable scenes as paintings, irrespective of what enters one's vision (people of all stripes, babies, animals, etc.): "'Bovine urine and rotten mushrooms can all enter the medicine chest.' The fan-shaped window that I created is the medicine chest of the man of elegance" (178).[147] Elegance thus depends on imaginative power and transformative inventions. Such inventions also sometimes test the limit of elegance, since functionality dictates attention to what is usually beyond the pale of aesthetic discourse. Li Yu devotes a section to "hiding dirt and covering up filth." What would a man of letters do if he must relieve himself while being seized with inspiration? Li Yu laments that a good line about to take shape may unfortunately be lost as a result. He devises a contraption—a small section of bamboo built into a wall next to his study—that allows him to urinate inside and lets the urine flow outside (163–64).

The prices of artworks and artifacts are occasionally mentioned and there are periodic warnings against extravagance, but the economic basis of aestheticized existence tends to be elided in the literature of connoisseurship. By contrast, Li Yu emphasizes his immersion in the marketplace. He allows the illustrations and description of windows and various designs to be copied, which can only boost sale of his books, but firmly objects to the reproduction of his stationery design and appeals to local officials to intervene, the production and sale of his trademark stationery being one source of his income (229). Keenly aware of branding—"attaching personal names to things" (*wu yi ren ming* 物以人名)—as cultural capital, he touts his design for a receptacle for ashes in incense burners and wants it named "Liweng's incense seal" (Liweng xiangyin 笠翁香印, 217). He wonders whether he bests Chen Jiru, whose name is also associated with various designs (including, unfortunately in Li Yu's opinion, one for toilets, 248).[148] His point of reference for branding is a late Ming cultural icon, but we are also reminded of how famous artisans boost the price of artifacts, as mentioned earlier.

Li Yu reiterates how his modest circumstances necessitate inventions and implicitly claims that his ingenious designs mark his superiority to the owner of fine things or even artistic treasures. To use "broken jars for window frame" (*wengyong* 甕牖) is the byword for poverty, for example, but to assemble broken jar pieces in an artful way is to evoke the crackle of valuable Ge, Ru, and Guan ware. Firewood is used to make gates in a humble abode, but to "do so by taking firewood worthy of entering a painting, so that the sparseness and density of the pieces are matched perfectly," is to create a scholar's gate (as distinguished from a farmer's): Li Yu calls it "transforming the vulgar into the elegant" (*biansu weiya* 變俗為雅, 202). In this sense the self is the source of aesthetic value, and this reasoning may explain the exclusion of antiques and art treasures from his work. It is not simply that he could not afford them. According to Li Yu, people value antiques because of their aura of antiquity, which promises communion with the ancients, who, however, might not have shared that obsession with ancient objects. In any case, books serve that purpose of communion much better than antiques. Further, antiques store and hide value. Their worth may be extreme but not apparent to the undiscerning (including the potential thief). But this opacity also suggests the assignation of value in such cases can be arbitrary.

The very table of contents of *Leisure Notes* announces new ways of contextualizing aesthetic sensibility. The book omits discussions of antiques, calligraphy, and paintings and begins with sections on dramatic performance and feminine charms, topics typically excluded from books on the art of living. By their inclusion, Li Yu signals the continuum between sensual pleasures and aesthetic sensitivity.[149] Late Ming informal writings often present women as aesthetic spectacle. Wei Yong's *Secrets Inside the Pillow* (*Zhen zhong mi*), for example, contains an essay classifying and evaluating the appropriate moods, inclinations, poses, settings, and paraphernalia of beautiful women. Li Yu's approach is more pragmatic. In the section on feminine charms ("Voice and Appearance"), he analyzes the basis of aesthetic and sensual appeal of women and offers advice on how women should improve their complexion, apply makeup, and choose hairstyles, socks, shoes, and articles of clothing.[150] By showing how women as aesthetic objects are fashioned or may be improved to enhance male pleasure, he dispels the aura of romantic longing.

There are no intense and unfulfilled desires in this world. Instead, a gentle eroticism translates (sometimes humorously) into a vision of affective nature and suffuses all aspects of aesthetic appreciation. Thus Li Yu claims that draping a virgin's skirt over an apricot tree not bearing fruit will lead to fecundity—hence its name "romantic tree" (*fengliu shu* 風流樹, 264–65)—and that watering the roots of lovers' blooms (*hehuan hua* 合歡花) every other day with water in which a couple has taken a bath will bring forth more beautiful flowers (274). Periodic rearrangement of furniture and utensils in a room introduces the joys and pathos of union and separation to the world of things: "It is to turn lifeless objects into affective objects" (232). Instead of the intense emotions and sentimentality sometimes evoked by humanizing things, Li Yu gives a technical and ironic turn to the idea. He declares, for example, that "wives and concubines are the divans among humans, and beds are the humans among divans" and proceeds to dilate on designs for bed nets: it is analogous to turning a plain woman into a beauty (208). To literalize the idea of "taking the plum as wife" like the recluse Lin Bu requires the creation of a portable paper-made "abode by the flower" (*jiu hua ju* 就花居) that allows the enjoyment of blooms in close proximity (262).

The sense of a world enlivened by sensibility feeds a measured and playful hedonism in Li Yu. In the section "Nourishing and Replenishing Life," he begins with injunctions on moderating pleasures so as to prolong them, then proposes the mental trick of imagining or experiencing a worse situation in order to enhance enjoyment, and ends with rather startling suggestions on cures for sickness, including the use of favorite food and objects of desire as medicine. Here the tone balances gaily between moral homilies on restraint and half-jesting encouragement of hedonism. By incorporating as elegant living what is conventionally unmentioned or unmentionable (bodily functions, economic calculations, the grosser sensual pleasures), Li Yu is also realigning self-consciousness with "the view from below" and celebrating the ingenious self that inverts hierarchies and crosses boundaries.

THE VULGAR CONNOISSEUR IN *JIN PING MEI*

For all the talk of "transforming the vulgar into the elegant," Li Yu does not really touch the negative associations of vulgarity with ignorance and pretension. He may argue for a less allusive and more accessible diction for the stage, but he is still thinking in terms of performance by family troupes in elite households, even as the "poor scholars" (*pinshi* 貧士) in his discourse still have the means to refashion a new brand of elegance. In other words, he stops short of being subversive.

The same may be said of the pointed critique of vulgar pretensions in mid–seventeenth–century stories like "The Fake Aficionado Formed a Covenant at Tiger Mound" (Huqiu shan jia qingke lianmeng), in *Stories Under the Bean Arbor* (*Doupeng xianhua*, tenth story), by Layman of Aina Incense (Aina Jushi), and "For He Who Borrowed the Tiger's Power, Curios and Antiques Brought Calamity, / Swooping Down in Attack like Eagles, Scholars Championed the Just Cause" (Jia huwei guwan liuyang, fen yingji shusheng zhangyi), in *Sobering Stone* (*Zuixing shi*, eighth story), by Ancient Wild Scholar of Eastern Lu (Dong Lu gu kuangsheng). In "The Fake Aficionado," a satire in broad strokes directed against the class of dealers and go-betweens in Suzhou who cater to the whims of the rich and powerful, one hanger-on surnamed Jia (homophonous with false), the "fake aficionado" named in the title, rallies his fellow dealers to form a "covenant" mimicking literary societies, pondering historical antecedents, and appropriating patron saints for their group. Jia is supposed to have acquired a literati veneer by virtue of having been a "study companion," but in fact the style of farcical caricature takes over, and he shows the grossest ignorance when he tries to sound like a connoisseur. The story paints a cynical picture in which both the scholar-officials (the would-be patrons) and their hangers-on are vulgar and immoral, and transactions in the supposed ornaments of literati culture only cover up the pimping of young boys and girls.

In the story from *Sobering Stone*, the main character, Wang Chen, is a convenient villain from the perspective of literati unease with unstable social boundaries. Wang is a servant who acquires literati skills and uses them to rise in the world after escaping the fury of a master intent on starving him to death upon discovery of his adulterous relationship with the master's concubine. The turning point of his fortunes comes when he accurately caters to the taste of powerful but uncultured eunuchs in the art market in Beijing: after the eunuchs dismiss Wang's landscape in the style of Ni Zan and Mi Fu and his cursive calligraphy, he produces with aplomb ornate paintings in the "blue and green style," gold-tinted images of flowers and birds, and calligraphy in the standard script. Having won their favor, he eventually rises to the position of imperially commissioned officer sent to Jiangnan to purchase artworks and antiques. Wang wreaks vengeance on his erstwhile master and others who slighted him by reporting their supposed ownership of items that should have been sold to the imperial collection. His greed and ruthlessness earn him jeering limericks from Suzhou scholars, and Wang decides to punish them by rounding them up to make copies of rare books and mistreating them in the process. Wang finally meets his comeuppance when the scholars band together to physically attack him. The confrontation eventually draws the attention of an upright official, who then investigates Wang's wrongdoings and puts him to death. The story is based on real events from the Chenghua reign.[151] Here collecting and connoisseurship are linked to misrule and the abuse of power. The person manipulating the emperor's misguided passion is himself an impostor who misappropriates literati skills to ignominious ends. In that sense the avenging scholars vindicate their moral and aesthetic values.

However, the most interesting prisms on the claims of normative taste and the paradoxes of self-conscious elegance are not these straightforward condemnations of vulgarity and depravity. It is when vulgarity itself becomes the venue for appreciating the texture of sights, sounds, smell, and touch in the fictional world, as in the case of *Jin Ping Mei*, that the questioning of norms becomes more probing and troubling. Many scholars have taken *Jin Ping Mei* as the obvious example of conspicuous consumption and its transgressive sociopolitical implications. Volpp observes: "Ximen's 'deviant consumption' of the python robe marks the symbolic transfer of power in *Jin Ping Mei* from the world of officialdom to the mercantile realm.... The trajectories of the python robes bear witness to the unseemly social aspirations of all those involved in their inappropriate circulation."[152] The appropriation of emblems of power, however, is not only political transgression but also aesthetic display. "Mandarin squares" with mythical animals that adorn official robes become part of female fashion in *Jin Ping Mei*. In a formal meeting with the partners of a future marriage alliance, Wu Yueniang wears "a full-sleeved robe of scarlet variegated satin, decorated with a motif of the four animals representing the cardinal directions paying homage to the kylin" (*JPM* 43.642; Roy 3:57). We are told that this pattern graces Yueniang's jacket as well as her robe in an itemized list of clothes tailored for the women in Ximen's family (*JPM* 40.502).[153] The final, unattainable object of Ximen Qing's desire, the beautiful Lady Lan, wears a robe with the same motif (*JPM* 78.1365; Roy 4:621). Does the implied author take pleasure in lingering over these robes? The violation of sumptuary laws seems irrelevant here: these designs are treated like other sartorial details or like the minutiae of the exceedingly ornate patterns on handkerchiefs that Pan Jinlian elaborates for her son-in-law Chen Jingji, when she requests their purchase almost as a kind of seductive challenge (*JPM* 51.774–75). One expects the authorial voice of *Jin Ping Mei* to showcase mercantile vulgarity and social ambitions or mock its debased characters' façade of elegance. While that perspective is undoubtedly present, we are also invited to linger on the sensual details of the plethora of things expressing the vagaries of desire.

The character that articulates the most fulsome appreciation of things in the book is the sycophant Ying Bojue, one of Ximen Qing's sworn brothers. This appreciation, always voluble and sometimes discerning, is inseparable from Ying's vulgarity and depravity. In numerous scenes, he is the consummate flatterer waxing enthusiastic over the material manifestations of Ximen Qing's wealth and power. Having gained the office of assistant judicial commissioner through lavish gifts to the grand preceptor Cai Jing, Ximen Qing revels in the paraphernalia of office. He shows off a new girdle to Ying Bojue, who is predictably impressed and exclaims:

Regarding the rest of them, enough said; but as for this girdle with its decorative plaque of rhinoceros horn, and this one of "crane's crest red," you couldn't find the like in the entire metropolis, though you had the money in hand.... This is the horn of the water rhinoceros, not the horn of the dry land rhinoceros. The latter is not worth anything. The horn of the water rhinoceros is called "Heaven-penetrating rhinoceros horn." If you don't believe me, bring a bowl of water, put the rhinoceros horn in it, and it will divide the water in two. This is a priceless treasure. Moreover, if you ignite it at night it will illuminate an area of a thousand *li*, and the flame will not be extinguished at night.
(*JPM* 31.438–39; Roy 2:216–17)

For Ximen Qing, the girdle matters because of its price (a hundred taels) and its provenance "from the household of Imperial Commissioner Wang on Main Street" (*JPM* 31.439; Roy 2:217), whose financial straits seem to render their superior status ripe for appropriation.[154] The Wang household commands the arc of Ximen Qing's desire, being the place where Jinlian started out as a maid and where Ximen revels in the illusion of power in sexual encounters with a social superior, Lady Lin, the widow of Imperial Commissioner Wang and the mother of Wang the Third, Ximen Qing's rival for the attention of the courtesans Li Guijie and Zheng Aiyue'er. Ying Bojue, for his part, is flattering Ximen Qing as preamble for requesting a loan on behalf of their common crony Wu Dian'en. Again, money and status are the real issues; the thing itself does not seem to matter much.

Zhang Zhupo scoffs at Ying Bojue for being a "fake connoisseur," and there is indeed some evidence of mix-up in his information. According to *Baopu zi*, if a person holding in his mouth a rhinoceros horn carved in the shape of a fish enters water, the water will part and he can also breathe in water. The only source that associates the "Heaven-penetrating rhinoceros horn" with "water rhinoceros" is Zheng Qiao's (1104–1162) *Comprehensive Records* (*Tongzhi*).[155] Some accounts mention a white or red line running from the rim to the tip of this type of rhinoceros horn, but none mentions "crane's crest red," a term usually used to describe species of flowers and fish. It is not clear whether the author is responsible for the confusion or that he is mocking Ying Bojue. It is also possible that he simply enjoys dilating on the lore of the "Heaven-penetrating rhinoceros horn"; he can parade his "broad learning about things" (*bowu* 博物) even as he mocks fatuous vanity and extravagance.[156] By contrast, the tone is more decidedly satirical when Ying gives his panegyric on Li Ping'er's expensive coffin boards named "Peach Blossom Cavern." Designed to impress Eunuch Xue, it is an obviously incongruous jumble of stories based on free and unwarranted associations with Tao Yuanming's (365–427) "Peach Blossom Spring" (*JPM* 64.1026).[157]

In another scene, Ying Bojue effusively praises a marble standing screen inlaid with mother-of-pearl and decorated with gold tracery, which, along with a bronze gong and a bronze drum, is brought to Ximen Qing's attention as an item that an imperial relative is trying to pawn for thirty taels. "Brother, just take a good look at these things. The pattern in the marble resembles a lion couchant, protector of the house, and the two stands for the bronze gong and the bronze drum are sumptuously decorated with varicolored designs and cloud patterns carved in relief, the workmanship of which is truly outstanding." Ximen hesitates, wondering whether the items will be redeemed. Ying reassures him: "His affairs are like a cart on a downward slope." Another crony Xie Xida chimes in: "The cinnabar-red painted lacquer is all done in accord with official specifications," and crows that the items are worth a hundred taels (*JPM* 45.662; Roy 3:86–88). Ximen Qing accedes to the pawning. Having set the screen up in the reception hall, Ximen looks at it right and left: "Its gold and blue-green hues weave a glow like colorful clouds" (*JPM* 45.662). Such is the limit of Ximen's powers of appreciation, but aesthetic appeal is in any case irrelevant. Ximen is swayed by the idea that a good bargain means that "for each thing there is a fated owner" (45.663). Many of the things Ximen Qing acquires become available because their erstwhile powerful and rich owners have fallen on hard times. Ying Bojue's role in these scenes of acquisition, as he dilates on the exquisiteness of the objects, is to mask relentless turns in the wheel of fortune as the basis of inevitable and rightful ownership.

Ying's connoisseurship is a unique blend of virtuosic knowledge and vulgarity. When Eunuch Director Liu, the manager of the Imperial Brickyard, sends Ximen Qing twenty pots of chrysanthemums, attention shifts quickly from the flowers to the pots. Zhang Zhupo comments: "The emphasis is on the pots: this is how vulgar people of the marketplace love flowers."[158] Yet Ying's knowledge about the pots is a tour de force: "These pots are double-banded wide-mouthed flowerpots, manufactured from the finest clay in the imperial kilns, and are both long-lasting and water-repellent. They are made from clay that has been strained through silken sieves and kneaded underfoot until it becomes a thick paste, just like that used in the firing of the finest quality of bricks in Suzhou. Where could one go to find articles of this quality these days?" (*JPM* 61.960; Roy 4:23). Roy pointed out that there was indeed an imperial brickyard that made bricks for palace construction located in Suzhou during the Ming dynasty.[159] The chrysanthemums may have traditional symbolic associations with lofty virtue and reclusion, but Ying is right that the economic and political significance of the gifts lies with the pots, which have a more immediate connection with the giver. His excursus on the making of the pots would not be out of place in the manuals of taste prevalent in the late Ming.

Sycophancy does not preclude heartfelt appreciation. Consider Ying Bojue's song on tea (*JPM* 12.153–54; Roy 1:228) and his paean to shad: "This fish of yours from Jiangnan is only in season once a year. If it gets stuck in the cracks between your teeth, when you manage to extricate it, it is still fragrant. It's not easy to come by. To tell the truth, I doubt if it is available even at court. Where else are you likely to find it except at Brother's place here?" (*JPM* 52.794; Roy 3:278).[160] He also recommends a recipe for its preparation (*JPM* 34.487). His effusive appreciation of the butterfat "abalone shell" pastry prepared by Li Ping'er (58.898) and by the courtesan Zheng Aiyue'er (67.1079) elevates gustatory satisfaction as a transformative experience, even while callously implying that women are replaceable: the pastry was Li Ping'er's specialty, and after her death it is Zheng Aiyue'er who continues to prepare the delicacy. Aiyue'er's offering plunges Ximen Qing into melancholy as he mourns Ping'er, but Ying Bojue manages to restore his good humor by tasteless jokes about being the beneficiary of Ximen's women.

If the implied author seems to intermittently speak through Ying Bojue's sensual appreciation despite his vulgarity, it is because there is no countervailing standard of elegance in the book. Or rather, elegance itself becomes vulgar. As Ximen Qing gains in wealth and power, the paraphernalia of refinement, such as calligraphy, painting, zithers, and antiques, comes to grace his surroundings. He eventually acquires four pages whose names (Qintong, Qitong, Shutong, Huatong) represent the standard ornaments of literati culture (zither, chess, calligraphy, painting). Ying Bojue offers the most detailed description of the Kingfisher Pavilion, Ximen's study decked out with literati pretensions, in a kind of indirect free style:

> Ying Bojue observed that facing each other on the upper and lower ends of the room were ranged two rows of six low-slung, bow-back, folding arm-chairs of the type called Dongpo chairs, embellished with Yunnan agateware lacquer, gilt nails, and wickerwork rattan seats. On the two side walls were hung four landscape paintings by well-known artists, mounted on ultramarine patterned damask with white satin borders. On one hand there stood a side table, the cabriole legs of which were carved in the shape of protruding "mantis belly" that tapered down into "dragonfly feet," and the top of which was inlaid with an oblong, letter-shaped, slab of marble, chosen for its pictorial quality. On this table was displayed an antique bronze incense burner in the shape of a gilded crane. In the center of the back wall there hung a plaque emblazoned with the three characters for Kingfisher Pavilion, with a pair of framed hanging scrolls suspended to the left and right, on the coated paper of which was inscribed the couplet: The breeze is tranquil, shadows of locust trees purify the courtyard; / The day is long, fragrance from an incense burner suffuses the latticework.... Ying Bojue wandered into the inner study, where he found standing on the floor a black lacquer summer bedstead with incised gold ornamentation and a decorative marble panel and fitted with bed curtains of blue silk. To either side of this were painted lacquer bookcases adorned with gold tracery, which were filled with conventional presentation gifts of privately printed books with brocade wrappers and bolts of fabric. There was also a desk, piled high with writing implements and books. Under the green gauze window there stood a black lacquer zither stand and solitary folding chair inlaid with mother-of-pearl. A letter case was also visible containing Ximen Qing's social correspondence, calling cards, and lists of people with whom Midautumn festival gifts have been exchanged.
> (*JPM* 34.484–85; Roy 2:284–85)

This passage appears only in the *cihua* edition. The editor of the Chongzhen edition would have been justified in cutting it out, for it contributes nothing to the plot. Yet it is a remarkable embodiment of vulgarized elegance. Ying does not pause to offer details on the paintings, lingering instead on the material for mounting them. The couplet and the incense burner suggest a mood of contemplative detachment, which is belied by the ornate side table and the chairs. The gold tracery on the bookcase seems to demand greater attention than the books, notable more for their brocade wrappers as vanity projects than for their content. Ying's attention is drawn to the list of gifts exchanged because transactions override all other modes of human connections in the book. It is fitting that Kingfisher Pavilion should be the setting for sexual trysts, monetary negotiations, and maneuverings to bypass legal constraints.

The scholars and officials who supposedly embody ideals of refinement are every bit as vulgar as Ximen Qing and his cronies despite the veneer of learning. The way Censor Song Qiaonian transparently hankers after Ximen Qing's "gilded Eight Immortals Tripod" (*JPM* 74.1234, 75.1255) is no different from the calculations of the marketplace. The mansions of the grand preceptor Cai Jing, his steward Zhai Qian, or Imperial Commissioner Wang may be more chock-full of precious objects and cultural artifacts, but we do not have the impression that they fulfill higher standards of elegance. Indeed, the grandest and most ambitious aesthete of all may be the Huizong emperor, but his Mount Gen Imperial Park is seen as the source of suffering and corruption rather than the realization of an aesthetic ideal.

In Ximen's dealings with scholar-officials, he affects elevated speech and cultural allusions. The result is not so much the exposure of his déclassé pretensions but the implicit castigation of all parties involved and the degradation of "high culture." In one memorable scene, Ximen Qing entertains Censor Cai, a top graduate, with singing girls:

> When Censor Cai saw them, he wanted to advance but could not, wanted to withdraw but did not manage, so he said, "Siquan [Ximen Qing's sobriquet], how can you show me such generous regard? I am afraid it will never do!" Ximen Qing laughed, saying, "How is this any different from Xie An's roaming in the Eastern Mountain?"

Censor Cai said, "I only fear that my talent does not measure up to Xie An, while you, sir, do possess the lofty spirit of Wang Xizhi." Thereupon, he held hands with the two singing girls beneath the moon, looking for all the world like Liu Chen and Ruan Zhao encountering goddesses in Tiantai Mountains. Upon entering the pavilion and seeing that it contained all the cultural artifacts that he remembered from his previous visit, he asked for paper and writing brush so that he might leave a composition for the occasion. (*JPM* 49.730–31; Roy 3:185–86)[161]

Xie An (320–385) and Wang Xizhi (303–361) are epitomes of cultural refinement from Eastern Jin (317–420). Xie An was famous for enjoying private life and consorting with courtesans in Eastern Mountains even as he rose to political prominence as prime minister and claimed major military victories against the rival regime in the North. Wang Xizhi is remembered as the supreme calligrapher. Wang and Xie appear together in a number of anecdotes demonstrating their affinities and implicit competition. In one of them they take opposite positions. Wang Xizhi laments the irrelevance or even deleterious consequences of the abstruse, speculative discourse called "pure conversation" (*qingtan* 清談) for the contemporary political crisis, while Xie An points to the fall of Qin (221–206 BCE) as a reminder that the reasons for political failure are manifold and "pure conversation" needs not shoulder the blame for undermining political will (*Shishuo xinyu* 2.70). If Xie An stands for the effortless combination of political engagement and romantic sensibility, Wang Xizhi emerges as the more cautious, corrective voice in this anecdote. Censor Cai may be alluding to this difference in comparing himself to Xie An and Ximen Qing to Wang Xizhi. What strikes the reader is not merely the incongruity of the analogies, for which Cai and Ximen represent obvious travesty. We are led to question the more general misuse of cultural allusions, for standard justifications of sensual indulgence as being compatible with, or even germane to, moral probity and political engagement appeal to exemplars such as Xie An. The vulgarization of the epitomes of cultural refinement tarnishes their symbolic power even as it mocks unworthy pretensions.

The downward shift of the tropes and emblems of elegance is ubiquitous in the book. When Pan Jinlian sings arias of longing as she plays the *pipa* during a snowy night, the delicate plaint of the pining woman familiar to the poetic tradition becomes a siren's song designed to goad Ximen Qing to leave the room of Jinlian's rival Li Ping'er (*JPM* 38.565–67). A chapter entitled "Ximen Qing enjoys a snowy scene in his study" (chap. 67) contains only a cursory reference to Ximen Qing noticing the snow; instead, we have a parade of characters engaging Ximen Qing in mundane business, from a masseuse to a supplicant who seeks Ximen Qing's intervention in a court case, from Scholar Wen who couches transactions of favors in polite language to Ying Bojue who maneuvers various negotiations to his own advantage. The snowy scene, instead of inspiring mournful contemplation (Li Ping'er has just died), becomes the setting for vulgar bantering and discussions of various delicacies, including milk with butterfat, "coated plums," and the aforementioned "abalone shell." In such cases of incongruity, one may argue that it is precisely the "vulgarization" that gives tired tropes a new life.

The incongruity between cultural artifacts and characters is ubiquitous. The Yang family residence with its textile business, where Ximen Qing arranges his marriage with Yang's widow Meng Yulou, boasts of tokens of refinement next to "a row of indigo vats for dyeing and two benches for fulling cloth": "Landscape paintings by well-known artists hung on the other walls. There was also a marble standing screen, to either side of which stood tall, narrow-necked, bronze vases of the kind used in the game 'pitch-pot'" (*JPM* 7.90; Roy 1:132; this passage is omitted in the Chongzhen edition). The most elegant décor described in the whole book may be the "Moon-Loving Studio" (Aiyue xuan) of the courtesan Zheng Aiyue'er (whose name means "moon-lover"), as seen through Ximen Qing's eyes:

> As he entered the parlor, he saw that there was a hanging scroll depicting Guanyin of the Ocean Tides in the place of honor on the facing wall, while on the walls to either side there were hung four scrolls depicting beautiful women in the four seasons, spring, summer, autumn, and winter, inscribed with the poetic lines: "Concerned for the flowers, one rises early in spring. / Enamored of the moon, one goes to sleep late at night. / Scooping up water, one finds the moon in one's hands. / Fondling the flowers, fragrance infuses

one's clothes." Above everything was suspended a couplet that read: "Rolling up the blind, one invites the moon to look in; / Tuning the cithara, one waits for the clouds to enter."
(*JPM* 59. 916–17; Roy 3:458; omitted in the Chongzhen edition)

Her bedroom is filled with the paraphernalia of literati culture, from the incense burner to the zither: "Upon a mica screen was depicted a landscape in varying shades of ink; / On a shelf of the nuptial couch was a pile of ancient and modern books" (*JPM* 59.918; Roy 3:460). The house of a high-class courtesan promises entry into the world of high culture, and the elegant décor here finds echoes in vernacular tales (e.g., "All the Famous Courtesans Mourn Liu Yong in the Spring Wind" [Zhong mingji chunfeng diao Liu Qi], in *Gujin xiaoshuo* 12, ca. 1621) and memoirs such as Yu Huai's (1616–96) *Miscellaneous Records of the Plank Bridge* (*Banqiao zaji*). But whereas the ornaments of literati culture seem fitting in these other examples, there is decidedly a sense of incongruity in *Jin Ping Mei*. The misappropriation of symbols of refinement is not merely a critique of pretension; it also tarnishes such symbols and showcase their powerlessness to elevate debased emotions.

If Ximen's relationships with courtesans are unabashedly crass, those of Principal Graduate Cai or Wang the Third are not any better, even though they may be dignified by the conventionally sentimental poems that those two write for their lovers (*JPM* 49.733, 77.1323).[162] If there are no higher standards of elegance and good taste (and the literati and scholar-officials as well as traditional ornaments of literati culture certainly do not seem to represent them here), what we are left with is the frank wallowing in sensual reality. Instead of seeing the endless descriptions as markers of moral outrage, we can imagine an author fascinated by the perspective of the vulgar connoisseur, who allows him to celebrate the pleasures of the senses and reframe or question normative elegance, even while leaving room for critical distance. He may be mocking Ying Bojue for failing to dwell on the famous landscape paintings in Kingfisher Pavilion, but like Ying he may find the cabriole leg of the side table well worth absorption and detailed description.

THE CONTRADICTIONS OF ELEGANCE
IN A LI YU STORY

If the vulgar connoisseur commands our attention and normative elegance seems to lose its relevance in *Jin Ping Mei*, what would a conscious investment in that relevance in an increasingly commodified and commercialized world look like? "The House of Elegant Ensemble" (Cuiya lou, literally "the house where elegant things and persons are gathered"), the sixth story in Li Yu's *Twelve Structures* (*Shi'er lou*, 1658), offers us playful yet probing reflections on this question. The story takes up the paradoxical balance and tension between transactional thinking and the ideal of elegance, sensual indulgence and more refined pleasures, conformity to and defiance of social norms and moral expectations. Here economic transactions initially augment a self-contained world of elegance, partly reprising the logic we saw in Li Yu's *Leisure Notes*, but it eventually succumbs to political pressure and the abuse of power.

Li Yu begins with a poem he wrote twenty years earlier, upon the request of an aged flower vendor, on the walls of his flower shop in Suzhou. In the poem he praises the vendor for combining the most vulgar of places (the market) with the most exquisitely refined thing (flowers). Li Yu then embarks on an excursus on the margin between refinement and vulgarity and characterizes the trade of books, incense, and flowers as "the three elegant things among what is vulgar" (*su zhong san ya* 俗中三雅). Antiques are not mentioned only because their inclusion is implied, for Li Yu refuses to regard incense, flowers, and books as merely "contemporary things" or "things of the moment" (*shiwu* 時物). (In other words, the shops probably also carry antique vases and incense burners, as well as rare books printed in earlier eras.) Li Yu opines: those involved in their transactions do so because of karmic ties: they were bees, bookworms, and musk deer in former lives.[163] If in their human incarnations they "only change their forms but not their character," however, they will only become "the three vulgar beings among what is elegant" (*ya zhong san su* 雅中三俗). In other words, if they follow their karmic burden of being busy among flowers, obsessed with books, or producing fragrance, they will be no different from other vulgar merchants. Only the combination of a sense of proper distance, aesthetic appreciation, and self-awareness can make the vendors of elegant things elegant persons.

This is but the preamble to a story, set during the Jiajing reign (1521–1566), that tells of the fate of three young men who master the art of elegance. Jin Zhongyu and Liu Minshu are both scholars who, distracted by many interests, have not succeeded in the examination system and have turned to trade. They share a lover, Quan Ruxiu, a much younger man from Yangzhou who is "more beautiful than a beautiful woman." Like Jin and Liu, Quan is a connoisseur with refined aesthetic sensibility, but he seems to have come from a humbler background—he does not seem to have taken the examination. "Jin and Liu valued their friendship and banished all distrust and misgiving. For the two friends sharing one catamite, not only were they free from jealousy, they even used him as a way to bring them together more closely. Others only noted that the two men had, with an addition, become three, little did they know that the three men had joined to become one" (*CYL* 130).

The spatial realization of this unorthodox ménage à trois is the House of Elegant Ensemble, and Li Yu takes pains to emphasize the multiple meanings of "elegance" here. Jin and Liu deliberately choose to engage in "the trade of elegant things" (*siwen jiaoyi* 斯文交易) so as to "not lose the proper modus operandi of the literati"—"trade in elegant things" confirms their identity as "literati merchants." They end up with three contiguous shops—Jin manages the bookshop in the middle, Quan the incense shop on the left, and Liu the shop for flowers and antiques on the right. Behind the shops is an elevated structure, the tastefully decorated House of Elegant Ensemble. "On all the evenings with pure wind and bright moon, they gathered there together—plucking away on string instruments, playing the flute, or singing. In all these their art was supreme, and all who listened were deeply affected" (130–31). They are the first to sample the best of incense, books, flowers, and antiques that pass through their shops. "What they stroked with their hands were antiques from periods no later than Qin and Han; what they hung on their walls were works of masters from Tang and Song or before. When they had their fill of enjoying these fine things, they sold them" (131). These are connoisseurs that seem to have an optimal relationship with their objects of appreciation: they show no excessive attachment that some decry as vulgar,[164] and they savor above all else their sensations and experience. The titular "ensemble" pertains to both aesthetic objects and the three men who seem to be the very epitome of refinement. Their togetherness adds erotic undertones to the word "ensemble."

Li Yu extends the epithet of *ya* to their fair and scrupulous mercantile methods. They would not buy things that are inferior, fake, or of dubious origins; nor would they sell things that are too cheap, too expensive, or too problematic (i.e., things that test a buyer's trust). By calling this the trading style that "preserves somewhat the elegant way" (*cun xie yao-dao* 存些雅道), Li Yu extends the meanings of "elegant" to encompass "proper" and "judicious" (*yazheng* 雅正). Propriety in mercantile dealings is conjoined with an unorthodox domestic arrangement. While Jin and Liu have their own wife and children in separate households, Quan lives in the shop and becomes their "wife" as Jin and Liu take turns to "appreciate and enjoy the flowers in the rear courtyard" (the standard euphemism for anal sex) under the excuse of guarding the shop. The combination of fair and open trade with semi-illicit pleasures, just like the quest for "elegance in vulgarity," speaks to the idea of elegance as the freedom to cross boundaries and to define an ideal space of liminality, self-expression, and self-fulfillment. The House of Elegant Ensemble is where Liu and Jin can be both literati and merchants, both embedded in sociopolitical reality yet detached from it, both heads of families and devoted lovers of a catamite.

The idyllic world of Jin, Liu, and Quan is rudely shattered by the predatory lust of Yan Shifan (1513–1565), son of the powerful minister Yan Song (1480–1567)—these historically corrupt and iniquitous characters are frequently represented as villains and rapacious collectors in Ming-Qing literature.[165] After various ploys to secure Quan's sexual service fail, Yan Shifan plots with the imperial eunuch Sha Yucheng to lure Quan to Sha's house and have Quan castrated.[166] Deprived of alternatives, the castrated Quan enters Eunuch Sha's service and, after Sha's death, joins Yan's household. Serving Yan Shifan as catamite grants Quan the opportunity to keep a careful record of his misdeeds. As is typical of Li Yu's oeuvre, the economic metaphor persists: having fallen victim to economic calculations that appraise him as mere "goods" (*huo* 貨), Quan employs a ledger in the form of an orihon to pursue justice. He is granted sweet revenge when, after Yan Song's impeachment, he becomes a palace eunuch and has the chance to enumerate the crimes of Yan Song and Yan Shifan in front of the Jiajing emperor, who thereupon abandons all plans of leniency and puts Yan Shifan to death. In fully revealing the treachery of Yan Song and Yan Shifan, Quan also elicits the emperor's heartfelt regret for having wronged the loyal official Yang Jisheng. (The historical Yang Jisheng [1516–1555] submitted a memorial detailing Yan Song's crimes to the throne, and he was tortured and eventually executed in 1555.) The story concludes with Yan Shifan's execution and his grotesque "objectification"—the transformation of his skull into a urinal.

As this cursory summary indicates, the story is divided into two halves—the homosexual romance and the celebration of connoisseurship and refinements in the first half and the story of Yan's crime and punishment, concomitantly Quan's victimization and revenge, in the second half. Scholarship on Li Yu is likewise divided, focusing on either homosexuality or political corruption and the abuse of power.[167] The bridge between the two halves is of course Quan, who sees himself as the connoisseur of beautiful things (Eunuch Sha praises him as "the premier elegant person in the capital") but is instead turned into the "beautiful thing" that can be traded. The language of connoisseurship provides the transition by confirming Quan's agency as the connoisseur as well as his degradation as the commodified object of connoisseurship. Yan Shifan's sycophants first arouse his lust by comparing Quan to other things in the shops: "The loveliest of all is that young shopkeeper, pure as ice and luscious as jade. So long as he is sitting there facing us, he *is* the famed incense, the unusual blooms, the antiques and the books. Why does one need to see any more goods!" (133). Yan forces Liu and Jin to give up Quan by imposing on them the logic of transactions. Yan takes the most expensive items from their shops without paying, and when Liu and Jin make inquiries, Yan's steward hints that payment will be forthcoming only if they offer Quan. Forced to choose between "the goods" and "the person," Liu and Jin opt for their lover, because "a thousand pieces of gold are easy to obtain, but beauty is hard to come by." But Yan's steward warns them that giving up their prized goods is scarcely a solution; he urges them to reconsider by comparing Quan to an object of connoisseurship:

> If you do not come to claim payment, then you clearly loathe him [Yan] and are trying to humiliate him. Is this a master you can afford to loathe or humiliate? Now if he wants to sleep with your wives, then you cannot be blamed for risking your very lives to refuse him. But here we are talking about nothing more than a "friend": even if you send him there for a bit of appraisal and appreciation (*shangjian* 賞鑒), it would be no different from offering him antiques, calligraphy, or paintings—even if there is slight damage, the price will not plunge. Why throw away a thousand pieces of silver and take a cup of vinegar[168] in exchange?
> (*CYL* 138)

The Chinese tradition offers many stirring stories about the primacy of friendship, including accounts of men who nobly sacrifice wife and children for their friends. But here the word "friend" means "lover"; by this reckoning, sexual relations devalue friendship and a male lover matters less than a wife. Jin and Liu are willing to sustain financial loss, but they balk at the prospect of endangering themselves and their families or ruining their livelihood. They ultimately acquiesce to the classification of Quan as a valuable item no different from antiques, calligraphy, or paintings.

Quan, more than his lovers, tries to pursue the promise of "elegance" to cross boundaries and define one's modus operandi. He refuses to become Yan's lover: "A chaste woman does not take two husbands. How can a chaste man serve three masters?" (138). The almost comical quip is belied by earnest attachment. Homosexual romance often reproduces the logic of heterosexual romance and presents the catamite as the counterpart of the chaste and loyal woman.[169] Here Quan redefines that mold by being equally devoted to his two "husbands," although the very proposition of "two husbands" threatens the logic of a romantic plot built on the figure of the chaste and heroic wife. How can devotion be absolute if its object is bifurcated? If the "two husbands" were "two wives," they could have sacrificed everything for Quan. But the hierarchy of gender roles as much as self-interest prevent Jin and Liu from doing so.

While Yan Shifan's steward uses the word "friend" with demeaning undertones, Quan reclaims the dignity of friendship for his relationship

Elegance and Vulgarity 141

with Jin and Liu. He refers to them as "friends with a sworn bond," recalling the sworn brotherhood of heroic sagas. The narrator commends his integrity for honoring the bond of friendship: "There are in the marketplace strange characters and unusual men. They are quite different from officials with gauze hats. . . . Refusing to go against their friends, they would rather offend powerful and important people" (134–35).

Ultimately, however, Jin and Liu betray Quan and choose to protect themselves. Quan is reduced to the status of an object, and his dehumanization is nowhere more horrifying than when Eunuch Sha, having drugged him and had him castrated, had his testicles thrown on the ground and eaten by a dog. A proper revenge requires commensurate debasement and "objectification" of his enemy. As mentioned, after Yuan's execution, Quan turns Yuan's skull into a urinal. "Back then, drooling,[170] Yan lusted after Quan and did this evil thing. Later, when Yan took his pleasure, he used a lot of saliva. That was why Quan repaid his fluid with urine, so that Yan would not lose his capital investment" (149). Li Yu concludes his story with the harangue that Quan hurls at Yan on the execution ground (149–50):

汝割我卵	You cut my testicles,
我去汝頭	I remove your head.
以上易下	Exchanging what's above with what's below,
死有餘羞	You die with shame that lingers.
汝戲我臀	With saliva you toyed with my buttocks,
我溺汝口	I will urinate in your mouth.
以淨易穢	Exchanging what's clean with what's filthy,
死多遺臭	You died leaving a foul name.
奉勸世間人	I urge you people in this world:
莫施刻毒心	Do not pursue your evil schemes.
刻毒後來終有報	Evil will in the end bring retribution:
八兩計謀換一斤	Eight taels of scheming will be repaid with a full catty.[171]

A story that begins by creating an ideal space with an "elegant ensemble" ends with deliberately gross references to gruesome mutilation, body parts, and body fluids. Li Yu's final message of retributory justice is fully satisfactory only if one takes Yan's crime and punishment as the crux of the story. Quan Ruxiu's name, which can be glossed as "the authority (or 'biding by expediency') to punish you," supports this reading.[172] But the story can also be read as a broader indictment of the obsession with elegance. Yan Shifan reminds us of the saying in the *Book of Documents*: "To toy with things is to lose one's will; / To toy with people is to lose one's virtue" 玩物喪志，玩人喪德. There is but a thin margin between "taking pleasure in things" and regarding people as mere instruments of pleasure. This opprobrium applies not only to Yan Shifan (whom Li Yu characterizes as a fake connoisseur, acquisitive but undiscerning) but also to Eunuch Sha, a connoisseur of gardens, antiques, and literati arts, and to a lesser extent even to Jin and Liu, inasmuch as their life of refinement also has darker undertones of exploitation.

The beginning concern with "elegance" (or redefining the boundary between "elegance" and "vulgarity") yields pride of place to the relationship between people and things, or rather the question of how a person can be reduced to an object in the name of refined sensibility. Quan's revenge uses macabre equivalences (the body as vessel, two body parts, two kinds of body fluids, two acts of ejaculation) to bring the question of value to its starkest instantiation. On one level Li Yu seems to equate connoisseurship with moral failure: Quan's two lovers choose self-preservation, and Quan is betrayed and mutilated. The House of Elegant Ensemble is premised on the notion of self-contained aesthetic pleasure but becomes its mockery and negation. Does Li Yu intend to thereby bring to the fore the economic and political pressures sidelined by the discourse of refinement? Yet the vindication of Quan ("the little loyal subject" [*xiao xiao zhongchen* 小小忠臣] who gains an imperial audience and steels the emperor's resolve to execute Yan Shifan and makes him blame himself bitterly for the unjust execution of Yang Jisheng), the aesthetic object and the object of desire that gains political agency and moral authority, may also be a circuitous affirmation of what it means to master or to be the center of a discourse of elegance.

REDEFINING ELEGANCE AND VULGARITY IN *HONGLOU MENG*

While *Jin Ping Mei* questions the meaning of elegance with its dependence on vulgar contextualization and Li Yu's story moralizes the contradictions of elegance with equivocation, *Honglou meng* brings to the polarity of elegance and vulgarity the full force of its commitment to and concomitant questioning of the lyrical ideal. The lyrical worldview toys with the idea that the self can defy social norms and assign value to things. Soon after Baoyu and his cousins and sisters move into the Grand View Garden, Tanchun tasks her half-brother Baoyu with buying her "interesting things" when he goes outside their garden and family compound:

> "Just like last time, when you got me the willow-branch basket, the incense box carved out of bamboo, or the little clay burner. I really liked them. But the others fancied them too and looted them as if they were treasures." Baoyu laughed. "So you want those things—they are not worth much. Just give five hundred coins to the lads and they will bring you cartloads of them." Tanchun said, "What would the lads know! You could pick out what is unadorned and not vulgar, the simple and unaffected items [1791 and 1792 editions: "things that are interesting and not vulgar"]—just bring me lots of them."
> (*HLM* 27.281)

Such a mode of reasoning would be unthinkable in *Jin Ping Mei*, where everything can be bought and sold and market value reigns supreme. No character would dream of elevating the value of "interesting things" by going against market consensus. Yet this becomes the dominant ethos in *Honglou meng*. This is not merely a matter of celebrating good taste; rather, good taste becomes the basis for an implied oppositional aesthetics, a kind of "us versus them" mentality. Baoyu and the girls in the Grand View Garden—the characters we sympathize with—consciously or inadvertently articulate the hope for rules and standards that set them apart from the world outside.

When Jia Yucun, the self-serving official whose name is homophonous with "fictive words and vulgar language" and who sets the plot in motion at the beginning of the book, comes to visit the Jia family, Baoyu is reluctant to meet him. Affirming the necessity of such social interactions, his cousin Shi Xiangyun cites the saying, "When the host is refined, the guest comes calling often." Baoyu responds: "Have done! Have done!

I do not dare to be called refined. I am but the most vulgar of vulgar people—I do not want to have dealings with such people!" (32.336). The self-declared "vulgarity" is a gesture of rejecting the understanding of "refinement" that links it explicitly to officialdom and, more broadly, rules of social engagement. The same disregard for worldly standards and the world of male sociopolitical values prompts Daiyu to dismiss the rosary of fragrant beads given to Baoyu by Prince Beijing as an object that "passed through the hands of a stinky man" when Baoyu offers the gift to her (16.152).

At the same time, Cao Xueqin's vision of aestheticized existence in the novel incorporates detailed descriptions of many fine things that seem to embody consensual views of elegance, as when Baoyu insists that fresh litchi should be paired with a white sardonyx plate (37.390). Beyond what meets the eye, the narrator delights in evoking past grandeur. Grandmother Jia corrects Wang Xifeng's misidentification of the "sunset clouds gauze" as the "pink cicada wing gauze," enumerating the pedigree of the former as "soft mist gauze" in one of four colors (the other three being "heavenly blue after the rain," "autumn fragrance," and "pine green") from an earlier era (40.422). Just as the exotic objects (including tributary things and European imports) intermittently mentioned in *Honglou meng* broaden the spatial reach of the fictional world, these relics of an even grander era extend its temporal depth.

Rarity contributes to the sense of unique appreciation. We see this also in the description of the "Hui pattern" embroidery screen that Grandmother Jia displays for the New Year celebration. Created by the well-born maiden Huiniang for her own pleasure, "it was not something one could buy in the marketplace. All the flowers embroidered on the screen were modeled on flower paintings by Tang, Song, Yuan, and Ming masters. That was why its style and colors had their basis in elegance, and the lush, sensual beauty of ordinary handicraft could not compare to it" (53.581–82).[173] Huiniang died young, and specimens by her are hard to come by, which further enhances the value of her embroidery. The panegyric here combines the conventional elevation of a "minor art" through literati ties (Huiniang's embroidered characters appear no different from actual cursive script) and the particular pathos of a maiden's untimely demise. Baoyu would have been drawn to this item, although his reaction is not mentioned. More to the point, such objects define views of elegance shared by the elite, and the aforementioned oppositional aesthetics does not apply.

In other words, the garden world shares the aesthetic judgment of the outside world but also tries to set itself apart. The same combination of distance and identification applies to its elegant activities. Literati pursuits integral to the conventional understanding of elegance are important to the garden world, yet the mixture of stylistic registers and repeated references to games create a playful distance. Or rather, it is the playful juxtaposition of elegance and vulgarity that defines a new brand of elegance, in a manner reminiscent of some examples discussed earlier. The "Crabapple Poetry Society" is initiated by Tanchun's elegant missive to Baoyu couched in elevated, classical diction, citing the imperative for the girls to mimic the famous literary gatherings in history, but its namesake and first topic is Jia Yun's gift: two pots of crabapple flowers accompanied by a fawning, comical, and barely literate letter (37.383–84). At its first formal meeting, elegant poems on chrysanthemums are juxtaposed with satirical doggerel-style compositions on crabs. In a similar vein, the description of the elegant, painterly poses of the girls as they compose poems on chrysanthemums is preceded by boisterous jokes between mistresses and maids that hint at all too real power politics in that world (38.400–02).

Tanchun issues a general warning (which she ironically directs also at Baoyu, the only male present): "It is not allowed to bring out words evoking the inner chambers—you'd better pay attention" (38.402). Scholars have often observed how the compositions of the poetry society appropriately give voice to character traits and concretize our image of the various girls, but the sense of role-play is also noteworthy. The girls take up poetic sobriquets, many of them gender neutral or even vaguely masculine. On the most basic level, some of the poems are written in the voice of a male persona. For example, Shi Xiangyun writes in "Facing Chrysanthemums" (Duiju): "With careless ease, I sit bare-headed by the fence / in the pure and cold fragrance, chanting lines and hugging my knees" 蕭疏籬畔科頭坐，清冷香中抱膝吟 (38.404). "Bare-headed" means removing the scholar's headscarf, and the posture of sitting here is typically masculine. Likewise, Daiyu's line in "Asking Chrysanthemums" (Wenju), "Muttering, hands clasped behind, I ask questions of the eastern fence" 喃喃負手叩東籬 (38.405), evokes the image of an obsessed scholar, slightly bent perhaps, posing questions to the chrysanthemums. In "Pinning Chrysanthemums" (Zanju), Tanchun imagines pinning chrysanthemums to the hair not of a woman but a male recluse: "His sparse hair is touched with cold from the dew on the three paths, / His hempen scarf takes on the scent of frost from nine autumns" 短鬢冷沾三徑露，葛巾香染九秋霜. The "three paths," mentioned in Tao Yuanming's "Return" (Guiqulai xi ci), evokes the recluse's abode. Of course, the choice of pronoun ("I" or "he") in the translation of these lines is somewhat arbitrary, since description and impersonation are equally plausible. Lyrical self-expression is bound up with role-play, and playfulness, by celebrating freedom of the spirit, tempers any notion of a deliberate quest for elegance.

Baochai refers to the poetry society as "a game" (*wanyi'er* 玩意兒, 37.395). The girls emphasize that they are "playing at being poets" and are mildly appalled by Baoyu's circulation of their poems outside the garden (48.517). Even Xiangling (Xue Pan's concubine), who is obsessed with composing verses and seeks out Daiyu as mentor and whose poetic self-fashioning raises her above her debased state,[174] claims to be "learning to write poetry for a lark" (48.517). The winter party for composing linked verse that marks the height of the garden's glory—a bevy of visiting cousins and relatives swell the ranks of poetry gatherings—is especially marked by riotous mirth and conviviality as the girls vie to be the first to come up with lines (50.532–38). The composition of linked verse is preceded by an unconventional feast of barbecue venison. When Daiyu laughingly expresses dismay, Xiangyun retorts: "What would you people know? 'The true gentleman of spirit has his own brand of romantic élan.' You all affect a fake loftiness and daintiness—nothing can be more tiresome! At this moment we are eating pungent meat to our heart's content, but we will come back with exquisite refinement of mind and words!" (49.531). Red Inkstone marvels at the deliberately incongruous juxtaposition: "Writing linked verse is a most elegant thing, but before the elegance he chooses to write about the really messy affair of young people eating bloody meat as a fitting match for the exquisite refinement of mind and words" (*ZYZ* 49.637). Handling raw meat is uncommon enough for the traditional Chinese elite for its juxtaposition with poetic composition to seem startling.[175] The author obviously relishes this apparent incongruity: as with the spirit of games and playfulness,

Elegance and Vulgarity 147

elevating carnivorous pleasure is about the freedom to redefine rules of taste.

Wang Xifeng happens upon the barbecue party and comes up with the opening line of the linked verse—an unexpected contribution from someone who describes herself as "nothing but a vulgar person who can write neither poetry nor prose" (*HLM* 45.477). She apologizes for offering only an "uncouth line" ("The north wind howled all through the night" 一夜北風緊), but the others encourage her: "The more uncouth the language the better. Just give us a line and you can go take care of your proper business" (50.532). Xifeng's connection with the poetry society goes back to an earlier invitation for her to become its "overseer." She sees through the agenda right away: "No need to fool me, I have already figured this all out! What is this nonsense about inviting me to be the Overseer? Obviously, you just want me to become the copper merchant bringing you cash! Having invented this poetry society, you need to take turns to host. You don't have enough to spend, so you have come up with this scheme to rope me in so that you can ask me for money. Did I get it right or not?" (45.475). She then argues that Li Wan, the widow of Baoyu's older brother, should foot the bill since she has a bigger allowance. Li Wan reproaches her for "pouring forth two cartloads of shameless words that should have been coming from the mouth of a good-for-nothing, muddy-legged, vulgar creature making precise calculations on his petty abacus" (45.476), but in fact Wang Xifeng's "vulgar words" offer a fair assessment of the situation.

The financing of the poetry society implies that the economic basis of elegance does not have to be a problem. Xifeng declares: "If I don't join the poetry society and spend a few strings of cash, wouldn't I be declaring myself in open rebellion against the Grand View Garden? Would I still survive here? I will come to my post first thing in the morning. Once I receive my seal of office, I will put down 50 taels of silver, and you can take your time hosting poetry society meetings" (45.477). But the garden world remains an alternative reality whose inhabitants are willfully ignorant of economic realities. Even a maid cannot tell how much exactly one tael of silver amounts to (51.577), and Baochai is the only one among the girls who can recognize a pawn ticket (57.636–37).

Can the world of beauty and aesthetic sensibility become economically viable? In Li Yu's "House of Elegant Ensemble," this is the issue taken up at the beginning of the story before political pressure and moral dilemma surface. In *Honglou meng*, the question of reconciling the aesthetic and the pragmatic comes to a head when Baochai and Tanchun devise schemes to turn the productive potential of the Grand View Garden to good account on the wake of intimations of shortages and economic difficulties (53.573–77). Their discussion of reform efforts is mediated through the language of learning. Baochai refers to Zhu Xi's essay, "On Not Giving Up on Oneself" (Bu ziqi wen), traditionally not included in Zhu's collection but incorporated into a 1662 edition. It contains these lines: "For all things under heaven are but things. But if a thing has one aspect that can be of use, it would not be discarded by the world. How can we say that humans do not measure up to things?"[176] "Not wasting things" is analogized with "not giving up on oneself (or literally, "not wasting oneself"), which harks back to the beginning image of the superfluous stone "lacking the talent to repair heaven" (*wucai butian* 無材補天). In other words, reversing wastefulness in the garden is based on a utilitarian vision of purposefulness at odds with the notion of seeking compensatory consolation in a world of aesthetic and romantic sensibility when one is deemed useless for failing to fit into larger schemes of meaning.

The concern for profit leads to the following curious exchange on the relevance of Zhu Xi or Confucius:

> Tanchun smiled and said, "Of course I have read it [i.e., Zhu Xi's essay]. It's nothing more than urging people to try hard. These empty metaphors and facile formulations cannot be all taken for real." Baochai said, "So Master Zhu too has empty metaphors and facile formulations? Every single line of his is true. Two days of managing affairs and you are already corrupted by material gains and desires, so much so that you even regard Master Zhu as 'empty' and 'facile'! Going forward, as you deal with greater things, you may regard even Confucius as 'empty'!" Tanchun smiled and said, "You are such a learned person, and yet you haven't read the Masters texts. Formerly Master Ji said, 'Those who ascend to the realm of official emolument and place themselves on the line of momentous decisions steal the words of Yao and Shun and turn against the ways of Confucius and Mencius...'" Baochai smiled, "And the next line?"

Tanchun laughed, "Now I am only taking what I want of the meaning by cutting up the passage—if I recite the following line, wouldn't I be condemning myself?"
(*HLM* 56.610-11)

The lines Tanchun quotes can be taken to mean that political responsibility and economic reality necessitate compromises. We can imagine that the line she does not quote contains a negative judgment of that argument. "Master Ji" (Ji is the clan name of the rulers of Zhou dynasty) does not exist. Why does Cao Xueqin deem it necessary to invent a fictitious Master to discourse on the dangers of profit when canonical Confucian writings do not lack such warnings? Perhaps the fictive text introduces a playful distance to a difficult issue. The *Analects* (4.5, 4.12, 7.16, 11.17) and *Mengzi* (1A.1, 4A.14, 6B.4, 7A.25) castigate the profit motive as morally dangerous; here it is recognized as being both necessary and in potential contradiction with the aesthetic and romantic spirit of the garden. When Li Wan chides Baochai and Tanchun for indulging in pedantic discourse instead of attending to the "proper business," Baochai replies, "The proper business is found in learning. If we do not raise the level of the discussion through learning, then we will sink to the vulgarity of the marketplace" (*HLM* 56.611). There is enough unease with the vulgarity of unvarnished, pragmatic calculations of profit for Baochai and Tanchun to playfully elevate the discourse through the language of learning. But the banter about defying Zhu Xi and Confucius, the fictitious Master, and the interrupted quotation indicate that profit as philosophy can be problematic. There is also intrinsic tension between "being a useless stone" and "creating a useful garden," between the notion elaborated in the preface that artistic creation is rooted in failure and an ethos of purposeful striving and pragmatic calculation. As it turns out, the eminently sensible reforms lead to conflicts as intrusive older female servants intent on protecting their profits end up policing and bullying the younger maids in the garden (chap. 59). The garden is sustained by the Jia family's enormous wealth but cannot really confront the economic mechanism of production and consumption.

The attempt to redefine elegance and vulgarity is entwined with the implicit desire that the garden world should set up its own rules and be distinct from the mundane realm: this nexus of ideas is developed with pointed attention to its contradictions in the episodes describing Granny Liu's second visit to the Jia family. Granny Liu's first visit (chap. 6) launches the narrative of day-to-day events in the fictional universe; hers is the defamiliarizing perspective that allows the reader to see what is for her novel things (such as the pendulum clock) and the lavish surroundings of the Jia family with fresh wonder. Her second visit (chaps. 39–41) takes us through another tour of the garden with more intimate glimpses into the living spaces of the main characters. She becomes the excuse for other characters to dilate on material details (such as the "soft mist gauze" mentioned earlier) and the mediator whose awe and incomprehension facilitate their renewed appreciation of things. Through her we ponder the relationship between gender and décor, as she mistakes Daiyu's room for a scholar's study and Baoyu's room for a young lady's boudoir. We see literati standards of elegance in full display (especially in Tanchun's rooms). Grandmother Jia, remarking that the young people are "not vulgar" (*busu* 不俗), shows her fine taste as she considers suitably lofty ornamental objects for Baochai's austere rooms. As a peasant woman in close encounter with undreamt of luxuries, Granny Liu magnifies for the reader the compelling materiality and preciosity of the garden world, from the piles of screens and lamps stored in the attic of Grand View Tower to the ivory and gold chopsticks, from the pigeon eggs to the fantastically elaborate eggplant dish.

Granny Liu compares the garden to a New Year painting, perhaps the only resource for visualizing a world of opulence for country folks (40.420–21). The sense of removal from the mundane is rendered more complex and paradoxical when the touring group comes to the convent of Miaoyu, a well-born young woman who practices Buddhist self-cultivation in the garden. Miaoyu offers Grandmother Jia tea in a "small covered teacup of porcelain in five colors with gold patina from the Chenghua reign," and when Grandmother Jia offers Granny Liu a sip of the tea (made with "rainwater saved from the previous year"), the most uncouth character and the most insistently pure one have momentary contact. Despite the great value of Chenghua porcelain,[177] Miaoyu is ready to discard the cup because of its "contamination" by Granny Liu. Baoyu suggests that the cup should be given as a gift to Granny Liu, and Miaoyu agrees only because she has not used that cup before: "If I had drunk from it, I would rather break it than give it to her" (41.439). Granny

Liu presents a mental obstacle for Miaoyu, while Miaoyu does not figure much in Granny Liu's mind. Red Inkstone suggests that if Granny Liu is motivated by the desire for financial gain, Miaoyu's obsession with "purity" masks the quest for fame and recognition (*ZYZ* 605).

If the Jia family considers itself well above Granny Liu, Miaoyu regards her convent as an inner sanctum set apart not only from the Jia family but also the garden world. Like Baoyu and some of the girls in the garden, but in a much more explicit, deliberate, and extreme fashion, she lives by the idea of setting up rules of value in her own world. Baoyu understands this logic very well. When Miaoyu invites Baoyu, Baochai, and Daiyu for tea in her inner rooms and offers Baoyu her own jade cup, Baoyu protests that he has been given a vulgar vessel. "Miaoyu said, 'This? A vulgar vessel? I don't mean to sound arrogant, but I am afraid you may not be able to find one such 'vulgar vessel' in your family.' Baoyu smiled and said, 'As the saying goes: Enter the village and follow its rules. When I come to your domain, I naturally adopt your standards and demote all things made of gold, jade, and gems as vulgar vessels'" (*HLM* 41.438).

Amid the "sensory overload" of Granny Liu's tour (and in deliberate contrast to it), the equivocal paean to elegance unfolds as a discussion of the taste of water. Miaoyu's regime of taste is so stringent that even Daiyu, usually the one expressing disdain, is mocked for her lack of discernment. When Daiyu asks whether the tea is made from "rainwater saved from the previous year" Miaoyu says scornfully,

> For all your refinement, you turn out to be a most vulgar person who can't even tell the taste of water. This is the snow on plum blossoms that I collected five years earlier when I lived at the Coiled Dragon Fragrance Temple at the Dark Tomb Mountain. All I got was what filled that porcelain jar in ghostly blue. I have been so chary of using it that I had it buried. It's only this summer that I opened it—I used it once; this is now the second time. How can you fail to discern the taste? How can rainwater saved from last year have this lightness and purity? How can it be worth drinking! (*HLM* 41.438–39)

This is almost a parody of the Ming-Qing discourse on water. Plum blossoms are sometimes described as "fragrant snow." Here the image of snow on plum blossoms recalls poems about making tea from snow and drinking tea among plum blossoms. Yet the disturbing echoes are unmistakable. What I translated as "Dark Tomb" is "Xuan's Tomb"—the Eastern Jin dignitary Yu Taixuan was supposedly buried at this mountain (famous for its plum blossoms) near Suzhou. *Xuan* means dark or mysterious. "Ghostly blue" is literally "ghost face blue"—it refers to the fluidly merging pattern of colors on porcelain produced by the legendary Jun kiln from the Song dynasty. The buried water reminds the reader of the burial of flowers discussed in chapter 1. Incomparable purity seems to be associated with death ("Dark Tomb" and "ghostly blue"). The preciosity of Miaoyu's taste and her obsession with purity may seem unnatural and excessive, yet it is but the sensibility of the garden world taken to its logical extreme.

The riddle on Miaoyu in the album Baoyu peruses during his dream visit to the Illusory Realm of Great Void portends her fate of degradation: "She wants to be pure, but can she remain pure? / 'Tis called emptiness, but is the emptiness real? / What a pity that she of substance as precious as gold and jade / Should ultimately be mired in mud and filth" 欲潔何曾潔，云空未必空。可憐金玉質，終陷淖泥中 (5.51). Her obsession with purity is strangely at odds with Buddhist notions of detachment and equanimity. In chapters 87 and 112, Miaoyu's repressed desire for Baoyu breeds rumors that eventually result in her abduction by bandits. As is often the case, nuances and intimations in the first eighty chapters become explicit melodrama in the last forty. Here the fact that Miaoyu offers Baoyu her own jade cup and the banter about jade being a "vulgar vessel" merely hint at unacknowledged emotional entanglements.

The unease with excessive purity and refinement is encoded in the name of the two antique cups with which Miaoyu serves tea to Baochai and Daiyu. Baochai's cup has a handle with the characters *banpaojia* 瓟斝 in seal script. A vaguely anachronistic inscription claims that this is the "treasured curio" (*zhenwan* 珍玩) of Wang Kai (3rd c.) from the Jin dynasty. A Jin aristocrat related to the imperial family by marriage, Wang Kai is featured in stories about extreme extravagance. There is also a line in small characters: "In the fourth month of the fifth year of the Yuanfeng reign (1078–1084) of Song dynasty (1082), Su Shi of Meishan saw this in the Imperial Treasury." Su Shi was in exile in Huangzhou in Hubei in 1082—a fact known to most literati because some of his most famous

Elegance and Vulgarity

works, such as the song lyric and the poetic expositions on Red Cliff, are dated to that year—and could therefore not be present at the imperial treasury in the Song capital Kaifeng.

The curious name of the cup has invited assiduous decoding. The nineteenth-century commentator Zhang Xinzhi takes the constituent components of the character *ban* 瓟, *fen* 分 (separate) and *gua* 瓜 (melon), to imply "splitting the melon" (*pogua* 破瓜), which means "sixteen" (the ancient graph for *gua* consists of two graphs for *ba*, meaning eight) but also has sexual connotations. He takes *pao* 斝, almost homophonous with *bao* 包 (to wrap), to mean "covering up" or "not showing one's feelings" (*baocang bulu* 包藏不露), and reads *jia* 斝, homophonous with *jia* 假 (false or fictive), as another marker of "fictive words and vulgar language" (*Jiayu cunyan* 假語村言),[178] the pun embodied by the character Jia Yucun, as explained in the preface to chapter 1.[179] Zhang Xinzhi argues that the vessel alludes to Baochai's secret passion for Baoyu. A *jia* is a bronze ritual vessel for holding wine in the form of a tripod with a handle and two pillar-like protrusions on the rim. *Ban* and *pao* are types of gourds. Shen Congwen (1902–1988) believes that *banpaojia* is made from a gourd trained to look like a *jia* or decked out like one. The use of wooden molds to control the shape of gourds became popular and increasingly elaborate from the late sixteenth century on. It was especially in vogue during the Kangxi and Qianlong reigns among court and aristocratic circles.[180] The inscriptions by Wang Kai and Su Shi, quite aside from their anachronism, are thus blatantly impossible, since they predate the fashion for gourd vessels by centuries. According to Shen Congwen, *banpaojia* encodes the pun *banbaojia* 斑包假 (a pattern covering up what is fake) to criticize Miaoyu's hypocrisy. Zhou Ruchang (1918–2012) agrees with the reading of the pun but argues that the cup reflects Baochai's reserve and the discrepancy between feelings and comportment in her character.[181] More generally, "fakeness" can pertain to the common associations of the *pao* gourd with simplicity, reclusion, and Daoist freedom.

The cup for Daiyu, made from rhinoceros horn, looks like an alms bowl, only smaller, and has three characters in pearl-drop seal script, *dianxiqiao* 點犀䀉. The pearl-drop script style recalls Daiyu's mythic existence as Crimson Pearl Fairy Herb, "crimson pearl" being a kenning for "tears of blood." The words *dian* 點 (dot) and *xi* 犀 (rhinoceros) evoke Li Shangyin's (813–858) famous line, "Our hearts, by the affinities of the magic rhinoceros horn, join in a dot" 心有靈犀一點通 (*QTS* 539.6163). But if *dianxi* suggests the ineffable communion of deep love, *qiao* 蠱, homophonous with *qiao* 喬 (fake, pretense), brackets it as something mediated by fiction. *Xiqiao* 犀蠱 is also a homophone for *xiqiao* 蹊蹺 (unexpected twist, perverse, strange), and Zhou Ruchang believes that it reflects on Daiyu's jealous and suspicious nature, especially since the word *dian* appears as *xing* 杏 (apricot, homophonous with *xing* 性, nature) in two manuscripts (*Gengchen ben*, *Qi xu ben*): the pun for *xingxiqiao* 性蹊蹺 (a perverse, strange nature) seems unmistakable. Shen Congwen argues that unlike *xing*, *dian* has a much more logical association with a cup made from rhinoceros horn and that *dianxiqiao* does not rely on homophonous puns for its meaning: instead it is the image of the white line that runs from the rim to the tip of the rhinoceros horn that suggests something "fake to the bottom" (*tou di jia* 透底假). (Rhinoceros horns with such a line is prized as "heaven-penetrating rhinoceros horns," as mentioned earlier. "Dot" refers to the cross-section of the line. The image of ineffable connection in Li Shangyin's poem is derived from this image of dot and line.) Shen believes that both cups convey criticism of Miaoyu: "She is actually somewhat unnatural, worldly, and disingenuous. Thus her purity and refinement are mostly superficial."

However, the ironic overtones are probably less specific. Both cups are linguistic constructions that defy visualization: a curvaceous gourd fashioned to resemble an angular, three-legged bronze ritual vessel and a shallow alms bowl made from a pointed rhinoceros horn. Rhinoceros horn cups, following its natural shape, are often tall. *Qiao* 蠱 is homophonous with a word (*qiao* 喬) that can mean tall. Rhinoceros horn bowls exist, but I have not found an example with an inward-curving rim typical of begging bowls. Both vessels encompass logical opposites: the *banpaojia* has vegetative origins but claims improbable antiquity and the symbolic endurance of ritual meaning, the *dianxiqiao* is made from a most precious substance but purports to be a begging bowl. That the rarest and finest things should be associated with the contortion of nature, impossibility, pretense, fiction, and perversity may reflect a more general unease with aesthetic perfection or spiritual freedom as precarious illusion.

If the insistence on purity and refinement cannot escape the delusion of subjective projection, then Granny Liu, the supposed embodiment of humble uncouthness, also upsets the hierarchical distinction of elegance and vulgarity. Daiyu compares her to a cow and a locust (*HLM* 41.436, 42.450), and Granny Liu embraces animal metaphors for herself with gusto as she plays court jester. During the feast in the garden, she exclaims: "Old Liu! Old Liu! With appetite hearty as a cow, I readily beat the old sow!" (40.425). For the wine game, she comes up with a suitably homespun insect image: "The great fire burns down the fuzzy worm!" (40.432). These creaturely references are apparently demeaning; at the same time, they seem to represent life force and vitality.

The paradoxical mutuality of illusion and reality, fiction and truth, ties Granny Liu and Baoyu. Their symbolic connection emerges through their respective tours of the garden and the repetition and juxtaposition of key motifs. The European-style plate glass mirror opposite Baoyu's bed seems to have induced his dream of his double, Zhen Baoyu (56.620–21); it also momentarily lulls Granny Liu into mistaking her reflection for the mother of her daughter-in-law (41.441), recalling the optical illusion of Baoyu, Jia Zheng, and his retinue during their first tour of the garden (17.171–72). Baoyu and Granny Liu are associated with the two sides of the double-sided mirror, which functions as a partition between the recesses of Baoyu's bedroom and a less private space. Granny Liu bumps her head against a European style painting of a girl that "sticks out," unprepared for the shock of verisimilitude and the illusion of depth and receding distance (41.440).[182] Baoyu has his "painting moment" when he imagines the loneliness of the beauty in a painting in a study and visits her, only to be shocked by moaning sounds that suggest her "enlivening": it turns out that his page Mingyan is making love to a maid (19.187). Granny Liu mentions firewood and a fire actually starts (39.416). A tale about an ill-fated girl that she casually spins sets Baoyu on a quest for its verification (39.416–18). When Baoyu is drinking tea and deliberating the taste of water with Miaoyu, Daiyu, and Baochai, Granny Liu loses her way as she looks for the latrine and stumbles into Baoyu's rooms, confused by the painting and the mirror. The inebriated Granny Liu ends up falling asleep on Baoyu's bed and befouling the air in his room. The contrast and tension between refinement and uncouthness are superseded by the dialectic of reality and illusion.

The meeting of opposites implicitly puts into question the social and aesthetic boundaries assumed by the regime of taste. The wooden cups brought out for Granny Liu are prized even more than gold and jade cups because of the exquisite images and cursive calligraphy inscribed on them, but she is not far off the mark when she declares a peasant's special affinity with wood (41.434–35). Red Inkstone comments: "Those who pretend to know should read this" (*ZYZ* 602), implying criticism of Granny Liu's aristocratic audience when they complacently laugh at her misidentification of the wood. Wily and strategic, Granny Liu nevertheless commands a genuine vitality that takes down constructions of elegance and vulgarity. We are reminded of Hazlitt's (1778–1830) definition of vulgarity as affectation, imitation, and conformism: "A thing is not vulgar merely because it is common. . . . Nothing is vulgar that is natural, spontaneous, unavoidable. . . . The true vulgar are the persons who have a horrible dread of daring to differ from their creed."[183] Granny Liu is calculating yet natural, while Miaoyu with her withering disdain for conformism ends up being constrained by the need to oppose it.

The fraught relationship between elegance and economic realities also comes to the fore. Right before Granny Liu's visit, the reader finds out that Xifeng has been lending the money for the maids' monthly allowance to earn interest (*HLM* 39.412), and we are taken through Granny Liu's rapid calculation that the cost of the crab feast (20 taels), the setting for the first poetry club meeting, would support a peasant family for a whole year (39.413). The garden world purports to set its own rules of taste and demands that the mechanism of production and consumption be gracefully concealed. In the midst of a bewildering abundance of things mentioned during Granny Liu's visit, it is the exchange of two fruits, the *yuan* citron and the Buddha's hand (a kind of ornamental citron),[184] between Ban'er, Granny Liu's grandson, and Xifeng's daughter (whom Granny Liu names Qiaojie), that is most portentous (41.437). Cao Xueqin probably intended Qiaojie to marry Ban'er as the Jia family suffers irreversible decline. A token of karmic ties, it heralds the collapse of the Jia family fortunes that will make such a union possible.[185] Conforming to or defying the consensus in forming one's own standards, negating or embracing the economic basis of taste, abiding by or transcending aesthetic and social boundaries become moot points in the shadow of decline and fall.

Elegance and Vulgarity

CHAPTER THREE

The Real and the Fake

As we have seen in chapter 2, the discourse on elegance and vulgarity is closely tied to the question of authenticity, not only because elegance is vindicated by discernment of the authenticity of aesthetic objects but also because the question of a person's genuineness or sincerity can expose the limits of the discourse of elegance, be it normative, moralized, self-conscious, or demotic. On a more fundamental level, stories about distinguishing the real thing from the fake often raise questions of value and judgment. When Zhang Chou, for example, parses "true appreciation" (*zhenshang* 真賞) that evaluates and "true discrimination" (*zhenjian* 真鑑) that distinguishes between the real and the fake, he is implicitly questioning the automatic equation of value with authenticity (*ZGSHQS* 4:137). Is value inextricably tied to authenticity? Who has the right to judge? Consider this passage from *Han Feizi*:

> Qi invaded Lu and demanded the Chan Cauldron. Lu sent its counterfeit. The men of Qi said, "This is a fake." The men of Lu said, "This is the real thing." Qi said, "Send Yue Zhengzi Chun here, and we will abide by the master's word." The Lu ruler asked Yue Zhengzi Chun [to testify to the authenticity of the cauldron]. Yue Zhengzi Chun said, "Why not send the real thing?" The ruler said, "I cannot give it up." He answered, "I also cannot give up my good faith."[1]

Yue Zhengzi Chun, mentioned in various early texts as an exemplar of probity and filial piety, has the moral authority to authenticate the Chan Cauldron. His ruler, unwilling to give up a prized cauldron of antiquity, asks him to lie. The valence of the word *ai* 愛, translated as "love" in modern Chinese, is often less emotive than proprietary in ancient usage and here connotes the resentment of prospective loss, hence its rendering here as "cannot give up." The story and its variants usually appear as pronouncements on the importance of good faith.[2] It operates on a stark equation. The cauldron is as important to the Lu ruler (and perhaps also to the dignity of the Lu state) as good faith and the reputation of good faith are to Yue Zhengzi Chun. One can be traded for the other. Judgments of an object's authenticity draw attention to the appraiser, leading to questions regarding the basis of his authority and the nature of an implicit transaction—what does he gain or lose as he proffers judgments?

THE AUTHORITY OF JUDGMENT

References to fakes arise as soon as the authenticity of an object becomes an issue. Ever since the Six Dynasties, anecdotes and treatises on calligraphy, painting, art objects, and antiques have included discussions of imitation, copies, and forgeries.[3] The implicitly self-congratulatory voice of the discerning connoisseur disparaging those duped by fakes seems to have become a staple by the Song dynasty. Thus Shen Gua (1031–1095) writes:

> Those who collect calligraphy and paintings in most cases proceed by nothing more than names. When by happenstance a piece is rumored to have come from the brush of Zhong Yao, Wang Xizhi, Gu Kaizhi, or Lu Tanwei, viewers would vie to buy it: this is so-called connoisseurship of the ears. And there are those who, when viewing paintings, touch them with their hands because of the claim that the color should not stick to the finger in good paintings. This is one grade below "connoisseurship of the ears": one can call it "fortune telling by gauging the bone structure and listening to the voice."[4]

Likewise, Mi Fu scoffs at collectors deceived by attributions to famous Tang artists. "People see paintings of horses and attribute them to Cao Ba, Han Gan, and Wei Yan; they see paintings of oxen and attribute them to Han Huang and Dai Song. It is truly laughable."[5] He claims to have seen only two authentic landscape paintings by Li Cheng (919–ca. 967) and is provoked by proliferating forgeries by "vulgar hands borrowing his name" to want to write a "Discourse on the Nonexistence of Genuine Works by Li Cheng" (Wu Li lun).[6] Mi Fu himself was a master copier and forger. Su Shi refers to his "clever theft and appropriation by force,"[7] and Song anecdotes tell of ruses whereby he borrowed paintings and calligraphy and returned his masterful copies to their owners while keeping the original.[8] Mi Fu also describes how the artist, collector, and imperial son-in-law Wang Shen invited him home to make copies of ancient masterpieces of calligraphy, only to have the copies mounted and passed off as original works later.[9] The prevalence of fakes goes hand in hand with heightened appreciation for artworks and antiques as the essential ornaments of literati culture.

So what is new in the Ming and Qing dynasties? There is the expected quantitative difference: from the mid-sixteenth century on, we have many more writings on forgeries and fraud in the market of artworks, antiques, and luxury goods (just as we have many more documents on almost any subject). The socioeconomic contexts of connoisseurship come to the fore: we see how personal rivalries, social networks, regional prejudices, and motives for profit shape aesthetic judgment. Many accounts present the prevalence of forgeries as simply a function of supply and demand. The rich and powerful, often lacking powers of discrimination but driven by the desire for acquisition, are shown to be easily taken in by fakes. Thus the corrupt minister Yan Song, who dominated Ming government from the 1540s to the 1560s, his son Yan Shifan, and rich Anhui merchants are often portrayed as undiscerning collectors duped by forgeries in these stories. (However, the record of the paintings and calligraphy owned by Yan Song and Yan Shifan, made upon their confiscation by the imperial court after their downfall, shows an impressive list of genuine works.[10]) Huizhou merchants also played key roles as patrons and collectors of art.[11] Their caricature or vilification may simply function as a necessary foil to the judgment of the connoisseur, often also the narrator and author. Another favorite target is the "social recluse" discussed in chapter 2, the literatus who did not hold office but who prospered through patronage and by marketing his skills as a connoisseur and a man of letters. He emerges in some accounts as the self-serving manipulator of value as he judges the authenticity of antiques and artworks.

Shen Defu gives us glimpses into these complex factors in his *Gleanings from the Wanli Reign* (*Wanli yehuo bian*). In his writings about collecting and connoisseurship, he is the implied hero who takes pride in his own judgment, unmasks the pretentious, and scoffs at the gullible. Shen relates somewhat complacently, for example, how he deflates his acquaintance Wang Zhideng's (1536–1612) pretensions as the latter boasts about his "antiques." Wang claims that the shabby black table in his house is where Wu Kuan (1435–1504)—a famous poet, painter, calligrapher, and scholar-official who, like Wang, hailed from Suzhou—once leaned and that the torn black hat on his wall was bestowed by the first Ming emperor (r. 1368–1398) on a monk from his hometown. Shen wrote: "He was trying to impress me. I smiled and replied, 'It could very well be so. Yet how are these any different from the greasy stained headscarf that the Daoist Hong Ya[12] left behind when he was enlightened and ascended to heaven, or the dilapidated jacket worn by the Tang general Li Sheng (727–793) when he vanquished the rebel Zhu Ci?' Wang blushed and could not say anything in response" (*WL* 3:655). Instead of addressing the question of authenticity, Shen subverts the equation of genuineness with worth. Beyond the obvious point that mere antiquity does not an antique make, Shen seems to take a special pleasure in exposing Wang's posturing.

Regional rivalries came to the fore, as noted in chapter 2. Shen Defu, who hailed from Jiaxing (in Zhejiang), held Suzhou literati and artists responsible for the rising number of forgeries: "Among the worthies of the earlier generation, none is as upright and scrupulous as Zhang Fengyi [Boqi], but even he cannot but make his living through dealing with forgeries. As for Wang Zhideng [Bogu], he's totally immersed in it, as if it were Ji Ran's economic policy" (2:655).[13] He considered northerners gullible (2:613). Zhang Fengyi (1527–1613) was a notable poet and playwright, famous among other things for appearing in theatrical performance alongside his son.[14] Wang Zhideng's lasting liaison and deep friendship with the courtesan Ma Xianglan was the subject of both ridicule and tribute.[15] Shen Defu accused him of using courtesans to curry favor with officials (3:713). Shen's opprobrium here, however, is directed less toward the unconventional or immoral behavior of Zhang and Wang than toward what he perceives to be the inevitable corruption of the literati whose livelihood depended on their reputation, social connections, and active participation in the market for artworks and antiques.

Having failed to advance beyond the lowest degree in the civil service examination, Wang Zhideng was a prototypical "social recluse." The claim of being able to appraise the authenticity of artworks was a lucrative affair but also a potential source of embarrassment. Shen Defu disparaged Wang's aesthetic judgment in another anecdote: Fan, a servant in the Cao household, acquired *The Drunken Daoists* (*Zui daoshi tu*), painted by the Tang master Yan Liben (d. 673). Wang Zhideng bought it from him at a cheap price but upon resale asked for a thousand taels of silver and would not settle for anything less than a few hundred. This drew a lot of attention from interested parties, but in fact Wang had bought a forgery copied by Zhang Yuanju from Suzhou, for which the cunning Fan had paid ten taels of silver, having sold the real thing for a high price. Yuanju was blind in one eye and, after suffering insults from Wang, disclosed the truth: "With two eyes you are blind when it comes to appraising ancient works, and yet you dared to mock my partial sight!" Wang was so embarrassed that he went into hiding (3:655). The fact that a servant—Fan was probably a steward—could participate in the art market suggests that connoisseurship, though presumably elitist, could be an equalizing force. (Did Fan become rich through shrewd investment in works of art?) This is a story in which the forger offers the bon mot and all parties concerned are fraudulent. The only person we trust is the narrator, Shen Defu, who claims to have seen both the real work and the copy (and can presumably tell the difference). His authority is based in part on nonparticipation in this web of transactions.

In unmasking a notable connoisseur like Wang Zhideng, Shen Defu implicitly set himself up as the indisputable authority. In another instance, he was persuaded to refrain from exposing a forgery. When Dong Qichang showed him a supposed Tang calligraphy masterpiece owned by Chen Jiru, Shen gave convincing reasons for being skeptical, but Dong convinced him to keep quiet for fear of embarrassing Chen. When reminded of his incipient faux pas years later, Shen was still remorseful (3:655–56). Dong Qichang was a high official and a leading artist and arbiter of taste, and Chen Jiru was a famous connoisseur and man of letters. In acceding to Dong's request, Shen accepted the implicit pact of social solidarity among those deemed qualified to judge art. Like Wang Zhideng, Chen Jiru was a social recluse who lived on his literary and artistic talents and reputation. How do we explain Shen's discretion in this case and scorn vis-à-vis Wang Zhideng? It might come down to personal feelings and relationships, although Wang's blatant profit motive could be a factor.

Recent scholarship has focused on literati disparagement of nouveau-riche merchants who drove up prizes in the art and antique market, bought forgeries, or became undeserving owners of genuine specimens. Such writings abound, but the more detailed and interesting critiques are often reserved for other literati. Personal and regional rivalries, which might have explained Shen Defu's animus for Wang Zhideng, were common. Shen notes how Dong Qichang and Zhu Jingxun, both notable connoisseurs, "undermined and attacked each other, and merchants and dealers got involved in their rivalry" (26.654). The Jiaxing collector Xiang Yuanbian is said to have mockingly called the famous poet and scholar Wang Shizhen and his younger brother Wang Shimao (1536–1588) "blind chaps." Xiang compliments himself and the calligrapher and connoisseur Zhan Jingfeng as being among the few who could boast of "having a pair of discerning eyes," but Zhan indicates his reservations vis-à-vis Xiang.[16] In another episode, Zhan Jingfeng tells how he bests Wang Shizhen in an argument about the dating of a stone relief in a temple. Present at the scene is another official from Huizhou. He is moved to exclaim: "'Formerly we said that only men of Wu had discerning eyes, now aren't we men of Xin'an [in Huizhou] the ones with discerning eyes!' His honor Yanshan [Wang Shizhen] fell silent."[17] In describing how Wen Zhengming's (1470–1559) paintings became fashionable and fetched high prices, Zhan Jingfeng claims that he started the trend, discerning the worth of Wen's works ten years ahead of Wu people. Three years later, Xin'an people followed suit, leading Yue (Zhejiang) people by another three years. He thus presents a pecking order for Suzhou, Huizhou, and Zhejiang in trend setting (although he himself hailed from Xiuning in Huizhou).[18]

The practice of producing catalogs that record colophons and include descriptions as well as judgments, common from mid-Ming onward, means that debates of authenticity were carried out in print. Sun Kuang (1574 *jinshi*), for example, records his disagreements with Wang Shizhen's colophons in his *Colophons on Colophons on Calligraphy and Paintings* (*Shu hua ba ba*). Wang Shizhen owned a real copy of Huaisu's (725–785) *Thousand-Character Essay* and obtained another version owned by a Ming prince. The style seemed slightly different, but he did not question its authenticity. Sun Kuang voices his skepticism and explains why it is easy to forge Huaisu's style: "But his style is nothing more than unrestraint and forcefulness, that is why it is easy to fake—for ultimately it lacks subtlety and depth." He sees the difference Wang observes as evidence of forgery but goes on to parse the value of fakes. He quotes the Ming official Yang Ershan, who spread the word among art dealers: "Bring them if you have forgeries—I will buy them. Authentic works are expensive; I would not be able to buy them."[19] Even so, Yang often managed to buy fine works. Evaluating forgeries requires more independent judgment, since one is no longer guided by the standards of historical verification. By implicitly embracing Yang's perspective of going beyond the dichotomy of authenticity and forgery, Sun Kuang puts himself forward as a decidedly better critic than Wang Shizhen.

Wang Shizhen, the preeminent man of letters of his generation, might have invited criticism of his aesthetic judgment because he was not an accomplished artist. Zhu Guozhen (1557–1632) mocks Wang's self-justification:

> Wang Yanzhou [Shizhen] was not good at calligraphy but loved to talk about it. He said, "There is an evil genie at my wrist but a god in my eyes." Naturally this is a clever person speaking—pleased with himself, confident of his mission, he staked out his position. Coming right down to it, however, is the evil genie only at his wrist? And the god in his eyes may also not be real. What kind of god would that be? Once this theory is propounded, those who cannot paint love to talk about paintings, those who cannot write poetry or prose love to talk about poetry or prose.[20]

Wang's idea that the critic's authority does not depend on his artistic abilities has a long and distinguished pedigree. Thus the claim in "The Diagram of Brushwork in Battle Formation" (*Bizhen tu*, ca. 4th–5th c., attributed to Madame Wei or Wang Xizhi): "He who excels in judgment does not write as a calligrapher, he who excels in calligraphy does not judge it well."²¹ Su Shi also wrote, "Although I do not excel in calligraphy, / No one knows it better than me. / Be content that I can divine its meaning, / It is, as I have said, something inimitable" 吾雖不善書，曉書莫如我。苟能通其意，嘗謂不可學.²² Zhu Guozhen, however, faults Wang's judgment by questioning this reasoning.

Mastery of the arts is, however, no guarantor of unerring judgment. In 1577 the Yunjian collector Gu Ruhe bought two supposed Liu Songnian (12th–13th c.) scrolls, which he showed to his friends with great pride. In Zhan Jingfeng's judgment, however, "not only were they forgeries, they were also muddled and vulgar." Zhan explained his judgment to Gu Ruhe, who in self-defense recounted how even such a master as Wen Zhengming could be fooled. Wen Zhengming had bought a Shen Zhou landscape and hung it in his great hall. Gu saw it and pronounced it authentic. Wen said, "Not only is it authentic, it shows Shen at his most self-assured. I just bought it for 800 coins. Isn't that a bargain?" Gu believed that Wen would not give it up even if he begged for it, so he just left. But when he got to the nearby Zhuan Zhu Lane, someone tried to sell him a scroll that looked like the one in Wen Zhengming's possession, and he bought it for 700 coins. Upon enquiry, the vendor said that he had sold the same to Wen. When asked by Gu, Wen, "ever eager to be right," refused to back down.²³ The literature of connoisseurship is driven by both social consensus and an agonistic momentum. The authority of aesthetic judgment depends in part on distance from actual transactions, but the "connoisseur as hero" narrative is deeply embedded in the socioeconomic contexts of connoisseurship: it is inseparable from social competition, monetary gain, and besting or manipulating market forces.

THE AURA OF THE REAL THING

The appraisal and appreciation of artworks and antiques were woven into the fabric of social and economic life. Tremendous cultural authority and economic benefit accrued to the power to distinguish the real from the counterfeit. Explanations for the detection of forgeries—telltale mistakes in the colophons, stylistic anachronism—are usually concrete, while eulogies of the genuine often invoke the ineffable. Shen Defu wrote of a genuine work by the master calligrapher Wang Xizhi: "Gazing at it for a long while, one can see that the spirit of the brush penetrates beyond the silk. Its aura is resplendent. Thus does one know that what the ancients said about '[the force] entering the wood by three centimeters' is no empty talk." He said of another masterpiece that "its soaring spirit dances in flight; it can no longer be fathomed by those of the mundane realm" (*WL* 3:657).

This kind of mystical language eulogizing the "genuine specimen" (*zhenji* 真跡) is typical of the literature of connoisseurship. Even concrete and vivid descriptions do not make the process of discernment more transparent. Consider Li Rihua's judgment of a genuine Huang Gongwang (1269–1354) painting: "The brushwork is hastily applied—it's completely artless and natural. This is just like Li Shi's younger sister in Huan Wen's house as she clutches her hair and makes her speech. Her hairpins are askew and her hair is in disarray, but her grace and allure are supreme.[24] Truly an amazing work."[25] The compelling image of a victimized woman who nevertheless overawes by her natural beauty and moral courage is taken from a concrete historical moment, yet it conveys a mood that remains in the realm of the ineffable and makes it hard to pin down the process of identification.

Even self-conscious attempts to theorize the judgment of authenticity cannot escape the vocabulary of intuitive communion. Zhan Jingfeng, after enumerating famous literati and artists who failed to discriminate between the real and the fake, contrasts other people's carelessness with his own purposeful gaze.

> I have said that even those acclaimed for their connoisseurship can err when it comes to distinguishing the genuine from the fake. That must be because they look too carelessly and set too much store by their own judgment, and so fail to go step by step to seek the essentials. That is why whenever I see a piece of calligraphy or a painting, I never fail to ask to borrow it for leisurely perusal. Having unrolled the scroll and viewed it several times, I would gaze at it intently and appraise it meticulously, concentrating my spirit and pouring my essence into the work, as if my body meets with the ancients and as if my heart harmonizes with the ancients, so that not the least doubt remains—only then do I make my ranking and offer definitive judgment.[26]

Zhan congratulates himself on his own felicitous judgment ("not failing even once in ten cases"). Yet this "method" is ultimately as mystical as the imagistic discourse we saw earlier.

This kind of mystical communion means that ancient paintings without colophons and signatures could gain attribution on the basis of reasoning that strikes us as cavalier. Shen Defu's friend showed him a large painting depicting elaborate palaces and a half-disrobed lady surrounded by female attendants. "He fretted over the absence of signature. He asked me: 'What should the painter's name be?' I said, 'This is a painting of Consort Yang following imperial decree to bathe at Huaqing Pond. You can just put down Li Sixun's (651–716) signature'" (*WL* 3:658).[27] His friend bought this painting for one piece of gold and sold it for a hundred. Shen often pokes fun at buyers who go by only the authority of signatures and colophons; here he seems to betray some satisfaction at how his judgment of attribution, authenticated by a fake signature, increases the market value of a painting a hundredfold.

Dong Qichang, who prided himself on having "the most discerning eyes over three hundred years,"[28] "assigned" Tang and Song masters to many scrolls bearing no names through what seemed to be no more than intuitive reasoning. In 1612 Dong identified a painting of snowy riverbanks with no signature as a work by the Tang poet and painter Wang Wei (701–761) and added a long colophon to it. He rhapsodized about Wang Wei's painting as the product of Buddhist enlightenment. For Dong, the scroll conveys how poetry and painting are intertwined and offers as intuitive "evidence" impressions from his travels and his grasp of Wang Wei's transcendent aesthetics:[29]

> Wang Wei has these lines, "The river flows beyond heaven and earth, / The mountain shimmers between being there and not being there" 江流天地外，山色有無中。 These are the supremely exquisite lines of a poet, yet they enter into the deepest mystery of painting. This painting is the loveliest brushwork of a painter, yet it enters into the deepest mystery of poetry. I once traveled with a short bamboo staff in Beigu Mountain: At the time of gathering dusk and faint shades, I let my eyes rest on the semidarkness, and I seem to see this scroll in front of my eyes. And when I chant the two lines by Wang Wei, this scroll is no longer an object of the mundane world.

The Real and the Fake

As this example indicates, identification is often no more than a matter of matching works with the cultural impressions or received wisdom about certain artists. Su Shi wrote in a colophon on a painting said to be by Wang Wei: "Savor Mojie's [Wang Wei's] poetry: there are paintings in his poetry. Observe Mojie's paintings: there is poetry in his paintings."[30] This has become an oft-repeated truism about Wang Wei. Dong elevates him as the first "literati painter."[31] His appeal to intuitive reasoning also underlies his theory of spontaneous and natural expression in the Southern School, which according to him is opposed to the emphasis on technical mastery in the Northern School.[32] Did such findings enhance his prestige (as inheritor of the Southern School) or bring him financial gain? If they did, then "true appreciation" can seem both mystical and worldly. In his discussion of Zhang Taijie's (b. 1588) forgery, *A Record of Treasured Paintings* (*Baohui lu*, 1634), J. P. Park observes that the advocacy of "legitimate lineage" and the desire to be the heir of an invented tradition promoted forgeries.[33] Intuitive reasoning—the affirmation of subjectivity by assigning value—is what makes a person "genuine," yet it might have contributed to the reputation of fakes. Could Dong have been guilty of inadvertently (or even deliberately) promoting forgeries? According to Shen Defu, Feng Kaizhi bought the scroll for a low price, but it became famous after Dong declared it a genuine work by Wang Wei and added his colophon. After Feng died, his son cut out Dong's colophon and attached it to a copy made by the master forger Zhu Xiaohai, and the counterfeit was sold for 800 taels of silver to a rich Huizhou merchant (*WL* 3:658–59).

The aura of the real thing notwithstanding, the nagging question of value remains. Li Rihua's friend Jin Yunpeng puts it thus: "The genuine is also fake if the genuine can be faked; the fake is genuine if the fake is compellingly genuine. When we come to the point where there is absolutely no difference, then we can say that the artwork comes from one hand, or we can say that it comes from many hands."[34] Evaluation may go beyond authenticity, as in the following anecdote about one Huizhou merchant's elusive quest for a real work by Dong Qichang:

> A merchant from Xin'an wanted to obtain Dong Qichang's calligraphy but was wary of forgeries, so he conferred with Dong's

henchman. The latter asked him to prepare lavish gifts and introduced him to Dong. After the proper rituals for host and guest had been performed, Dong ordered his page to grind ink. The ink thickened, and Dong then rose, waved his brush, and gave the calligraphy to the overjoyed merchant, who bowed in thanks, brought it home, and hung it in his hall. All the visitors who saw it marveled at it. The following year, the merchant again came to Songjiang and happened to pass by Dong's official residence. He saw a person entering on a palanquin. Someone said, "That's Minister Dong." The merchant saw his face: it bore absolutely no resemblance to the man who did the calligraphy for him the year before. He waited for him to come out and looked at him carefully: the difference was indeed unmistakable. He could not help crying out loud about the wrong he had suffered. Dong stopped his palanquin and asked why he was distressed; the merchant wept and tearfully told the story from beginning to end. Dong smiled and said, "You, sir, have been duped! I sympathize with your sincerity: now just come in with me and I will do the calligraphy for you." Overjoyed, the merchant bowed again and again. Only then did he get the real specimen. He returned and boasted about it to others, yet connoisseurs often claimed that the earlier work was superior.[35]

The merchant seeks the most irrefutable test of authenticity: the chance to witness the artist at work. But what if the artist himself is a fake? Can we be certain that he is fooled the first time or the second time or on both occasions? The underlying tone of disparagement for the rich but undiscerning Huizhou merchant is unmistakable: he is unsure of his judgment; that is why he insists on witnessing the artist wielding his brush. He wants to impress his visitors, but the connoisseurs among them offer a confounding conclusion: the acknowledged fake seems to be aesthetically superior. Not only is the quest for the genuine specimen arduous and unpredictable, its final worth is sometimes open to debate. By dramatizing the difficulty of objective verification and questioning its equation with worth, the anecdote (itself of doubtful veracity) seems to leave subjective illumination as the only alternative for apprehending the aura of the real thing.

The Real and the Fake 169

THE FORGER, THE COPIER, THE AUTHORIZED DELEGATE

Li Rihua comments on the pleasures of connoisseurship: "Authenticating the real thing is of course joyous, but uncovering (*qiong* 窮) the counterfeit is also satisfying."[36] The word *qiong* means to uncover, to fully understand, or to get to the bottom of something: it implies assiduous attention or even fascination. Fakes could be just honest imitation. Zhao Qian (16th c.) mastered the style of Zhao Mengfu's calligraphy; demand for these acknowledged fake Zhao Mengfu works was so high that he became rich enough to build his own collection.[37] His buyers might harbor the intention to deceive, but Zhao is free from such suspicion. A family of stone carvers who produced perfect calligraphic masterpieces that "could be mistaken for the real masters" earned the patronage and friendship of Wen Zhengming, Wang Shizhen, and his brother Wang Shimao. They were artisans honored for having "the scholar's flair."[38] Gao Lian praises imitation antique bronze vessels from Suzhou (especially the ones produced by Xu Shousu) for their elegance and notes that they cost as much as half of real antiques. While real antique vessels will have to be "hidden objects" (*cangpin* 藏品), imitation antique vessels can be "useful objects" (*yongpin* 用品) or "objects of appreciation (*shangpin* 賞品). Gao Lian opines: "Failing to obtain something from antiquity, one can with such things imagine the spirit of ancient times. How can one say that they are not worthwhile?" (*ZSBJ* 517). Gao Lian also praises Ming imitation of Song Ding wares, especially the ones made by Zhou Danquan (533). The fact that the names of artisans who produced masterful fakes are recorded in *biji* implies recognition of their artistry.

Adjudicating forgeries may be difficult precisely because the ideal connoisseur, the masterful artist, and the supreme forger share the same mental processes and appeal to the same rhetoric. According to Li Rihua, the forger Zhu Xiaohai started out repairing old paintings and "restoring signatures" (*bukuan* 補款) and ended up producing forgeries. "Zhu always encloses himself in a room and sat quietly, taking up the brush only after fully grasping the essence [of the artwork]. He truly bedazzles like an actor who has mastered perfect imitation."[39] The description of intense contemplation suggests the forger's spiritual communion with the artist. From the beginnings of aesthetic thought in the Chinese tradition, imitation is recognized as a key path to master tradition. Gu Kaizhi (344–406), the subject of several anecdotes on how painting should "capture a likeness by conveying the spirit" (rather than strive for mere verisimilitude), nevertheless discusses in detail how to make a perfect copy.[40]

By the late Ming the discourse of imitation sometimes employs the vocabulary of freedom and mystical union. According to Dong Qichang, "For the masters of recent times, they don't have one brushstroke that does not resemble the ancients. Unfailing resemblance means that there is no deliberate resemblance. One may say that there is no conscious craft of painting."[41] Along the same lines, Dong defines stylistic independence as perfect imitation, appealing to the merging of tradition and individual difference, a recurrent topic in Chinese aesthetic thought: "One departs from the model even further because the resemblance is absolutely complete."[42] Elsewhere Dong compares the imitation of a calligraphy model to a sudden encounter with a strange being: the key is to capture the spirit with one glance.[43] The connoisseur, collector, and scholar-official Sun Chengze (1593–1676) introduces a more agonistic note when he claims that the key to learning calligraphy properly is "spiritual imitation" (*shenmo* 神摹): the learner must put the ancient's genuine specimen on the desk and walk around it, observing it from different angles and distance, until he can re-create the ancient's creative process, "as if he were standing next to the ancient and seeing how he applied his brush." "Then unleash crack troops to go after the model—even if one cannot destroy the enemy, one would have pressed close to the city wall." The military metaphor here reminds us that the goal of the imitator is to replace the original. According to Sun, one should imitate "as if one wishes to create a forgery to deceive others."[44]

The continuum of imitation and creation may explain the admiration for forgers. When the Suzhou artist Huang Biao sent Wang Shizhen a piece of calligraphy with the fake signature of Zhao Mengfu, Wang "showed it to his guests, many of whom considered it Zhao's work." Wang seemed to delight in the successful deception, although he removed the fake signature while keeping the piece in his collection and remarked that Huang's style, though polished (*shu* 熟), "appeared more vulgar upon familiarity."[45] Jiang Shaoshu (17th c.) had no such reservations when he praised forgeries produced by Huang Biao and his son Huang Jingxing, lamenting the likelihood that they will be forgotten (since they did not sign their own names) unless he draws attention to them.[46] Huang Biao characterizes his mission as "re-creating the image to continue what is being broken off."[47] Jiang Shaoshu regards disciples who reproduce their masters' styles (sometimes doing so in the latter's name) as "supplementary schools" (yupai 餘派), as inevitable as "the year that must have its intercalary month" (YSZ B.16a–17a). On the purchase of counterfeit Dong Qichang paintings produced by Dong's friend Zhao Zuo, Jiang Shaoshu comments: "One can say this is buying Wang and obtaining Yang" (i.e., Yang Xin's [370–422] calligraphy rather than that of Wang Xianzhi [344–386])—this is not the real thing perhaps, but nevertheless a superior specimen.[48] Jiang's admiring entry on Zhao Zuo follows closely on that on Dong Qichang—the two passages are also of comparable length.[49] It is all a matter of contexts and perspectives: a Mi Fu forgery of Wang Xizhi, for example, is valuable for being Mi Fu's work despite its genesis in the intention to deceive.[50]

There were numerous writings lauding "the stamp of authenticity" (zhenqi 真氣) as well as the connoisseur's ability to tell the real from the fake, yet it was an open secret that many famous artists relied on helpers who produced works in their name. Tang Yin is said to have asked Zhou Chen to paint on his behalf, and many paintings attributed to Tang Yin could have been by Zhou Chen.[51] Wen Zhengming put his signature on paintings done by his two sons (Wen Jia [1501–1583] and Wen Peng) and by his disciples Zhu Lang, Qian Gu (1508–1579), and Ju Jie, and tacitly tolerated other counterfeits. "There were many in the Suzhou area who made their living by relying on (his indifference to counterfeits)."[52] In a letter to Qian Gu, Huang Jishui (1509–1574) asked Qian to paint a fan and then sign as "Wen Zhengming."[53] In another anecdote, a buyer who intended to ask Zhu Lang to paint in Wen Zhengming's name sent the gifts to Wen by mistake. Wen said, "Would it be acceptable if I paint the real Wen Zhenming work, just so that it will pass for the fake one by Zhu Lang?"[54] Wen's letter asking Zhu to "come by his house and settle (on his behalf) an elegant debt (qingzhai 清債)" has been preserved.[55] Superior forgers brought their work for him to sign.[56] Wen Zhengming's refusal to unmask forgeries is remembered as charity and magnanimity.[57] Likewise, Wang Shizhen regards Shen Zhou's willingness to put his signature on forgeries of his paintings as proof of his liberality and generosity.[58]

Assertions and anecdotes about how Dong Qichang had "authorized delegates" (*dai bi ren* 代筆人), other artists who paint on his behalf, are especially numerous.[59] Dong Qichang recognized that forgeries of his work proliferated but did not seem to mind. He refused to unmask a man from Wu, a forger who painted in his name. "Wherever I go, scholar-officials often take what they have collected of my works to show me. I know in my heart that they are forgeries but do not argue about it, for this can wait for the discerning one [literally, "Ziyun"] in a later era."[60] The phenomenon of Dong "outsourcing" his calligraphy and paintings can be interpreted in opposite ways. It can be seen as his complicity in market forces and his cynical attempt to appropriate other artists' works and to monetize his reputation,[61] or it can be understood as his cavalier disregard for social and economic obligations as he immersed himself in the aesthetics of detachment and transcendence, what Dong describes as "heading straight for the Land of the Enlightened with one leap."[62] Dong implies such disdain when he claims to have allowed his friends to use his name and fake his works as a form of financial assistance: "My calligraphy and paintings, having undeservedly gained a reputation in our times, have not infrequently brought succor to my starving friends."[63] Indeed, this may well be the fundamental paradox of Daoist or Chan Buddhist aesthetics—rising above mundane cares may seem, from another perspective, perilously close to worldliness or even readiness to exploit others' expectations.[64]

The ways whereby Wen Zhengming or Dong Qichang allowed or authorized forgeries are indicative of broader cultural trends. In the realm of texts and literary production, we see forgeries of or interventions with earlier texts as well as famous contemporary literati whose names became veritable engines of textual production. A good example is Dong's friend Chen Jiru, who turned his own authorship (or rather, brand) into a kind of cottage industry, supporting a host of penurious writers who composed on his behalf. According to Qian Qianyi, Chen sent these poor and obscure scholars from the Wu and Yue areas, divided into clans and groups, to "find passages and choose lines ... taking trivial words and obscure stories and bringing them together as books."[65] As a result, his fame spread far and wide, reaching distant lands and penetrating all levels of society. High officials recommended him for office when he was in his seventies.[66] Chen's epigrammatic sayings were especially popular: there were numerous late Ming imitations; some were passed off as his work. He was often quoted, sometimes without proper attribution. In all these malleable permutations of and fluid transitions between the real and the fake, one is tempted to infer consequent anxieties, uncertainties, or moral questions. However, the mood of many of these accounts is matter-of-fact, depicting complex social relations and economic considerations that make people countenance and even appreciate copies, imitations, and counterfeits.

THE PERFIDIOUS CONNOISSEUR

If the valorization of the connoisseur's superior knowledge sometimes makes victims of fraud seem like mere fools, moral judgments return in full force in accounts of the connoisseur's perfidy and rapacity. Versions of the story about how a forgery of *Going Up the River at Qingming Festival* (*Qingming shanghe tu*) by Zhang Zeduan (ca. 11th–12th c.) brings Yan Song's wrath on the official Wang Shu (1507–1560), father of the famous poet and scholar-official Wang Shizhen, reveal potential tension between the discourse of connoisseurship and its moralization.

The earliest extant reference to this story is found in Xu Xuemo's (1522–1593) *Reminiscences from Emperor Shizong's Reign* (*Shi miao shi yu lu*, ca. 1583): an unnamed official from Taicang presented a forgery of *Going Up the River* to Yan Shifan (Yan Song's son), who employed one Tang Biaobei (meaning "Tang who mounts scrolls") to adjudicate the authenticity of artworks that came into his collection. Expecting but failing to receive a bribe, Tang declared the painting a forgery, which led to the downfall and execution of the Taicang official.[67] Describing the scroll as a *youwu* 尤物, a supreme specimen with dangerous allure, Zhan Jingfeng notes: "On account of it, Wang from Taicang invited calamity and Minister Yan hounded someone to death."[68] The identification of Yan's victim as Wang Shu (who hailed from Taicang) became current only in the early seventeenth century.

In 1610 a friend showed Li Rihua *Going Up the River*. After recording the various colophons on the scroll and explaining the existence of different versions and copies, Li proceeds to tell how it changed hands. The scroll was once in the possession of the minister Lu Wan (1458–1526). After Lu's death, his widow guarded it jealously and had it sewn inside her pillow. Her nephew Wang Zhenqi begged to see it. She relented but banished ink and brush during his perusal for fear that he would make a copy. Aided by his fantastic memory and skills as a painter, Wang managed to produce an excellent copy after sessions of contemplation spanning two or three months. Just then Yan Song was trying to acquire this painting, and Commissioner Wang Shu, trying to please Yan, bought Wang Zhengqi's copy for eight hundred taels of silver without realizing it was a forgery. Yan was overjoyed and asked the mounter Tang to restore the painting. Having realized that this was a forgery, Tang demanded from Wang a bribe of forty taels of silver to keep the secret. When the incredulous Wang refused, Tang exposed the forgery. Enraged, Yan Song brought about Wang's eventual downfall and execution.

Li Rihua's comments pertain to Yan Song's aesthetic judgment rather than his moral failure: "Now Wang was but one who tried to muddle ahead with his official career, it was fitting that he lacked discernment. But Yan Song had broad learning and refinement even when he was young and reached the height of wealth and rank in his later years. Having gathered and examined numerous works, he should have been able to tell the difference right away. As for Wang's forgery, it must have required an experienced hand to uncover. The supreme craft of the copy thus meant it was far from ordinary." Instead of simply condemning rapacity or abuse of power, he recommends the categorical separation of aesthetic appreciation from power politics. "Can it be true that the flames of power and the waves of profit should not in any case borrow any resources from pure and precious objects? It is said that the Wei Lord Yi's obsession with cranes is worse than Ji Kang's and Ruan Ji's indulgence in wine.[69] Judging from this, those enamored of ancient art should not use it as a means to gain power and glory. And those who occupy proud and prominent positions should also follow this logic and yield to humble scholars."[70]

In Shen Defu's version of this story (*WL* 3:827), Tang, famous for his expertise in mounting scrolls, serves Yan Song and is also acquainted with Wang Shu. Tang urges Wang to buy the scroll and offer it as a gift to Yan. Upon being entrusted by Wang with the task of the purchase and failing to obtain it, Tang buys a forgery produced by the aforementioned

Suzhou artist Huang Biao. The elated Yan invites friends to admire this prized acquisition. Among the guests is Wang's jealous rival, who then exposes the fraud and unleashes Yan's fury against Wang. Shen adds that according to some, it is Tang who reveals the truth because of grudges against Wang Shizhen and his brother. Like Li Rihua, Shen condemns Yan in passing but seems more curious about the furor over a scroll painted by a mere "craftsman of the Academy."[71] The aesthetic of *Going Up the River*, based on the interest in verisimilitude and urban life, is very different from that of literati paintings. Both Li and Shen observe that a Song emperor had probably commissioned paintings on street scenes along River Bian, and Zhang Zeduan's work was the best among them. Both note the existence of different copies. Unlike other artists shrouded in the lore about their style and personality, we know next to nothing about Zhang Zeduan. What does the "genuine specimen" mean in this case? Does the term still retain the aura of the artist's "genuine spirit"? Does it simply mean the acknowledged winner in a group of commissioned paintings? Again, aesthetic questions almost overshadow moral ones.

The historical veracity of these accounts is open to question.[72] They seem to have been elaborated on the basis of the following: Yan Song's ownership of the scroll,[73] the enmity between Yan Song and Wang's father as well as Wang himself,[74] and Wang Shizhen's familiarity with both the original and its copy. In a colophon on *Another Version of Going Up the River at Qingming Festival* (*Qingming shanghe tu bieben*), Wang notes that the real copy was owned by a minister (i.e., Yan Song) and confiscated and taken into the imperial treasury, where it was beloved by the Longqing emperor (r. 1567–1572). According to Wang, Huang Biao created a commendable copy owned by Wang's younger brother. Huang's work seems to have been based on a version of *Going Up the River* by another palace artist.[75] Wang notes in the next entry that Yan plotted someone's death in his attempt to acquire the scroll.[76] Wang Shizhen also addressed two poems to a mounter named Tang, praising his expertise in mounting scrolls; there is no hint of any enmity.[77] Tang's involvement in Yan's abuse of power cannot be ascertained. His culpability in these stories is a function of his connoisseurship: as the one who judges the authenticity and value of artworks, he holds (and therefore can abuse) power beyond his social station. His villainy, somewhat incidental in the accounts by Li Rihua and Shen Defu, takes center stage in Xu Xuemo's brief account, which is repeated with further circumstantial details in Xu Shupi's (17th c.) *Minor Records* (*Shixiao lu*). The official who failed to bribe Tang Biaobei, who then declared Wang's copy of *Going Up the River* a fake, is identified as Wang Shu.[78] Xu recounts (with some skepticism) how Tang reaches his judgment: a group of gamblers in the scrolls are shouting "six" with their mouth open. This means that they are speaking Fujianese ("six" is "lok" in southern dialects) when in fact they should show pursed lips as Bianjing natives ("six" is "liu" in northern dialects).[79] Perhaps it is fitting that Tang, as an artisan, should eschew the appreciative language eulogizing the ineffable and discuss evidence of authenticity in much more concrete terms.

The plotline of persecuted innocence is more starkly drawn in Gu Gongxie's (18th c.) account.[80] Here Wang Shu owns the authentic scroll, which Yan Shifan forces him to give up. Unable to part with it, Wang has a copy made and sends it to Yan. The ingrate Tang, whom Wang saved from penury and recommended to Yan earlier, exposes the forgery. The reasoning is again pegged to details: Tang points out that the tiny claws of the sparrow should not span two tiles. That such an oversight would disprove the authenticity of the scroll implies that stringent verisimilitude down to the minutest detail is the ultimate criterion for artistic excellence. Again, that seems to be an artisanal perspective.

Whereas the voice of the connoisseur appraising *Going Up the River* almost distracts from the moral urgency of the anecdotes by Li Rihua and Shen Defu, focus on the represented connoisseur (Tang) in the accounts by Xu Shupi and Gu Gongxie particularizes his skills, heightens his villainy, and sharpens the moral conflict.[81] The late Ming classical tale "Tang Biaobei" by Cheng Kezhong (d. ca. 1600s–1610s) explores another perspective: here the connoisseur is also the antagonist, but instead of moral polarity we have a fascination with trickery.[82] Poetic justice is realized when the trickster is tricked; and trickery seems to be the last resort for those who try to counter the abuse of power. Since the story is not well known, I have translated it below.

Cheng Kezhong, "Tang Biaobei"

When Yan Song [Fenyi] was in charge of government, his son Yan Shifan [the junior supervisor of works] oversaw the household and had the authority to grant or deny favors. Shifan also excelled in connoisseurship; hence he gathered all the precious gems and treasures under heaven as well as every masterpiece of calligraphy and painting from Jin and Tang dynasties. His only regret was that he lacked the right man to mount artworks in his collection. At that time Wang, a Suzhou official and the grandson of the former grand tutor Wang Wenzhen, had through hereditary office become the supervisor of affairs.[83] Wang frequented Yan Song's home, and it was said that he and Yan Shifan called each other brother. Shifan entrusted Wang with the search for the said man, and Wang thus recommended Tang Biaobei, whom he knew and whose abilities he praised in the highest terms. Shifan offered two hundred taels of silver to get Tang fired up for the work, and when Tang arrived the two got along very well.

Living by Shifan's side and attending to him at meals, Tang gained his favor. He was inordinately respectful as he shuttled back and forth between the Yan and Wang households, consistently calling Yan and Wang "masters" in his dealings with them. Both men trusted him because he was competent without being boastful. Wang was secretly pleased that he managed to install his aide right next to the powerful man. But Tang, a mean-spirited fellow, found out that Wang had an heirloom that was a rare treasure—a Han dynasty jade cup kept in a purple gold bowl that weighed almost twenty measures. He secretly informed Yan Shifan, who then enjoined him to try to get it.

Wang figured: "This is a treasure handed down from my ancestors—something I value more than life." He thus prevaricated: "Positions and wealth are granted through the chief minister's beneficence and the good office of the supervisor of works, how indeed do I dare to begrudge the cup? If you, sir, make me the fortunate intendant in charge of waterway transportation, I would raise the cup to drink to your long life and offer it." According to the law, there was no way that one could through clandestine channels get such an important appointment. Wang was simply using this as an excuse to deflect the issue. Yan Shifan said, "You, sir, should just let the matter rest for now. I will request my father to promote you to the rank of grand imperial officer in the Ministry of Ritual and junior supervisor of works commissioned to oversee river management. The position commands the same authority as that of an intendant, only the salary is higher." Wang agreed. Just then he managed to find a piece of uncarved jade as creamy white as lamb fat. Paying a hundred taels of silver, he engaged the service of a fine jade carver from Yunnan, who rushed day and night to make and polish a cup that looked absolutely no different from the one Wang kept at home. Wang offered it along with the bowl. Yan Shifan was overjoyed, and Wang was thrice promoted in one year, reaching the rank of minister of ritual.

One day, Tang came by to visit, and Wang, while chatting with him, let slip these words: "You, sir, are my old friend. How grand to have one of my own by the supervisor's side! The cup was the former belonging of our own grand tutor. I would not have exchanged it even for fifteen cities! Why would I set much store by empty titles?" Tang asked in surprise: "How could you say that? Isn't the one in the supervisor's house the real thing?" Wang explained to him what happened and shouted for the cup: "Bring the cup! I will honor Mr. Tang's exertion." Tang had long wanted to undermine Wang so that he could monopolize Yan Song's attention. The following day, he told Yan Shifan: "Wang took you for a nobody, Master. That with which he gained high office was a fake. Last evening, when we drank, your humble servant saw the real thing. It was ten times better." Furious, Yan shook his sleeves and rose. Tang said, "Wang did not bring his family, and the chests and trunks are all inside his bedchamber. If you, Master, go to visit him tomorrow morning and bring along ten burly servants to search his rooms, you'll get the real cup!" Yan Shifan assented.

He went on his way in the morning. Wang had an old family servant who, looking into the distance from a crack, saw that Yan did not come with any friendly intent and said, "He must be coming for the cup!" He hastily put the cup in his chest, jumped over a low wall and hid outside. Yan entered and, before sitting for too long, rose and held Wang's hand: "The minister of ritual is a position of the third rank, and yet it is not as good as a wine cup. How could you bear to deceive me with a forgery?" Wang replied, "I have said before that I could not sufficiently repay the chief minister's beneficence channeled through you, sir, even if I were to give up my life. How dare I test the blade with my neck? Moreover, it is as if the intricate carving on the cup came from one with supernatural power. How could a mundane jade worker be capable of it? I don't have my family with me, and my chests and trunks are all here. Please look through them." Yan searched the premises and found twelve other cups, all of inferior quality. Wang rose and made his case: "Others are just jealous that I have received great favors. It will be my good fortune if you, sir, do not let the words of petty-minded men influence you." Even then Wang did not realize that Tang had set him up.

Yan Shifan returned in shame and reprimanded Tang severely. Tang had no way to clear himself of blame. Some days later, he visited Wang again. Wang said, "The other day I stepped on the tiger's tail and almost did not survive. But the cup is fortunately still here. Bring the cup and let me drink another round with Mr. Tang." After Tang left, Wang's old family servant said, "You, young master, do not hide your belongings carefully enough.[84] How do we know that Tang did not bring about the perilous situation the other day? Your servant is just worried that disaster will overtake us tomorrow." Wang stamped his foot as the truth dawned on him: "That's it! That's it! What is to be done?" His servant said, "At dawn I will take the cup and secretly return home. Following that, you should plan to leave office and go back home." As morning came, right after the family servant left the city, Yan Shifan mustered a hundred imperial guards on horseback and came for another search, but again to no avail. Yan Shifan was ashamed to have lost the amity with an old favorite and suspected Tang of petty interference. The doubts and uncertainties on his mind could ultimately not be resolved.

Wang, for his part, planned to find a way to wreak vengeance on Tang and surreptitiously spied on his dealings. Just then a man from Kuaiji brought three scrolls of Tang and Song paintings [to the capital]. Tang purchased them with 150 taels of silver but sold them to Yan Shifan for 800. Wang secretly summoned the vendor of the paintings: "Bring me the scrolls and I will pay you double the amount. If Tang is unwilling to return them, you should pretend to stab your forehead with a knife. He will be frightened for sure and will relent." The vendor did as he was told. Tang presented the case to Yan, who was in any case reluctant to part with 800 taels of silver.

After Wang obtained the scrolls, he set things up grandly and invited Yan Shifan to honor him with a visit with these words: "The slave Tang turned against our beneficence and instigated discord between us. That he got to enter your service was due to my oversight. By chance I have obtained three scrolls and with them I beg to redeem my error." Yan Shifan rose in surprise, "Where do the scrolls come from? Their worth is not insignificant. How did they come to be in your possession?" Wang said, "An official's son from Zhejiang wanted to seek a minor office in the capital but had no wherewithal to do so. He was about to sell these and use them as presentation gifts, but they were almost seized by a miscreant. He was so afflicted that he wanted to kill himself—only then did he escape the tiger's jaws. I bought them for 90 taels of silver. They do not deserve the honor of your perusal." Yan said, "That slave Tang is so devious! We should let the great hound chew his liver! These scrolls entered my chest. He induced me to pay 800 taels of silver for them. Claiming that even that amount was insufficient, he came to ransom them. Little did I expect that they cost only ninety taels." Wang said, "Relying on your aura and authority, Tang had demanded 3,000 taels from me. He resented me for not yielding the sum and thus used the cup to sow discord. Fortunately, because your honor is benevolent and discerning, I managed to stay unharmed. The amount Tang amassed in his coffers is not insignificant. He was always using your honor's name to threaten others and to extort from them. I fear this will not bode well for the chief minister." Yan Shifan was upset, stopped drinking, and left. He further summoned the imperial guards on horseback to surround Tang's abode and appropriated the 85,000 taels of silver in his possession, claiming other goods as being related to these charges. He had Tang beaten until there was not a patch of intact skin left and exiled him to distant Miyun. When all these things happened, Tang had not stayed for that long in the capital. To this day, by way of cursing a man one has recommended, one still says: "Do not be like Tang Biaobei of Wumen!"[85]

The name Tang Biaobei, first mentioned in Xu Xuemo's account, becomes pointedly symbolic here. His craft of mounting (biaobei 裱褙) is homophonous with words meaning "surface" (biao 表) and "back" (bei 背) and underlines the discrepancy between appearance and actuality, the manipulation of the meanings of objects and the misjudgment of character. Biaobei is also sometimes written as biaobei (裱背 or 表背), in which case the graph bei 背 means both "to put white silk or paper at the back" and "to betray." Tang betrays (bei) his first patron by using his presumed authority to tell the real thing from its surface (biao) imitation. Textual records indicate that a family of mounters, surnamed Tang, were famous for their craft, acted as art dealers, and had active social ties with the scholar-officials of the Lower Yangzi area.[86] Perhaps an artisan who is supposed to have appropriated literati accomplishments without necessarily possessing the knowledge or cultivation sustaining them is a figure ambiguous enough to invite vilification.

In all versions of this story (except for Gu Gongxie's account), Wang is at least partially responsible for his misfortunes, having tried to curry favor with Yan Song and Yan Shifan by presenting a forgery. It is only in "Tang Biaobei," however, that the ambiguities of his role come fully to the fore. Here Wang does not initiate the gift-giving, and he seems more justified in resisting Yan's demand for his jade cup, an heirloom that goes beyond aesthetic appreciation and represents filial duty or lineage continuity. He is thus more of a potential victim. At the same time, we learn how he hopes to use Tang to get close to Yan. Other accounts imply his hopes for advancement, here he explicitly requests a promotion and concretely profits by offering Yan a forgery. Whereas other versions of the story credit Tang with the expertise to see through a forgery, here Wang twice discloses his trick of substitution to Tang, apparently reveling in his success at besting the powerful Yan Shifan. Wang's vanity and lack of judgment thus become more glaring. Foiling Tang's attempts to expose him, Wang manages to use the connoisseur's tricks—the arbitrary definition of value and the manipulation of prices—to give Tang his comeuppance. In that sense, the protagonist takes on the traits of the antagonists. Yan Shifan's abuse of power or Tang's perfidy and avarice are lampooned, but Wang, the supposed agent of justice, is also fully implicated in the calculations that tie connoisseurship to patronage, corruption, and deception.

MORALIZED TRANSACTIONS IN
AN OFFERING OF SNOW

The anecdotes and stories discussed in the previous section have all been identified as possible sources for (or, in the cases of accounts by Xu Shupi and Gu Gongxie, variants bearing the imprint of) the play, *An Offering of Snow* (*Yi peng xue*, hereafter *Snow*), a thirty-scene *chuanqi* play by the Suzhou playwright Li Yù. Yan Shifan as the rapacious collector who abuses his power and Tang Qin (also called Biaobei) as the dealer, middleman, and connoisseur persist as antagonists in the play. A jade cup replaces *Going Up the River* as the object of contention, which recalls Cheng Kezhong's "Tang Biaobei,"[87] and has led scholars to identify an anecdote about family feuds and intrigues caused by an antique jade cup, discussed in the introduction, as another possible source for the play. Irrespective of whether we can establish any of them as the intended historical referent (*benshi* 本事), there is little doubt that these (mostly contemporaneous) stories recounting how the circulation of real and fake antiques or artworks chart social and political relationships share common concerns with *Snow*. However, the economic calculations in these stories yield pride of place to a looming moral compass in *Snow*.

Qi Biaojia (1602–1645) saw a performance of the play in Suzhou in 1643.[88] Included in various anthologies of oft-performed scenes and performance guides with musical notations, it has continued to be popular onstage as Kun opera and regional opera.[89] Like many other *chuanqi* plays, the title here designates an important symbolic object that determines the plot—in this case a white jade cup named "An Offering of Snow."[90] Why might a cup work better than a scroll as a plot device (and a prop) in the play? As in "Tang Biaobei," the jade cup as heirloom adds a dimension of filial duty to possession. In addition, the play emphasizes its antiquity and political meaning: the cup was made from Bian He's jade, buried with the First Emperor of Qin (r. 220–210 BCE), presented by a general to the Tang emperor Xuanzong (r. 712–756), kept in the imperial treasury until the end of the Song dynasty, and obtained by the protagonist's ancestor during the chaos of the Yuan dynasty (*YPX* 2.9). Unlike objects whose history is often no more than an account of its buyers, sellers, and transactions, "An Offering of Snow" is tied to the motif of recognizing worth (Bian He defends the jade's authenticity with life and limbs in well-known stories from the Warring States),[91] political power, and historical continuity. The jade cup also has enough imagistic association with ritual vessels to warrant an ironic juxtaposition. Tang Biaobei declaims after obtaining what he takes for the real jade cup: "The jade cup in the box is weighty like cities, / The ritual vessels in court are as trifling as mud" (8.30).[92] The very pursuit of the jade cup by Yan Shifan and Tang Biaobei signifies the perversion of cultural values symbolized by ritual vessels.

The play begins with Mo Huaigu of Qiantang (Hangzhou), restless with his hereditary office as the supervisor of affairs, planning to go to the capital to seek a more important position by cultivating his connection with Yan Shifan. Mo encounters and takes under his protection the destitute Tang Qin, who has been reduced to penury because of his vices and tries to eke out a living by mounting scrolls. They set out for the capital, along with Mo's concubine Xueyan and his servant Mo Cheng. There Yan Shifan entertains Mo Huaigu at a banquet, during which Mo recommends Tang to Yan as they watch a performance of *The Wolf of Zhongshan* (*Zhongshan lang*), a short play by Kang Hai (1475–1540) about how an ingrate wolf tries to kill its savior—the transparently analogical play within a play announces themes of deception and betrayal. *Snow* then shows marked parallels with the tale "Tang Biaobei": Tang tells Yan about a priceless jade cup ("An Offering of Snow") that Mo owns, Yan covets it, and Mo agrees to give it up on condition that he be appointed the commissioner for the transportation of grains along the Grand Canal, acting on the assumption that such an important appointment will likely not materialize and he will not be called on to give up his jade cup. Mo does get his appointment, however, and ends up sending Yan a replica of his cup, but he later inadvertently reveals the truth to Tang Qin. Upon Tang's urging, Yan searches Mo's abode but fails to find the cup because the servant Mo Cheng, sensing trouble, has fled the premises with it.

From this point on the play introduces moral choices absent in "Tang Biaobei" and other possible sources. Fearing Yan Shifan's vindictiveness, Mo Huaigu abandons his post and flees with Xueyan and Mo Cheng to Jizhou (present-day Tianjin), where his friend Qi Jiguang serves as military commander and offers him refuge.[93] Yan sends his men to pursue Mo, accusing him of "stealing the divine ritual vessel,[94] leaving his post without permission, toying with the state, and deceiving the ruler" (13.45).

Mo is arrested by Yan's men at Jizhou and faces execution. His servant Mo Cheng offers to die in his place, and Qi Jiguang helps to deceive the executioners with the substitution. Mo Huaigu, under the alias Gui Fu (meaning "return and restore" or "return and avenge a wrong"), flees to Chaohe River, where he seeks the protection of Qi's friend Adjutant Wei. Mo Cheng's severed head is sent to the capital, where Tang Qin declares it a fake, and Xueyan and Qi Jiguang are arrested and brought to the capital. Xueyan agrees to marry Tang Qin in return for his testimony that the head is real and then assassinates him before committing suicide on the wedding night. In the meantime, Mo Huaigu's family in Qiantang has been implicated in his supposed crime. Mo's son Mo Hao escapes with his tutor, while his mother goes into exile with the servant Wen Lu, who assumes Mo Hao's identity. Mo Hao, under the name Fang Getian, passes the examination and submits a memorial to the throne impeaching Yan Song and Yan Shifan for corruption and abuse of power. The emperor miraculously sees the justice of his case: the Yan family falls from power, the Mo family is restored to its former position, and Mo Hao (under his alias Fang Getian) is appointed circuit commissioner. Unbeknownst to Mo Hao, his parents have accidentally met at the grave designated as Mo Huaigu's (where Mo Cheng was actually interred), and the two have joined Qi Jiguang in Jizhou. Mo Hao confronts Qi, expecting to wreak vengeance for the latter's supposed betrayal of Mo Huaigu, and is instead reunited with his parents. In this final scene, Yan Shifan's severed head, "circulated and displayed at the nine frontiers" as warning against treason (30.102), arrives at Qi's camp, and the jade cup, hitherto in Qi's keeping, is restored to the Mo family.

Li Yù is the most prominent figure in a group of dramatists associated with Suzhou during the Ming-Qing transition. Their works sometimes have a markedly topical focus as they draw from recent and contemporary history, addressing social problems and political developments from late Ming to early Qing.[95] This group of playwrights, active from the 1620s to the end of the seventeenth century, did not hold office, belonged to a lower social echelon, and captured the liveliness of urban culture with a diction more expressive than allusive. According to Jiao Xun (1763–1820), Li Yù started out as a servant or the descendant of a servant in the household of the chief minister Shen Shixing (1535–1614), and he "went to great lengths to vindicate servants by granting them agency" in *Snow*.⁹⁶ Others question this version of Li's "class origins," noting his friendship with the most famous literati of his day: Qian Qianyi, Wu Weiye, and Wu Qi (1619–1694) all wrote prefaces for his plays or exchanged poems with him.⁹⁷ What Jiao Xun painted in affirmative and heroic terms has also been decried by modern scholars as "slave morality," a servant's internalization of a value system that valorizes hierarchical distinctions and self-abnegation.⁹⁸ Such gaps between supposed authorial intention and modern perception are not uncommon. What seems incontrovertible is that social inferiors, whether as villain or heroes, define the dramatic conflict in *Snow*.

The name of the male lead, Mo Huaigu, has been glossed as a warning: "do not cherish antiques." To be obsessed with antiques is like futilely holding snow with one's hands.⁹⁹ His sobriquet is "Wuhuai" (literally, cherishing nothing), and that of his son, "Getian." Wuhuai and Getian are the names of ruling lineages in high antiquity. Tao Yuanming invokes them at the end of his autobiographical account, "Master Five Willows" (Wuliu xiansheng zhuan): "Does he (Master Five Willows, the transcendent recluse) belong to the Wuhuai lineage? Or does he belong to the Getian lineage?"¹⁰⁰ If Mo Huaigu and his son live up to the detachment embodied by their sobriquets, they should not care for worldly possessions like the jade cup. Alternatively, the jade cup would have belonged to a vision of aesthetic self-containment and withdrawal from public affairs, which is indeed presented at the beginning of the play: Mo Huaigu comes onstage declaiming his interest in learning and connoisseurship, being surrounded by Qin and Han bronzes as well as ancient books and paintings (*YPX* 1.5). Mo, however, chooses to enter the world of power politics, bringing the cup into a web of transactions that trap him in bad faith. He complacently declares as he gains a prestigious post in exchange for the fake cup: "The jade cup has numinous power!" (9.31). As in Cheng Kezhong's "Tang Biaobei," Mo Huaigu's apparent satisfaction with the appointment introduces ambiguities that preclude our understanding of his role as simply that of an innocent victim.

To reestablish moral clarity, Li Yù magnifies Tang Qin's abuse of power and apotheosizes Mo Cheng and Xueyan as martyrs of virtue, mapping their roles through their relationship with the jade cup. Tang Qin embodies the volatility of social distinctions, which is dramatized by his frequent change of costumes. He comes onstage in rags, but Mo

Huaigu, after discovering Tang's talent with mounting scrolls and his knowledge of antiques, offers him "a set of headscarf and robe" appropriate for scholars (1.7–8). When Mo recommends Tang to Yan Shifan during the banquet, he sends word to Tang that he "should change into a servant's clothes and cap before seeking an audience" (5.17). The servant's attire is matched by Tang's extreme obsequiousness (he advances on his knees and kowtows), but when Yan finds out that Tang has been wearing a scholar's clothes in Mo's household, he grants him the same privilege. With such costume change, Tang advances to the status of "assistant in elegant matters" (*qingke* 清客). When Mo Huaigu obtains a new post in exchange for the fake cup, Tang also gains the post of military commissioner as the facilitator of the transaction, and he visits Mo wearing an official's gauze cap and a formal robe (9.30–31). Social roles are no more than change of costumes: this basic fact of theatrical spectacle gains symbolic quotient for someone who embodies the discrepancies between surface and meaning. As noted, Tang's name and his craft of mounting are homophonous with words meaning "surface" and "back" or "betrayal"; here it is also the tool of deception. He introduces himself thus: "No matter how brand new the calligraphy and painting, I can make their fake ancient pedigree most convincingly real. Even with bits and pieces of torn silk, my set up can bring out a whole new life" (1.7). Tang's perfidy is also transparently symbolized by the performance of *The Wolf of Zhongshan* when Mo introduces him to Yan.[101] With such doubleness he usurps the authority to determine what is "the real thing," whether it be the jade cup (8.29, 9.33, 10.35) or Mo Huaigu's head (16.56, 18.60–65). Xueyan juxtaposes these two acts as his greatest crimes: "As for the presented jade cup, you relentlessly questioned its veracity; having ended his life with a trap, you furthered judged the authenticity of the severed head" (20.71).

As antidote to this vision of murky distinctions and moral turpitude, Li Yù presents Mo Cheng and Xueyan as exemplary characters. They share with Tang Qin the status of being Mo Huaigu's servants; unlike Tang they adhere adamantly to that role. (Mo Cheng says that his family has "for generations received the masters' beneficence" [14.48]. Xueyan speaks of being raised by Mo's wife [3.11]; she is likely a maid who had become a concubine.) Mo Cheng dies in Mo Huaigu's place at the climactic midpoint (scene 15); Li Yù clearly intends this act of self-sacrifice to uphold the moral framework of the play. Scenes from *Snow* included in popular seventeenth- and eighteenth-century anthologies focus on Mo Cheng's sacrifice, Xueyan's vengeance, and eulogies of their loyalty. The *Zui baiqiu* selections further heighten the sacrifice of absolute loyalty by making the master-servant bond even more hierarchical—Mo Huaigu repeatedly abuses Mo Cheng as "unworthy slave" (*goucai* 狗才). Late Ming and early Qing literature abounds with examples of "loyal servants" (*zhongpu* 忠僕) or "righteous servants" (*yipu* 義僕). Some scholars have suggested that this phenomenon addresses anxieties about social unrest as evinced by incidents of late Ming rebellions of indentured servants (*nubian* 奴變).[102] How should the servant's self-sacrifice be understood? Arguments against "slave morality" seek redeeming traits of altruistic courage or reciprocity.[103] But perhaps the issue is less how the moral actions Li Yù upheld can be justified from modern perspectives than the contexts and implications of Li Yù's moral compass.

The closest analog of the master-servant relationship is that between ruler and subject. Of the five cardinal relationships, the virtue of loyalty binding the subject to the ruler is the only one justified neither through biological and family ties nor through reciprocity. (The discourse on loyalty in Warring States sources does emphasize reciprocity, but the demands on the subject become increasingly absolute and one-sided, especially in the late imperial period.[104] Filial, fraternal, and conjugal devotion, while based on the hierarchy of parent and child, younger and older kin, husband and wife, are also bound by kinship or sexual union. Friendship is based on reciprocity.) In that sense, the subject's loyalty toward the ruler is the most abstract of all virtues, and the one most easily corroded. In the wake of Ming collapse, the poet Fang Wen (1612–1669) wrote: "What cannot be destroyed over ten kalpas is the hankering for wealth and position, / Of the five cardinal ties none is as fake as that between ruler and subject" 萬劫不消惟富貴，五倫最假是君臣. Late Ming discourse on loyalty dwells not so much on its fragility as on its extreme demands—the latter may be a response to the former. The violent deaths of officials who died for their remonstrance with the ruler or for attacks against corrupt ministers and eunuchs turned loyalty into a blood sport: the assumption seemed to be that the more gruesome the death, the more remarkable the loyalty. Such is the logic that unfolds in another famous Li Yù play, *The Register of the Pure and the Loyal*

(*Qingzhong pu*). It eulogizes the official Zhou Shunchang (1584–1626), who is tortured and executed for attacking the corrupt eunuch Wei Zhongxian (d. 1627); it also glorifies five plebian heroes who lead a riot protesting Zhou's arrest and die as martyrs.

Unlike *Register*, *Snow* does not explicitly celebrate loyalty by linking it to political courage. The self-sacrifice of servants is, however, dignified with political analogies. Mo Cheng invokes the example of Ji Xin (*YPX* 14.48), who broke a critical siege for Liu Bang (the first Han emperor, r. 202–195 BCE) by pretending to be him and getting killed. He is also compared to the loyal Zhao retainers of antiquity who make supreme sacrifices for the surviving son of their master (the Zhao Orphan).[105] An admiring chorus likens Xueyan to Warring States assassins like Zhuan Zhu, Jing Ke, and Nie Zheng (20.72).[106] The general Qi Jiguang's repeated avowals of loyalty to the Jiajing emperor as he faces accusations of having deceived the court by allowing Mo Huaigu to escape (17.59–60, 18.61–63) also imbues the latter's persecution and Mo Cheng's sacrifice with political significance. Qi is willing to "embrace death for a friend's sake" as he compares himself to loyal defenders of the realm who die defying the enemy.[107] Xueyan feigns willingness to marry Tang Qin not only to pursue vengeance but also to save Qi Jiguang. Qi Jiguang's involvement thus adds grander associations of political integrity to personal loyalty. In the scheme of loyalty, it also does not matter that Mo Huaigu is a flawed character and perhaps does not deserve the absolute devotion and self-sacrifice of Mo Cheng and Xueyan. The same can be said of the Jiajing emperor. It is customary in virtue stories to have undeserving objects of devotion—an unfeeling parent or mother-in-law, a cruel husband, or a benighted ruler would simply heighten the merit of the filial child or daughter-in-law, the chaste wife, or the loyal subject, who would be persisting in their loyalty against all odds. When Mo Hao, as a newly minted official, submits a memorial to impeach Yan Song, he "removes his cap and bears an axe" (27.90), indicating that he expects to be found guilty and to face execution: that was indeed the fate of many officials who opposed the historical Yan Song. Violence, self-sacrifice, and unquestioning adherence to absolute standards are recurrent refrains in the discourse of political loyalty, and Li Yù seems intent on elevating the servants' personal loyalty as political loyalty by force of association and analogy.

What do Mo Cheng and Xueyan gain in return for their sacrifice? Their "reward" is posthumous fame and honor. They become, by dying, the equal of their masters: this is self-assertion or agency at the price of self-annihilation. Echoing the Warring States Wu prince Guang's words to Zhuan Zhu as the latter sets out to assassinate Guang's enemy ("My body is your body" [*Shiji* 86.2518]), Mo Huaigu says to Mo Cheng: "If I manage to survive and return to my hometown, your parents will be my parents, your descendants will be my descendants" (*YPX* 14.49). Mo Cheng dons his master's clothes as he faces execution: "I take off the servant's shorts / and put on the official's cap. / My body in chains, / my arms bent and shriveled: / Feeling the blade, I can only swallow the blood. / Do I dare to tell my name?" (14.49).[108] Mourning Mo Cheng, Xueyan embraces the severed head and uses the same language of lamentation as if she were mourning Mo Huaigu: "But under the same cover with these bones, on the same pillow with this skull, through nine deaths I will stay with him" (18.62–63). Unlike the secret substitution in Mo Cheng's case, Xueyan's assassination of Tang Qin and subsequent suicide are acts of courage that immediately garner public eulogies. Mourners at her grave declare that she puts the elite to shame: "So many in cap and gown bow to the woman: / Who is willing to give his head at the frontier battlefields?" (21.75). On another level, however, Xueyan's death is also a substitution—this role of heroic vengeance and self-sacrifice should have been enacted by Mo's wife. Echoing this pattern of substitution, the servant boy Wen Lu takes Mo Hao's place and goes into exile with Mo Huaigu's wife, allowing Mo Hao to escape and take the examination. A counterfeit cup has set in motion a series of substitutions.

The fake cup looks identical to the real cup but cannot replace it, but a different head (Mo Cheng's) can replace the intended one (Mo Huaigu's): Li Yù does not intend any irony, but the implied logic that a person's identity can be less unique than that of a jade cup, or that a servant should, in the name of loyalty, die for a master because of forces set in motion by the latter's reluctance to yield a prized possession, must seem jarring to the modern reader. For Li Yù, however, it is a matter of reinstating a moral scheme. Corrupt transactions (a fake cup in exchange for an appointment; demanding a life for being cheated over a cup) can be corrected only through moralized transactions of absolute loyalty—a servant dying in his master's place; a dependent giving up his or her life as a way of asserting agency and gaining a posthumous name and vindication.

AN ECONOMIC SOLUTION IN *IDEAL MATCHES*

In *Snow*, obsession with the nonpareil jade cup and the furor over its forgery are associated with greed, abuse of power, and misplaced pride. Moral compass is restored through a series of substitutions of the real by the counterfeit: namely, servants and social inferiors who take the place of their betters in enduring suffering and embracing death. As mentioned earlier, these are "pretenders" whose charade fulfills the absolute demands of loyalty. The real and the fake versions of the jade cup and of the severed head thus enact an uncompromising restitution of the moral fabric in *Snow*. By contrast, *Ideal Matches* (or *Imaginary Matches, Yizhong yuan*) by Li Yu displaces the moral implications of polarizing the real and the fake. While Li Yù prunes the economic calculations of his source materials to create a more starkly defined moral equation, Li Yu embraces them as the potential solution to some of the contradictions in late Ming sensibility and social reality.

Ideal Matches carries a preface dated 1659 by Fan Xiangwen and another undated preface by the woman poet Huang Yuanjie (ca. 1620– ca. 1669).[109] Huang sums up Li Yu's intention of enacting poetic justice, especially for ill-fated women of talent: "Driven by the fervid passion for cherishing talents and trusting the dispassionate observation of love, he [Li Yu] summoned the fragrant souls and numinous spirit of these four persons and let them all find fitting mates" (*YZY* 318). The deliberate contrast between "fervid passion" (*reqing* 熱情) and "dispassionate observation" (*lengyan* 冷眼) implies an inversion of the formulas for treating romantic love. Love is treated "coldly" (*leng* 冷) with calculations, both by the protagonists and by Li Yu; the "burning" (*re* 熱) issue is the just requital for talent. The play is Li Yu's "gift" of compensatory consolation to four famous historical personages well known for their painting and calligraphy: the scholar-official Dong Qichang, the social recluse Chen Jiru (both mentioned earlier), and the courtesan artists Yang Yunyou and Lin Tiansu. The four historical characters did know one another. Numerous literary exchanges between Dong and Chen are found in their collections, and both Dong and Chen wrote about Yang and Lin with appreciation and empathy.[110]

Much of what we know about Yang and Lin comes from the writings of the Huizhou literatus, collector, publisher, and merchant Wang Ranming (given name Ruqian, 1577–1655), who gets written into the play as the matchmaker Jiang Huaiyi.[111] Huaiyi is the sobriquet of Jiang Qiuming 江秋明, which is orthographically very close to Wang Ranming 汪然明. (The graphs for "Jiang" 江 and "Wang" 汪 are similar, with one stroke less for Jiang. "Ran" 然 and "qiu" 秋 can look very similar in cursive script. "Ming" 明 is a character shared by both names.) Wang Ranming's collection, *The Hall of Spring Stars* (*Chunxing tang shiji*), also called *Thatched Hall Under Spring Stars* (*Chunxing caotang ji*), includes *Studio of Listening to Snow* (*Tingxue xuan ji*), which started out as a collection of poems about Yang Yunyou composed by Wang Ranming and his friends and turned into an elegiac volume mourning her death (ca. 1630s). It includes poems on Wang's arrangements for her funeral and commemoration as well as other poems of mourning. Determined to honor Yang's memory, Wang also asked his friends to write colophons on her paintings.

In the summer of 1623, Wang Ranming "built an abode of meditation for the Daoist Yun (i.e., Yang Yunyou)," which suggests that he took her under his protection. In the mid- or late 1620s, she left Hangzhou to get married. That marriage did not end well. Yang's line, "An official's dark gauze cap is ultimately an unfeeling thing" 烏紗總是無情物, cited in *Listening to Snow* (3.18a), suggests that this husband who betrayed her held office or abandoned her once he gained office. One of Huang Yuanjie's comments in the play alludes to Yang's marriage to a man for whom Yang purchased an official appointment (*YZY* 21.390). Yang returned to West Lake around 1628. The poems Wang Ranming wrote upon her return, when he invited her to paint on his boat (called *The Convent of Karmic Joy*), suggests empathy with her misfortunes and tactful encouragement. Here is one of them:

WANG RANMING, "ASCENDING *THE CONVENT OF KARMIC JOY* WITH YANG HUILIN (YUNYOU) ON A WINTER DAY" 冬日同楊慧林登隨喜庵

此日何如鳥出籠	How does this day compare to a bird leaving its cage?
況同輕艇欲凌空	What's more—we share a light boat about to soar to heaven.

| 相看莫道傷心事 | Looking at each other, let's not speak of heartbreak |
| 且把湖山入畫中 | And just put the lake and the mountains into the painting.[112] |

Listening to Snow begins with two colophons by Dong Qichang. The first one (1629), written when Yang Yunyou was still alive, assesses the place of Lin Tiansu and Yang Yunyou in the tradition of literati painting. Dong compares Lin and Yang to the Northern Tradition and Southern Tradition in Chan Buddhism, respectively, implicitly ranking Yang above Lin: "But for Tiansu's supreme elegance, I can see its limits, while Yunyou's gentle, free spirit is uniquely filled with strength and resonance. If her talent can be allowed to develop, there would be no way to fathom its limits." He compares Yang to a bird going around a tree three times without finding a resting place, alluding to Cao Cao's "Brief Song" (Duange xing). "If it were not for Ranming and a few other fine men who have become her staunch defenders, how can a brick be ground into a mirror [i.e., how can the impossible become possible]?"[113]

Dong Qichang's second colophon, written for an album of Yang's landscape paintings, praises her talent and laments her untimely death. "There is Wang Ranming, whose staunch defense of her in life and death does not stem from blind infatuation. He treasures the traces she left behind, as if they were the pendants the goddesses untied at the Han River, and passes them around her devotees, so that they can listen together to the music of Xiang Shores. This is heartfelt sincerity—he is a true friend of the departed. Just be careful not to show these paintings to the vulgar and undiscerning."[114] The pendants of the goddesses, referring to an evanescent encounter with an elusive object of desire, can sometimes have mildly erotic undertones.[115] Here it is transformed into Yang's artistic legacy, whose appreciation and commemoration also gain an ethical dimension. The spirits of Xiang Shores are the daughters and wives of legendary sage kings (Yao and Shun): their music mourning Shun conveys a higher moral purpose. As a tribute to Yang's artistic achievements, *Listening to Snow* tones down romantic, sensual imagery and derives its pathos from poems commending Wang's friendship with Yang and Dong's appreciation of her works.

If aesthetic appreciation promises to displace romantic innuendoes in *Listening to Snow*, the two are entwined in Wang Ranming's earlier collection, *Dream Grass* (*Meng cao*), which is devoted to Lin Tiansu. *Dream Grass* begins with Wang Ranming's "Account of a Dream by the Secluded Window" (Youchuang jimeng, 1622). In his dream, Wang enters a grand residence. A dignified old man welcomes him and takes him through winding corridors to a studio called "Listening to Snow." Surrounded by exquisite objects and calligraphy and paintings "worthy of the connoisseur," Wang sees a divinely beautiful woman accompanied by a maid. The old man introduces her as his daughter and asks Wang to find a fitting husband for her. When the old man leaves the room, Wang sees that the woman is holding a fan painted with flowers in the Song-Yuan style. Her maid says that Lin Tiansu painted the fan, which her mistress loves. Wang replies that he too owns several of Lin's paintings. The maid asks to see them, and Wang takes out a silk handkerchief painted by Lin.

> "Tiansu painted these willows to bid me farewell when she returned (to Fujian). Should I use it as a gift?" The woman turned her back and smiled, "Tiansu bade you farewell with this handkerchief, how can you give it up so lightly? If you don't mind my scrawl, I will inscribe a poem on it for you." Joy and fear mingled in me, and I did not know what to do. She leaned against a low table, lowered her head, tenderly wetted the brush, and wrote a quatrain: "Willow branches in the gentle spring breeze: / Who made these into a poem on a painting? / The long branches are waiting for you to break them off. / Do not say that you meet only at the moment of parting." 嫋嫋春風楊柳枝，誰人寫入畫中詩。長條好待君攀折，莫謂相逢是別時。

Just as Wang plans to write a poem in response, the old man takes his seat at the feast, and in the commotion the woman vanishes. Wang wakes up and composes a poem to the same rhyme: "Painted on a sheet of light silk are willow branches / That for no reason turned into a poem in a dream. / Vainly I recall the moment of desire by the rain-soaked window— / These seem to be the poems of Zhangtai, matched in longing." 一幅輕綃畫柳枝，無端翻作夢中詩。雨窗漫記銷魂處，髣髴章臺唱和詩。[116]

The rest of *Dream Grass* consists of contributions from eight male poets, including Dong Qichang and Chen Jiru, and from the courtesan poet Wang Wei (ca. 1595 ca. 1647). These include poems about Wang Ranming's dream, as well as poetic commentary and colophons on *Dream Grass*. As this poetic chorus shows, Wang's dream is ambiguous enough to invite different interpretations. Chen Jiru, who comes up with the title *Dream Grass*, which alludes to the story of how Emperor Wu of Han clutches the "dream grass" so that he can dream of his deceased consort Lady Li,[117] implies that Wang Ranming's dream expresses longing for Lin as the absent beloved: "Could it not be that Tiansu worries about your inconstancy / And summons the illusion of the beauty to test you?" 將無天素愁郎變，幻出如花來試君? At the same time Chen emphasizes that their bond is literary and religious: "Ranming and Tiansu have a friendship based on literature and it lies beyond the mundane realm. Tiansu returned to Fujian, and Ranming could not stop thinking of her. She thus took shape in his dream. I would say that the maiden in the Hall of Listening to the Snow is none other than Tiansu—the five Spirits of Strength magically brought her to test you, and that is all."[118] Dong Qichang in his colophon implies that Lin Tiansu left because of emotional entanglements or their rumors: "Why did Tiansu show such feminine constraint and return to Sanshan (Fujian) after only one visit to Wulin (Hangzhou)? I was about to scold her when Ranming staved off criticism for her."[119] Why would *Dream Grass* "stave off criticism"? Does it explain Lin's departure by giving expression to Wang Ranming's contradictory feelings for her? Does it confirm that the relationship between Wang Ranming and Lin Tiansu goes beyond insinuations of desire?

In her preface to *Liu Rushi's Letters* (1640), written after Yang's death, Lin Tiansu praises Wang Ranming as a knightly figure whose friendship with courtesans confirms his superior sensibility: "Formerly, when I sojourned in West Lake, I often saw Ranming picking blossoms at the fragrant embankment or leaning against fair ones on painted boats. He enjoyed his ease among mountains and waterways, a veritable knight in yellow clothes.[120] . . . Another ten years passed, and I returned to Sanshan. Ranming sent me scrolls of paintings, and I knew that among his companions at West Lake was the beauty in the painting,[121] Yang Yunyou, and many were jealous of him."[122] The friendship between Wang and Lin entered a new phase in the 1640s, when Wang seemed to be suffering from financial difficulties. He visited Lin in Fujian, who gave him many gifts (including her own paintings), possibly as a way of offering financial assistance.¹²³

Lin Tiansu seems to be simultaneously the implicit object of longing, the voice of reproach, and the mediator of desire. Tsao Shu-chuan suggests that the woman in the dream may actually be a cypher for Yang Yunyou, considering the name of the studio ("Listening to Snow") and the associations of willows (*yangliu* 楊柳) with her name. (Other poems in *Dream Grass* also seem to encode her name.) This would imply that Lin left because of the rivalry between her and Yang. What seems certain is that *Dream Grass* points to the contradictions of desire in the relationship between the literati and courtesans—we see an intriguing mixture of longing, evasiveness, guilt, eager expectations, and fear of commitment.

Wang Ranming knew Li Yu and might have furnished him with details about the lives of Yang Yunyou and Lin Tiansu.¹²⁴ Wang was still alive when Li Yu wrote the play, which may explain why he is the only major character depicted through an alias. By then Dong, Chen, Yang, and Lin had all died. Wang Ranming's appreciation of Yang and Lin became an integral part of his social ties with well-known figures like Dong Qichang and Chen Jiru. Perhaps this explains Li Yu's decision to turn him into the matchmaker, which was indeed Wang Ranming's self-appointed role as he brought suitors to the famous courtesan Liu Rushi's attention.¹²⁵ While Dong and Chen comment on Wang's relationship with Yang and Lin in *Spring Stars*, the situation is reversed in Li Yu's play, with Wang bringing about the union of Yang and Lin with Dong and Chen, respectively.

On the most obvious level, Li Yu's play refines away the dark sides and sordid details in the lives of the historical characters involved. No mention is made, for example, of the riots in 1616—sparked by popular anger about the brutal conduct of Dong Qichang's family members or servants—that razed Dong's family compound in Songjiang.¹²⁶ Wang Ranming's writings about the historical Yang and Lin indicate that they suffered frustrations and disappointments despite their reputation for talent. But in *Ideal Matches*, the betrayed courtesan (Yang) becomes a girl from a respectable family and marries Dong, while the lonely courtesan (Lin) becomes an independent agent who finds a worthy mate in Chen. Both end up with optimal ways to assert their agency and put their talents to good use. There might have been competition between their historical counterparts, but here Lin facilitates Yang's marriage with Dong. The aesthetic appreciation of the historical Dong and Chen for Yang and Lin is translated into romantic unions.

These unions come to fruition only after many twists and turns in the plot. The play begins with Dong Qichang and Chen Jiru fulfilling their "pact of escaping fame" (*YZY* 2.323) at West Lake and pondering the option of finding "ghost painters" who can help them field endless requests for their artwork (2.324–25). In the same locale, Yang Yunyou, the daughter of a poor scholar, ekes out a living by forging Dong Qichang's paintings. Meanwhile Lin Tiansu, a famous courtesan from Fujian, has come to West Lake looking for love and recognition; her forte is to paint in Chen Jiru's style. Dong and Chen come upon the forgeries by Yang and Lin at the shop run by the monk and art dealer Shikong and are so impressed that they want to find the forgers. Shikong, hoping to marry Yang and perhaps also Lin, jealously conceals their identities. Posing as matchmaker, Shikong then comes to Yang's father and proposes to arrange her marriage with Dong Qichang, having secured the service of one Huang Tianjian (Huang the Natural Eunuch or Huang Castrated by Heaven [*tianjian* 天監]), rendered impotent by venereal disease, to pose as Dong. Shikong's plan is to take Yang to Beijing and marry her there. He covets her beauty as well as the financial potential that her talent promises: he reckons that her skills in forgery are tantamount to "an inexhaustible dowry" (3.326) and will also let him build connections with famous literati. Duped by Shikong, Yang's father agrees to let her depart for Songjiang (Dong's hometown) right after her marriage with the fake Dong Qichang (Huang Tianjian). During their boat journey, Yang realizes she has been swindled and plots revenge. With the help of Huang Tianjian and Shikong's maid Miaoxiang, she drugs Shikong and they throw his body into the river. The three of them then go to Beijing, where Yang flourishes as a painter. For protective cover, Yang continues to keep Huang as her nominal "husband" and even buys him an official appointment. It is only upon returning to West Lake that Yang sends Huang away and resumes her status as an unmarried young woman.

Interwoven with the scenes enacting the vicissitudes of Yang's fortunes is the unfolding story of Lin Tiansu. Through the intervention of Jiang Huaiyi, a friend of Chen and Dong, Lin Tiansu meets Chen Jiru and the two plight their troth. Lin wants to arrange for her parents' burial in Fujian and adopts male disguise for her southward journey. Mistaking her for a scholar, bandits in need of a record keeper kidnap her, and she survives (in male disguise) as their secretary in the bandits' mountain lair. Lin's letter eventually reaches Chen, who, however, seems helpless, until Jiang Huaiyi offers to appeal to his friend, the General Pacifying the Seas, for help. The deal is sealed when Chen Jiru sends the general a poem inscribed on a fan. Persuaded that the inclusion of the poem in Chen's collection will grant him immortality, the general launches an expedition against the bandits: the easy price of the rescue mission, premised on the momentous importance of even casual compositions of those who enjoy literary fame, is classic literati fantasy.

In the meantime, Jiang Huaiyi has been trying to arrange the match between Dong Qichang and Yang Yunyou. Being told by Yang's father about Yang Yunyou's marriage with the person he believes to be Dong Qichang, Jiang takes umbrage and believes that Dong acted in a clandestine fashion because he was wary of competition. Yang's father realizes he has been deceived only when he finds the real Dong Qichang, who takes him in, feeling guilty that "real calamities have come about because of an inflated reputation" (16.375). After the misunderstandings have been cleared up, Jiang sends a matchmaker to propose marriage on behalf of Dong Qichang (who in the meantime has left for the capital to take up an important post) upon Yang's return to West Lake, but Yang, fearing another trap, refuses. Lin Tiansu, who has been restored to Chen Jiru, is persuaded by Chen and Jiang to dress up as a man to woo Yang Yunyou (for fear that Yang may end up marrying someone other than Dong Qichang). She discloses the truth and her intention to bring about the match between Yang and Dong only after Yang "marries" her. Dong and Yang finally meet in a wedding ceremony in the final scene.

Variations on the theme of the paradoxical inversions of the genuine and the counterfeit are typical of *chuanqi* plays, especially Li Yu's oeuvre, but here they proliferate in an especially extravagant fashion and find a key metaphor in the real and fake work of art. At the beginning of the play, Dong complains about the burden of artistic fame: "All day long I fan away sweat with the force of wind and pour ink like rain—even that does not suffice to satisfy the demands of dilettantish aficionados'" (2.322). Chen joins Dong in his lament, for although he manages to resist the imperial court's summons to take up office, he finds "the polite debts of brush and ink" impossible to turn down (2.324). They decide to seek out skillful forgers of their works and keep them at hand to take over burdensome obligations, their rationale being that their instruction would suffice to infuse "true meanings" into the forgeries: "The 'Orchid Pavilion' is passed around everywhere, / Who can tell which is the genuine specimen? / So long as the sutra passed through the Buddha's hands, / It counts as the true interpretation" (2.325).[127]

Other main characters are similarly enmeshed in the boundaries between the real and the fake. The monk and art dealer Shikong, whose name can mean "truly empty" 是空 and is homophonous with *shikong* 實空, "indeed empty" or "the substance that is empty," traffics in forgeries and acts as middleman for Yang. For Shikong, such shady dealings (whose Chinese equivalent, *tuokong* 脫空、托空, also puns with his name) are symptomatic of false appearance and deviousness. For Yang Yunyou and Lin Tiansu, however, the counterfeit defines a path to truth. Yang forges Dong Qichang's works, but her forgery is also true self-expression. She paints a desolate wintry landscape in Dong's style, adding to it her dilapidated house, an old man returning home (her father), and a woman inside the house braving the cold to chant poetry (herself).[128] The quatrain she inscribes is transparently self-referential, especially the third line: "Blowing on cold hands, I transmit my likeness in the thatched house" 呵凍自傳蓬戶影 (3.327). She exclaims afterward: "He [Shikong] asked me to mimic Dong's painting, how did I come to write my own poem?" She adds Dong Qichang's signature and seal only after concluding that the undiscerning Shikong or some ignorant prospective buyer is not likely to notice the incongruities. Using Dong's name seems almost like an afterthought; the implicit reasoning being that the people who can be fooled deserve to be deceived. Yang thus internalizes Dong's style and makes it her own through distinctive self-representation. When Dong later encounters this painting, he describes it as "a forgery that reveals true emotions" (5.334). Imitation is also her way to forge a union with a projected ideal lover: "Turning to paper, I seek the man who can become a fitting mate!" (3.327).

For Lin Tiansu, a Fujian courtesan who has come to West Lake to seek her fortune, the valence of forgery is different—it is her way to seek true appreciation. She is the Fujianese southerner who wants to test the aesthetic judgment of sophisticated Jiangnan literati, but she also wants to claim due recognition. She declaims: "Let's mix fish eyes with pearls, / and see who has the Persian's discerning eye?. . . Wang Xizhi's calligraphy is superior to Xiao Cheng's. / Why did Xiao, for no good reason, steal Wang's name?" (4.331). Xiao Cheng was a notable calligrapher unjustly dismissed by the scholar and calligrapher Li Yong (678–747). By fooling Li Yong with his convincing forgery of Wang's calligraphy, Xiao Cheng challenged Li's judgment.[129] Through allusion to Xiao Cheng's story, Lin Tiansu invokes the forger's agonistic ambition and desire to be recognized. She professes trepidation about producing fake Chen Jiru paintings so close to Chen's hometown, yet she also seems to be eager for unmasking, especially if that means honest comparisons that vindicate her talents.

Who can tell the genuine from the fake? *Ideal Matches* offers us scenes of judgment and appraisal. "Test of talent" (*shicai* 試才) is a common trope in fiction and drama; the civil service examination is sometimes enacted onstage as a public performance of talent.[130] It is a measure of Li Yu's playful inversion of theatrical conventions that the middle scene(s), usually devoted to emotional climaxes or decisive turns in the plot, are taken up with parodies of the "test of talent" trope in *Ideal Matches*. In scene 14, "Exposing the Shameful Charade" (or "Exposing the Buffoon" [Luchou]), Yang Yunyou subjects her supposed husband, the fake Dong Qichang (Huang Tianjian), to tests of his knowledge about painting and poetry. Huang Tianjian, played by the clown, is reduced to bawling. His exposure embodies the comic reversal of true recognition. Before dismissing Huang as a fraud, Yang is not above suspecting "Dong Qichang" of "brandishing a label to sell lies" (*xuan biao mai huang* 懸標賣謊), perhaps because "all eyes in the world might as well be blind" (14.364).

In scene 15, "Entering the Military Tent" (Rumo), Lin Tiansu in male disguise is kidnapped by bandits who, while needing a record keeper, are yet wary of "fake scholars" and see fit to administer a test. After farcical exchanges on impossible tests, the bandits settle on singing, because they "have heard that recently famous men of letters are all capable of taking up roles on the stage."[131] After Lin Tiansu sings an operatic aria, the bandits exclaim: "Marvelous! The voice is melodious and the manner refined. This is a man of letters for sure!" (15.368). Beyond the obvious joke that the literati may not claim to matter more than entertainers, Lin's performance, just like Huang's failure, is the inversion of noble self-revelation and true recognition. At the same time, these two climactic middle scenes about fakery and masquerade also reveal the truth. By exposing the charade of the fake Dong Qichang, Yang Yunyou begins her journey of self-assertion. By pretending to be a literatus, Lin Tiansu also finds new powers.

Appraising worth is a problematic proposition, perhaps in an even more profound way, in the scenes marking the relationship between the male and female protagonists. In scene 5, "Encountering the Paintings" (Huayu), Dong Qichang and Chen Jiru come upon the forgeries by Yang Yunyou and Lin Tiansu and are cast into momentary confusion as they try to remember whether they have in fact painted those works. Dong exclaims about Yang's work, "The painting does seem to be authentic, but the calligraphy of the signature is a bit too deliberate and makes one somewhat suspicious": "Hard it is to appraise whether it is real or not, / It leaves one convinced yet suspicious" (5.334). The marker of difference—the covert signature, as it were—is Yang's self-referential poem describing her poverty, which makes Dong wonder why the same talent should confer on him wealth and honor while denying recognition for the unknown woman artist. This injustice strikes him much more forcibly than the forger's intention to deceive. Chen is similarly confused: the copy of his style is perfect while betraying a "feminine charm." The signature seems the only clue: "Could it be that I shied away from putting down my own name / and asked someone else to write it?" (5.334).

Poems and paintings conveying a person's essence and functioning to mediate longing recur as a standard trope in romantic fiction and drama. Here the encounter with forgeries of one's work raises new questions. How does donning a mask or imitating another facilitate self-expression? Is there an inalienable essence that ties a work to its creator? What is the truth behind forgeries—the fact of deception or the mystique of perfect recognition? Instead of being outraged or dismissive, Dong and Chen probe the perimeters of their own endeavors and value the forgeries as the creations of kindred spirits. The projected romance is, however, based on practical calculations. Having established that Lin Tiansu painted the fan bearing his signature, Chen declares: "I will marry her so that she can wield the brush on my behalf" (5.336). Dong's aria in the final scene (30.416–17), when he meets and marries Yang Yunyou, alludes to the same arrangement.

In scene 5, Dong and Chen are the connoisseurs who assign value. The power in the gaze of appraisal again comes into play, only on a grander scale, when Yang Yunyou sets up shop as a "performing painter" in Beijing (scene 21, "Rolling Up the Curtain" [Juanlian]). At first Yang paints behind curtains, but her clients clamor to have the visual obstacle removed, charging that a man hiding behind the curtains is wielding the brush for her.[132] Even after the curtain is raised, they demand to have the skirt of the desk removed—the ostensible reason is the absurd allegation that a man hiding under the desk is helping her; the real issue is of course their prurient interest in the smallness of her bound feet. The spectacle of the woman artist painting is eroticized and becomes part of her aura as object of desire—Li Yu implicitly shares the same aesthetics in the arias devoted to this theme.[133]

Yang is fully aware of the implicit transaction. These patrons claim to be interested in her art, but their real concern is whether she is for sale. Instead of venting her indignation (which she can ill afford since these are the buyers of her paintings), she exploits the situation and turns the table on them by becoming their appraiser. For each spectator she offers a painting that sums up his character. For a particularly insistent and lecherous client, she paints on his handkerchief a monkey stealing fruit to mimic his "painted face with furtive glances" (the character is played by the *jing*, the comic villain with a painted face). For a more rustic and honest onlooker, she paints "a fisherman and a woodcutter who abide by their lot." She compares an aged admirer to "a lean crane facing the wind" and captures the impossibility of his desire with a scene of "the plantain in winter" (plantains flourish only in the summer). She seems to convey measured approval for a man with a faraway expression and a flowing beard, painting "a lone pine on a hill" as his objective correlative (21.388). The man who receives the painting of a monkey stealing fruit fantasizes about Yang's meaningful gaze, but his companions remind him: "She did not look only at you, we have all been looked over by her" (21.389). The demonstration of Yang's skill as a painter—the confirmation of its truth through public scrutiny—potentially reduces her to the status of a commodity, but she counters it by returning the gaze of evaluation, objectifying her clients and evaluating the worth of the gawkers through painted images that bypass their economic power as buyers of her paintings.

Yang sells her paintings for survival but also as one way to meet the right man, although the only upshot is the unwelcome attention of one persistent suitor (the aforementioned recipient of the monkey painting). Upon her return to West Lake, she sets up "tests of talent" to choose a fitting mate. The conceit in *Ideal Matches* is that the test of aspiring suitors, a standard convention in late imperial literature,[134] does correct the fiasco of the earlier test that exposed a fake "Dong Qichang" (scene 14) and yield a candidate of talent and beauty—only this is a woman (Lin Tiansu) in male disguise (scene 28, "Trick Marriage" [Kuangyin]). Cross-dressing is a common plot twist in romantic fiction and drama. Li Yu uses the scene to spin ever more paradoxical inversions of the real thing and the counterfeit. Lin Tiansu presents herself as a male suitor but reveals her identity through a quatrain on "Mulan Joining the Army," the poetic topic set by Yang Yunyou: "She dons armor and takes the place of another in the army, / Forcing men to retreat—none knows her as a woman. / Do not say that repairing heaven is not a woman's task: / The goddess Nügua was after all not a man" 蛾眉披甲代行師，掃退群雄不識雌。莫道補天非女職，媧皇原不是男兒 (28.406). This is genuine self-expression (recalling her exploits among bandits) but also equivocation that lies like truth.

At the same time, the scene presents perfect self-revelation and mutual recognition. Yang Yunyou reverses the logic of her "objectification" and feminizes her supposedly male suitor: not only does Lin have to pass tests of poetic talent and painterly skills, she is asked to "take a few dainty steps" to demonstrate the ethereal grace of her gait. Male connoisseurship of female charms often pays attention to the style of walking, which is considered the best clue to the size of bound feet.[135] In some ways the fake courtship enacts a moment of ideal self-fulfillment for both: Yang Yunyou gets even with the world by exercising the power of choice and by treating her prospective husband like a woman, while Lin Tiansu gains the satisfaction of acting like a man and a knight-errant by controlling the fate of others. In an earlier scene, when Chen Jiru and Jiang Huaiyi marvel at Lin's convincing male disguise, she sings of the power of her "inner man": "Who is the male phoenix? Who is the female one? / If your spirit can envelop your body, / Then the female would become male. / To gain a form erect and distinguished, / First let your spirit soar. / What's more, there are very few real men in the world, / Most of them are but varieties of women" (13.358). Male disguise is for Lin not merely expediency, it confirms her indomitable spirit.[136]

In that sense the ideal match *is* between Yang Yunyou and Lin Tiansu, perfectly paired in fulfilling their respective fantasies of power and agency as well as talent and beauty: "talent brings them together, / painterly skill is the matchmaker" (28.408). They also share a similar fate, suffering adversities while preserving their chastity (27.404). Furthermore, this is the most romantic scene in the play: unlike the scenes devoted to the relationship between the male and female protagonists, empathy and mutual recognition here are divested of economic and practical considerations. A mood of intimacy develops: both Yang and Lin disrobe, for the moment of truth can only be dramatized when the cross-dressed Lin reveals her luxuriant tresses, slender waist, and bound feet. Li Yu toys with the idea that the illusion is punctured only when blissful union is most tantalizingly close. In the scheme of the play, Lin's disguise is a necessary ruse to bring about the union of Yang and Dong. However, the details of the deception, lovingly realized, allow Li Yu to play with the idea of the ideal match between the two women and its impossibility.

The fraudulent can be comically unmasked (e.g., Huang Tianjian in scene 14), but, more often than not, deception can be earnest (as with forgeries by Yang and Lin) or plain good fun (as when Lin fools the bandits or woos Yang). Liars inadvertently tell the truth, as when Shikong claims that Dong wants to marry Yang (7.342). Even the artist cannot confidently establish the hierarchy of his real work and the counterfeit (5.334–35), and appraisal turns out to be as much power play as aesthetic judgment (21.387–89). Why does Li Yu delight in such inversions and shifting boundaries? On the most basic level it is a celebration of artistic license; his self-congratulation that the playwright can right the wrongs of history as he arranges ideal matches. He brings this up in the opening aria summarizing the play: "The matches onstage do not rely on heaven; / they belong to a special Romantic Ministry" (1.321). He declares in the final aria in the last scene: "All thanks to a man of letters who recreates heaven, / Regrets can be retold, but not in vain, from the beginning." The exit verse reiterates the point: "Master Li is undaunted by poverty all these years: / Accustomed as he is to fighting Heaven with his fragile brush. / Beauties are snatched back and restored to men of talent, / And teary eyes can be transformed into a smiling countenance" (30.417).

This self-conscious valorization of theatricality is also Li Yu's way of addressing some of the contradictions in late Ming sensibility and social reality, notable in the economic transactions pertaining to the art market and the world of courtesans. As mentioned earlier, Dong Qichang identified many long lost "genuine works," reaching his conclusions by a somewhat mysterious process. He might have been guilty of inadvertently promoting forgeries. Both Chen and Dong seem to have monetized their reputation by employing others to write or paint on their behalf. Chen Jiru celebrated the forgeries of Dong Qichang as a mark of his greatness. He was also witness to the dramatic increase in the market value of Dong's calligraphy and painting. "As for paintings and calligraphy [in his name], less than one out of ten come from his hands. But as for those making a living by borrowing his name, their forgeries often circulate in the capital and spread all the way to foreign peoples. Fragments of his works sell for pieces of gold. He is the only one whose works have risen in reputation and value a hundredfold in my lifetime. This too is wondrous."[137] What is being marketed is also the image of the artist in demand. One account tells of the eighty-year-old Dong Qichang in 1629 at West Lake: "He could scarcely meet the demands even as he wrought his brush with flying speed. Ink soaked his sleeves: he was truly one of the immortals."[138] Huang Zongxi also described boats lining up for miles as prospective clients waited to obtain Chen Jiru's calligraphy.[139] One could lament how "the genuine spirit" is compromised by transactions (no matter how politely concealed), but Li Yu chooses to celebrate the image of the performing artist as a mode of self-expression and the vindication of the value of art.

Late Ming courtesans were romanticized as alluring goddesses and eulogized for their talents and passions, at the same time the reality of dependence and economic transaction was never far off.[140] Writings on Yang Yunyou and Lin Tiansu share this dual focus, as shown in the earlier discussion of Wang Ranming's *Spring Stars*. As mentioned, apparently at least one of Yang's marriages ended unhappily. Extant sources are silent on whether Lin married; she might have made a living by selling her paintings as she dwindled into middle age. The male literati liked to project a self-image as knight-errant (*xia* 俠) or "knight in yellow clothes" (*huangshan ke* 黃衫客) in the courtesans' world, offering succor to courtesans in distress, playing matchmaker, and glorying in the tension between friendship and sexual innuendoes. That was the role that Wang Ranming played (or imagined playing) vis-à-vis Yang Yunyou and Lin Tiansu, and that is how the historical Lin Tiansu referred to him in the aforementioned preface to *Liu Rushi's Letters*. In fact, he did not seem to have been able to do much to allay their disappointments and frustrations, as evident in his writings about them discussed earlier. Besides being familiar with the paradoxical combination of romance and transaction in the lives of courtesans (as an integral part of his social world), Li Yu would have known the particulars about Yang and Lin through his friendship with Wang Ranming and with Huang Yuanjie, whose comments on the play indicate familiarity with Yang's story. In some ways Li Yu is fulfilling Wang Ranming's ambition to play the role of the knight errant through the character of Jiang Huaiyi. Of course, on another level it is Li Yu who, by bringing about the ideal unions, truly realizes the fantasy of being "the knight in yellow clothes," as he declares in the opening aria: "Talented scholars had their love karma shriveled in former lives, / beauties drowned in regrets in earthen springs. / For them the hero in yellow clothes clamors for justice. / Chanting, the knight of the brush strokes his beard in excitement" (*YZY* 1.321).

Artistic expression, aesthetic appreciation, and romantic passion are sometimes lauded as ways of being genuine that rise above economic considerations, yet as the lives of the historical Dong, Chen, Yang, and Lin demonstrate, these categories could be determined by economic realities and the calculations of transaction. In *Ideal Matches*, the economic problematization of genuineness becomes its own solution. The literatus and scholar-official permitting (or facilitating) forgeries of their own works are seeking room for genuine self-cultivation. Their forgers encode their real hopes and fears through forgeries. Courtesans no longer negotiate the treacherous margin between agency and commodification: in the play, moments of danger and potential degradation facilitate heroic action. The specter of prostitution becomes artistic self-revelation and authoritative judgment, as when Yang Yunyou paints in front of her gawking suitors. Romantic union is also the perfect economic transaction: women artists struggling for survival are now gainfully employed, using their talents and their bodies to earn security and social standing. Men of letters and scholar-officials enjoying fame as artists turn their names into brands and repeatable performances by their concubines and thereby claim the artist's freedom from external demands.

It is in light of these complexities that we can fully appreciate the irony of the grand finale in scene 30, "Encountering the Real One" (Huizhen). The title indicates that after her marriage with the fake Dong Qichang and suspicious refusal to marry the real Dong, which results in her "marriage" with the cross-dressing Lin Tiansu, Yang Yunyou finally gets to meet "the real one" (i.e., the real Dong Qichang). The term *huizhen* also means, from the male perspective, "encountering the goddess (or the courtesan)" and recurs in romantic-erotic poetry and fiction.[141] Dong and Yang are meeting for the first time, but they share a history of "spiritual intercourse" (*shenjiao* 神交, 30.415) mediated by their respective paintings. This perfect understanding prompts Dong to dismiss the quest for the "genuine specimen" in art: "If, having one who will wield the brush in my name by the bedside, / I still try to create the real 'Orchid Pavilion,'[142] / the effort will be in vain, as I must realize. / From now on the jade brush will not be mine to hold: / All will be given to the female hero" (30.416–17). The ideal match in question is thus not only between a beauty and a talented scholar but also one uniting the artist and his forger.

BEYOND THE ECONOMIC SOLUTION

Does the proliferation of forgeries, copies, and imitations lead to more general anxieties about the "fakeness" of people, social practices, or conventional morality? We recall the iconoclastic thinker Li Zhi's (1527–1602) indignation about insincerity and bad faith in his world: "For if the person is fake, then there is nothing that is not fake. As a result, if one speaks fake words to fake people, then they are glad. If one talks about fake affairs to fake people, then they are glad. If one discusses fake writings with fake people, then they are glad. If there is nothing but fakes, then there is nothing but gladness. If the stage is filled with fake people, how can the short ones [who cannot really see what is on stage] tell the difference?"[143]

The ubiquitous fake replicas of ideal prototypes in a work like *Jin Ping Mei*—from literati refinement to heroic brotherhood—render the very proposition of normative elegance problematic. Nevertheless, there is no particular attempt to link "fake things" to "fake people" in *Jin Ping Mei*. By contrast, Ding Yaokang (1599–1669) makes an apparently logical leap from forgeries to hypocrisy and venality in his sequel to *Jin Ping Mei* (*Xu Jin Ping Mei*), focusing on literati pretensions and fraudulence that put authorship and the authority of attribution into question: "Even more laughable are those who borrowed the good poems and fine prose of others and have them published as their own works, or put down the signatures of famous masters on their own calligraphy, paintings, or writings. And then there are those social recluses and elegant hangers-on who produce fake books, sell fake calligraphy and fake antiques . . . and then there are those fake gentlemen of renown, fake cohort of examinees, fake students of the academy, fake successful candidates. . . . Hence it is said: what suits people of this world are fakes, not the real thing."[144] During the Ming-Qing transition, when princes sank to anonymity (if they survived), when the cases about the real and fake crown prince and the real and fake Consort Tong in the Hongguang Court sowed confusion,[145] and when the claim of remnant Ming courts to legitimate mandate (i.e., the question as to whether they could be considered real heirs of the Ming dynasty) continued to raise hopes and fears, questions of distinguishing the real and the fake seemed fraught with political dangers and contradictions.

Perhaps what is remarkable is how rarely the materials we discussed venture into such moralizations or politicization. For example, Shen Defu's disparaging remarks about Wu literati may seem to come close to Ding Yaokang's opprobrium, but he also chronicles valid aesthetic judgment by himself and others. He also seems blissfully unaware of irony as he assigns the name of a Tang master to an unknown work. More generally, there is in the discourse on connoisseurship a focus on aesthetic judgments that sometimes displaces moral considerations. In some cases, the arbitrariness of values even leads to a fascination with trickery and price manipulation, as in some *biji* anecdotes and Cheng Kezhong's tale "Tang Biaobei." The moral dimension of distinguishing the real from the fake surfaces in some writings about the rapacity of the powerful as they hanker after authentic masterworks; we see this forcefully delineated in *Snow*. Dramatic tension based on erasing or manipulating differences (between the real and the fake jade cup, the real and the substitute head), orchestrated by Tang Qin, finds resolution in another kind of substitution: a servant (Mo Cheng) and a concubine (Xueyan) who embrace martyrdom by fulfilling the role of their master and mistress.

In contrast to such stark moral equations, *Ideal Matches* proposes a celebration of the unstable boundaries between the real and the counterfeit: the counterfeit does not usurp the position of the real; instead, the two seem complementary. Economic calculations and transactional romance, instead of being decried as a corruption of sincerity and authenticity, become the foundation of optimal pleasures and contentment. In some ways, Li Yu's radical solution stands outside the mainstream of Chinese literary tradition. *Ideal Matches* continued to be performed in Kun opera and eventually Beijing opera and other regional operas as a love story and a comedy of errors;[146] the ironic implications of celebrating the artist's union with his forger and of proposing the complementarity of the genuine artwork and its counterfeit do not take center stage.

The question of the real and the fake, when it is not moralized, tends to be absorbed into metaphysical ruminations about reality and illusion. Li Yu's genius is to bring genuine emotions and earnest self-expression to the creation and appreciation of the counterfeit. The more dominant mode, however, is to put subjectivity in the very crucible of reality and illusion—that is, turn desire into the engine of subjective illumination that can transform reality into illusion and vice versa. When the dialectics of reality and illusion is intertwined with that of love and its transcendence, we enter the world of *Honglou meng*.

The mutual implication of these two sets of dialectics (reality and illusion, love and its transcendence) in *Honglou meng* has been discussed in terms of the parameters of lyricism and fictionality.[147] But illusionistic play is also aesthetic pleasure, as we see in Li Yu's *Leisure Notes*. Shang Wei links the fascination with illusionism in *Honglou meng* to trompe l'oeil in contemporary visual culture in court and aristocratic circles.[148] We recall that the visit of the imperial consort to the Grand View Garden takes place at the coldest time of the year, but artificial flowers and birds made from silk and feathers brighten the bare branches. It is as if nature-defying imitations can be a superior marker of imperial glory.

More generally, the play with perspectives, distance, pictorial allusions, and optical illusions is endemic to Chinese garden aesthetics.[149]

Illusion as aesthetic pleasure is built into the narrative of *Honglou meng*, especially in the chapters devoted to Grand View Garden. Conjured up through dreams, memories, and private myths, the Grand View Garden is maze-like, full of mirrors, reflections, visual tricks, and sudden changes in perspective—it seems to reflect the pleasures of actual gardens even as it embodies the dialectics of reality and illusion. In other words, the aesthetics of illusion in *Honglou meng* is built on Daoist and Buddhist metaphysics but also lingers lovingly on the pleasure of confusion and steers clear of explicit moralization. Baoyu's room, with its plate glass mirror and illusionistic painting of a girl, is the realm where visitors get lost and momentarily fail to recognize themselves (*HLM* 17/18.171–72, 41.440–41) and where he can dream of visiting his double Zhen Baoyu, who is also looking for him (56.619–21).[150] Optical illusion and the mirroring process are experienced as enchantment rather than the beginning of enlightenment—this is true even in the most symbolically overdetermined scene, when Jia Baoyu dreams of his double Zhen Baoyu. A dream that can provoke questions on the limits of consciousness and the boundaries of selfhood does not have its subversive potential turned into something truly disturbing, although the fact that it comes in the wake of the discussion of economic reforms in the garden (see chapter 2) may drive home how the tension between aesthetics and economics (and attendant ruminations on elegance and vulgarity) is bracketed by questions of illusion and reality.[151]

Illusion is linked to fakery only when it seems to support a moral agenda, as when Baoyu and his father Jia Zheng debate the meaning of "naturalness" (*tianran* 天然) during their first tour of the garden (17/18.167). A corner of the Grand View Garden is made to look rustic, with a thatched house and domestic animals. Jia Zheng sighs in admiration and declares that the vision of "nature" inspires him to consider the eremitic ideal. Baoyu, on the other hand, points out how artificial rustic charm is the opposite of "naturalness." This part of the garden will later be named "Sweet Rice Village," and Baoyu's widowed sister-in-law Li Wan will live there with her son. Li Wan became a widow at a very young age and makes peace with her fate by abjuring desire, her heart turning into "withered wood and dead ashes" (4.36) in the aristocratic household. By the standards of her society, Li Wan is a praiseworthy and virtuous woman. A well-born woman who loses her husband has no choice but to remain a loyal and chaste widow for the rest of her life. Cao Xueqin seems to use the "fake naturalness" of her abode to question what conventional morality passes off as inevitable and natural.

If the pleasure of illusion prevails despite (or perhaps because of) the sense of its transience and fragility and the paradoxical mutuality of reality and illusion persists in the first eighty chapters, the polarity and hierarchy of the real and the fake come to the fore in the last forty chapters. Baoyu loses the jade he is born with and is reduced to a state of befuddlement or even semi-idiocy. A fake jade presented to the family deepens his confusion. Throughout the novel, the jade has a double life as a reminder of Baoyu's mythic origins as the stone deemed unfit to repair heaven and as an object with magical potency. By the end of the novel, the jade as the magical object embodying Baoyu's consciousness dramatizes a trajectory of renunciation: the Monk restores the jade to Baoyu, but he will want to give it back, a symbol of renouncing desire (jade [*yu* 玉] is homophonous with desire [*yu* 欲]). The ending of the novel is concerned with reestablishing order, and rival conceptions of order—such as Confucian engagement and Buddhist or Daoist renunciation—find moments of reconciliation. The problem of desire has been tamed through the trajectory of the real thing—the real jade that is lost and found, only to be given up when Baoyu embraces enlightenment.

CHAPTER FOUR

Lost and Found

In charting the discourses on elegance versus vulgarity and on the real versus the fake from late Ming to early Qing, I included postconquest examples from Li Yu's corpus. Li Yu's distinct spin on these issues seems to be part and parcel of his delight in ingenuity and in inverting conventional paradigms, although one may also read his unique combination of irony, pragmatism, and measured hedonism as a response to the late Ming emphasis on exquisite sensibility and genuine expression. Any overly neat dichotomy of cultural trends before and after the dynastic transition must be treated with caution, however. As mentioned in chapter 2, manuals and treatises on objects and refined living continued to flourish into early Qing, although informal essays did diminish in number. Only one aspect of the discourse on things showed the unmistakable stamp of political turmoil—the accounts of how artworks or material objects are lost in the conflagration of Ming collapse and of how they sometimes come into the possession of new owners. The figure of the collector-connoisseur, so central to late Ming sensibility, acquires new sociopolitical meanings in early Qing. He is now the purveyor of memories, the defender or critic of aesthetic absorption, or the participant in social networks inviting political interpretations.

OWNERSHIP AND LOSS

Ownership is ephemeral and illusory: this is the recurrent refrain in the literature of connoisseurship. In *Famous Paintings*, Zhang Yanyuan chronicles the destruction of imperial collections due to warfare and political disorder. His own family collection suffered a no less grievous loss. Zhang's grandfather was pressured to yield some of the finest works in his collection to the throne in 818 when a jealous eunuch spread word about its excellence. More works were lost in the 820s during the rebellion of the regional commander Zhu Kerong. In that sense, Zhang Yanyuan's *Famous Paintings*, preserving what he "appraised with his mind and eyes," is the textual bulwark against oblivion. Possessions are like "mist and clouds passing before one's eyes" (*yanyun guoyan* 煙雲過眼), a term that first appears in Su Shi's "Account of the Hall of Treasured Paintings" (see chapter 1). What remains are textual traces. From Li Qingzhao's (1084–1155) "Postscript to the *Record of Bronzes and Stones*" (*Jinshi lu* houxu) to Yuan Haowen's (1190–1257) "Treatise on Bygone Things" (Guwu pu), the loss of personal possessions prompts nostalgic retrospection as well as philosophical ruminations on the meaning of ownership and the intersection of individual loss with dynastic collapse.

Zhou Mi (1232–1308) borrowed Su Shi's phrase to entitle his inventory of private art collections in Hangzhou, *Record of Clouds and Mist Passing Before One's Eyes (Yunyan guoyan lu)*. Unlike earlier catalogs that categorized artworks according to artist or subject matter, Zhou Mi used ownership as the organizational principle. Since the Mongol conquest accounted for the dispersal of the Song imperial collection as well as the private collections of rich and aristocratic families, Zhou's catalog of current and previous owners inevitably evokes a mood of ephemerality and the pathos of dynastic collapse. Going beyond the loyalist reading, Ankeney Weitz argues that *Records of Clouds and Mist* also testified to the social interactions between the literati nostalgic for the fallen Song and the new elite of the Yuan regime.[1]

Zhou Mi's work is often cited as precedents for early Qing works that dwell on the fate of objects and their owners. A notable example is *Notes from the Resonant Rock Studio (Yunshi zhai bitan)* by Jiang Shaoshu (ca. 1580–ca. 1650s).[2] Jiang held office under the Ming and also served in the

Hongguang court. His studio name is probably linked to his interest in rocks.³ Unlike Zhou Mi's catalog, Jiang's book offers detailed descriptions in a manner typical of contemporary treatises on artworks and curios. A pervasive mood of impermanence entwined with a deep understanding of the possessive drive as well as the pleasure of connoisseurship accounts for its pathos.

Jiang Qing, in his preface to *Resonant Rock* (1649), praises Jiang Shaoshu as one who "takes pleasure in things without indulging in things, finds enjoyment for his mind without allowing its stagnation in absorption." This is a standard defense evoking, for example, Su Shi's "Record of the Hall of Treasured Paintings" (see chapter 1). As evidence he mentions a few examples of loss and destruction enumerated in the book and avers an implicitly cautionary note. The collector and artist Xiang Yuanbian, for example, put numerous seals on the artworks he owned and kept careful record of transactions (as mentioned in chapters 2 and 3), but these attempts to confirm possession failed to protect the Xiang collection from dispersal. During the wars of Ming-Qing transition, "the Xiang family collection that took generations to accumulate was thoroughly plundered by the local commander Wang Liushui and nothing remained. Is it not vain to make a thousand-year plan? The supreme specimens of things should be all regarded as mist and clouds passing before one's eyes" (*YSZ* B.17a–18a). Along the same lines, an entry on a gathering in 1637, when Jiang's friend He Qingqiu described a jadeite inkstone he inherited from his father, ends with the wholesale destruction of He's possessions when roving bandits overran He's hometown Suizhou (A.12a–12b).

At stake are not simply the vicissitudes of personal fortunes but the very symbolic quotient of objects in an age of disorder. An imperial jade "seal of mandate" (*yuxi* 玉璽) inscribed with lines about the mandate of heaven was discovered in Henan in 1624. But this supposedly auspicious omen, instead of confirming heaven's favor and auguring prolonged Ming rule, only highlighted the abuse of power—the eunuch Wei Zhongxian ordered all provincial officials to come to the capital to offer congratulations—and certainly did nothing to forestall the fall of the Ming dynasty twenty years later. Jiang Shaoshu is skeptical about authenticity of the seal, supposedly created during the Qin dynasty and passed on through generations to rulers who could claim legitimate mandate. He believes that the seal vanished when the last Yuan emperor "fled with it to the desert" (A.17a–18b).

There are also examples of sentient objects responding to the contemporary crisis. In 1646, when Jiang Shaoshu was in Nanjing, his friends told him about the current copper shortage and noted that cauldrons in the imperial treasury were destined for smelting. Three cauldrons, weighing six to seven hundred catties each, were heard to cry out at night, "just like dragons murmuring in a secluded valley." Some monks heard about this and managed to raise funds to redeem them: "Because of that the weighty vessels of a thousand years escaped the pit of fire and ascended to the realm of lotuses, forever guarding a Buddhist temple" (A.20a–20b). Mysterious affinities govern the union and separation of things. Li Binzhai, who inherited a rare jade box from his father, accidentally encountered its cover among random items offered by a vendor. This fateful conjoining of component parts, however, did not mean that the treasure stayed in the family. Li died without progeny, and the box was sold to the early Qing collector Ji Yuyong, in whose studio Jiang got to see it (A.8b–9b).

In some cases, the fall of the Ming is the unstated but unmistakable backdrop to the fate of things and their owners. How did political upheaval affect notions of ownership? Jiang Qing mentions in the preface that Jiang Shaoshu resigned from his official position in 1645 when others were still vying for power and position, "preserving his heaven-endowed nature" and finding consolation in studying and evaluating calligraphy, paintings, and other objects of art in a secluded garden east of his abode (1a–2a). In telling of the fate of the "King Wen [of Zhou] cauldron" (A.4a–6b), supposedly datable to the eleventh century BCE, Jiang describes it in detail and eventually casts doubt on its authenticity, noting that he had the chance to see it in the summer of 1645, when he was "escaping the heat" in clan fields close to the house of the antique dealer He Rixian, who had the cauldron in his possession at that point. (He Rixian had obtained it from the widow of the merchant and official Huang Zhengbin, his friend and would-be partner in a venture to open a shop for antiques and artworks in Suzhou.) No mention is made of the Qing conquest of the South and the collapse of the Hongguang court at that juncture. Han Siwei, a former Ming official, wanted to buy the cauldron in 1645, but "just then he was heading north"—that is, he was going to Beijing to take up office under the Qing. In Beijing Han met Wang Yong, brother of the calligrapher and scholar-official Wang Duo (1592–1652), another "turncoat." In 1648, when Wang Yong was on his way to take up office at Jinqu (Zhejiang), he met Jiang Shaoshu and showed him his rich collection of paintings and antique vessels. Jiang was ecstatic, "it was as if I had entered the mythical garden Xuanpu." Not long after, He Rixian died and Wang Yong bought the cauldron. In this account there is no mention of politics, but clearly connoisseurship offered psychological escape from political turmoil, and the new collectors were often those who chose to serve in the Qing government.

One of the longest entries in the book is devoted to a white Ding cauldron-censer (A.12b–17a), so-called because it was produced in the Ding kiln in the early twelfth century during the final years of the Northern Song. The history of its ownership in early and mid-Ming testifies to the cultural authority of the elite from Danyang (in Jiangsu), whence Jiang hailed.[4] Jiang Shaoshu's maternal grandfather, Sun Zhen, owned it at one point. Jiang records with relish the literary gathering of his maternal great grandfather (Sun Zhen's father Sun Yu) with famous Suzhou literati, including Tang Yin and Zhu Yunming (1460–1526). Tang's poem, carved on the rocks at Sun's house at Southern Mountain, had faded with time. Jiang lovingly records it and adds his own harmonizing poem.[5] It might have been through the social ties of Sun Yu and his brother Sun Fang (1511 *jinshi*) that the Dingware censer acquired an inscription by the famous scholar-official Li Dongyang (1447–1516) on its stand. In other words, the early history of this vessel evokes glorious family history as well as notions of rightful ownership and tasteful appreciation.

The Sun family suffered when Japanese pirates attacked Danyang in 1555 and lost much of its collection. The Dingware censer came to be owned by Tang Hezheng (1571 *jinshi*), son of the famous scholar-official Tang Shunzhi (1507–1560). The artisan Zhou Danquan, famous for his uncanny ability to create replicas, asked to observe the Ding ware, measured it against his hand, and copied the design.[6]

> He returned half a year later and took out a censer from his sleeve, saying, "As for the white Dingware censer in your family, I have obtained another one." Tang Hezheng was greatly shocked and compared it with the one in his collection. There was not the

slightest difference. When placed on the stand of the old censer, it fit seamlessly. Tang asked whence it came. Zhou Danquan said, "When formerly I asked to borrow it for viewing, I used my hand to measure it twice. The reason I did so was to assess its size and weight. The truth is I made a replica—I would not deceive you." Tang sighed in admiration, bought it for forty taels and kept both the copy and the original at home.
(*YSZ* A.13b–14a)

Sometime later, during the final years of the Wanli reign (1572–1620), the rich merchant Du Jiuru, who "angled for rare items to enhance his fame," insisted on seeing the Ding vessel, which was now in the possession of Tang Hezheng's grandson Tang Junyu.[7] Junyu "in jest" showed him the replica. Du was so enamored of it that he forced Tang to sell it to him for a thousand taels of silver and rewarded the middleman with two hundred taels. Ashamed of the deception, Tang sent someone to tell Du the truth, but the latter thought it was a ploy to get the Dingware back. Tang had no choice but to show the real specimen: "It was just like Curly Beard meeting the Tang emperor Taizong. Although both possessed the mien of dragons and tigers, the one that glowed with an aura was naturally distinct from ordinary ware. Thus does one know that Du Jiuru's obsession was nothing more than the way Lord She loved dragons:[8] it was not true appreciation, and in his generosity and understanding Tang Junyu far surpassed others" (A.14b).

At this point the narrative is somewhat unclear: we are told that, upon Du Jiuru's death, the vessel was passed on to his son Du Shengzhi. Was this the real Dingware censer or the replica? Presumably it was the former, although the narrative is silent on whether Tang Junyu finally sold the real Dingware to Du. The narrative then turns to the exploits of the devious art and antique dealer Wang Yueshi, who obtained the Dingware censer from Du Shengzhi through calculated and well-timed loans.[9] Wang tried to control the market for Dingware by collecting similar items, perhaps as a way to pass off counterfeit Dingware as authentic—the rarer such items became, the harder it would be for critical consensus to emerge. Among Wang's victims was the collector and scholar-official Ji Yuyong, who unleashed his fury on Wang when he discovered that Wang had sold him a fake vessel. Jiang Shaoshu notes elsewhere that Ji, a distinguished calligrapher and painter, did not turn away dealers who brought him fakes, reasoning thus: "I just follow my own inclinations. If I inclusively seek fine works long enough, authentic works would naturally come to me. This is just like the buying the bones of a fine horse at Yantai and finally obtaining the steed that gallops a thousand miles."[10] In this case, Ji might have been offended by how Wang held his judgment in contempt. Wang did not bother to produce a replica; he sold Ji a square censer with four legs. A friend who had seen the real Dingware told Ji that it was a round tripod. The furious Ji enjoined another official to have Wang arrested. Wang escaped imprisonment by fobbing Ji off with more counterfeits.

The Dingware censer was finally destroyed amid an undignified squabble. Wang's cousin Huang Zhengbin, the aforementioned collector and an official with a merchant background, entrusted Wang with the sale of a Ni Zan painting. Suspicious of Wang's tricks, Huang added a seal mark in a hidden corner of the painting. When Huang's servant Foyuan came to fetch the painting, Wang replaced the original with a copy. Foyuan noticed that the painting and the way it is mounted looked the same, but the seal mark was missing.

> Foyuan, a shrewd person, lied: "My master is coming not only to take the painting back, he also wants to take a look at the Dingware censer and discuss its price." Just as Wang Yueshi gave the censer to Foyuan, Huang Zhengbin arrived. He said to Wang, "The painting has not been sold for all this time, and you should be returning the original to me. Why are you resorting to your tricks?" Wang slapped his forehead and swore. Huang asked him, "I made a private mark—where is it now?" Just as they were arguing and blaming each other, Foyuan held on to the censer from the side and twined his fingers in the ears of the censer to show that it would not be returned. Wang tried to grab it, and the censer fell on the ground and broke like a tile. Wang hurled himself against Huang in extreme anger and frustration and injured Huang's ribs. At the time Huang Zhengbin had just been driven away by the Hongguang emperor and he was deeply unhappy. Further, he was humiliated by Wang Yueshi, and he passed away overnight.
> (YSZ A.16a–16b)

Wang Yueshi made his way to Hangzhou, where the Prince of Lu (Zhu Changfang), one of the Ming princes around whom remnants of anti-Qing resistance gather, sent his attendant Yu Qiyun to Wang to make enquiries about the Dingware censer. Wang Yueshi sold a fake version to the prince for two thousand taels of silver, with Yu taking a cut of four hundred taels. The Prince of Lu, leading a doomed cause, was then "in the midst of dislocation," and a clumsy kitchen servant was put in charge of the prince's treasures. When the prince asked to see the censer, one foot broke off as the servant removed it from its box; the servant was so terrified that he drowned himself. Not long after, Yu threw the broken censer into the Qiantang River.

Jiang comments in the voice of "the Unofficial Historian" (A.16b–17a): a cauldron is a "weighty vessel" with ritual significance and firmly established bronze prototypes—there is no place for ceramic imitations. He also notes with disparagement recent trends that elevate not only Song ceramics but also ceramics from the Xuande and Chenghua reigns, implying that such inflated value is symptomatic of the disorder of the times.[11] The story of the Dingware censer is a series of substitutions of the counterfeit for the real. While Zhou Danquan maintains artistic integrity in producing a replica, Tang Junyu may have been momentarily tempted by the lucrative ruse he almost practices on Du Jiuru. When Wang Yueshi enters the story, the deception becomes calculated and the motive is frankly mercenary. The Dingware censer that comes into his possession, which may or may not be authentic, allows him to control the market and produce forgeries. The final tussle that destroys the censer exposes greed at its most petty. Its replica continues to wreak havoc and destruction.

Jiang Qing in his preface cites Huang Zhengbin's demise as a cautionary tale demonstrating the absurdity of losing one's life over mere things. The political implications of the conclusion of this somewhat rambling account are also tragic and chilling. Many officials (especially members of Donglin and Fushe) initially supported the Prince of Lu over the Prince of Fu (Zhu Yousong) as the head of the rump Ming court in Nanjing after Beijing fell to the rebels and then the Qing in the spring and summer of 1644. The Prince of Fu prevailed and reigned as the Hongguang emperor for a year (June 1644–June 1645). When the Hongguang court collapsed, the Prince of Lu assumed the mantle of "supervisor of

Lost and Found 219

the state" in Hangzhou for five days before he surrendered to Qing troops in the sixth month of 1645.[12] He was taken north to Beijing and executed in 1646. The Prince of Lu was interested in Buddhism, amassed a collection of rare and precious objects, and was skilled in calligraphy, painting, and music. His works include a book on Ming imperial princes, a study of phonology, a treatise on calligraphy, and a chess manual, and he produced many bronze vessels and zithers following the styles described in the early twelfth-century catalog *Comprehensive Illustrated Account of Antiques from the Xuanhe Reign* (*Xuanhe bogu tu*).[13] In many ways he conforms to the stereotype of the artist tragically miscast as ruler, but his heedless quest for Song ceramics in the midst of cataclysmic collapse also shows a pathetic obliviousness. Not only does the Dingware censer highlight fatuous possessiveness, it almost becomes a political allegory as it captures the arc of Ming decline and fall.

PUBLIC AND PRIVATE SYMBOLISM

Tenuous ownership of art or precious things in the midst of political turmoil prompts ruminations on loss and ephemerality, but what remains, even if they are ordinary things, leads to redefinitions of possession or empathetic identification: sometimes in the context of public and (or) private symbolism.[14] Thus the scholar and thinker Chen Que (1604–1677), who lived in reclusion after the fall of the Ming, describes his staff as a friend who shares his fate and seems to embody historical vicissitudes in "The Account of the Dragon Staff" (*Longzhang ji*).[15] The staff is fashioned from a tree limb Chen found in Shaowan Mountain in 1641: "Its head is bent and its neck bowed. Its shoulders seem to be bearing weight. Its body is straight and its end long, while its knees protruded slightly. Knobs big and small number 116. At the length of seven *chi* and eight *cun*, its shape was astonishing and its aura luminous."[16] Resisting attempts to wrest the staff from him—two senior clansmen resort to theft—he eventually exchanges it for a convalescing friend's zither, only to eventually redeem it.

During the wars of Ming-Qing transition in 1646, the staff is twice stolen but mysteriously returns floating on water. "In the course of eight years, it met with calamities five or six times. Its shoulders and thigh were wounded, yet it still raises its head and stretches its feet, serving proudly as the model for all staffs.[17] I empathize with its vicissitudes and lament its misfortunes; thus I have told its biography. Human affairs are all like this. How can it be merely the fate of one staff!" In "Inscription on the Dragon Staff" (Longzhang ming), Chen uses the language of friendship and directly addresses the staff. He imagines its respectful attitude at the moment of encounter: "You bent in reverence; / our chance meeting became a joyous bond" 俯躬若敬, 傾蓋交歡. The trials and tribulations the staff suffers confirm their shared desire for withdrawal:

迄乎今夏	We reached this summer,
我病子閑	When I was sick and you, idle.
虜抄盜劫	Raiders raided and bandits abducted you;
兩遇兇殘	Twice you met with violence.
投水潛逸	You threw yourself into water to escape,
言歸故山	Returning to the mountain of old.
我于子薄	I have treated you with too little regard,
子則我敦	But you have shown me deep devotion.
八年之中	Through these eight years,
歷盡苦艱	You have endured endless hardships.
誓不遺子	I vow to never leave you,
終老盤桓	And together we will reach the end of our days.

In thus anthropomorphizing his staff, Chen Que may not sound very different from the obsessive characters discussed in chapter 1. But here the "biography" of the staff is bound up with historical upheavals from 1641 to 1648; the experience of losing and regaining it becomes Chen Que's profession of faith in his own tenacity in troubled times.

The political meanings of ruminations on things are even more evident in the scholar and philosopher Wang Fuzhi's (1619–1692) "Encomia on Miscellaneous Things" (Zawu zan).[18] Wang writes about sixteen objects that are either obsolete or removed from his milieu and invests them with allegorical meanings. He explains in the preface: "Sitting listless during a rainy day, I think back on things tied to specific customs and locality. They are either no longer in existence or they remain in the human realm but are impossible to come by in a desolate mountain. I tell of their origins and purpose and write rhymed encomia for them. As for the various things linked to important affairs, they are not within my purview. Indeed, being moved by one falling leaf, one can know autumnal melancholy."

Wang Fuzhi starts with the hair pouch (*faji* 髮積, literally, "storing hair"). "Made from paper in the shape of the demon catcher Zhong Kui, it is bearded and holds bamboo strips in its hands. Hung on the wall, its back is emptied to keep hair that falls off from combing." Zhong Kui is a Daoist deity who quells ghosts and demons. He is holding sewn bamboo strips, the medium for writing in early China, because in some versions of Zhong Kui lore he is an unsuccessful scholar or a prize candidate scorned because of his ugliness. According to the *Classic of Filial Piety* (*Xiaojing*), "One's body, hair, and skin are gifts from one's parents, one should not dare to ruin or harm them. This is the beginning of filial piety."[19] By this logic, even the hair that falls off from combing has to be kept. Gathered and stored in the hair pouch, it will be buried with the person when he or she dies. The Manchu conquest was experienced as a crisis of culture and tradition in part because of the mandated change of costume and hairstyle. The decrees enforcing such changes provoked widespread resistance, which in turn led to ruthless reprisals. The hair pouch lost its meanings under Qing rule. Men's pate, shaven except for a tuft of hair, meant that hair was no longer a protected or cherished thing.

The rhyme that follows imagines the death of Zhong Kui, perhaps because he is no longer able to protect one's hair:

神力憤盈	His divine power brims with anger;
食妖充餒	He devours demons to satisfy his hunger.
謂髮離顛	He says that once hair has left the head,
其類維□	One is akin to [blank].
顧顛已□	Look: the head is already [blank],
寇繁有徒	Legion is the number of followers.
玄冠赭袍	He with the black hat and the red robe:
云胡其徂	How does he come to die?

The subject of hair goes to the heart of acceptance or rejection of Qing rule, and the blanks were probably censored words. The first blank square was likely a disparaging word, perhaps "slave" 奴 (*nu* or some other word that rhymes with *tu* [followers]), and the second blank square likely had the word for "bald" (*tu* 禿) or, more likely, "shaven" (*kun* 髡), the latter referring to an ancient punishment. "Legion is the number of followers" is a line from the *Documents* referring to those who ignore the worthy and attach themselves to the powerful.[20] Here it refers to hair cut off as well as the multitudes who have accepted the new hairstyle. Wang did not shave his head and seemed to have escaped punishment by living in strict reclusion in remote mountains.

Besides the hair pouch, Wang uses several other objects to consider transformations of the physical body and their implications for moral choices and existential dangers. The cooling hairpin (*qitong* 氣通, literally "letting air go through") puts hair up in the summer to counter the heat, and heat (*re* 熱) becomes a metaphor for hankering after gain or fame (literally "burning within" *rezhong* 熱中): "As for those burning within and covered in sweat, / They are not within your purview" 熱中汗背, 非爾所審. The hairpin, also rendered obsolete by the new hairstyle, is in any case irrelevant for those all too eager to embrace the new order.

The incense cylinder (*xiangtong* 香筒), carved from sandalwood, ivory, or bamboo, is kept in the wide sleeve of Ming costume. Wang draws on the symbolic associations of fragrant and foul-smelling plants with virtue and deviance in the *Verses of Chu* tradition to praise the incense cylinder:

香魂化虛	The soul of fragrance becomes evanescent:
留之以凝	keep it by letting it come together.
褎衣閑閑	Wide clothes bringing ease
偕爾寢興	rise and rest in your company.
□□之夫	Men who [blank]
蕭葦之逐	pursue malodorous weeds.
無所置爾	There is no place to keep you
袪如□□	when the sleeves are like [blank].

The first two blank squares likely describe devious and despicable men attracted to foul smells (perhaps "men who chase stench" *zhuchou zhi fu* 逐臭之夫).[21] The "malodorous weeds" symbolize moral failure, following the significatory scheme established by the *Verses of Chu*. The narrow sleeves of the Manchu costume have no place for the incense cylinder, and the erased words at the end probably describe the tapered sleeves. Again, an accouterment ruled out by sartorial changes is invested with moral and political meanings.

Lost and Found 223

The objects Wang Fuzhi describes are quotidian and sometimes local, yet their broad historical significance is often unmistakable. Demon repellant (*gui jian chou* 鬼見愁, literally, "demons would see this and fret") is a fruit found in Wudang Mountain in Hubei. Its dried seeds can be made into a kind of rosary. Wang claims that children are made to wear them to ward off evil spirits and seems to associate that power with keeping at bay barbarians at the margins of the empire:

鬼愁不愁	Whether demons fret or not
人亦不知	is not what humans can know.
如彼明王	Be like that king of bright virtue
守在四夷	who guards against barbarians at the four frontiers.
爾不我佩	"If you do not wear me,
鬼愁何有	why would the demons fret?"
使爾今存	"If only you exist now,
人胥疾首	All enemies will in pain bow."

Lines 3 and 4 seem out of place with the abrupt shift of focus from an almost jocular beginning to the momentous question of guarding against invaders from beyond the frontiers. The shift turns the demon repellant into the crucible of imagining counterfactual history, sustaining the dialogue in the second half. The fruit speaks, imagining how disaster might have been avoided. The poet in reply fantasizes about the magic pellet that would bring enemies to submission.

Some historical references are more covert. Wang writes about the mineral silk lantern (*liaosi deng* 料絲鐙). A Yunnan specialty, mineral silk is a translucent substance derived from amber and amethyst.[22] The mineral silk lantern is made by "joining together six panels" (*liufang hecheng* 六方合成), possibly evoking the common six-sided Ming hat said to have been designed by the first Ming emperor, who sees it as a symbol of "unifying the six dimensions" (i.e., the world) (*liuhe yitong* 六合一統).[23] Its provenance from Yunnan has special significance for Wang Fuzhi, since he served the Prince of Gui or the Yongli emperor (Zhu Youlang [1623–1662]) in Yunnan, the final holdout of Ming resistance. The lantern becomes a symbol of Ming rule and its continuation in Yunnan:

元夕張鐙	The lantern of Lantern Festival
漢明始創	was first created by Emperor Ming of Han.
窮工取麗	Exquisitely crafted and ornate,
既光且綺	it is luminous and beautiful.
爭月搖星	Vying with the moon and the stars for brightness
石繭火機	is mineral silk with its seeds of fire.
以陰以雨	Under cloudy skies and in the rain,
奪我容輝	my face is robbed of its light.

Some believe that the Lantern Festival began in the Han dynasty with sacrifices to the god Taiyi.[24] Since Emperor Ming of Han (r. 57–75) is said to have sent an envoy to India to bring Buddhist scriptures, the custom could have been associated with Buddhist rituals. Here Wang might have chosen the reference based on the Han emperor's posthumous honorific "Ming." The penultimate line is from "Valley Wind" in the *Classic of Poetry*; in that poem the image evokes the desolation and rancor of the abandoned woman. Cloudy skies and rain robbing the lantern of brightness (the meaning of "Ming") become the doleful symbol of Qing conquest.

In some cases, the historical significance of the object is explicitly stated. The highly valued silk from the heavenly silkworms (*tiancan si* 天蠶絲) of Guangxi, another area that was for a while under the control of the forces of the aforementioned Prince of Gui, has a golden sheen, and its strands are longer and stronger than ordinary silk. Woof and warp in the weaving of silk threads have always constituted the metaphor for ordering the world. Here the strength of this silk links it to images of fastening and upholding the tenets of kingship:

弗飽女桑	This silkworm does not feed on mulberries,
弗眠葦曲	nor does it sleep in round rush pans.[25]
柔堅絁耀	Soft, enduring, and glowing red,
綴彼金玉	its silk threads string pieces of gold and jade.
乾綱既裂	The tenets of sovereignty have already been broken,
孰與維之	what can hold them together?
千金一繭	The cocoon worth a thousand pieces of gold
不及貂狸	does not measure up to the furs of raccoons and foxes.

Lost and Found

These strong silk threads string the gold and jade implements of ritual; the silk radical is also a constituent component of the words for cords or principles (*gang* 綱, here translated as "tenets") of government and for the act of fastening or holding things together (*wei* 維). Animal furs, newly favored because of Manchu customs, have usurped the place of silk, another trope for the conquest as the inversion of values.

With even more direct reference, Wang mourns the drum of peace (*taping gu* 太平鼓, a kind of tambourine) that makes street music for the Lantern Festival. For Wang, its name evokes the glory of the fallen Ming:

三百韶華	Three hundred years of splendor
河清海謐	when the River runs clear[26] and the sea is calm.
歡情踔厲	Buoyant feelings of joy
播于始吉	were spread at auspicious beginnings.
天山笳哀	The fife notes are mournful at the Heavenly Mountains,
漁陽撾斷	At Yuyang the sticks break from beating war drums.
凡今之人	Of all the people in this world,
孰肯念亂	who is willing to think of the disorder?

Fife notes belong to the music of nomadic invaders from the North. The war drums of Yuyang allude to the An Lushan Rebellion (756–763), which marked the decline of the Tang dynasty. Both are music of disorder that challenges the good cheer of the drum of peace. The final two lines, both taken from poems about like-minded brethren or lack thereof in the *Classic of Poetry*,[27] describe repression or forgetfulness of violence that make a mockery of the drum of peace, which presumably continues to be the music of the Lantern Festival.

Wang Fuzhi's "Encomia on Miscellaneous Things" may be fruitfully compared with his inscriptions (*ming* 銘) on eleven things that define his existence as a scholar, a recluse, and a Ming loyalist (dated 1670).[28] Five of these are implements related to writing (brush, inkstone, ink stick, elbow rest, cover for an inkstone). The rest include a staff, a duster, a chess set, a comb, his "Studio of Observing Existence" (Guansheng ju), and its south window. While the encomia and the inscriptions are both broadly speaking allegorical, and both use modes of direct address, imaginary dialogue, and personification, the inscriptions adhere more closely to the tradition of directly articulating intent (*yanzhi* 言志). A typical example is Wang's "Inscription on an Ink Stick" (Mo ming):

莠讕浮嚻	Because of mean slander and shallow clamor,
惜爾如珍	I cherish you like a treasure.
微言苟伸	So long as subtle words can find expression,
爾不吝滅爾身	you do not begrudge annihilating your body.

His "Inscription on the Cover of the Inkstone" (Yangai ming) likewise pursues a direct analogy:

黃塵玄埃	Brown dust and dark dirt:
切近其災	coming close to them is calamity.
苟藏身之已密	So long as the body is already hidden,
彼於我何有哉	what can they do to me?

It is when the history of the object takes center stage that we find the more elliptical style with embedded references to the historical context typical of the encomia discussed earlier. Thus Wang wrote about a comb given to him by a former general of the Yongli court: "General Huang Jintai of Xin'an took the tonsure and is called Master of Great Brightness. He asked me to write a short biography of him and gave me a tortoiseshell comb as gift. He said, 'I have been keeping it for a long while. There is none but you, sir, to whom I can give this gift.' I was moved by his regard and wrote an inscription for it." Huang became a monk and shaved his head after the defeat of the Yongli regime; for him, the comb reminds him of a lost cause. The inscription takes up the question of "to whom this gift can be given," and the answer seems to be couched both in Wang's voice and in the voice of the comb.

我瞻斯人	I look at these men,
皆可贈者	they can all be given this.
達多迷頭	Daduo lost his head—
非無頭也	It's not that he didn't have a head.
豈其遠而	How can it be that far—
神農虞夏	The way of Shennong, Yu, and Xia?

Lost and Found

Any man can be given this comb; the difference would lie between combing a full head of hair and a tuft of hair left to make a Manchu-style braid. In *Surangama Sutra*, Yanruo Daduo sees his beautiful reflection in the mirror, becomes angry with his head for not recognizing it, and runs away demented. The Buddhist parable for losing sight of one's true nature and confounding illusion with reality here refers to those who have lost their integrity. For those who have "lost their heads," the comb is irrelevant. Shennong, Yu (king Shun), and Xia (king Yu) are ancient sage kings. They are the ones Boyi and Shuqi call out to when they starve themselves to death on Shouyang Mountain as they refuse to eat the grains of Zhou, a regime they perceive as unjust and violent. The song of Boyi and Shuqi (*Shiji* 61.2123), oft-invoked emblems in Ming loyalist writings, can also speak for Wang Fuzhi:

神農虞夏	Shennong, Yu, and Xia,
忽焉沒兮	Have all of a sudden vanished.
我安適歸矣	Where can we return?

Whereas Wang's inscriptions deal with familiar objects from the scholar's studio that figure as recurrent topics in literati compositions, the encomia are concerned with accoutrements of grooming or things tied to specific festivals and localities. The historical and emotional weight they are made to bear is sometimes unexpected and almost idiosyncratic. Whether the associations are customary or surprising, however, Wang's trenchant loyalism makes the symbolic quotient unmistakable. For many members of the literati, by contrast, loyalist sentiments are likely to be expressed in less pointedly political ways. For them, writing about things is a favored mode for conveying mournful reflections on the dynastic transition and nostalgia for the late Ming world. Varying degrees of accommodation with the new order seek refuge in indirect expression, which nevertheless leaves room for political interpretations.

A good example is Chen Zhenhui's (1604–1656) *Miscellaneous Accoutrements for the Autumn Garden* (*Qiuyuan zapei*, 1648). Writing about sixteen objects that stir his imagination and longing either as things that remain as consolation for his life as a recluse or are lost because of recent cataclysmic changes, Chen's ruminations focus on his personal experience. Yet Chen's friend Hou Fangyu (1618–1655) takes pains to highlight the historical and political meanings of Chen's work in his preface.²⁹ This transition from private to public symbolism exemplifies the interpretive choice of contemporary and later readers.

Chen Zhenhui, Hou Fangyu, Fang Yizhi, and Mao Xiang, all famous young scholars of distinguished pedigree in the 1630s and 1640s, were called at the time "the four noble sons."³⁰ They were fully immersed in the refined pleasures of the Lower Yangzi area and were all known for consorting with famous courtesans. After the fall of the Ming, Chen Zhenhui chose reclusion, and Hou reluctantly took the examination under the Qing in 1651. Chen's covert disaffection and Hou's outward compromise might have led to Chen's choice of indirect expression and Hou's emphasis on uncovering hidden intention. Hou is known to many readers as the protagonist of the most famous play about the Ming-Qing dynastic transition, Kong Shangren's (1648–1718) *Peach Blossom Fan* (*Taohua shan*).

Chen begins with "the *jie* tea behind the temple" in his native Yixing (in Jiangsu). He praises its lightness and delicacy, which he associates with purity and quietude. For Hou, delicacy has social implications: "The friendship of noble men is gentle and delicate. He (Chen) is criticizing those who cling to the powerful." Delicacy or blandness in taste is pitted against profit and power (*nong* 濃 means, literally, "strong taste"). Chen dwells on the beauty of local orchids and their picking and sale in early spring. Hou infers Chen's identification with the "solitary fragrance" of orchids, following the symbolism of the *Verses of Chu*. In Chen's piece, the appeal of "Master Pang's hazelnut tree" at the Lotus Temple in Yixing derives in part from the legend that the Tang Buddhist Layman Pang Yun planted it. Hou suggests Chen uses the Buddhist reference to "articulate his intent to go beyond the mundane realm." Chen writes with relish about the "bamboo mushroom" as a delicacy for the mountain recluse, noting that its freshness is ephemeral and easily compromised. It would not be edible even a day after picking. For Hou, this is akin to subsistence on the wild ferns of Shouyang Mountain for Boyi and Shuqi, the archetypal loyalists who refuse to "eat the grains of Zhou." He obviously treats the plant's dependence on its place of origins as transparent analogy for the reluctance of the conquered to transfer loyalty to the new regime.

Hou's interpretive bent is to historicize and politicize, particularly when Chen offers more circumstantial details. For example, Chen praises the fragrant *yuan* citron for being superior to the Buddha's hand citron, which is prized only because it comes from a faraway place (Fujian). He quotes his son Chen Weisong's quatrain on the fruit and continues, "Ever since the turmoil, Buddha's hand, autumn orchid, and jasmine have not reached us for five years. Even if they are around, they are beyond the reach of a poor scholar in the mountains."[31] This makes him treasure all the more the fruit of the fragrant *yuan* trees in his own courtyard. Hou infers a more specific reference to anti-Qing resistance in southern China and perhaps even Chen's frustrated desire to join it: "He writes about the fragrant *yuan* citron to mark blocked communication with Fujian and Guangdong, and to lament that it is servants who pluck the fragrant fruit." "The servants' hands pluck the fragrant fruit" 摘香童僕手 is a line from the Chen Weisong quatrain quoted in Chen Zhenhui's entry. While the original is a vignette on the enjoyment of the fruit, Hou uses usurping servants to imply an unjust political order, perhaps even hinting at their analogy with the Qing conquerors.

The only object in Chen's list that has an explicit connection with the Ming dynasty is the "Pecking Parrot Gold Cup" from the Chenghua reign in the possession of Chen's uncle Wu Wenqing (d. 1650). Even here the tone of lamentation is muted: "Beholding this remnant of an era of peace, one cannot help feeling the emotions of listening to pipa music from the Tianbao reign."[32] Enjoying the Chenghua cup is like listening to Tang music from the era before the disastrous An Lushan Rebellion. For Hou, this is a "ritual object from the former dynasty" that makes one long for a bygone era of peace. Chen seems, however, more attuned to its aesthetic properties, comparing Chenghua pottery with the slightly more flamboyant but equally valued Xuande ware and declaring Song Ding-ware to be unparalleled, referring to a white Dingware cup that he manages to keep despite the turmoil of dynastic transition.

The note of personal loss is most marked in Chen's entry on Xiang bamboo brushes. It is also most densely allusive. Chen's uncle was an official in Guangxi in 1628 and brought back hundreds of them. Chen gave them away liberally to friends like the minister Wen Zhenmeng (1574–1636) and the scholar Wu Yingji (1594–1645).

> Over twenty years, they have almost all been lost. What remain are less than ten. Looking to Guangxi in the distance, how is it

different from unattainable heaven? But with the turmoil and devastation I have experienced in midlife, what use is there for Jiang Yan's five-colored brush or Prince Xiangdong's silver brush? Furthermore, good friends within the realm have mostly passed away, like the iron-forging Ji Kang and like Wang Huizhi remembered through his zither music. The spirit of *Encountering Sorrow* composes verses in vain, and the grave for brushes has been sealed. Beholding a Xiang bamboo brush, I am overcome by the boundless emotions roused by Su Shi's jest about being worn down by brushes and Ji Kang's lamentation over the last Guangling tunes. Only the tears flow on, like Yang Tan's tears mourning Xie An at the gates of Xizhou and like the tears of Shun's wives staining Xiang bamboo. How is this different from the Tang poet Lu Guimeng leaving a record of the brocade skirt?[33]

King Shun's wives, identified with the goddesses of River Xiang in some legends, weep for Shun's death, and their tearstains leave the bamboo of River Xiang mottled.[34] Xiang bamboo is thus a name that evokes mourning. After being given a five-colored brush in a dream, Jiang Yan (444–505) dreams of a man who calls himself Guo Pu (another well-known poet) demanding its return. He wakes up to find himself depleted of inspiration.[35] Prince Xiangdong (Emperor Yuan of Liang, r. 552–555) uses silver brushes to write about those of pure virtue.[36] If the display of literary talent seems no longer relevant and the record of virtue not to be taken for granted in troubled times, the brush's mission may be confined to mourning. Ji Kang is mentioned twice, first by way of being identified as the one with strange obsessions (forging iron) and then as the consummate zither player playing the tunes of Guangling for one last time before his execution. Wang Xianzhi (344–386) and Wang Huizhi (338–386) are both masters of the zither, and Xianzhi mourns Huizhi by plying untempered tunes on Huizhi's zither (*Shishuo xinyu* 17.16). The stories about Ji Kang and Wang Xianzhi, as well as that of Yang Tan mourning for Xie An (*Jinshu* 79.2077), encode the longing for the true friend (*zhiyin*, literally, the one who understands the music). Hou Fangyu presents Chen Zhenhui's mourning as being pointedly political: "He laments the minister (Wen Zhenmeng) as the wise man gone too soon and the loyal and righteous martyrdom of Wu Yingji." Chen does not elaborate on the death of Wen and Wu, erstwhile recipients of the Xiang bamboo brushes he used to own in abundance. Hou emphasizes the political meanings of their death: Wen during his brief tenure as minister tried to turn the tide of Ming decline to no avail, and Wu led the protest against the miscreant Southern Ming minister Ruan Dacheng (1587–1646) and died in anti-Qing resistance in 1645.

In some cases, Hou's allegorization seems to leave authorial intention behind. Chen is bemused by how the colorful rocks at Amber Creek in Six Dimensions Mountain become fashionable collectors' items during the late Ming, but Hou cites a line from the *Classic of Poetry* ("My heart is not a rock" 我心匪石) that brings to mind the rock's constancy ("It cannot be turned" 不可轉也) and implies Chen's profession of steadfast integrity. In the entry on folding fans, Chen records changes in fashion and notable artisans making fans. For Hou, the fact that folding fans originated in Korea means that Chen is pointedly "recording the change of institutions" due to foreign influence. The last two entries on azaleas and the crabapple blossoms of Yongding are lost,[37] but according to Hou the former is about omens fulfilled, and the latter identifies the crabapples with political upheavals: "He details their beginnings, their decline, and their revival to show that there is a reason to rise and decline, this is so not only with things."

The emphasis on sensuous details and personal recollections of things in Chen's work is subsumed under political purpose in Hou's preface. In the process, the vignette-like components of a reclusive existence become deliberate gestures of self-definition through objective correlatives. This balance or tension between private and public symbolism often emerges in the interpretation of works from this period. Indirectness and subtlety serve the purpose of political caution and mediate ambivalent emotions with sensory impressions of apparently trivial things. The preponderant interpretive bent from contemporaries and posterity, however, is to politicize and to allegorize.

OBJECTS FROM THE FALLEN DYNASTY

Accounts of the vicissitudes of ownership give us glimpses into momentous historical changes, as Jiang Shaoshu's book demonstrates. Perhaps this kind of pathos is nowhere more evident than with imperial objects whose fate is determined by political turmoil. During the chaotic years of the Ming-Qing transition in mid-seventeenth century, some objects from the Ming imperial palace were lost, resurfaced in the marketplace, and subsequently ended up in the possession of new owners. Typically, such objects inspire lament and nostalgia for the fallen dynasty. Sometimes they are regarded as emblems of Ming history or its final years of decline and fall. Writing about such objects becomes a way to reflect on history, to articulate one's convictions, or to defend one's political choices, and poetic exchanges on these objects sometimes chart the relationships within socio-literary communities. Even as Ming imperial objects inspire historical retrospection, their symbolic quotient is often determined by the moral or political self-definition of their new owners.

Jiang Cai's (1607–1673) poem about a ram-shaped paperweight used by the Chongzhen emperor (r. 1628–1644) exemplifies how Ming loyalism and alienation from the new regime is articulated through an object with imperial aura. Jiang Cai was a scholar-official who, through his forthright remonstrance and critique of the powerful minister Zhou Yanru (1593–1644), incurred the wrath of the Chongzhen emperor. He was savagely beaten, imprisoned for two years (1642–1644), and demoted to a military outpost in Xuanzhou (Anhui). Through these dark days, his younger brother Jiang Gai (1614–1653), also an official and noted man of letters, offered succor and attempted intervention, to no avail. When Jiang Cai was on his way to Xuanzhou, Beijing fell to the rebels. Jiang Cai and Jiang Gai eventually settled in Suzhou.[38] The long title of the poem describes the circumstances whereby the jade ram enters Jiang's possession.

THE JADE RAM ON MY DESK IS AN OBJECT FROM THE FORMER DYNASTY. SOME TIME AGO, MY YOUNGER BROTHER GAI BOUGHT IT IN A TEMPLE MARKET. AS HE LAY DYING, HE TOOK IT OUT AND GAVE IT TO ME. LOOKING AT IT, I AM MOVED TO COMPOSE A POEM. 案頭玉羊一具，前朝物也。昔弟垓得於廟市，易簀之際，出以貽贈。覽之感賦。

咸陽烽火倍堪傷	Mourning flames of war in the capital, grief deepens evermore.
御府銀鈎宛宛藏	The calligraphy from imperial precincts is palpably hidden.[39]

薊北山川豺虎窟	Among northern mountains and rivers is the lair of jackals and tigers,
天涯生死鶺鴒行	Living and dying at world's edge are brothers sharing a common cause.[40]
裴楷甲第今荒草	Pei Kai's mansion is now rampant with weeds,[41]
蘇武丁年故乳羊	For Su Wu in his prime, there was then the lambing ram.[42]
為語兒曹好珍惜	Send words to our sons and progeny: treasure it well,
吾家傳笏尚盈牀	Our family's court audience tablets still fill the whole bed.

The very presence of the jade ram on Jiang Cai's desk is a reminder of temporal and spatial displacement. Its rightful place should have been the palace; its moment of glory, the reign of the last Ming emperor. Its vicissitudes embody the sufferings of many; for Jiang, the jade ram recalls the fall of the Ming dynasty as well as the loss of his brother. The Chongzhen emperor was a notable calligrapher.[43] Jiang imagines imperial calligraphy elusively embedded, though hidden, in the jade ram, since it used to rest atop sheets of paper with the emperor's writing. Its link to loss and devastation is heightened by "the vanished jade ram" as the symbol for political collapse in the literature of omens.[44]

"The lair of jackals and tigers" in line 3 alludes to Du Fu's depiction of the Tang capital Chang'an overrun by rebels.[45] The fall of Beijing first to the rebels and then the Qing (line 3) results in the wanderings of the Jiang brothers (line 4)—the parallelism of "jackals and tigers" with "wagtails" (translated as "brothers" because "wagtails on the plain" is the image associated with the plight of brothers in a poem from the *Classic of Poetry*) means that the bond of brothers offers solace in the midst of political turmoil. A few months before Jiang Gai died, he had written to Jiang Cai offering the latter a residence he had just purchased—hence the reference in line 5 to Pei Kai (237–291), the Jin scholar-official who is said to have yielded a house he built to his older brother. Su Wu (ca. 140–ca. 60 BCE) is a Han envoy detained for nineteen years in Xiongnu territories. Braving harsh conditions and Xiongnu intimidation, he remains steadfast in his loyalty to the Han. The Xiongnu sends Su Wu to herd sheep, threatening to detain him indefinitely, for "only with rams lambing would he get to return [to the Han court]" (*Hanshu* 54.2463). Through the allusion to the Su Wu story, the jade ram is now also associated with the "lambing ram," an impossible occurrence that becomes the specter of permanent exile. Jiang Cai hailed from Laiyang in Shandong, but does it make sense for him to compare his "displacement" in Jiangnan with all its cultural splendor to Su Wu's detainment in the wilderness of Xiongnu territories? At issue perhaps is the idea of inner exile or a homeland rendered alienating by Qing conquest. This is a recurrent theme in early Qing poetry.[46] Thus Fang Yizhi's son Fang Zhongtong wrote: "Say no more about how hard it is to find your foothold in the world: / The central plains today have all become alien lands" 休道世間難著足, 中原今日總他鄉.[47] Gu Yanwu lamented, "Today's Daliang is not the realm of old, / At Yi Gate is Hou Ying, sunken in sorrow" 今日大梁非故國, 夷門愁殺老侯嬴.[48] Wu Zhaoqian was bemused by postconquest Jiangnan: "The Gusu Terrace, overrun by deer, is not my land, / East of the River are gowns and caps different from those of former travelers" 胥臺麋鹿非吾土, 江左衣冠異舊遊.[49]

An object with tantalizing proximity to imperial aura through the Chongzhen emperor's writing ends up in the temple market and eventually on Jiang Cai's desk. Its dislocation evokes a more pervasive displacement and destruction, an association confirmed through the esoteric literature on omens and the Su Wu story. How does one reclaim the sense of "being in the right place"? There is personal space, of course, as signaled by one's abode ("Pei Kai's mansion"). One may also seek refuge in the memory of one's family history of being loyal Ming subjects. "Court audience tablets filling the bed" (*man chuang hu* 滿牀笏) alludes to a story about the Tang official Cui Yiyuan (8th c.), whose bed is said to have been piled high with such tablets during his family feasts, such is the abundance of officeholders in his extended family.[50] Here Jiang Cai pointedly uses the word "still" (*shang* 尚), implying that such tablets are from the Ming dynasty. If his descendants are to cherish the jade ram, they should do so by holding on to memory of the family's glorious service of the Ming dynasty. In other words, he seems to cherish the hopes of his progeny becoming "hereditary loyalists" (*shixi yimin* 世襲遺民). Given his deliberations on exile and homelessness, it is perhaps ironic that Jiang Cai should insist on being buried at Xuanzhou, where he was headed for demotion and exile, as decreed by the Chongzhen emperor. We can only wonder at this stubborn, unquestioning loyalty (*yuzhong* 愚忠). But perhaps to embrace this displacement—the exile decreed by the last Ming emperor—is but the final confirmation of the deep malaise he feels in the new political landscape.

In Jiang Cai's elegy for Jiang Gai, he explains that he did not take up Jiang Gai's offer of an abode in Suzhou. Jiang Gai urged him on his deathbed to move to Suzhou to take care of his family, and Jiang Cai eventually moved there in 1659. He bought the property that had belonged to Wen Zhenmeng, renaming it "Jingting Mountain Abode" (Jingting shanfang),[51] and eventually "Garden of the Arts" (Yipu).[52] The beauty of this garden estate is praised in guidebooks, essays, and poetry. Many of these poems are addressed to Jiang Cai's younger son Jiang Shijie (1647–1709), who inherited the Garden of the Arts in 1673. Chen Weisong (1625–1682) wrote in a note to his preface to a collection of poems on the garden: "[Garden of the Arts] is one of the most impressive landmarks in the Suzhou area. Xuezai (Jiang Shijie) studies there; arrayed on both sides are ancient cauldrons, tea utensils, wine vessels, and various curios."[53]

Among Jiang Shijie's prized possessions is a porcelain cosmetics box painted in cobalt blue from the Xuande era (1425–1435). The box, said to have originated from the Ming imperial palace, was the subject of numerous poems and song lyrics, including works by Wu Qi (1619–1694), Wang Wan (1624–1691), Yu Huai (1616–1696), Mao Qiling (1623–1716), and Chen Weisong. According to Mao Qiling, the history of this box came to light only when a former eunuch from the Ming palace recognized it in the marketplace. Mao sees symbolism in its very shape—rectangular and rimmed by double edges, the perimeter seems a miniature replica of the palace moat: "Just like the moment when the Consort Lihua is done with adornment, / And the palace moat, with faint traces of balm, encircles the palace walls" 宛如麗華鬭粧罷，宮溝淺膩縈苑牆.[54] Zhang Lihua (d. 589), consort of the last Chen emperor, is a famous femme fatale in Chinese history, but Mao Qiling's allusion stops short of equating Ming rulers with benighted last emperors. The image seems to be chosen for its sensual evocativeness rather than its implied moral judgment.

In these poems, the Xuande reign becomes the symbol of early Ming prosperity and power. Yu Huai goes one step further and juxtaposes the porcelain cosmetic box with the Xuande emperor's paintings—both signify the artistic attainment of a great age.[55] He also sees in its blue lines and clear glaze a symbol of restraint: "There were no ladies in the sojourning palaces" 別館離宮無粉黛. The feminine associations of the cosmetics box are thus divested of any hint of decadence or sensual indulgence. It has survived intact in an era when "remnants of rouge and powder fill the capital, / Vendors sell broken inkstones and cracked zithers" 殘脂賸粉滿長安, 斷研零琴市兒賣, suggesting a tangible link with the past. The pathos of Ming decline and fall is captured in the fate of the box as it ends up in the marketplace, its worth properly appraised only because a former palace lady (or a eunuch in some accounts) recognizes it as an imperial object. All the poems on the topic reiterate this idea, perhaps most poignantly in Chen Weisong's song lyric.

TO THE TUNE "MAN TING FANG," ON THE XUANDE PORCELAIN COSMETICS BOX, PAINTED IN COBALT BLUE, WRITTEN FOR JIANG SHIJIE OF LAIYANG[56] 《滿庭芳》詠宣德窯青花脂粉箱為萊陽姜學在賦

龍德殿邊	By the side of the Dragon Virtue Palace,
月華門內	Within the Moonlight Gate,
萬枝鳳蠟熒煌	Ten thousand phoenix candles blazed.
六宮半夜	In the Six Palaces, in the middle of the night,
齊起試新妝	They all rose to try a new mode of adornment.
詔賜口脂面藥	By imperial decree were rouge and balm bestowed.
花枝裊	Like blooms on swaying branches,
笑謝君王	They smiled and thanked the emperor.
燒瓷翠	Warming blue porcelain,
調鉛貯粉	They mixed colors and stored power,
描兩鴛鴦	Painting two lovebirds.
當初溫室樹	Back then, as with trees in the Warm Chamber,
宮中事秘	The secrets of palace affairs
世上難詳	Could hardly have been known in the world.
但銅溝漲膩	But balm-streaked water rises beyond the Bronze Moat
流出宮牆	And flows outside the palace walls.
今日天家故物	Today the former imperial object
門攤賣	Is displayed and sold at the gate
冷市閑坊	Of an empty marketplace by a desolate road.
摩挲怯	Timidly caressing it,

> 內人紅袖　　The palace lady with red sleeves
> 慟哭話昭陽　　Wails and speaks about the Bright Sun Palace.

The juxtaposition of past and present is defined through focus on two temporal moments. The first half reenacts the gentle pleasures of palace life during the Xuande reign and depicts the gift of the cosmetics box as a mark of imperial beneficence. As in the other poems on the topic, the expectant and grateful palace ladies convey no sense of sensual excess. The second half charts the movement of the box from inside to outside the palace, from being the embodiment of closely guarded secrets to shameful exposure. The beginning lines of the second stanza (lines 12–14) allude to the Han minister Kong Guang (65–4 BCE), who is so discreet that he would remain silent even when asked innocuous questions about the trees in the Warm Chamber Palace (*Hanshu* 81.3354). Hiddenness stokes longing and protects the aura of imperial mystique. "Balm-streaked water" (line 15) recalls Du Mu's (803–852) poetic exposition on the Efang Palace of Qin: "The Wei River, overflowing, is streaked with balm: / It is the discarded water used to wash away rouge" 渭流漲膩, 棄脂水也.[57] Du Mu sees heedless sensual indulgence and intoxication with power as the seeds of Qin downfall; many believe that he is also criticizing contemporary excesses in the Tang court. Here the intent is not critical: the association with the palace moat seems to have been summoned by the shape of the box (as mentioned earlier) and by the idea of revealing what should have been hidden. Du Mu ends his piece on Efang Palace with these famous lines: "The men of Qin did not have the time to lament themselves, and posterity lamented them. If while lamenting, posterity did not heed Qin as mirror, then it would be making its own posterity lament it" 秦人不暇自哀, 而後人哀之。後人哀之而不鑒之, 亦使後人而復哀後人也. In Chen Weisong's lyric, there is no tangible "lesson of history" because "balm-streaked water" flowing outside the palace walls (lines 15–16) does not refer to excesses and moral failure but stands for the collapse of order, the breakdown of boundaries that results in the ultimate indignity of the cosmetics box becoming a common item traded in the marketplace. The former palace lady's lamentation means that pathos leaves no room for historical judgment (lines 20–22).

Chen Weisong's song lyric cannot be dated with certainty. He eventually took the 1679 examination but often expressed nostalgia for the fallen Ming. Among those who addressed poems to Jiang Shijie about the cosmetics box were Qing officials like Wu Qi, Wang Wan, and Mao Qiling. The only Ming loyalist among them was Yu Huai, whose poems about Jiang Cai and Jiang Gai (Jiang Shijie's father and uncle) indicate a deep friendship with the family.[58] In Jiang Cai's corpus, there is almost no poem addressed to Qing officials, although the lack did not rule out social connections, for it might have been the result of deliberate exclusion, a function of Jiang Cai's self-definition as a loyalist. While Jiang Cai's son Jiang Shijie did not seek office under the Qing, he is certainly open to cultivating social ties with Qing officials, often through poems expressing nostalgia for the Ming, as exemplified by the poetic exchanges on the Xuande cosmetics box and on his garden. According to his friend Li Guo (1679–1751), Jiang paid a hefty price for the box and offered it as a present to the courtesan-poet Chen Susu.[59] The romance between Jiang and Chen inspired Zhu Suchen's play *Moon Over the Qin Tower* (*Qinlou yue*), whose publication (ca. 1680) might have been financed by Jiang Shijie.[60] An object fraught with historical memory has become, with a generational shift, a love token, although the melancholy overtones of the romance have also been linked to Ming loyalism.[61]

With writings on the cosmetics box, nostalgia and lamentation rule out the critical edge in historical reflection, even when the allusion to Du Mu's "Poetic Exposition on Efang Palace" might have seemed to warrant it. As mentioned, the Xuande reign is lauded in these works as an era of peace and prosperity. But Ming Qing poetry, fiction, and miscellanies also refer to the Xuande emperor's wayward obsession with cricket fights. He went to great lengths to acquire unusual specimens, inviting accusations of political irresponsibility or even of sowing the seeds of Ming decline. According to Shen Defu, the Xuande emperor

> was most conversant with this sport. He once sent a secret decree to the Suzhou magistrate Kuang Zhong, demanding a thousand crickets. For a while there was this saying: 'Crickets chirp and creak, these the Xuande emperor must seek.' Even to this day people know about it. I have heard that, among the low-ranking officers in the military outpost at Suzhou, there were even those who, by catching crickets, attained hereditary office on a par with those who cut down or captured the enemy. These days Xuande era porcelain

cricket pans are considered treasures, priced at a level no less than that of Song dynasty Xuanhe pans.
(*WL* 2:625)⁶²

Sometime between 1654 and 1656, when Wu Weiye (1609–1672) was a Qing official in Beijing, he saw a cricket pan that had belonged to the Xuande emperor in the collection of his friend Sun Chengze (1592–1676), like him a former Ming official who served the Qing and whose recommendation was instrumental for the imperial summons that resulted in Wu's appointment.⁶³ Wu then wrote "The Song of the Xuande Emperor's Gold Inlaid Lacquer Cricket Pan" (Xuanzong yuyong qiangjin xishuai pen ge, *WMC* 1:61–63).

As mentioned in chapter 1, the minister Jia Sidao, blamed for hastening the fall of the Song dynasty, was also obsessed with cricket fights. Emperor Duzong (r. 1265–1274), the de facto last Song emperor, shared Jia's passion and was dubbed the "Cricket Emperor." For an object with such disastrous associations, it is almost surprising that Wu Weiye does not sound more sharply critical. He refrains from offering a forthright denunciation of the cricket pan as a symbol of unseemly frivolity and woeful neglect of government. Indeed, this critical perspective is at first deliberately muted. The poem begins thus:

宣宗在御昇平初	When the Xuande emperor ruled, in those early years of peace and prosperity,
便殿進覽豳風圖	The scroll *Airs of Bin* was presented for his perusal at the palace of repose.
暖閣才人籠蟋蟀	Palace ladies in cozy side chambers put crickets in cages
晝長無事為歡娛	And, in long days unhurried, found pleasure in them.

Wu Weiye introduces the subject with crickets in canonical classics and in a famous painting. "Seventh Month" ("Airs of Bin") in the *Classic of Poetry* contains this line: "In the tenth month, crickets come under our bed" 十月蟋蟀入我牀下. The image conveys a rustic charm in the context of the litany of agricultural labor in "Seventh Month." For the Xuande emperor to look at Zhao Mengfu's pictorial rendering, *Airs of Bin* (now no longer extant)—and perhaps to specifically pay attention to the "crickets under the bed" in "Seventh Month"—is to be reminded of the duties of governance and the proper relationship between the ruler and his subjects. The aura of refinement and decorum persists in the ensuing description of palace ladies amusing themselves by keeping crickets. According to Wang Renyu (10th c.), during the Tang emperor Xuanzong's reign, palace ladies kept crickets because they were enthralled by the music of their chirping sound.[64] Instead of dwelling on the perverse projection of martial fantasies to cricket fights, Wu Weiye deliberately summons the associations of crickets with gentle diversions. The tone becomes more caustic with the description of the luxuries lavished on the crickets. "Dingzhou porcelain with flower patterns was the fiefdom bestowed on them, / Jade grains and jasper ambrosia were offered as their food and drink" 定州花瓷賜湯沐, 玉粒瓊漿供飲啄. To use Ding porcelain ware from the Song dynasty—priceless treasures by the Ming—to keep crickets is not only extravagant but also politically dangerous: "fiefdom" suggests the inversion of value. If a pastime is dignified with the vocabulary for affairs of state, it can only mean that political concerns have in turn become trivialized.

The conflation of mettlesome crickets with famous generals and of the cricket pan with historical battlefields is the conceit that runs through the whole poem and the source of irony and pathos. With allusive and metaphorical virtuosity, Wu Weiye spins endless insect puns and effaces the boundaries between men and crickets. The Xuande emperor's perspective, marked by a shift to his voice, is the source of this inversion or confusion (lines 13–16):

君王暇豫留深意	The ruler, savoring leisure, was raptly attentive:
棘門霸上皆兒戲	"Jimen and Bashang are all but child's play.
鬥雞走狗謾成功	Vain is the boast of success with cockfights and hound races,
今日親觀戰場利	Today I survey with my own eyes victory on the battlefield."

To counter Xiongnu incursions, Emperor Wen of Han (r. 180–157 BCE) sent three generals to guard the outposts Jimen, Bashang, and Xiliu near Chang'an in 158 BCE. When he inspected troops under Zhou Yafu's

(199–143 BCE) command at Xiliu, he was moved to exclaim: "Alas! This is a true general! The armies at Jimen and Bashang I saw earlier are nothing but child's play. Their generals could suffer raids and be captured. As for Yafu, who can threaten him?" (*Shiji* 57.2074–75). The line with which the Han emperor praises Zhou Yafu's martial prowess here marks the Xuande emperor's recognition of his crickets' worth, with the irony deepened by the reference to "child's play." He considers cricket fights superior to cockfights and hound races (all three were popular forms of gambling) because it best captures the euphoria of victory on the battlefield.[65] I have translated lines 14–16 as the emperor's words or thoughts; they could have been rendered as "indirect free style." Either way, the perspective of the emperor is unmistakable.

Wu Weiye then uses images from cricket fights to reenact the military struggles that paved the way for the founding of the Ming dynasty, with a tantalizing suggestion that these are historical memories unfolding as scenes imagined by the Xuande emperor. Victors and losers all find their cricket analogs. Victorious Ming troops, "broad-browed and tall, spread two wings, / with teeth gnawing, legs straight, and whiskers like spears" 坦顙長身張兩翼，鋸牙植股鬚如戟 (lines 17–18). With a two-pronged army, "spread out as left and right wings" 張左右翼, the Zhao commander Li Mu (d. 229 BCE) defeated the Xiongnu. "Whiskers and eyebrows like spears" 鬚眉如戟 is a conventional description of manly valor. As for the defeated contenders for the throne during the Yuan-Ming transition, "To what end do they hide among the grass? / This is a menial breed under the stove—scarcely worthy to be our rivals" 草間竊伏竟何用，竈下廝養非吾羣 (lines 23–24).[66] The erstwhile Mongol ruler driven into northern deserts is "a yellow-whiskered barbarian who quakes to see the victors, / Head bent and legs broken, his spirit flees" 黃鬚鮮卑見股栗，垂頭折足亡精魂 (lines 31–32).[67] The Xuande emperor's passion is apparently dignified and justified through this web of historical references, but the crickets also become grotesque echoes of early Ming military glory.

The Xuande emperor anthropomorphizes crickets as he imagines them as early Ming war heroes. But defeats in real battles reduce humans to insects (lines 44–48):

二百年來無英雄　　For two hundred years there have been no more heroes.

故宮瓦礫吟秋風	Among the ruins of former palaces are chirps in the autumn wind.
一寸山河鬭蠻觸	For one inch of territory, the Man fought the Chu,
五千甲士化沙蟲	As five thousand armored soldiers turned into sand and insects.

In a famous parable on relativism, perceptions, and perspectives in *Zhuangzi*, the kingdoms of Man and Chu, situated on the right and left tentacles of a snail, respectively, fight for land, resulting in the death of tens of thousands in the process (*Zhuangzi jishi* 25.891). In *Master Embracing Simplicity* (*Baopu zi*), Ge Hong (284–364) describes the magical transformations of King Mu of Zhou's troops as his southern expedition drags on indefinitely—the gentlemen are turned into gibbons and cranes, the common people into grains of sand and insects.[68] Lines 47 and 48 thus juxtapose hypothetical philosophical detachment with all too real violence and destruction. The parable in *Zhuangzi* urges us to regard gain and loss as inconsequential, but in that battle between Man and Chu, as well as King Mu's interminable campaign, the horror of dehumanization, summed up in images of metamorphosis, cannot be resolved through philosophy. Pushing the metaphor of cricket fight to its limits, the collapse of the Ming is presented as a calamitous yet avoidable series of events, comparable to the gratuitous cruelty children inflict on crickets: "What of the puny bodies in the thicket? / Captured, they have by mistake fallen into children's hands" 灌莽微軀亦何有, 捉生誤落兒童手 (lines 49–50). Dehumanizing insect analogies leave little room to mourn even the heroism of martyrs: "Bandits, like swarms of ants, pierced walls and bore away rotten flesh, / Bones of battles, even when remembered as noble, decayed all too soon" 蟻賊穿墉負敗胾, 戰骨雖香嗟速朽 (lines 51–52). Heroes are no more; only chirping crickets remain among the ruins of palaces to lament loss and devastation (lines 44–45).

The dominant mood of the poem remains elegiac rather than critical. The Xuande emperor's obsession may indicate a heedless inversion of priorities and even portend dynastic decline, but the cessation of cricket fights, insofar as it is part of a general collapse and indiscriminate destruction, arouses deep sadness. (The favored pastime of the new regime was apparently falconry, although in time cricket fights would become very popular again.) Wu presents the irrelevance of the cricket pan as an inevitable corollary of the chaos and devastation of dynastic transition (lines 59–62):

秘閣圖書遇兵火	The books of hidden imperial chambers met with the flames of war,
廠盒宣窰賤如土	Guoyuan lacquer boxes and Xuande porcelain are worthless as mud.
名都百戲少人傳	Few continue the hundred amusements in the famed capital.
貴戚千金向誰賭	Where can noble relatives place their bets of a thousand gold pieces?

The empty, displaced cricket pan, now in the possession of Wu's collector friend Sun Chengze, symbolizes the fall of the Ming dynasty in the final lines (lines 63–70):

樂安孫郎好古癖	Master Sun of Le'an is obsessed with love of antiquity,
剔紅填漆收藏得	And has collected lacquer ware of sublime artistry.
我來山館見雕盆	I came to his mountain abode and saw the inlaid bowl—
蟋蟀秋聲增歎息	The sounds of cricket in autumn made me sigh ever more.
嗚呼	Alas!
漆城蕩蕩空無人	The lacquered city walls, all smooth, are empty, without a soul.
哀螿切切啼王孫	Grieving insects, with urgent cries, lament the fate of princes.
貧士征夫盡流涕	Poor scholars and men at war all shed tears—
哀哉不遇飛將軍	What a great pity that the Flying General met no recognition.

When the second and last emperor of Qin (r. 210–207 BCE) wants to paint the city walls, entertainer Zhan offers remonstrance by ostensibly agreeing with him: "Although the people will fret about the cost of painting the city walls, it will be wonderful. The painted city walls will be all smooth—the raiders will not be able to climb up" (*Shiji* 126.3203).

Here the lacquered walls, smooth and even, also represent indictment of excesses and extravagance—but the raiders have breached the walls and conquered. The autumnal cries of insects, the symbol of desolation and death in the Chinese literary tradition,[69] here gains pathos and urgency because of the accidental phonetic association of crickets (called *wangsun* 蚟孫 in the Chu dialect, according to Yang Xiong's *Fangyan*) with princes (*wangsun* 王孫, line 68).

With a further twist, Wu Weiye compares the crickets that have vanished from the bowl to Li Guang (184–119 BCE), the Han "Flying General" who met with no recognition in his era. The idea of recognizing worth or the failure to do so reverberates throughout the poem. Fighting crickets are compared to early Ming commanders like Xu Da (1332–1385) and Chang Yuchun (1330–1369), who were recognized by the first Ming emperor Zhu Yuanzhang (r. 1368–1398) and laid the foundation for the Ming empire. The Xuande emperor focuses all his attention on crickets, whose extraordinary treatment reflects on the plight of talented men who are not recognized. The martial prowess of crickets was cultivated because of imperial delusions, and as a result the real "Flying General" was not to be found. The problem of mismanaged talents is especially glaring in the final years of the Ming. The last line can also be read in another way: "What a pity that they (i.e., the poor scholars and men at war) have not encountered the Flying General." For a country in the throes of crisis not to have heroes like Li Guang spells calamity for all, not just "poor scholars and men at war" (line 69). The crickets that are now ignored and no longer fighting in the pan may paradoxically also be compared to the unrecognized Li Guang. Recognizing worth depends on distinguishing the real and the fake, a particularly fraught question during the dynastic transition, as noted in chapter 3. The only acts of recognition still possible are those of the collector Sun Chengze and the poet-historian Wu Weiye. Wu thereby confirms the cricket pan as the embodiment of tenacious historical memory and of the uneasy balance between historical judgment and elegiac lamentation.

CONNOISSEURSHIP, POLITICAL CHOICES, AND SOCIAL TIES

As the previous examples show, writings about things often involve gatherings and social networks. Jiang Shijie belonged to a family of notable

Lost and Found 245

loyalists and never sought office under the Qing, but his social ties with Qing officials are evident in the poems on the cosmetics box. Aesthetic appreciation can define a kind of common ground for the literati irrespective of their political choices. Prominent early Qing scholar-officials, such as Sun Chengze, Zhou Lianggong (1612–1672), Gong Dingzi (1616–1673), Liang Qingbiao (1620–1691), and Wang Shizhen (1634–1711), all had loyalist friends, and some of their literary exchanges involve artworks, artifacts, and ornaments of literati culture. The dynastic transition saw a shift of collections from the South to the North. Prominent Jiangnan families declined, and their massive collections were dispersed (as in the case of the Xiang family collection mentioned earlier); the buyers were often Qing officials, many of them northerners. "The Han members of the early Qing government were likely to be predominantly northerners."[70] In tracing this phenomenon, Fu Shen and Liu Jinku focus on famous paintings and calligraphy, but the same seems to be true of other antiques, curios, and artifacts as well.[71]

Sun Chengze was one of these northern collectors. He was a prolific scholar who wrote extensively on history, philology, and neo-Confucian learning, but he is now remembered chiefly for the connoisseurship and judgment he shows in the accounts of calligraphy, paintings, and rubbings he owned or saw in *Record of Whiling Away the Summer in the Gengzi Year* (*Gengzi xiaoxia ji*, hereafter *Gengzi*). Written between the fourth and sixth month in 1660, after Sun retired from office, this work shows how collecting and connoisseurship acquired a new pathos in early Qing. During the dynastic transition, artworks that had belonged to the Ming imperial palace or great family collections flooded the marketplace. Living in Beijing at the time, Sun had ample opportunity to exercise his judgment in the new art market. This is how he describes one of his "rescue operations":

> Jing Hao specializes on landscape and was first among ancient and modern masters. With the disaster of 1644, famous paintings filled the marketplace—the only thing that could not be found were paintings by Jing Hao. One day I saw someone coming out of the former palace carrying tattered scrolls—Jing Hao's painting was among them. But it was already in a very sorry state. I got a superior craftsman to remount it, and I found that underneath the white

silk was another more densely woven piece of silk. This too was extraordinary. The mountains and trees are all delineated in fine strokes with a worn-down brush and shaped like ancient seal script and clerical script. Its style is austere and archaic in the extreme. This is not what Guan Tong and Fan Kuan can match up to. I ordered Pu'er to put it away and store it in the Sea Clouds Chamber.[72]

Jing Hao's (10th c.) paintings were already extremely rare by the seventeenth century, but Sun Chengze in his initial disappointment sounded as if he had expected to see Jing Hao's works among the damaged pieces carted out of the former palace. The expertise and vocabulary of connoisseurship have not changed (an "austere and archaic style" has always been prized), but the issue is now saving treasures from ruination and oblivion. In another case, Sun bought a precious Li Gonglin painting from an ignoramus, who got it from the Ming palace but could not even read the artist's seal.[73] There are similar entries about purchases at the marketplace or unlikely street corners, about obtaining famous calligraphy and paintings from "the former palace," sometimes when these works are already damaged almost beyond recognition.[74] The asking price was in many cases modest; those who raided collections and tried to resell often did not know the value of their goods.[75]

Sun Chengze also describes the gatherings centered on appreciating artworks that survived political turmoil:

> After 1644, the bronze camels are to be found among brambles, and the jade bowl has also entered the human world. Two or three of us, who share the same interests, daily collect fragments of calligraphy, paintings, or rubbings in order to lodge our ardent, restless sorrow. I have the "Ink Karma Studio" situated east of my chamber. Some brought items from their collections for an occasional visit. I have thus been fortunate enough to behold many famous works from ages past. Summoning them to mind, I sort out my recollections.[76]

The Jin calligrapher and general Suo Jing (239–303), foreseeing chaos, pointed to the bronze camels in front of the Luoyang palace gates and sighed, "I will meet you again among brambles" (*Jinshu* 60.1648). The emergence of the "jade bowl," a funereal item from the Han imperial grave at Maoling, alludes to the exposure, during dynastic collapse, of what should have remained hidden.[77] These are clichés that nevertheless seem singularly apt. "Ardent, restless sorrow" (*laosao* 牢騷) is vague enough to encompass lamentation for the fallen Ming or a more general melancholy. Some exegetes have used the term *laosao* to gloss the title *Lisao* 離騷 (usually translated as *Encountering Sorrow*), the ancient Chu poem traditionally interpreted in terms of Qu Yuan's political frustrations and engagement with the crisis facing the Chu state.[78] But a less political reading of the term is entirely plausible. The last fascicle of *Gengzi* names other collectors. Sun's list includes the poet and scholar-official Zhu Yizun (1629–1709). During a period when Zhu still identified as a Ming loyalist, he seemed to have developed a friendship with Sun in part because of his connoisseurship.[79] The kind of social networks exemplified by Sun Chengze (and Jiang Shijie above) were probably typical. Collecting and connoisseurship define a sociocultural space wherein political differences can be, at least temporarily, suspended.

Sun rose to high office under the Qing and retired in 1653. In the preface to *Gengzi* in 1660, he styles himself "The Recluse of the Valley of Retreat" (Tuigu yisou). He describes a life of unhurried refinement and lofty detachment. "I wander for a while and again enter my study. I take one or two famous works of calligraphy and painting and linger over them in appreciation, fully taking in their mood and meaning. And then I put them back in their original place, close the door, bate my breath, and sit."[80] The convergence of connoisseurship with withdrawal from politics is an important aspect of Sun's self-representation as well as his friend's depiction of him. In "The Song of the Valley of Retreat" (Tuigu ge) addressed to Sun, Wu Weiye rhapsodizes about Wu's estate, the Valley of Retreat, and imagines it as the space of freedom and escape.[81] Wu wrote this poem in spring 1654, shortly after he came to Beijing. In the tenth month of the same year, he became a Qing official and served for two years. Wu Weiye's post-1644 writings are filled with lament for the fall of the Ming dynasty, nostalgia for the world before its collapse, and, since his northward journey to take up office in 1653, regrets and anguish over his own irresoluteness and compromises. Wu contrasts his own sense of entrapment with Sun's liberation upon retirement.

使我山不得高	I have been consigned to where the mountains cannot be high,
水不得深	The waters cannot be deep,
鳥不得飛	Birds cannot fly,
魚不得沉	Fish cannot sink.
武陵洞口聞野哭	At the entrance to Wuling Cave, one hears crying in the wilds.
蕭斧斫盡桃花林	The blighting axe has hacked away all of Peach Blossom Forest.
仙人得道古來宅	The ancient abode where immortals have attained the Way
劫火到處相追尋	Is where kalpic fires have arrived, as one seeks the recluse.
不如三輔內	It is better to stay within the domain of the capital,
此地依青門	At this place by the Blue Gate—
非朝非市非沈淪	Where it is neither court, nor market, nor yet sunken oblivion.

The Wuling Cave and Peach Blossom Forest, which signify the escape from history in Tao Yuanming's famous "Peach Blossom Spring," are here ravaged by violence and devastation. The Valley of Retreat on the outskirts of Beijing, by contrast, is presented as a liminal space commanding Olympian perspectives.[82] Collecting and connoisseurship thus promise to mediate the contradiction between service and withdrawal: this is of course a wonted theme especially prominent in late Ming writings, but the choice is now much rifer with anguish for some (like Wu) because of the dynastic transition.

The political choices and social ties of the elite are sometimes mediated through the vocabulary of connoisseurship. A good example is the poetic exchanges between Mao Xiang (1611–1693) and Fang Gongqian (1596–1666) on a Xuande censer. Censers supposedly dating from the Xuande era became much sought-after treasures from the late sixteenth century on. *Catalog of Cauldrons and Ritual Vessels from the Xuande Era* (*Xuande dingyi pu*), allegedly an official document from the Ministry of Works produced during the Xuande reign and included in the *Four Treasuries*, was actually not mentioned before the eighteenth century and likely not compiled until then.[83] The attribution of *Disquisition on Xuande*

Censers (*Xuanlu bolun*) to Xiang Yuanbian (1525–1590), also included in the *Four Treasuries*, is obviously spurious.[84] The earliest reliable reference to Xuande censers is found in Gao Lian's *Eight Treatises* (*ZSBJ* 448, 450).[85] In *Scenes from the Capital* (*Dijing jingwu lue*), Liu Tong (1634 *jinshi*) and Yu Yizheng (active 1615–1635) offer detailed descriptions of Xuande censers, including the multiple rounds of refinement that contribute to their glow.[86] Suffice it to say that by the time Fang and Mao were writing on the subject in 1662–1663, the lore about the Xuande censer as the epitome of Ming culture was firmly in place.

Mao Xiang hailed from Rugao (Jiangsu) and was the scion of a distinguished scholar-official family. Active in the Revival Society (Fushe) and Incipient Society (Jishe) during the late Ming, he retired from public life under the Qing but continued to host literary gatherings and theatrical performances in his estate, Painted-in-Water Garden (Shuihui yuan), which he built in the early 1650s. His anthology of writings by himself, his family members, and his friends, *Collected Writings of Kindred Spirits* (*Tongren ji*), compiled during the mid-Kangxi period (1673–ca. 1692), testifies to the evolution of literary communities that included both Ming loyalists and Qing officials.

Fang Gongqian, who belonged to the prominent Fang family in Tongcheng (Anhui), passed the provincial and capital examinations in the same years (1618, 1628) as Mao Xiang's father Mao Qizong (1590–1654). Fang served in the Hanlin Academy and the Bureau of Palace Affairs under the Ming and eventually held the same office under the Qing.[87] Implicated in the Case of Examination Scandal in 1657, Fang Gongqian and his family (except his sixth son Fang Yicang) were exiled to Ningguta in Manchuria.[88] Before he left, Fang entrusted his prized Xuande censer to his son Yicang. When, upon imperial pardon, he returned to Beijing in 1662, Yicang brought the censer to meet him. Fang composed "Seeing the Xuande Censer Again, Three Poems" (Zaijian Xuande lu sanshuo) for the occasion.[89]

Fang Gongqian sees his own survival mirrored in the enduring glory of the censer: "In my mind there is the strange glow / That becomes more palpable with stroking" 意中光怪在, 拂拭更離離; "Hard and brittle, we have lived through separation and chaos: / Our mutual gaze takes in our unravaged bodies" 堅脆經離亂, 相看不壞身. Fang acquired the censer forty-three years earlier (1619): "What's more, it was cast during the former dynasty, / And has for long been cherished in our era" 況復前朝鑄, 久為當代憐. Fang's perception of the dynastic transition is inextricably intertwined with the reversals of his fortunes under the Qing. The promise of political power or literary fame seems all too vain. He implies that both cataclysmic historical changes and personal vicissitudes urge him to embrace detachment: "I can only rub my worn eyes / As incense burns day and night at the pine shrine" 好拭摩娑眼, 松龕晝夜煙.

In 1663 Fang Gongqian and his family moved to Yangzhou, where Mao Xiang went to meet him and wrote "The Song of the Xuande Bronze Censer, Composed on Behalf of Collegial Uncle Fang Tan'an" (Xuan tonglu wei Fang Tan'an nianbo fu, *MPJ* 1:132–33).[90] In his elegy for Fang Gongqian (1666), Mao Xiang looked back fondly on this meeting: "Seeing my father's good friend again was like seeing my father. I was beside myself with commingling sadness and joy.... When it comes to appraising the refinements of culture, discussing and editing our compositions, exchanging poems on the Xuande censer, there was not one gathering not filled with joy, not a word that is not excessive praise [for me].... Three generations gathered in amity in one hall. This is truly a joyous occasion countering twenty years of suffering" (*MPJ* 1:455–57).

As Yasushi Ōki pointed out, "The Song of the Xuande Bronze Censer" affirms the friendship between Mao and Fang through the cultural and historical meanings of the censer.[91] On a more basic level, it demonstrates Mao's empathy with Fang and the compromises he made (lines 1–6):

龍眠先生鬚鬢皤	The Master of Longmian,[92] hoary of beard and temples,
兩朝鼎貴稱鳴珂	Attained glory and honor in two dynasties.
絲綸世掌遭遷播	His family has held office for generations, yet exile befell him.
邗江賣字書掔窠	Selling calligraphy at Yangzhou, he writes in great bold strokes.[93]
生平好古入骨髓	Throughout his life, his love of antiques is bone deep,
玩好不惜三婆娑	On cherished objects his attention repeatedly lingers.

Although Mao Xiang identified as a Ming loyalist, his sons did take the civil service examination under the Qing, and here Mao warmly praises Fang's history of serving both the Ming and Qing dynasties. Generations of office-holding (literally, holding onto "imperial decrees" [*silun* 絲綸]) is no protection against the reversal of fortunes, and Mao Xiang implies that Fang's undeserved demotion and exile just underline the dangers of public life irrespective of the dynastic transition.[94] Mao Xiang, likewise famous for his "big graphs with bold strokes" (*boke* 擘窠), also sold his calligraphy in Yangzhou at one point. In that sense, Mao and Fang, despite their different political choices, confirm a sociocultural solidarity that includes calligraphy and the appreciation of antiques and objects of art.

A good portion of the poem is devoted to the style, color, and history of Xuande censers. The vocabulary is so technical that Mao wrote an accompanying piece, "Notes on 'The Song of the Xuande Bronze Censer'" (Xuan tonglu ge zhu), by way of explanation (*MPJ* 1:429–30). Both Mao's poem and his "Notes" borrow extensively from Liu Tong's *Scenes from the Capital*. Liu Tong wrote about various makers of imitation Xuande censers, the inner glow of the genuine specimens that cannot be faked, and "the calamities visited on authentic form (literally, 'original color')"— these include the practice of adding burnt cracks, fashionable during the early and mid-sixteenth century, and the late sixteenth- and early seventeenth-century trend of excessive polishing driven by the misguided belief that "the nature of bronze" is thereby properly revealed. All these points are repeated with slight modifications in Mao's writings. For example, Liu avers that real Xuande censers have an inner glow comparable to human skin. Mao Xiang further anthropomorphizes the censer: "The strange glow of the censer is truly marvelous: / Toned muscles, fine flesh, and a spirit pure and harmonious" 有爐光怪真異絕, 肌膩肉好神清和 (lines 7–8). In "Notes," Mao adds feminine metaphors and elaborates the distinction between the real and the fake:

> What is most wondrous about Xuande censers is its color. The fake ones have an outwardly dazzling color, while the real ones have an inwardly blended color: a wondrous light emanates from its dusky blandness—just like a beautiful woman's skin, so soft that it can be gently pinched.[95] Burn incense in it for a while, and it shows an

ever-changing luminosity. Even if it has no contact with fire for a long time, and even if it is put in filth and mud, once cleaned it remains the same as before. For the fake ones, even if they are nourished by flames for decades, they will look dull and leaden once the flame is gone.

Mao Xiang's friend Du Jun comments on these beginning lines: "This is a judicious judgment of the character and literary accomplishment of people past and present." On the "improving techniques" that end up eroding the "true essence" of Xuande censers, Du opines: "As with everything, trying to meet the expectations of vulgar people can only bring about ruin" (*MPJ* 1:429–30). Du Jun thus implies an analogy between the genuine Xuande censer and genuineness of character, and the moral implications are further developed in Zhang Chao's introduction to Mao Xiang's "Notes" in *Collectanea of an Enlightened Era* (*Zhaodai congshu*).⁹⁶ According to Zhang, in extreme cases of forgery "the censers are cut in two, half of it genuine, half fake, like a man in two segments." We recall that those who vacillated and served both the Ming and the Qing dynasties were also called "men in two segments" (*liangjie ren* 兩截人). When the poet and scholar Sun Zhiwei (1620–1687) was about to take the examination in 1679, Du Jun wrote a letter to remonstrate (unsuccessfully) with him: "Do not be 'a man in two segments.'"⁹⁷

Mao Xiang seems less interested in the possible moral analogies between the genuine censer and singleness of purpose or unswerving loyalty. Instead he focuses on the pathos of "true appreciation" (*zhenshang* 真賞) based on a deep empathy with the drama of destruction and rebirth in the lore about the origins of Xuande censers. Legend has it that during the Xuande reign, a fire broke out in a palace hall used for Buddhist rituals, and the metal from the melted statues, which contained gold and silver, was used to cast new vessels (including censers). Liu Tong quotes the account in *Scenes from the Capital* only to dismiss it as spurious and offers an alternative explanation for the aura of Xuande censers: after being told that six rounds of refining bronze would produce a special glow, the Xuande emperor decreed that the bronze should be refined twelve times. Mao Xiang repeats both "explanations," qualifying his credence with the expression *huoyun* 或云 ("it is said") in the poem. In the "Notes," he prefaces the account of the fire with *chuan* 傳 ("legend has it"), adding that other gems and treasures melted and merged with the metal, which is then recast as bronze vessels. Images of regeneration in the wake of conflagration seem to resonate with the generation who lived through the vicissitudes of the Ming-Qing transition.

The poem concludes with the idea that the survival of the Xuande censer makes it a condensation of historical memory and personal memory (lines 33–42):

平生真賞惟懺閣	For the true appreciation of a lifetime, none matched the Repentance Studio.
同我最好沈江河	The best ones accompanying me sank in the River.
撫今追昔再三歔	Feeling the present, seeking the past, I sigh yet again,
憐汝不異諸銅駝	Pitying you, the censer, as being no different from those bronze camels.
一爐非小關一代	A censer is no small matter—it is tied to a whole era.
列聖德澤相漸摩	We touch the sages' virtuous legacy—a mutual polishing.
我今為公作此歌	Now for you, sir, I compose this song,
萬事一往何其多	For myriad things—all too many—that are bygone.
歌成乞公書大字	The song being done, I beg you, sir, to write it in big graphs,
明日且換山陰鵝	For which tomorrow I will just offer the geese of Shanyin.

In another essay, Mao Xiang wrote about the joys of connoisseurship as he examined the collection of Zou Zhilin (1574–1654), which included masterpieces of painting and calligraphy as well as Xuande censers, in his Repentance Studio. The memory of plenitude, however, just reminds him of personal loss—his best Xuande censers were lost during the chaos of 1644 and 1645 as the family crossed the Yangzi River fleeing turmoil and battles. As mentioned above, the proverbial "bronze camels" among brambles symbolize dislocation and devastation—yet here it is also a token of miraculous survival that provides a tangible link to the past (lines 35–36). The very nomenclature of the censer ties it to what was remembered as a "glorious era" (*shengshi*

盛世) in Ming history, and the image of "mutual polishing" (*xiang jianmo* 相漸摩) means that stroking the censer is to have the "virtuous legacy" (*deze* 德澤) "rubs off" on the connoisseur. This magic of "mutual transformation" continues and historical memory persists because the censer lives on as a poem and as a work of calligraphy (lines 39–41). Following the example of the Shanyin Daoist who, knowing Wang Xizhi's partiality for geese, barters them for Wang's calligraphy, Mao professes to prepare for a proper recompense in order to receive the gift of Fang's calligraphy. In fact, of course, the poem itself is a gift for which the calligraphy is the recompense. The web of exchange continues: Fang writes a poem to thank Mao Xiang on behalf of the censer ("Wei Xuan lu xie Pijiang"), for "a mere thing is also moved by its soulmate" 物亦感知己 (*MPJ* 2:1172): "Word is that the censer was cast in the palace a long time ago, / Thanks to your appreciation its authenticity is confirmed" 爐傳宮鑄舊, 得子品題真. In return Mao wrote another poem to thank Fang for his poem (1:174). In some ways this is just standard poetic exchange among literati, but it also demonstrates how the censer defines an aesthetic space shared by those who made different political choices and how historical memory is self-consciously mediated through poetry and calligraphy.

For Mao Xiang, the Xuande censer also evokes palpable experiences: "Fit for incense, fit for flames, fit for table and mat: / How can it be merely a matter of appreciation or poetic composition?" 宜香宜火宜几席, 寧惟鑒賞堪吟哦 (lines 29–30). Du Jun comments: "Fully living the censer's true meaning—shallow people would not be to articulate this." Ōki noted that Mao Xiang's personal memories of the Xuande censer—perhaps the ones that sank in the River—involve his beloved concubine Dong Bai.[98] In *Reminiscences of the Plum Shadows Convent*, Mao's recollections of his life with Dong, Mao describes burning incense in the Xuande censer in Dong's company: "The censers were always hot from earlier use, and their color was like liquid gold and grain-colored jade. We carefully poked and moved an inch of ember, on top of which we put fine sand and then the chosen incense for steaming" (*MPJ* 1:589).[99] They are fully immersed in the aroma of the incense in an enclosed room, banishing awareness of political turmoil. Together they craft incense pellets, and the very characters Dong carves on a bracelet allude to the name of a pattern on the Xuande censer.[100] What does it mean for historical memory and romantic love to be thus intertwined through objects? It is one of the questions we will explore in the following section.

THE TRAJECTORIES OF AESTHETIC OBJECTS IN *SPRING IN MOLING*

As embodiment of both historical and romantic memories, the Xuande censer belongs to broader arguments about the confluence of romantic love, aesthetic appreciation and creation, political integrity, and historical reflections—arguments that Mao Xiang implicitly upholds, for example, in his memoir of his life with Dong Bai and in his writings about his Painted-in-Water Garden.[101] Links to the fallen dynasty embodied by objects can thus dignify or justify their romantic-aesthetic associations. From another perspective, romantic love can invest objects with private meanings, domesticate them, and save them from the weight of history. The consequent escape promises to resolve the contradictions of implacable historical memory. Wu Weiye's play, *Spring in Moling*, portraying the many interconnected but also conflicting dimensions of objects laden with historical memory and changing hands in dizzying ways, illuminates these issues.

Spring in Moling carries an undated preface by Wu Weiye (under the pseudonym Master Reclusive Gardener [Guanyin zhuren]) (*WMC* 2:727–28) and a preface by Li Yizhi (The Recluse of Yuyuan [Yuyuan jushi]) dated the seventh month of 1653 (3:1495–97).[102] By then the play had been published. Two months later, Wu began his northward journey along the Grand Canal to take up office under the Qing. Based on references to the play in Wu's corpus and in contemporaneous writings, the completion of the play can be dated to 1650 or 1651.[103] Contemporary readers and viewers of the play as well as Wu Weiye himself emphasize how the play's elegiac and nostalgic tone conveys political lamentation (*WMC* 2:560, 3:14940-95, *MPJ* 2:1491, *QMZ* 5:523). Moling (Jingling or Nanjing), the capital of the Ming dynasty from 1369 to 1420 and again during the Hongguang reign (the so-called Southern Ming, 1644–1645), is linked to Ming rule and Jiangnan culture, which Wu Weiye laments and celebrates in his poems and song lyrics (*WMC* 1:24-27, 176-80, 2:533–38, 3:1151). The protagonist caught in a moment of dynastic transition and facing difficult political choices suggests autobiographical echoes. Did Wu Weiye remain an "inner loyalist" despite serving the Qing for two years (1654–1656)? Is the play about Ming loyalism or acceptance of the new order? Instead of yielding simple either/or answers, the significant objects in the play, at once aesthetic, romantic, historical, and political, articulate nostalgia, compromise, ambivalence, and contradictions. Focus on a symbolic object is one of the conventions of southern drama—it may cause strife, bring lovers together, signal virtue or vice, or determine the plot in other ways. *Spring in Moling* stands out in multiplying such objects—there are four—and in lavishing attention on their appearance, history, trajectory, appreciation, cultural significance, and affective power.

On one level the plot of *Spring in Moling* adheres to the model of romantic southern drama: it traces the vicissitudes and eventual union of young lovers. Set in 987–988 (*MLC* 3.1239), its political and historical context is the fall of the Southern Tang (937–975) and the rise of the Song dynasty (960–1279). Southern Tang, with Jinling (Nanjing) as its capital, was a regional power whose territories included the Lower Yangzi area and the modern Jiangxi and Anhui provinces. Its last ruler, Li Houzhu, was famous for his poems, song lyrics, calligraphy, musical sensibility, and impressive collection of books, paintings, and calligraphy. His reign was overshadowed by Song dominance, and he lived the final three years of his life as a Song captive.[104] The protagonists in *Spring in Moling* both have deep connections with Southern Tang. The hero Xu Shi is the son of the late Southern Tang minister Xu Xuan, and the heroine Huang Zhanniang is the daughter of a Southern Tang general, Huang Ji. Huang Ji's sister (and Zhanniang's aunt) is Li Houzhu's consort Huang Baoyi, who oversees his collection of books and calligraphy.[105] Xu Xuan and Huang Baoyi are both historical characters.

The romance between Xu and Huang is orchestrated by Southern Tang ghosts. Holding the infant Huang Zhanniang on his lap in 972, Li Houzhu pledged to choose a husband for her when she grows up (*MLC* 3.1239). The union of Xu and Huang has the blessing of the ghosts of Li Houzhu and Huang Baoyi and gains momentum through the intervention of the Daoist priestess Geng, honored for her esoteric arts in Li Houzhu's court (8.1256, 10.1262, 11.1265–66, 13.1269 71).[106] The love story unfolds through four objects from the Southern Tang court: the Yutian jade cup, the Yiguan mirror, the calligraphy of Zhong Yao (151–230) and Wang Xizhi (303–361), and the Burnt Groove Pipa. These objects, all

Lost and Found 257

mentioned in the play's summary (1.1236), change hands multiple times; their trajectory and disputed ownership determine the plot. In addition, Xu Shi's property, the Yiguan House, while properly speaking not an object, is part of this web of exchange and boasts of a special connection with the Southern Tang court, with its name inscribed by Li Houzhu. (Yiguan House is named after Xu Xuan's prized possession, the calligraphy of Master Yiguan [late 2nd c.].[107])

Characters are presented through their relationship with these objects and the culture of connoisseurship. The male protagonist Xu Shi is introduced along with his Yutian jade cup. He comes onstage declaring his melancholic immersion in objets d'art as he finds refuge from political displacement in antique shops. The dynastic transition has left him desolate, and he seeks consolation and sense of purpose in his skills as a connoisseur. His friend Cai You praises Xu Shi's jade cup as "the foremost objet d'art in Jiangnan" and describes its artistry and quality with a technical vocabulary indicating expertise. Xu Shi, however, emphasizes its ties with history, loyalty, and ritual authority by comparing the jade cup, a royal gift to his late father Xu Xuan, to ancient bronze wine vessels (2.1237). Xu Shi claims that his father was then basking in royal favor, and the Southern Tang was at the height of its power. (In fact, Li Houzhu, ever since his accession to power, had accepted Song sovereignty.) Yutian (Khotan, present-day Xinjiang), an oasis kingdom on the Silk Route, is famous for its jade.[108] Yutian jade evokes memory of legitimate mandate (*zhengtong* 正統) and dynastic power by implicitly affirming the connection between Southern Tang and the Tang dynasty, which received tributary gifts from Yutian. Historians debate whether the Southern Tang should be considered a legitimate successor of the Tang dynasty. In *Spring in Moling*, however, there is a deliberation conflation of the Southern Tang with the Tang dynasty.[109]

In a parallel scene, the heroine Zhanniang is presented as the inheritor of Southern Tang cultural heritage (3.1239–40). Her father entrusts to her keeping the Yiguan mirror, a gift from his sister, the imperial consort Huang Baoyi. He also gives her as models to be copied the calligraphy of Zhong Yao and Wang Xizhi, masterpieces that bear the seal of Li Houzhu's "Pure Heart Hall" (Chengxin tang) and colophons by Huang Baoyi and Xu Xuan. The Yiguan mirror, named after the calligrapher Master Yiguan, is associated with calligraphy, cultural accomplishment, and courtly heritage and thus goes beyond the standard associations of the mirror with beauty, love, and illusion. As in *The Peony Pavilion* by Tang Xianzu (1550–1616), the act of looking into the mirror and perceiving oneself as object of desire stirs up longing, and as she looks into the mirror Zhanniang sings lines reminiscent of Feng Xiaoqing, *The Peony Pavilion*'s famous reader who, trapped in a loveless marriage, finds no object for her love beyond her own reflection: "I cherish you for sedulously bringing forth smiles; / You cherish me, as we see each other's ill fate" 我憐卿送笑殷勤, 卿憐我相看薄命 (*MLC* 5.1246).[110] It is at this juncture that her maid Niaoyan mentions Xu Shi's earlier unsuccessful attempt to borrow the Zhong-Wang calligraphy, whose mention prompts Zhanniang to add her own colophon despite professing misgivings that the calligraphy may one day be lent to Xu Shi. (If Xu Shi or other men get to see the colophon, Zhanniang would be guilty of immodest self-display.) The awakening of desire is thus tied to appreciation of masterpieces of calligraphy from Li Houzhu's collection.

The logic of romantic drama stipulates the exchange of objects that embody the spirit of the lovers. In *Spring in Moling*, this is fueled by Xu's obsession with the calligraphy of Zhong and Wang, in exchange for which he offers Huang Ji the Yiguan House, but Huang Ji demurs and demands the Yutian jade cup as well. Romance thus begins as a negotiated transaction of valuable items. Xu Shi's grandiose gesture reminds us of some famous late Ming collectors: Wang Shizhen is said to have exchanged property for a Song printing of *Hanshu*, and Wang Xiyuan, as mentioned in chapter 2, gave up an estate for four Shen Zhou scrolls. Wu Weiye praises the lofty sensibility of his friend Sun Xiaowei because he sold acres of land in order to buy antique vessels (*WMC* 2:759–60). When Xu Shi comes onstage, he proudly places his expertise on judging calligraphy above his friend Cai You's knowledge about "solid goods" (*yinghuo* 硬貨) like "copper and jade" (*MLC* 2.1236–37), and the contemporary discourse of connoisseurship often did rank calligraphy highest among objects of appreciation. To exchange concrete things offering security and comfort for calligraphy with intangible spirit confirms his superior sensibility.

Xu Shi reasons thus: "I am not casting into darkness the gift bestowed by the former dynasty: / This is all for the sake of supreme calligraphy. / I will naturally find fine jade in the writing.[111] / What's more, I have the duty to collect my late father's ink traces" (7.1253). Xu Shi's rationale for giving up "the gift bestowed by the former dynasty" is that he is exchanging it for another object from the collection of the Southern Tang court, one that moreover contains his father's colophon ("ink traces") and would therefore assuage filial longing. He is also not consigning the cup to the "darkness"[112] of oblivion and ignorance, for Zhanniang is a true connoisseur.[113] Huang Ji, for his part, is initially unwilling to agree to the exchange, but Zhanniang convinces him to give up the calligraphy on the ground of Xu's connoisseurship. Xu Shi imagines Zhanniang's appreciation of the cup and envies its fate of being held by the beauty, thus reprising the reasoning of Tao Yuanming's "Poetic Exposition on Stilling the Emotions" (Xianqing fu),[114] in which the speaker imagines being transformed into various objects close to the beloved lady. Beyond the fantasy of proximity, however, empathetic identification effaces the boundaries between the connoisseur and the object of appreciation: Xu Shi, even as he gives up the jade cup, infuses his spirit into it.

Zhanniang moves into Yiguan House and, while admiring the Yutian jade cup, sees in it the image of Xu Shi (9.1259–61). This communion of spirit becomes mutual when Xu Shi discovers Zhanniang's image in the Yiguan mirror (14.1272–75), which he has received from an old lady (the Daoist priestess Geng in disguise) in a shop for antiques and curios during a market fair celebrating Li Houzhu's birthday, a melancholy reminder that the mirror is an object that has survived the decline and fall of the Southern Tang. (The comic villain Zhen Qi, homophonous with "truly marvelous" or "True Curio" [Zhen Gudong], whose ugliness is described with a string of technical epithets reserved for bronzes, pottery, inkstones, and steles [4.124–144],[115] has designs on Zhanniang and tries to steal the mirror. Geng intercepts his theft and gives the mirror to Xu Shi.) The alternative title of the play, *Double Reflections* (*Shuangying ji*), testifies to the importance of the theme of love that defies bodily boundaries. (The word *ying* 影 in the play carries multiple meanings: shadow, image, likeness, reflection, and spirit.)

The consequences of the "spirit journeys" for Xu Shi and Zhanniang are not commensurate, however. While Xu Shi suffers only a mild sense of distraction, Zhanniang lies in a coma-like state. Whereas he sees the image of her holding the jade cup (and looking at his image) in the mirror, she sees only him because she is looking at him from *within* the mirror. Earlier she saw only his image in the jade cup (but not the image of him seeing her in the mirror, since by then she has lost the mirror, and her spirit has gone along with it). Her spirit is at once more present in Xu Shi's world and more markedly evanescent. In a kind of parallel reflection, Xu and Huang speak to the image of the other onstage together (17.1281–84). While Xu Shi addresses the mirror and Zhanniang initially looks at the cup, it is Zhanniang's spirit that has come to Xu Shi's place of sojourn in Luoyang. She is presented as a phantom heroine unable to feel her own physical presence—she tries to hold the Zhong-Wang calligraphy and trim the candle but cannot; she speaks but Xu Shi does not hear her.[116] To Xu Shi, Zhanniang remains only an image in the mirror, apparently heeding his pleas and turning around—when she is looking at the cup, Xu Shi sees only her back—and moving her gaze to the calligraphy as he reads out her name, but still mute and removed. For Zhanniang, however, Xu Shi is no longer a figure in the cup; he is palpably real as he reads out Zhanniang's name on the colophon of the calligraphy.

This asymmetry persists as the supernatural agents arrange their marriage. Zhanniang's spirit enters the Southern Tang palace in the underworld to meet her aunt Huang Baoyi and learn of predestined karmic ties (18.1284–85), while Xu Shi encounters the ghosts of Li Houzhu and his entourage hunting in the mountain near Luoyang and learns of his marriage destiny (20.1291). (The historical Li Houzhu was buried in Luoyang.) In other words, while Zhanniang is absorbed by the vanished world of the Southern Tang, Xu Shi continues to function in the human world, into which bygone historical characters venture as phantoms. The two are married in the immortal (or ghostly) realm with the blessing of Li Houzhu and Huang Baoyi at the midpoint of the play (scene 22). Lamenting that the jade cup and the Yiguan mirror are no more than "the moon in the water and flowers in the void," Li Houzhu proposes to use a final treasure, the Burnt Groove Pipa, to cement their ties. The pipa from the Southern Tang court has become part of the Song imperial collection. The Daoist priestess Geng steals it from the Song treasury and offers it to Zhanniang, who learns to play with lessons from Huang Baoyi (26.1308–9).

As Zhanniang is strumming the pipa and telling of her stories, Zhen Qi bursts on the scene. Xu Shi is arrested for stealing imperial property and Zhanniang's spirit vanishes (scene 27). Zhen Qi is but one of several somewhat perfunctory villains in the play. The other villains include Zhang Jian, Dugu Rong, and Liu Chang's ghost. Zhang Jian, a eunuch in league with Zhen Qi, arranges to send Zhanniang into the Song court as a palace woman and seeks to incriminate Xu Shi. (Since Zhanniang is lying in a coma, however, her maid Niaoyan goes in her place.) Dugu Rong, whom Xu Shi seeks out as a potential patron, borrows the Zhong-Wang calligraphy but refuses to return it. The ghost of Liu Chang, formerly king of another regional kingdom, Southern Han (917–971), tries to thwart the marriage of Xu Shi and Zhanniang and kidnaps Zhanniang's spirit as she wanders homeward. The focus on aesthetic judgment displaces more dramatic and implacable moral confrontation, and political differences never emerge as a cause of contention, as Sun Chengjuan pointed out.[117] Thus Zhen Qi, mocked for his own ineptitude, is merely jealous of Xu Shi's connoisseurship. Dugu Rong swindles the Zhong-Wang calligraphy but abjectly returns them upon hearing of Xu Shi's success.

All obstacles begin to fade away when Xu Shi faces down his accusers, exonerates himself, and gains the title of top candidate with a poetic exposition on the Burnt Groove Pipa (29.1318). Xu Shi initially refuses the title, claiming that he needs to first find Zhanniang, but is eventually persuaded to serve the Song emperor, who bestows the pipa on him and enjoins the eunuch Zhang Jian to find Zhanniang within three days. (Thus both Li Houzhu and the Song emperor foster Xu's marriage, recalling Wu Weiye's moment of glory when the Chongzhen emperor gave him special leave to return home for his wedding in 1631 [*WMC* 3:1434].) The maid Niaoyan has entered the palace in Zhanniang's place holding on to the jade cup and has come under the protection of Zhang Jian, who offers her to Xu Shi as the woman he is seeking. Xu Shi ends up taking Niaoyan as his concubine, and through her help finds Zhanniang, whose spirit has returned to her body. The play ends with the marriage of Xu Shi and Zhanniang in the human world and with their visit to Li Houzhu's temple on the occasion of the latter's birthday. In that final scene Li Houzhu, Huang Baoyi, and the Daoist priestess Geng come onstage as immortals. The former Southern Tang music master Cao Shancai strums the Burnt Groove Pipa and sings to them of the vanished glory of Southern Tang palaces but also affirms the transcendence of immortals. He is to remain in the temple with the pipa and to honor the memory of the Southern Tang court with music.

If the account of the play seems almost bewildering, it is because Wu Weiye develops his unwieldy plot by multiplying antagonists and subplots. The multiplicity of symbolic objects seems at first blush another manifestation of the problem. An object that functions as a love token and charts the separation and union of lovers is a standard ploy in romantic Southern drama and sometimes becomes the title of the play. Why does Wu Weiye deem it necessary to have four such symbolic objects? On this issue he can be absolved of excess, however. He needs all four to explore different dimensions of the relationship between past and present, momentous historical changes and private happiness, lamentation for a lost world and accommodation with the new order.

If Wu Weiye's concern is merely to depict love that transcends physical limits, he needs only the cup and the mirror. The obvious models would be *The Peony Pavilion* and the Yuan play, *The Fair Maiden's Departed Soul* (*Qiannü lihun*), by Zheng Guangzu (late 13th–early 14th c.). Indeed, echoes of both abound in *Spring in Moling*. The difference here is that the objects bearing the images of the beloved acquire their magic from a bygone world and a ghostly realm. Transition between image and reality (or two-dimensional and three-dimensional existence) is made possible by the fluid line between past and present. By focusing on the provenance of these objects from the Southern Tang court, Wu Weiye charges romantic love with elegiac remembrance of the fallen dynasty. Such convergence would imply that fulfillment in love is also a kind of refuge for those lamenting a lost world. However, for Wu to address questions of political choice and its intersection with aesthetic claims, as well as tensions between the old world and the new, he needs the calligraphy and the pipa, both of which are mentioned in historical sources.

Various accounts of Southern Tang history note that Li Houzhu and his father were both accomplished calligraphers and that they amassed a vast collection of masterpieces of calligraphy, including many works by Zhong Yao and Wang Xizhi.[118] Huang Baoyi, who also excelled in calligraphy, was put in charge of the Southern Tang collection of books and calligraphy. It is noteworthy that Li Houzhu and Huang Baoyi are the overseers of the earthly romance in the supernatural realm. The great loves of Li Houzhu's life are supposed to be his chief consorts, the two Zhou sisters. When the first Empress Zhou died at the age of twenty-nine, Houzhu wrote a moving elegy.[119] Her younger sister, the second Empress Zhou, barred Houzhu from intimacy with other palace ladies, including Huang, who had initially enjoyed his favor. Huang is said to have survived by serving Zhou with self-abnegation and by carefully adhering to her duties as guardian of Houzhu's collection.

Instead of the jealous and extravagant second Empress Zhou,[120] who perhaps fits better stereotypes of a grand romance and dynastic decadence, Wu presents Huang as Houzhu's soulmate. The result is a more distinctive association of Southern Tang with aesthetic creation and cultivation. The implied analogy between Southern Tang and the Ming dynasty means that despite dynastic collapse, the latter could also claim a high place in arts and letters. As mentioned earlier, the Chongzhen emperor excelled in calligraphy, and several Ming emperors were noteworthy painters. More to the point, Wu Weiye may be paying tribute to the brilliant creativity of late Ming Jiangnan literati culture, for which he played a vital role. At the same time, there may be a sense of unease about the association of aesthetic passion with political irresponsibility in postconquest retrospection on the late Ming, as suggested by Li Houzhu's excessive attachment to his collection: "Alas! Don't say that it's but a scholar's lot to love calligraphy and painting. Even I, who could give up being ruler over the realm, could ultimately not let go of the few treasured things that I had valued my whole life. That calligraphy [the one in Xu Shi's possession before its misappropriation by Dugu Rong] is the most esteemed object of my appreciation" (*MLC* 26.1309).

When Nanjing was about to fall, Li Houzhu supposedly said to Huang Baoyi: "These are all the things I treasure. If the city cannot hold out, you should just burn them. Do not let them disperse." The collection was burnt in a huge conflagration when Nanjing fell.[121] Xia Chengtao questions the authenticity of this story, citing as evidence Li Houzhu's lamentation of the book burning by Emperor Yuan of Liang (r. 552–555) when the Liang capital was besieged, an episode already discussed in chapter 1.[122] Of course critique of another's error does not forestall one's own folly—the Liang emperor had decried how Wang Can (177–217) burnt his books when Jingzhou fell. The story about book burning might have been told to serve the narrative of dynastic decadence and self-destructive aestheticism. Whatever the cause, the dispersal and destruction of treasured possessions during the chaos of dynastic transition were all too real. Song catalogs of what remained of Southern Tang collections indicate that only a mere fraction survived.[123] Books seemed to have fared better: Emperor Taizu, founder of the Song dynasty, is said to have obtained sixty thousand scrolls as "remnants of the conflagration."[124]

It is against the weight of such memories of destruction that Wu Weiye offers his version of preservation and cultural continuity. The Zhong-Wang calligraphy, bearing colophons by Huang Baoyi, Xu Xuan, and Huang Zhanniang, makes its circuit in *Spring in Moling*, affirming romantic love and historical memory. When Xu Shi takes the scrolls to Luoyang to seek the Song official Dugu Rong's patronage, however, they take on more ambiguous political meanings. Xu Shi's father Xu Xuan was Dugu Rong's examiner, and Dugu Rong attained the *jinshi* degree in 972, the same year that Li Houzhu held the infant Huang Zhanniang on his lap (12.1267). The fact that he has switched allegiance to the Song dynasty does not occasion comment and criticism in the play. In reviving the connection with Dugu, Xu Shi acts like, and is perceived as, a prospective dependent, although he claims to be only a "sojourning traveler."[125] As mentioned, Dugu Rong's misappropriation of the scrolls is one of the subplots in the play. He borrows them and refuses to return them, with a view to presenting them to the Song court to advance his own career, for he has heard that "the court ordered Wang Zhuo to collect calligraphy masterpieces past and present" (12.1267).

The historical Wang Zhuo (ca. 928–969), a noted calligrapher, served in the courts of Later Han (947–950, the Turkic Shatuo regime), Later Zhou (951–960), and Song. The salient point here may be less Dugu Rong's perfidy than his reasoning. The new Song regime (just like the Qing) was eager to augment its credentials as the inheritor of a great cultural tradition. Many former Southern Tang officials, including the historical Xu Xuan, participated in ambitious early Song cultural projects, such as the compilation of *The Best from the Garden of Literature* (*Wenyuan yinghua*), *Imperial Reader for the Era of Great Peace* (*Taiping yulan*), and *Extensive Records for the Era of Great Peace* (*Taiping guangji*).[126] In *Spring in Moling*, Dugu Rong eventually returns the calligraphy scrolls to Xu Shi, who sends them to Huang Ji as betrothal gifts (40.1353), but their potential place in the Song court resonates with the justification of serving a new regime in the name of preserving cultural continuity.

Like the calligraphy scrolls, the pipa encompasses personal and historical dimensions, mediates conflicting loyalties, and charts a complex relationship with both the Southern Tang and the Song. More than the calligraphy that reminds us of Li Houzhu the collector, it has direct ties to Houzhu the poet by producing the music of his lyrics and may claim to conjure visions of the past with songs of remembrance. Both Houzhu and the first Empress Zhou were accomplished composers and musicians. In appreciation of Zhou's skill with the pipa, Houzhu's father, Emperor Yuanzong, bestowed on her the Burnt Groove Pipa.[127] On her deathbed, Empress Zhou gave Houzhu the pipa, and Houzhu buried Zhou with a gold-flecked sandalwood groove pipa that she loved.[128] The "Burnt Groove" evokes Cai Yong's (133–192) Scorched Tail Pipa. Legend has it that when Cai Yong heard a crackling sound as a piece of paulownia wood from Wu was being burnt, he recognized its worth, rescued it from the fire, and turned it into the Scorched Tail Pipa, which produced sublime music (*Hou Hanshu* 60B.2004). As for the Burnt Groove Pipa, "some said that it was cut from burnt wood, some said that it was preserved because it survived a fire."[129] Both the "scorched tail" and the "burnt groove" associate artistic excellence with danger and ruin. At the same time, both imply that the scar of surviving destruction is a proof of worth. Negativity and redemption converge in aesthetic creation: this becomes an important premise in *Spring in Moling*.

In historical accounts, the musical accomplishments of the Southern Tang court are associated with indulgence and impending doom. The Southern Tang looks back to the allure of the "Rainbow Skirt and Feathered Coat" from the reign of the Tang emperor Xuanzong, a musical symbol of both splendor and dynastic crisis.[130] The musical tradition of the "Rainbow Skirt" was lost in the aftermath of the An Lushan Rebellion. Houzhu obtained its notation, and music master Cao (presumably the inspiration for Cao Shancai) was able to "follow the notation and roughly approximate the music." Empress Zhou corrected the errors in Cao's version and created appealing "new music based on rapid hand movements."[131]

> Secretary of Central Affairs Xu Xuan heard it and asked: "Stately tunes should end slowly, and these sounds are too hurried. How did

this happen?"[132] Cao replied, "The original version was actually slow, but someone in the palace changed it. All the same, this is not an auspicious omen." A year or so later, Empress Zhou's son died, as did the empress shortly thereafter. Houzhu's kingdom sank into decline. It is the human heart that gives rise to music. Good governance or political disorder respond to gentle and measured tunes or urgent and violent ones. How can those be empty words![133]

There is unstated rivalry between Empress Zhou and Musician Cao. The historian affirms Zhou's music as superior, Cao's version being riddled with errors and no more than a rough approximation of the "Rainbow Skirt." But ultimately he seems to side with Cao, who is given the chance to air prescient judgments, recalling warnings against "sharp and urgent sounds" as portents of political disorder in canonical texts.[134] In some other accounts, Houzhu is said to have neglected affairs of state because of immersion in music.[135] He elaborated an old tune, "Nian jiashan" ("Thinking of home and realm"), by adding a finale. But the word for "finale" (*po* 破) also means "break," and "Nian jiashan po" 念家山破 can mean "Thinking of the breakup of home and realm." This is also regarded as "an omen of defeat."[136]

In *Spring in Moling*, Wu Weiye dispenses with all associations of the Burnt Groove Pipa with excess, indulgence, and political irresponsibility. Music is distinctively tied to memory of and longing for a lost world. Cao Shacai, a former musician from the Southern Tang court, evokes prototypes such as Li Guinian, the Tang musician whom Du Fu encounters in the wake of the An Lushan Rebellion (*QTS* 232.2562, *MLC* 6.1248). Early Qing literature is filled with references to musicians and entertainers who lived through the dynastic transition—notably the music teacher Su Kunsheng, the storyteller Liu Jingting, the singer and entertainer Wang Zijia, and the pipa player Bai Yuyu.[137] They are purveyors of memories and historical knowledge; encounters with them and their performance typically prompt nostalgia, lamentation, and reflection on the possibility of aesthetic mediation.[138]

Cao Shancai performs twice in the play. On the first occasion, he plays on an ordinary pipa, singing songs based on lines from the lyrics by Li Houzhou and his father. The undiscerning audience, consisting of Zhen Qi and his cronies, hear only "peng-peng clangor." It is Zhanniang, overhearing Cao's playing in the adjacent house, that enquires whether these are Houzhu's lyrics (6.1250). Cao refers to himself as the "has been" (*guoshi de ren* 過時的人), and performance here dramatizes temporal displacement. Appreciation comes only from Zhanniang, identified with the Southern Tang through family history and sensibility. To Cao, however, she remains hidden in her chamber; for the performer, the possibility of appreciation in the new era remains tenuous.

By the time Cao Shancai performs again at the end of the play, he is a Daoist ready to serve in the temple honoring Li Houzhu. Strumming the Burnt Groove Pipa, he recalls the particulars of Houzhu's visit to the Sheshan Temple (next to Houzhu's temple), Xu Xuan's composition in court, and Huang Baoyi's calligraphy and music in the palace. A devout Buddhist, Houzhu had built the Sheshan temple, and Cao contrasts Houzhu's palpable presence in the past with its present erasure: "But now, / The new dynasty has replaced the old one, / and the reign titles are completely gone from imperial inscriptions.[139] / Only the sounds of the River remain, embracing the old temple, / As cold tides hang on the pagoda's shadow" (41.1356). Houzhu's temple, built by Song imperial decree upon Cai You's submission of a memorial on the miraculous union of Xu and Huang (which confirms the potency of Li Houzhu's spirit), is in a sense the recompense for that negation.

Cao Shancai describes his relationship with the Burnt Groove Pipa, a gift from Xu Shi, in romantic and conjugal terms: "I will turn the 'Song of Roosting Crows' into the 'Tune of the Phoenix Seeking Its Mate,' / Just like how you, husband and wife, are matched by fairy glue. / For the time to come I will embrace it aslant, / And sleep with it, / Carefully keeping guard at the monk's modest hut" (41.1358). Li Bo's (701–762) "Song of Roosting Crows" (Wuqi qu, the title of a *yuefu* ballad) presents the heedless pleasures of the ancient Wu king and his beloved Xi Shi while hinting at mutability and impending doom (*QTS* 162.1682). "Phoenix Seeking Its Mate" (Qiufeng cao) is the song of courtship and seduction traditionally attributed to the Han poet Sima Xiangru (ca. 179–117 BCE).[140] By this logic, the song of ardent longing will replace that of ironic critique and historical reflection. "Fairy glue," made from phoenix beaks and horns of unicorns, can reconnect broken bowstrings.[141] Conventionally employed as a metaphor for a man marrying again after his wife's death, here it refers to the pipa strings, and by extension connections with the past, that can be restored even if broken. Cao claims to seek the past and its tenacious memory, embodied by the Burnt Groove Pipa, as his mate. According to Ma Ling's *History of the Southern Tang* (*Nan Tang shu*, completed ca. 1102–1105), Li Houzhu wrote a poem mourning Empress Zhou on the back of the Burnt Groove Pipa:

佹自肩如削	You have come: of course your sloping shoulders
難勝數縷條	Can hardly bear the weight of these few silken strings.[142]
天香留鳳尾	Heavenly fragrance lingers on the phoenix tail peg,
餘暖在檀槽	Remnant of warmth remains on the sandalwood groove.[143]

Cao's aria follows the same logic and anthropomorphizes the pipa as he embraces it aslant, turning the lost world of the Southern Tang into the object of desire.

The spirits of Li Houzhu, Huang Baoyi, and the Daoist priestess Geng appear onstage right after Cao's song about the pipa, as if such a profession of faith about memory must literally conjure the past. Their visitation vindicates the power of attachment to the past but also facilitates reconciliation with the new order.

CAO: *(kneeling)* Your Majesty, can you recognize your old servant?
HOUZHU: You are Cao Shancai in the Court of Immortal Music. I remember eighteen years ago, also on the third day of the third month, *(pointing to Xu Shi)* your father presented a lyric, entitled "Ten Thousand Years of Joy," for my birthday. Shancai turned it into a song on the pipa, and Baoyi raised the Yutian jade cup to drink to my health. How can I forget!
CAO: *(crying)* Just now your humble servant strummed the Burnt Groove Pipa, telling of how things were for your royal highness.
HOUZHU: Alas! So what you were strumming just now was the Burnt Groove Pipa? It has been a long time since I listened to your music. Play me another song and describe the scenes after I left.
CAO: As you decreed.
HOUZHU: What about my Pure Heart Hall?
CAO: *(singing, to the tune "Houting hua")* The Pure Heart Hall is piled with horse fodder,

HOUZHU: And the Palace of Glorious Ensemble?
CAO: *(singing)* The Palace of Glorious Ensemble is choked with tangled weeds.
HOUZHU: What about all the trees in the royal palace?
CAO: As for the trees, *(singing)*: They have been cut down and used as firewood.
HOUZHU: Those books and scrolls are what I loved most.
CAO: As for the books, *(singing)*:
    They are torn apart, with none to mend them.
        But thanks to the son-in-law who can put up a show, a fancy top candidate, we managed to earn *(singing)*
    This spot of a temple with incense and offerings.
        I too have become a Daoist in the temple.
HOUZHU: This is no small undertaking.
CAO: *(singing)* At the Three Mountains, angry waves roil,
    Crows beat their wings against the tips of branches.
    In the empty city, rancorous ghosts howl.
    What I fear is that
    The ruler will sit in sorrow,
    And I must therefore
    Strum this pipa until dawn.
HOUZHU: The ways of the world are naturally like this. Now that I have tasted the fruit of immortality, the loss no longer weighs on my mind. Xu Shi, today we are going to the Peach Feast of the Queen Mother of the West and have stopped here for a while. Now we must be on our way.
(*MLC* 41.1356–60)

The performance of songs remembering the decline and fall of dynasties will be featured prominently in the most important plays of the next generation: Hong Sheng's (1645–1704) *Palace of Last Life* (*Changsheng dian*, scene 38, "Strumming the Ballad" [Tanci]) and Kong Shangren's *Peach Blossom Fan* (*Taohua shan*, final scene, addendum to scene 40, "Lingering tunes" [Yuyun]).[144] In the latter, completed more than four decades after *Spring in Moling*, the storyteller Liu Jingting offers an overview of Ming decline and uses other ill-fated southern dynasties as analogs to trace the demise of the Hongguang court in his song, "Autumn in Moling" (Moling qiu). Untempered by the redemptive promise enacted by aesthetic objects in *Spring in Moling*, the vision of decline and fall in "Autumn in Moling" is much starker—perhaps the difference in mood is already implied in the seasonal markers. (The historical Li Houzhu was born and died on the seventh day of the seventh month.[145] By moving his birthday to the third day of the third month, Wu Weiye effectively combines the commemoration of his birthday with spring sacrifices and evokes the promise of hopeful spring renewal.) The affecting scenes of desolation in Cao's song are obviously echoed in the music teacher Su Kunsheng's description of postconquest Jinling in "Lament for Jiangnan" (Ai Jiangnan) in the final scene of *Peach Blossom Fan*. However, whereas the grief in Su's song is untrammeled (perhaps the historical distance is liberating), mourning in *Spring in Moling* is checked by Li Houzhu, the very person whose fate should invite pity and lamentation.

For the music master Cao, temporal displacement is healed by spatial restitution: the demarcation of a new space for playing the pipa in order to allow proper mourning and commemoration. That space is created because the spirits of the Southern Tang orchestrated the union of Xu and Huang, and Xu as top candidate has won the emperor's attention. In that sense the pipa is the perfect instrument for conjuring the past as well as for integration into the new order. Its transfer from the Southern Tang court to the Song imperial treasury marks the pathos of dynastic collapse. Li Houzhu orchestrates its theft from the Song treasury to augment the romantic bliss of Xu Shi and Zhanniang and to indirectly push Xu Shi into serving the new dynasty. It is because Xu is accused of stealing the pipa that he has to exonerate himself with a poetic composition on it, through which he becomes a top candidate and gains a path to officialdom under the new regime (*MLC* 29.1318).

The duality of the pipa and, as mentioned, that of the calligraphy scrolls finds reverberations in the complexity or inconsistencies in the character of Xu Shi. Interpretations that emphasize "the pathos of decline and fall" (understood as lamentation for the fall of the Ming) draw attention to the male protagonist's link with the historical Xu Shi, the grand-nephew of Xu Huiyan, the valiant martyr who died fighting the Jurchens. But there is little of the resistance fighter in the Xu Shi in the play, and there is certainly no hint of him rejecting the legitimacy of the Song dynasty. The only foe he vanquishes is the ghost of Liu Chang, the former ruler of Southern Han. Liu Chang and his consort, the Persian woman Mei Zhu, caricatured as brutish and barbaric, are set up as foils for the refinement of Li Houzhu and his court. The play presents them as fitting rivals for each other in the underworld—neither of them challenges Song rule. In other words, the battle is between culture and barbarity, not between Southern Tang and Song.

Xu Shi does show initial reluctance in accepting the title of top candidate, which seems to be an honor thrust upon him. His ostensible excuse is the need to find Zhanniang, but it is obviously his unease about serving two masters that deters him: "You, the Song Emperor, are pressing me hard, / But who will excuse my lies in front of the Sovereign Li (i.e., Li Houzhu)?" (31.1326). The prologue describes examination honors as "a dream in the spring wind," and his examination composition is curiously perfunctory. Yet Xu Shi's success in the Song court has the implicit blessing of Li Houzhu, who waves aside Xu's profession of loyalty: "It's a different world now" (26.1309). With the Song emperor's insistence, Xu Shi eventually accepts office without too much soul-searching; he might have been persuaded by the examples of his prospective colleagues Dou Yi and Lu Duoxun (31.1325), two historical characters who served other regimes before the Song.[146] In thus accepting the rationale of serving two dynasties, Xu Shi is close to the historical Xu Xuan, a Southern Tang official who served the Song for thirty years but continued to show concern for Houzhu during his captivity under Song rule. He wrote a moving tomb inscription for Houzhu and two elegiac poems mourning him.[147] In *Spring in Moling*, lamentation and commemoration also represent a mode of accommodation with the new order.[148] Here Xu Xuan is dead by the time Xu Shi is introduced; a passing comment from Dugu Rong suggests that he did briefly serve the Song (12.1267).

The historical Xu Xuan has no son. His younger brother Xu Kai, like him an official and a renowned man of letters, did not serve the Song. Xu Kai had a son, Xu Shilang, who opened a teashop filled with the calligraphy of Xu Xuan and Xu Kai in front of the Sheshan Temple in Nanjing.[149] In *Spring in Moling*, Xu Shi is called "Shilang" on several occasions. Does Wu Weiye intend any reference to the historical Xu Shilang, who represents the choice of reclusion? When Xu Shi comes onstage, he implies withdrawal from politics by avowing interest in objets d'art and "elegant things." He spends time in shops for antiques and curios and sings arias with a gentle melancholy. He chides his friend Cai You for valuing jade and bronze vessels above calligraphy and paintings and discusses with him the merits of Jie tea "behind the temple" (2.1236–37)—all these are topics that recur in the literature of connoisseurship, including works by Wu Weiye's friends.[150] As we have seen, however, the promise of aesthetic objects to define an alternative to political participation is uncertain in the play.

The historical characters Xu Shi, Xu Xuan, and Xu Shilang encompass a range of choices (heroic resistance, political accommodation, withdrawal) whose possible combination is explored in the character Xu Shi in the play. The supernatural figures that seem both spectral and transcendent introduce ambiguities and offer resolutions. Xu Shi's heroic defense of Houzhu is not directed against his real enemy (the Song emperor) but displaced as a battle with Houzhu's ghostly rival Liu Chang. Political accommodation with the new order seems sanctioned or even orchestrated by Li Houzhu. A life of aesthetic appreciation and withdrawal from politics as an option recedes as the play unfolds, although the Southern Tang objects inspiring that ideal continue to manifest their power in other domains, including romantic love, historical memory, and political ambition.

Of the three options outlined, political accommodation is most dominant in the play, perhaps because it is most flexible and complex, allowing a measure of heroic loyalty toward Houzhu (as realized in the ghostly battle with Liu Chang) as well as inward distance (commensurate with the idea of withdrawal). In that sense the historical Xu Xuan may be the closest analog of the character Xu Shi. Xu Xuan's devotion to Houzhu and defense of his memory while serving as a Song official as well as his aesthetic, literary, and scholarly accomplishments might have made Wu Weiye regard him with special sympathy as a kindred spirit. Historians are divided in their judgment of Xu Xuan. In Ma Ling's *History of the Southern Tang*, Xu Xuan is put in the chapter entitled "Biographies of Those Who Turned to the Light" ("Guiming zhuan"). Although he admires the literary and artistic achievements of the Southern Tang court, Ma Ling dismisses its claim to sovereignty as misguided, and by his reckoning officials who switched allegiance to the Song dynasty chose legitimate mandate ("turned to the light"). By contrast, Lu You (1124–1209) considers Southern Tang a legitimate successor of the Tang dynasty (hence his designation of the Southern Tang rulers' biographies as "basic annals") and disparages the disloyalty of those who served two dynasties. There is no chapter devoted to Xu Xuan; he is mentioned briefly in a chapter on Xu Kai, whom Lu You regards as a more worthy model of loyalty because he did not serve under the Song. Ma Ling, writing before the debacle of the fall of Song territories in the North to the Jurchens, embraced the perspective of Song mandate and celebrated Song unification of China. Lu You, writing more than a century later, empathized with the Southern Tang as the analog of Southern Song, the bearer of legitimate mandate and the defender of culture threatened by a belligerent northern regime.

Wu Weiye was keenly aware of these debates. His friend Mao Jin (1599–1659) published Lu You's history.[151] Another friend, Li Qing (1602–1683), combined the histories by Ma and Lu, together with other sources on the Southern Tang, in one publication.[152] Wu's acquaintance Mao Xianshu (1620–1688) wrote *Forgotten Stories About the Southern Tang* (*Nan Tang shiyi ji*).[153] Zhou Zaijun (b. 1640), the oldest son of Wu's friend Zhou Lianggong (1612–1672), published detailed annotations on Lu You's history (*Nan Tang shu zhu*). One of the sources included in Zhou Zaijin's book is the Ming loyalist Wu Yan's *Chronicle of the Transmission of Mandate Under the Three Tangs* (*San Tang chuanguo biannian*), which upholds Southern Tang as the legitimate successor of the Tang dynasty, perhaps thereby implying support for the legitimate mandate of the Southern Ming regimes around which remnants of anti-Qing resistance gathered.[154]

The justification of and unease with political accommodation account for a kind of evasiveness in the presentation of Xu Shi, and his complex relationship with the lost world of Southern Tang and the new Song order is embodied by the fate of the four objects discussed in this chapter. Their trajectories of being "lost and found" delineate the promise of self-contained romantic bliss, the functions of mourning and commemoration, and the possibility of bridging conflicting loyalties. These objects are stolen, swindled, exchanged, or miraculously bestowed and restored in the play. Of all their circuits, it is perhaps Xu Shi's exchange of the jade cup and his house for the Zhong-Wang calligraphy that is most significant, for it sets in motion the events that lead to his romance and participation in the new regime. Yang Chung-wei observed that the subtle changes in Xu's attitude toward the jade cup as he prepares to give it up and his justification of the exchange as "cultural responsibility" (the calligraphy being a more fitting complement for a literatus) addresses the ambivalence and mental adjustment of political compromise.[155]

The trajectory of objects also determines the movement of the characters. Armed with the Zhong-Wang calligraphy, Xu Shi goes first to Bianjing (present-day Kaifeng) and then to Luoyang to seek the patronage of Dugu Rong. A play on the dilemma of "serving two dynasties" needs only two geographical focuses: Bianjing (the Song capital) and Nanjing (the Southern Tang capital). Why introduce Luoyang? Luoyang is where Li Houzhu is buried, and where Xu Shi engages with the ghostly cohort of the Southern Tang court. But Luoyang also recalls the poet Lu Ji (261–303), who hailed from the southern kingdom of Wu and, after the fall of Wu, lived in reclusion for ten years before going north to Luoyang to serve the newly ascendant Jin dynasty. When Wu Weiye attained the *jinshi* degree and entered the Hanlin Academy, he compared himself to the talented Lu Ji (*WMC* 3:1434). In *Spring in Moling*, however, Lu Ji is invoked with pointed reference to reclusion (*MLC* 2.1236) and his Luoyang journey to seek recognition and answer the summons of the new dynasty (11.1265). These political implications are ameliorated by the cup and the mirror, which turn Luoyang into the place where the Xu-Huang "romance of reflections" unfolds.

When Dugu Rong's misappropriation of the Zhong-Wang calligraphy leaves Xu Shi in political limbo, it is the trajectory of the Burnt Groove Pipa that brings about a resolution. Stolen from the Song imperial treasury in Bianjing and given to Xu Shi and Huang Zhanniang, it becomes an instrument for expressing love but also precipitates Xu's persecution and vindication. Arrested for its theft, Xu ends up being rewarded with it when his composition on it earns him the title of top candidate. Xu gives the pipa to Cao Shancai, who will play it to commemorate Li Houzhu in his temple in Nanjing. From being the instrument of political integration into the new Song order, the pipa is returned to its original player and becomes the means for commemorating the bygone world of Southern Tang. Its dual role reconciles acceptance of the present with lamentation of the past.

After taking on layers of romantic and political meanings, aesthetic objects find their home with the reunited lovers and the temple for Li

Houzhu in *Spring in Moling*. In *Peach Blossom Fan*, the great play about the Ming-Qing dynastic transition written about four decades after *Spring in Moling*, the creation, transferal, and destruction of the peach blossom fan, the symbol of romantic and political passion, define nostalgia for and critique of late Ming culture. By then, historical distance allows a direct depiction of that period, and acceptance of firmly established Qing rule renders political accommodation a nonissue. The object symbolizing the passions of a lost world palpably summoned can thus be torn to shreds to make way for religious renunciation at the end of the play.

BEYOND THE HISTORICAL MOMENT

What kinds of passions and uncertainties are involved when one's sense of purpose and belonging is tied to things that are lost and found and sometimes lost again? The idea of "lost and found" speaks to the experience of loss, devastation, and renewal during the political turmoil of the Ming-Qing dynastic transition. From masterpieces of artworks to their imitations, from imperial objects to quotidian ones, from private to public symbolism, stories of ownership yield self-conscious ruminations on how things become meaningful. One may claim that the fate of objects (being lost or found) provides the venue for understanding personal vicissitudes and historical changes. One may emphasize the meanings of "finding" as acts of recognition that rescue lost works from oblivion and thereby confirm cultural continuity. One may seek escape from an alienating political reality in the enjoyment of things or their transformation into havens of private meanings.

Writing about loss also puts another spin on the notion of ownership: in the end what can be "owned" is the memory of things realized through writing. The culture of collecting and connoisseurship puts great emphasis on the collector's and connoisseur's appreciation of the world of things, bringing self-observation and self-appreciation into the accounts of such experience. In this sense, only upon loss can possession be genuine, because the actual context, the social dimension of ownership, is thereby dissolved. By the same token, what is lost can be repossessed through memory and writing, for it is in the vagaries of consciousness in retracing lost dreams that possession can best be established. The early Qing literature of remembrance, notably Zhang Dai's *Dream Memories of Tao'an* and *In Quest of Dreams at West Lake* (*Xihu mengxun*), describes things and places with loving precision.[154] The notion of collecting memories (whether personal or mediated) in order to repossess a lost world affirms the powers of the dreaming, imagining, or remembering self. *Honglou meng* is built on that reasoning. The beauty and allure of things are heightened by loss, even as loss opens the venue for critical retrospection. *Honglou meng* is thus indebted not only to late Ming sensibility (with its focus on dreams and subjectivity) but also to the fate of that sensibility in the wake of dynastic collapse.

Epilogue

In *Spring in Moling*, temporal disjunction is healed by the creation of the Li Houzhu Temple, the space for mourning and memory. Song sovereignty facilitates its creation, but it also seems to exist outside it. The spirit of Houzhu claims not to care about his own tragic history, but Cao Shancai can now commemorate, relive, and conjure the Southern Tang by playing music on the Burnt Groove Pipa in the temple. In that sense the temple is above all Cao's domain. The space one can own is one created through one's imagination, memory, performance, or writing. For all the potential contradictions in *Spring in Moling*—the lamentation of Cao Shancai seems more convincing than Houzhu's equanimity—the temple as the locus of remembrance and ritual reverence seems stable and well defined.[1] The Burnt Groove Pipa finds its place, a kind of interstitial space between the lost world and the new order: an aesthetic object is made to bear the burden of history and fulfill its political destiny. One may even argue for a neat "division of labor" for the four objects in the play. As mentioned in chapter 4, whereas the jade cup and the mirror chart romantic love, the pipa and the calligraphy are tied to political choices. Of the two political objects, the pipa embodies historical memory and nostalgia even as it paves the way for Xu Shi to prove his talent under the new regime, while the calligraphy masterpieces facilitate participation in the new order by affirming cultural continuity between Southern Tang and the Song.

The complex relationship between politics and aesthetics represented by the Burnt Groove Pipa obtains throughout chapter 4. Not only do aesthetic objects embodying imperial aura and Ming glory, such as the Chongzhen emperor's jade ram paperweight and the Xuande censer, inspire mourning and reflections on historical vicissitudes, even objects associated with frivolous or even dangerous pleasures, such as the cosmetic box from the Ming palace or the lacquer pan used by the Xuande emperor for cricket fights, are appreciated as precious and tangible links to a lost world. Personal loss is often intertwined with national calamity, but what remains after political upheavals can still become the components of an ascetic yet aesthetic existence, as Chen Zhenhui implies in *Miscellaneous Accouterments for the Autumn Garden*.

This is an aestheticism of loss, whereby the denial of luxury and abundance only leaves more room for memory and imagination. At the same time, those who managed to continue their late Ming lifestyle while maintaining distance from the new regime could also claim that aesthetic pleasure has a political dimension, inasmuch as their loyalism is marked not only by fealty to the fallen dynasty but also by affinities with the refinements of late Ming culture. Mao Xiang's continued interest in collecting and connoisseurship, evident in his social and cultural activities at the Painted-in-Water Garden he built in the 1650s, testified to this kind of sensibility and reasoning.

Mao Xiang offered refuge to Ming loyalists but also socialized with Qing officials in his garden. Appreciation of fine things crops up as a topic in the literary exchanges with both groups, who were sometimes present at the same gatherings. Aesthetics and politics intersect in another way when political passions seem to retrospectively redeem aesthetic obsessions. A number of Ming officials famous for their taste and sensibility, such as Ni Yuanlu (1593–1644), Fan Jingwen (1587–1644), and Qi Biaojia (1602–1645), embraced martyrdom. Qi Biaojia built Yushan, his famous garden estate, and wrote about his obsession with its design and construction.[2] He drowned himself in the pond in Yushan, leaving behind a testament stating that he wanted to die as a Ming martyr, after the Hongguang court collapsed in 1645. Yushan became a more deeply politicized space after the fall of the Ming, since Qi's sons, Qi Lisun (1627–ca. 1663) and Qi Bansun (b. 1632), used it to offer refuge to Ming loyalist fugitives like Wei Geng (d. 1663) and Qu Dajun (1630–1696).[3]

The fate of Yushan as aesthetic space and political space reminds us how the Ming-Qing dynastic transition is a salient point of reference for many of the examples discussed in this book. Thus "The House of Elegant Ensemble," the Li Yu story discussed in chapter 2, explores the dark sides of connoisseurship by showing how the supposedly self-contained world of aesthetic enjoyment is but a fatuous and fragile illusion. The economic and political pressures repressed in the discourse of refinement come back with a vengeance. Written in the 1650s but set in the mid-sixteenth century, it looks back at the late Ming world of political corruption versus aesthetic pleasure with ambivalence—the latter cannot escape moral compromises, but its embodiment ultimately rises to heroism. Retrospection across the divide of the Ming-Qing transition also informs Li Yu's play *Ideal Matches*, discussed in chapter 3. The late Ming world of courtesan romance, artistic genius, and aesthetic appreciation is shown to have been embedded in economic realities and the calculations of transactions. Li Yu offers an economic solution to the conundrum of late Ming sensibility—the fact that artistic talent or romantic passion is monetized and commodified is no longer a cause for hand-wringing but the basis of optimal pleasures. In some ways this is one early Qing answer to the accusation that late Ming indulgence in romantic-aesthetic values had built-in contradictions that undermined the equilibrium of the self and of the polity. The claims of the aesthetic as a category of significance and its uneasy relationship with economic and political values are also fundamental to our understanding of *Honglou meng*. Written in the eighteenth century, it may seem far removed from mid-seventeenth-century political turmoil. In fact, it inherits the tension between the beautiful and the useful, between the aesthetic and the moral or political as sources of meaning that characterizes some late Ming writings as well as early Qing reflections on the late Ming.

The relationship between the aesthetic and the political is paradoxical: there is both mutual dependence and latent opposition, and the boundary between the two can be both fluid and fixed. The binaries of the chapter titles in this book function in comparable ways. The relationship between people and things can be liberating, degrading, dangerous, or transcendent; contradictory perspectives sometimes come together in ambiguous ways. The discourse on subjectivity and the discourse on things are intertwined in important moments in the history of Chinese thought. Treating people as things or things as people does not simply yield predictable versions of cynicism or lyricism, as the residual compassion in *Jin Ping Mei* and the ironic skepticism in *Honglou meng* demonstrate. Elegance and vulgarity would seem to exist in obvious polarity, yet multiple and shifting criteria of judgment, especially on the value of social consensus and individual difference, yield versions of the elegantly vulgar or the vulgarly elegant. The real and the fake is another set of categories that should involve easy distinction but takes us to a world that both elevates and problematizes the genuine. While mythologizing the aura of the authentic, the Ming-Qing cultural milieu also granted cultural authority to the forger, the copier, and the authorized delegate. Both the moralization of the distinction between the real and the fake and the refusal to moralize it take us to ultimate questions of value and the authority of its assignation. Finally, lost and found would seem to suggest opposites without any paradoxical turn—that is, until we consider the fate of objects from a lost world whose value lies in evoking loss and whose presence announces absence, the meaning of ownership confirmed through loss, or the seductive yet problematic claims of memory, imagination, and writing to preserve a lost world by holding on to the contours of its things.

Notes

INTRODUCTION

1. Xie Guozhen found a manuscript version of *Huacun tan wang* that contains variants and lists Wang Wenbo as its author. See his *Jiang Zhe fangshu ji*, in *Xie Guozhen quanji*, ed. Xie Xiaobin and Yang Lu (Beijing: Beijing chubanshe, 2013), 5:619–20.
2. Scholars and officials identified with the Donglin group were committed to orthodox moral teachings associated with Zhu Xi (1130–1200) and were vociferously opposed to corruption (exemplified among others by the eunuch Wei Zhongxian). Their moral fervor, however, was sometimes colored by unfair partisanship.
3. The Eastern Depot (Dongchang) started as the emperor's personal bodyguard unit and evolved into an apparatus for surveillance and torture controlled by palace eunuchs.
4. All translations in this book are my own, unless otherwise stated.
5. Wu Qizhen was a good friend of Cheng Jibai's son and saw the Dingware vessel among what remained of Cheng's collection. See *Shu hua ji*, *ZGSHQS* 8:35. Among the other collectors named, Xiang Yuanbian is known to have offered five hundred taels to try to buy a Dingware censer from Zhang Dai's uncle. See Zhang Dai, *Zhang Dai shiwen ji*, ed. Xia Xianchun (Shanghai: Shanghai guji chubanshe, 1991), 320.
6. Lu Yitian, *Lenglu zashi*, ed. Cui Fanzhi (Beijing: Zhonghua shuju, 1984), 302–3. According to Wu Qizhen, Cheng was ensnared in a vendetta Wei waged against another official and died in 1625 (*Shu hua ji*, *ZGSHQS* 8:35).
7. See the stories and plays about Yan Song and Yan Shifan as ruthless and rapacious collectors discussed in chaps. 2 and 3 of this book.

8. On Huizong as collector, see Patricia Ebrey, *Accumulating Culture: The Collections of Emperor Huizong* (Seattle: University of Washington Press, 2008).
9. This story also appears in other seventeenth-century miscellanies. See *YSZ* A.9a–11a; Cao Jiazu, *Shuo meng*, cited in Jiang Ruizao, *Xiaoshuo kaozheng*, ed. Jiang Yiren (Hangzhou: Zhejiang guji chubanshe, 2016), 88–89; Li Shaowen, *Yunjian zashi*, included in Yao Hongxu, *Songfeng yuyun*, *Siku quanshu cunmu congshu bubian* (Jinan: Qi Lu shushe, 1997), 8.13a–14a.
10. See chap. 4 of this book.
11. See Timothy Brook, *The Confusions of Pleasure: Commerce and Culture in Ming China* (Berkeley: University of California Press, 1998); Craig Clunas, *Superfluous Things: Material Culture and Social Status in Early Modern China* (Honolulu: University of Hawai'i Press, 2004).
12. See, e.g., Jonathan Hay, *Sensuous Surfaces: The Decorative Object in Early Modern China* (Honolulu: University of Hawai'i Press, 2010); Dorothy Ko, *The Social Life of Inkstones: Artisans and Scholars in Early Qing China* (Seattle: University of Washington Press, 2016); Judith Zeitlin, "The Cultural Biography of a Musical Instrument: Little Hulei as Sounding Object, Antique, Prop, and Relic," *Harvard Journal of Asiatic Studies* 69, no. 2 (December 2009): 395–441.
13. See Yang Zhishui, *Shijing mingwu xinzheng* (Beijing: Beijing guji chubanshe, 2000); Yang Zhishui, *Gu shiwen mingwu xinzheng hebian* (Tianjin: Tianjin jiaoyu chubanshe, 2012); Yang Zhishui, *Wu se: Jin Ping Mei du "wu" ji* (Beijing: Zhunghua shuju, 2018).
14. See Tina Lu, *The Coin and the Severed Head: Ownership and Fungibility in the Seventeenth Century* (Cambridge, Mass.: Harvard University Asia Center, forthcoming); Sophie Volpp, *The Substance of Fiction: Literary Objects in Ming-Qing China (1550–1750)* (New York: Columbia University Press, forthcoming).
15. I have used a tone mark to distinguish Li Yù (chap. 3) from Li Yu, discussed in chaps. 2 and 3.

1. PEOPLE AND THINGS

1. See Yao Xiaosui et al., eds., *Yin xu jiagu keci leizuan* (Beijing: Zhonghua shuju, 1989), 961–64; Multifunction Chinese Character Database.
2. See Wang Guowei, "Shi wu," in *Guantang jilin* (Beijing: Zhonghua shuju, 1991 [1959]), 1:287. *Wu* is said to mean "mixed-color silks" in *Zhouli zhushu* 27.420.
3. Duan Yucai explains (quoting Dai Zhen's *Yuan xiang*): "The people of Zhou used the Ladle and Cowherd Asterisms to head the Asterial Order." See *Shuowen jiezi zhu* (Shanghai: Shanghai guji chubanshe, 1981), 2A.10a (53a).
4. Qiu Xigui, *Gu wenzi lunji* (Beijing: Zhonghua shuju, 1992), 70–74. Qiu disagrees with Wang Guowei's reasoning but finds his conclusion convincing.
5. *Song ben Yu pian biaodian zhengli ben: fu fenlei jiansuo* (Shanghai: Shanghai shudian chubanshe, 2017), 428. Gu's definition echoes the *Classic of Changes (Yijing)*,

"Xu gua": "What fills heaven and earth are naught but the myriad things" (*Zhouyi zhushu* 9.187).

6. For example, *Laozi jiaoshi*: "The Way is the repository of myriad things" (62.256); "Profound indeed—it [the Way] seems to be the ancestor of myriad things" (4.19). But the Way itself is also said to be a thing ("As a thing, the Way...") (21.88). See also the commentary on the Qian hexagram ("it provides the resources for the beginning of myriad things") and on the Kun hexagram ("it provides the resources for giving rise to myriad things") (*Zhouyi zhushu* 1.10, 1.18). The *Xici Commentary* describes the creation of hexagrams as being rooted in observation of heaven, earth, the body, and the world of things "to match the true nature of myriad things by categories" (*Zhouyi zhushu* 8.166).

7. A quick comparison: *wu* occurs 348 times in *Zhuangzi*, whose 64,606 characters make it almost twice as long as *Mengzi* (34,685 characters), where it appears 23 times. *Xunzi* (91,000 characters) is almost 150 percent of the length of *Zhuangzi* and has 156 occurrences of *wu*. *Liji* (99,020 characters) is slightly longer than *Xunzi*, and *wu* appears 119 times. In the much shorter *Laozi* (4,899 characters), *wu* appears 35 times.

8. This point is also developed in Cheng Xuanying's (7th c.) gloss on *Laozi* 21: "The Way cannot be separated from things, things cannot be separated from the Way. There is nothing outside the Way, and no Way outside of things." *Jijiao Cheng Xuanying Daode jing yishu*, in *Meng Wentong wenji*, vol. 6, *Dao shu jijiao shi zhong* (Chengdu: Ba Shu shushe, 2001), 417.

9. The punctuation here follows Qian Mu's *Zhuangzi zuanjian* (1.5) and Wang Shumin's *Zhuangzi jiaoquan* (1.27), not Guo Qingfan's *Zhuangzi jishi* (1.32).

10. *Wu* as verb can also mean "manage" in early texts, as in *Zhouli zhushu* 13.198: "to manage the affairs of the land" (*yi wu di shi* 以物地事). See also *Xunzi*, where *wu* as verb can mean "to make distinctions among things" and "to encompass all things": "Those skilled with things use things to make distinctions among things; those skilled in the Way encompass all things in dealing with things" (*Xunzi jianshi* 21.301).

11. The reading is different if we follow Guo Xiang's line breaks: "He who is in possession of a great thing cannot treat things as [mere] things. It is because he is not a thing that he can turn things into [mere] things." Wang Shumin follows Guo's line breaks and suggests the emendation of the line "he is not a thing" as "he does not turn things into [mere] things" (*Zhuangzi jiaochuan* 1:404).

12. *Zhuangzi zuanjian* 1.5, 6.51.

13. An illuminating contrast might be the line "the myriad things will transform on their own" in *Laozi* (*Laozi jiaoshi* 37.146). In *Laozi*, transformations inevitably fulfill the Way, while in *Zhuangzi*, there is a voice deliberating the movement between states of being.

14. See Xu Fuguan, *Zhongguo yishu jingshen* (Taipei: Xuesheng shuju, 1981 [1966]).

15. *Wenxuan* 17.763, trans. Stephen Owen, *Readings in Chinese Literary Thought* (Cambridge, Mass.: Harvard University Asia Center, 1996), 96. The idea of turning the focus of sensory perception from external things to inner illumination also appears in *Chunqiu fanlu* 57.331, *Laozi Heshang gong zhangju* (*Zhengtong Daozang* 20:129), *Yue jue shu* 7.137, 18.325, and *Shiji* 68.2233.

16. Liu Xie, *Wenxin diaolong zhu*, comp. Fan Wenlan (Hong Kong: Shangwu yinshu guan, 1986 [1960]), 26.493.
17. See *Shangshu zhushu* 3.47; *Zuo Tradition/Zuozhuan: Commentary on the "Spring and Autumn Annals"* (hereafter *Zuo*), trans. and annot. Stephen Durrant, Wai-yee Li, and David Schaberg (Seattle: University of Washington Press, 2016), Xiang 27.5, 2:1202–3. In the latter case, it is about using received text to convey one's intent or ambition.
18. See, e.g., the implied causation and sequence in Liu Xie's formulations: "giving form to things to express intent" (*tiwu xiezhi* 體物寫志) and "being moved by things and intone intent" (*ganwu yanzhi* 感物吟志). Liu Xe, *Wenxin diaolong* zhu, 8.134 and 6.65, respectively.
19. Zhong Rong, *Zhong Rong Shipin jianzheng gao*, annot. Wang Shumin (Taipei: Zhongyan yuan Zhongguo wenzhe yanjiusuo, 2007), 47.
20. *Wenxuan* 17.762–64.
21. *Wenxin diaolong zhu*, 46.693.
22. Liu Xie writes about "empty quietude" (*xujing* 虛靜) as the crucial condition for nourishing literary creation. The term has been linked to both *Zhuangzi* and *Xunzi*.
23. *Wenxin diaolong zhu*, 8.136.
24. *Wenxin diaolong zhu*, 46.693.
25. On the filiation of Six Dynasties literary thought to late Warring States and Han correlative thinking, see Cheng Yu-yu, *Yinpi lianlei: wenxue yanjiu de guanjian ci* (Taipei: Lianjing chuban gongsi, 2012).
26. On the reading of *cai* 財 as *cai* 裁, see *Xunzi jijie* 6.97. Wang Niansun (*Jingyi shuwen*) reads *cai* as *cheng* 成 (to bring to fruition) (cited in *Xunzi jijie* 6.97).
27. The counterpoint to this discourse of deliberate control may be the kind of "moral magnetism" imagined in *Guanzi*: "Rectify one's form and be adorned with virtues, and one will encompass the myriad things. They come flying on their own; their limits cannot be fathomed by the spirit" (*Guanzi* 37.647). "By holding on to the principle of oneness, one can rule over myriad things" (*Guanzi* 37.647, 49.777).
28. In "Refuting the Twelve Masters" (Fei shier zi), Xunzi attacks Zisi (Confucius's grandson) and Mengzi for making up theories based on old lore and calling them "five phases" (*Xunzi jianshi* 6.60–61). There is no reference to "five phases" in the received text of *Mengzi*. While the specifics of teachings and texts associated with Zisi can no longer be known, they could have been associated with "five phases" and the kind of cosmological correspondences that were to flourish in Han texts like *Chunqiu fanlu*.
29. The phrase *wanwu* (myriad things) appears fifty times in *Xunzi* and only once in *Mengzi*. (*Xunzi* is almost thrice the length of *Mengzi*.)
30. *Mengzi zhushu* 13A.229.
31. *Mengzi jizhu* 13.350.
32. Zhu Xi elevated the *Analects*, *Mencius*, *Great Learning*, and *Doctrine of the Mean* as the Four Books in late twelfth century. The Four Books with Zhu Xi's commentary became the basic texts for the civil service examination after 1313.
33. In "Great Learning," "Investigation of things" sets in motion the following (in order of sequence): "extension of knowledge" (*zhizhi* 致知), "making one's thoughts

sincere" (*chengyi* 誠意), "rectification of one's mind" (*zhengxin* 正心), "cultivation of one's person" (*xiushen* 修身), "bringing order to one's family" (*qijia* 齊家), "governing one's state" (*zhiguo* 治國), and "bringing peace to the world" (*ping tianxia* 平天下). This series of connected and sequential endeavors is commonly referred to as the "eight items."

34. *Liji zhushu* 31.895, trans. Andrew Plaks in *Ta Hsüeh and Chung Yung* (London: Penguin Books, 2003), 44.
35. *Daxue zhangju* 6–7, trans. Wm. Theodore de Bary in *Sources of Chinese Tradition* (New York: Columbia University Press, 2000), 1:729.
36. Zhu Xi, *Zhuzi yulei* 60.1437.
37. Zhang Zai, *Zhengmeng* ("Da xin"), in *Zhang Zai ji*, ed. Zhang Xichen (Beijing: Zhonghua shuju, 1985), 24.
38. Shao Yong, *Shao Yong ji*, ed. Guo Yu (Beijing: Zhonghua shuju, 2010), 49; cf. 152, 179–80.
39. Wang Yangming, *Chuanxi lu zhong*, in *Wang Yangming quanji*, ed. Wu Guang et al. (Shanghai: Shanghai guji chubanshe, 1992), 76.
40. Wang Yangming, "Bixia chi ye zuo," in *Wang Yangming quanji*, 786.
41. See Cheng Yi's "Four Admonitions," (Si zhen), quoted in Zhu Xi's commentary on the *Analects* (*Lunyu jizhu* 12.132).
42. "Lü ao," *Shangshu zhushu* 13.184. This is one of the so-called archaic script chapters "discovered" in the early fourth century. These chapters are late compilations that also contain much earlier materials from the Warring States.
43. See *Guoyu*, "Zhou yu" 1.1: King Mu of Zhou successfully attacks the Rong, but the tokens of victory (four white wolves and four white deer) also cost him the submission of domains on the margins.
44. See *Han Feizi* 7.112, 10.194–95, 30.800; *Guanzi* 26.478, 32.567–68; *Huainanzi* 7.242; *Lüshi chunqiu jiaoshi* 16.969; *Shiji* 32.1492. In *Huainanzi* (12.379, 13.452), *Lüshi chunqiu jiaoshi* (18.1168), and *Liezi jishi* (8.250), Yiya is credited with the power to distinguish the taste of the water from two tributaries even after they merge. Lord Huan has many harem favorites, whose sons compete for the succession. Yiya supports one son's bid to challenge the heir apparent (*Zuo* Xi 17.5, 1:326–27). In some accounts, maggots crawl out of Lord Huan's room as his decaying corpse lays unburied in the midst of unrest (*Han Feizi* 2.112, 36.801, 37.826, 831; *Shiji* 32.1492).
45. *Zuo* Min 2.5, 1:238–39. Wang Zhong notes that giving the cranes a place inside the imperial carriage was equivalent to granting them the rank and salary of a marshal (239). Versions of this anecdote appear in various Warring States and Han texts (*Lüshi chunqiu jiaoshi* 11.588, *Han shi waizhuan* 7.292, *Xinshu* 6.126, *Xinxu* 8.279).
46. *Xin Tangshu* 34.881; Chen Hong, "Dongcheng laofu zhuan" (*TPGJ* 485.3992–95); Zhang Dai, *Tao'an mengyi*, ed. Huai Ming (Beijing: Zhonghua shuju, 2008), 3.58.
47. *WL* 2:625; Pu Songling, "Cuzhi," in *Liaozhai zhiyi huijiao huizhu huiping ben*, ed. Zhang Youhe (Shanghai: Shanghai guji chubanshe, 1983), 1:484–90.
48. *LDMHJ* 6. Zhang Huaiguan's "Er wang deng shu lu," anthologized in Zhang Yanyuan's *Fa shu yao lu* (*ZGSHQS* 1:61), offers the same account. In that passage,

we have "the way of civilization and martiality" instead of "the way of learning and refinement." The account in *Taiping yulan* (619.2911, 748.3451) has "140,000 scrolls" instead of "240,000 scrolls."

49. See chap. 4.
50. Patricia Ebrey describes how Song Taizu (the founding Song emperor) "seized the treasures and documents of the courts he defeated and sent them back to his capital at Kaifeng." Ebrey, *Accumulating Culture: The Collections of Emperor Huizong* (Seattle: University of Washington Press, 2008), 32–34.
51. On the authorship and editions of these catalogs, see Ebrey, 355–72.
52. Ebrey, 43, 75.
53. The Ming novel *Water Margin (Shuihu zhuan)* turns the transportation of large and curiously shaped rocks from Jiangnan to Kaifeng at great expense into one of the provocations "driving bandit-heroes to Liangshan."
54. *Er Cheng yulu* 11.61a, cited in *Jinsi lu*, 2.26.
55. *Er Cheng yulu* 17.9b; *Zhuzi yulei*, 5.90, 97.2496.
56. *Er Cheng yulu* 17.9b; Huang Zongxi, *Song Yuan xue'an*, j. 14, in *Huang Zongxi quanji* (Hangzhou: Zhejiang guji chubanshe, 2005), 3:698.
57. Elsewhere the Cheng brothers show their affirmation of devotion to the classics, historical learning, and literary writings. Likewise, Zhu Xi both disparaged historical scholarship and affirmed it in different contexts. See Chen Dengyuan, *Guoshi jiuwen* (Beijing: Zhonghua shuju, 1958), 2:372–74. On the attitudes of Confucian thinkers toward historical scholarship, see Xiang Yannan, *Cong lishi dao shixue* (Beijing: Beijing Shifan daxue chubanshe, 2010), 54–66.
58. See Zhao Yuan, "Shuo 'wanwu sangzhi': dui Ming Qing zhiji shiren de yizhong yanlun de fenxi," *Zhongguo wenhua*, no. 2 (2009): 114–31.
59. On the different (even opposite) meanings of the term *wuhua*, see Zhao Qiang, *Wu de jueqi—qian xiandai wanqi Zhongguo shenmei fengshang de bianqian* (Beijing: Shangwu yinshuguan, 2016), 62–71.
60. The translation of the name of the hexagram follows Richard John Lynn, *The Classic of Changes: A New Translation of the I Ching as Interpreted by Wang Bi* (New York: Columbia University Press, 2004), 329–34. Xu Shen designates *xian* 咸 as the phonetic component of the character *gan* 感, defined as the act of "moving a person's heart" (*Shuowen jiezi zhu*, 10B.46a [513a]).
61. *Zhouyi zhushu* 4.82.
62. Zhu Xi, *Jin si lu*, 3.38, 43.
63. Cheng Hao, "Shao Yaofu xiansheng muzhiming," in *Er Cheng wenji*, 4.1a–3b.
64. *Er Cheng yulu*, 17.7a–7b; *Jin si lu*, 3.44.
65. *Lunyu jizhu*, 4.94; *Zhuzi yulei*, 34.871.
66. *Lunyu jizhu*, 4.94; *Zhuzi yulei* 18.419.
67. "The millet is not fragrant, bright virtue alone is fragrant" (*Zuo* Xi 5.8, 1:276–77). This quotation, said to be from the *Zhou Documents*, is incorporated into "Junchen," one of the ancient script chapters of *Documents* (*Shangshu zhushu* 18.274). In another passage in *Zuozhuan*, the fragrance of ancestral sacrifice is linked to "the absence of slander and villainy" (*Zuo* Huan 6.2, 1:96–97).

68. Ronald Egan's translation, in *The Problem of Beauty: Aesthetic Thought and Pursuits in Northern Song Dynasty China* (Cambridge, Mass.: Harvard University Asia Center, 2006), 17.
69. Ouyang Xiu, "*Jigu lu* zixu," in *Ouyan Xiu quanji* (Beijing: Zhongguo shudian, 1986), 1:287.
70. See Egan, *The Problem of Beauty*, 7–59; Shi Zhenghao, *Songdai jishi tupu yanjiu* (Zhengzhou: Henan daxue chubanshe, 2017), 70–74. As Egan pointed out, Ouyang Xiu's collection was the first of its kind.
71. Quoted in Zhai Qinian, *Zhou shi*, *juan shang*, in *Congshu jicheng chubian* (Shanghai: Shangwu yinshu guan, 1935), 11. Zhai claimed that Li was the first among scholars to pay attention to the learning of bronze vessels from the Three Dynasties. Li Gonglin likely drew the images in his *Kaogu tu*. Cf. Shi Zhenghao, *Songdai jishi*, 76–80.
72. See Zhai Qinian, *Zhou shi*, *juan shang*, 13–16; Jeffrey Moser, "The Ethics of Immutable Things: Interpreting Lü Dalin's 'Illustrated Investigations of Antiquity,'" *Harvard Journal of Asiatic Studies* 72, no. 2 (December 2012): 259–93; Shi Zhenghao, *Songdai jishi*, 81–83. On Lü's ritual thought, see Nie Tao, "Lü Dalin *Liji jie* zhong de 'Qu li' quanshi ji xueshu tese fenxi," *Jingxue yanjiu luncong* 25 (June 2020): 67–93.
73. Lü Dalin, "*Kaogu tu* zixu," in *Kaogu tu (wai wu zhong)* (Shanghai: Shanghai shudian chubanshe, 2016), 2. To "use one's understanding to meet the poet's intent" (*yi yi ni zhi* 以意逆志) is how Mencius describes the proper way to understand the *Classic of Poetry*.
74. See Yuan Haowen, "Guwu pu," in *Yuan Haowen quanji*, ed. Yao Dianzhong and Li Zhengmin (Taiyuan: Shanxi guji chubanshe, 2004), 93–95; Jiao Hong, "Ke *Kaogu Bogu* ertu xu," in *Danyuan ji*, ed. Li Jianxiong (Beijing: Zhonghua shuju, 1999), 138–39; Gu Yanwu, "Guqi," in *Rizhi lu jishi* (Zhengzhou: Zhongzhou guji chubanshe, 1990), 21.507–8; Tang Zhen, "Shan you," in *Qian shu jiaoshi*, annot. Huang Dunbing (Changsha: Yuelu shushe, 2011), 201; Yao Jiheng, preface to *Haogu tang jiacang shuhua ji* (ZGSHQS 8:712). In the cases of Yuan Haowen and Yao Jiheng, the rationale for appreciating ancient vessels is used to justify attachment to other antiques and artworks.
75. Ouyang Xiu, *Ouyang Xiu quanji*, 1:277–78. For a translation and discussion of this piece, Ouyang Xiu's poem on the rock, and implicit debates on the justification and critique of "petromania," see Ronald Egan, *The Literary Works of Ou-yang Hsiu* (Cambridge: Cambridge University Press, 1984), 41–42, 101–2; Xiaoshan Yang, *Metamorphosis of the Private Sphere: Gardens and Objects in Tang-Song Poetry* (Cambridge, Mass.: Harvard University Asia Center, 2003), 138–43.
76. Su Shi, *Su Shi wenji biannian jianzhu*, annot. Li Zhiliang (Chengdu: Ba Shu shushe, 2011), 2:129–32. For a full translation and discussion of this piece in the context of Song art collecting, see Egan, *The Problem of Beauty*, 162–236.
77. See Su Shufen, "Su Shi yu Wang Shen jiaoyou kaoshu," *Furen guowen xuebao* 37 (October 2013): 75–106.
78. In a colophon (1094) on a painting by Huang Tingjian, Su Shi quoted Huang's disparagement of Wang Shen's taste when Wang asked Huang for inscriptions: "What

matters the most for calligraphy and painting is ineffable resonance (*shenyun*). It's not that what you own are not bought at a high price, what one may fault is only the lack of ineffable resonance" ("Shu Huang Luzhi huaba hou sanshou zhi er," *Su Shi wenji biannian jianzhu*, 9:630).

79. Mi Fu, "Shu zijin yan shi," in *Mi Fu ji*, ed. Huang Zhengyu and Wang Xincai (Wuhan: Hubei jiayu chubanshe, 2002), 105. It is not clear whether Mi Fu should be trusted here.
80. On the poetic exchanges around the Qiu Pool Rock (or rocks), see Yang, *Metamorphosis*, 179–96; Egan, *The Problem of Beauty*, 218–36; Yao Hua, "Su Shi shige de 'Qiuchi shi' yixiang tanxi," *Wenxue yichan*, no. 3 (2016): 155–65.
81. "Nine Blossoms" refers to a range of nine peaks in Anhui; here it calls attention to the rock as miniature mountain peaks. The conceit of mountains contained in a bottle gourd is standard Daoist imagery.
82. One Song scholar who saw an image of "Nine Blossoms in a Gourd" wondered at Su Shi's preference: it did not seem that extraordinary to him. See Fang Shao (b. 1066), *Bozhai bian*, in *Congshu jicheng chubian* (Beijing: Zhonghua shuju, 1991), 187.
83. It is possible that Dong Qichang was the copier rather than the author of this treatise. See Li Congqin, "*Gudong shisan shuo* zuozhe xianyi ji qi sheji sixiang," *Anhui Shifan daxue xuebao (renwen shehui kexue ban)*, 2013.6 (41): 779–86. The treatise (section 9) classifies *gudong* into eleven ranks and four categories: "gold and jade; calligraphy, paintings, rubbings, and carvings; pottery and lacquer ware; horizontal lutes, swords, mirrors, and inkstones" (*DQC* 3:195–96).
84. *Gudong shisan shuo* (*DQC* 3:192).
85. *Gudong shisan shuo* (*DQC* 3:192).
86. Shu Min's preface, in Wang Zuo, *Xin zeng gegu yaolun* (1459) (Hangzhou: Zhejiang renmin meishu chubanshe, 2011), 1.
87. Cao Zhao's preface, in Wang Zuo, *Xin zeng gegu yaolun*, 2.
88. Xu Youzhen, *Xu Youzhen ji*, ed. Sun Bao (Hangzhou: Zhejiang renmin meishu chubanshe, 2015), 33–34.
89. Fei Yuanlu, *Zhaocai guan qingke*, 24a–24b.
90. Zhong Yao is said to dig up Wei Dan's coffin in order to obtain Cai Yong's calligraphy buried with Wei. This story is also told in Su Shi's "Account of the Hall of Treasured Paintings" discussed earlier. In one anecdote, Mi Fu threatens to jump into the river when Cai You refuses his request to exchange Wang Xizhi's calligraphy for a painting that Mi owns (Ye Mengde, *Shilin yanyu* [Beijing: Zhonghua shuju, 1984], 155; Mi Fu, *Mi Fu ji*, 242).
91. Qian Qianyi, "*Qinshu* xu" (*QMZ* 2:952–53). Yan Tiaoyu excelled in playing the zither and also collected some famous zithers, including a Tang specimen. Qian also wrote prefaces to the collections by Yan and his brothers (*QMZ* 2:951–54). For Yan's biography, see Zhang Pu, *Qilu zhai heji*, ed. Zeng Xiao (Jinan: Qi Lu shushe, 2015), 437–38.
92. Yuan is alluding to Tao Yuanming's (365–427) "Account of Peach Blossom Spring" (Taohua yuan ji).
93. *Baopu zi neipian jiaoshi* (Beijing: Zhonghua shuju, 1981), 13.245.

94. *Huangdi suwen lingshu jing* (Beijing: Zhongyi she, 1923), "Shui zhang," 9.1b; *Chao Yuanfang yixue quanshu*, comp. Wang Xudong (Beijing: Zhongguo zhongyiyao chubanshe, 2018), "Pi bing zhu hou," 156–57.
95. Lin Bu (967–1028) was a Song poet and recluse famous for his love of plum blossoms; Mi Fu is remembered among other things for his eccentricity and love of strangely shaped rocks (see later discussion).
96. Wu Congxian, *Xiaochuang ziji*, annot. Guo Zhengfan (Beijing: Zhonghua shuju, 2008), 151.
97. Zhang Dai, *Tao'an mengyi*, 4.80; "Wu yiren zhuan," in *Zhang Dai shiwen ji*, ed. Xia Xianchun (Shanghai: Shanghai guji chubanshe, 1991), 267–68.
98. Zhang Chao, *Youmeng ying*, ed. Duangan Muming (Hefei: Huangshan shushe, 2011), 143.
99. Ji Kang's obsession is also mentioned in Su Shi's "Account of the Hall of Treasured Paintings," discussed earlier.
100. See Liu Xiaobiao's notes to *Shishuo xinyu* (*Shishuo xinyu jianshu* 20.4, 705). By using the same word, *pi*, to juxtapose his own focus on a canonical classic with the fixations of Wang Ji and He Qiao, Du Yu seems to suggest that intensity of mental focus forges a common ground for what may otherwise pass for totally different dispositions (intellectual passion, love of animals, and greed).
101. *Songshi* 444.13124; Ye Mengde, *Shilin yanyu*, 155.
102. *Tan'gai*, in *Feng Menglong quanji*, ed. Wei Tongxian (Nanjing: Fenghuang chubanshe, 2007), 6:152.
103. Lu Shusheng, "Yanshi ji," in *Wan Ming ershi jia xiaopin*, ed. Shi Zhecun (Shanghai: Shanghai shudian, 1984), 18–19.
104. Fang Ziqian (given name Risheng), a famous chess player and phonologist, was the tutor in Li's household. The poet called Half-Stone Studio was Shao Jianzhang (sobriquet Shaowen). He lived in obscurity, and only a few of his poems are preserved in anthologies.
105. The vase is of the pear-shaped kind called *danping*. See Xu Wei, *Xu Wei ji* (Beijing: Zhonghua shuju, 1999), 2:592–93.
106. *Shangshu zhushu* 6.82.
107. Lu Shaoheng, *Zuigutang jiansao* (1624) (Taipei: Jinfeng chuban gongsi, 1986), 123. This book is also listed under the title *Xiaochuang youji* and attributed (wrongly) to Chen Jiru.
108. See *Shijing* Mao 55, "Bend of River Qi": "There is the resplendent noble man: / As if cut, as if chiseled, / As if carved, as if polished" 有匪君子，如切如磋，如琢如磨 (*Maoshi zhushu* 5.127).
109. Yuan Hongdao, "Liuqiao taohua," in *Wen zhi*, comp. Liu Shilin (Changsha: Yuelu shushe, 1998), 164. (This essay is not included in *YHD*.) Cf. *YHD* 1:824; Chen Jiru, *Chen Meigong xiaopin*, 155.
110. Tian Yiheng, "Bie hua ren," in *Liu qing rizha* (Shanghai: Shanghai guji chubanshe, 1985), 33.14b–15b (1074–76).
111. Jin Junming, "Ji lan si ze," in *Wan Ming xiaopin wen xuan*, ed. Zhu Jianxin (Shanghai: Shangwu yinshu guan, 1937), 3:214–18.

112. See Du Guangting, "Qiuran ke" (*TPGJ* 193.1445–48). There are several dramatic iterations of the story during late Ming.
113. Zhang Dai, *Tao'an mengyi*, 8.155–56.
114. Qian used the word "redeem" to indicate his disdain for the Huizhou collector (likely a merchant). Qian was Xie's examiner. According to Quan Zuwang (1705–1755), Xie and Qian became enemies because both were pursuing the courtesan Liu Rushi. Chen Yinke questions this and argues that the sale raised funds for the Vermilion Clouds Tower, which Qian built for Liu Rushi (*Liu Rushi biezhuan* 2:396–99).
115. Qian Qianyi, "Ba *Qian Hou Hanshu*" (*QMZ* 3:1780–81). Qian is alluding to lines from Li Houzhu's famous song lyric to the tune "Pozhenzi" when Southern Tang crumbled and he was taken to the Song court: "Most bitterly, on the day I took leave of the ancestral temple in woeful haste, / the Music Registry was still playing the song of parting / And I waved away tears, facing the palace ladies" 最是倉惶辭廟日，教坊猶奏別離歌，揮淚對宮娥. Some have criticized Li Houzhu's grief facing palace ladies (instead of his people or the ancestral temple) as being itself the mark of dynastic doom; see Su Shi, *Dongpo zhilin*, ed. Wang Yufen (Hohhot: Yuanfang chubanshe, 2006), 64–65.
116. These are discussed in Judith Zeitlin, *Historian of the Strange: Pu Songling and the Chinese Classical Tale* (Stanford, Calif.: Stanford University Press, 1993), chap. 3; Wai-yee Li, *Enchantment and Disenchantment: Love and Illusion in Chinese Literature* (Princeton, N.J.: Princeton University Press, 1993), chap. 3.
117. A starker contrast can be drawn between these stories and stories about random things [e.g., household items, utensils] becoming human without developing any emotional connections with the human characters in the stories. For a list of twenty-four such stories in *Taiping guangji*, see Cao Huajie, "*Taiping guangji* jingguai gushi muti yanjiu," M.A. thesis, Jimei University, 2013, 51.
118. On comparisons between the two versions, see Tian Xiaofei, "A Preliminary Comparison of the Two Recensions of *Jin Ping Mei*," *Harvard Journal of Asiatic Studies* 62, no. 2 (December 2002): 347-88; *Qiushui tang lun Jin Ping Mei* (Tianjin: Tianjin renmin chubanshe, 2003). Citations in this book are principally from *Jin Ping Mei cihua*, but I also refer to an edition with collated commentaries (*Huiping huijiao Jin Ping Mei*, hereafter *Huiping*) based on the Chongzhen edition.
119. As Ximen Qing's unofficial concubine, Chunmei is entitled to some clothing and jewelry when she is sold. Yueniang gives her nothing because of her role in facilitating the affair between Pan Jinlian and Ximen Qing's son-in-law Chen Jingji. The go-between, Auntie Xue, makes a tidy profit when she resells Chunmei to the commandant Zhou Xiu for fifty taels.
120. Jinlian is brought to Ximen Qing's house in a sedan chair accompanied by four lanterns (*JPM* 9.115). Yulou comes in a large sedan chair and four pairs of red gauze lanterns (7.97). For Ping'er, Ximen Qing sends a large sedan chair, a bolt of red satin, four pairs of lanterns, and four servants (19.265).
121. David Tod Roy's translation, *The Plum in the Golden Vase, or Chin P'ing Mei* (Princeton, N.J.: Princeton University Press, 1993–2013), is based on the *cihua*

edition. Translations are mine when page numbers from Roy's translation are not included.
122. Roy translates this as "court affection."
123. In that sense, Jinlian's acquisitiveness is less about wealth or the things themselves than her own obsessive desire. The Chongzhen edition commentator notes the dismissive way Jinlian refers to the powerful eunuch Huang Jingchen, defender-in-chief of the palace command: "The words 'Eunuch Huang' are uttered so coldly. Thus one can see that in the hearts of truly passionate women and truly lustful women, wealth does not matter" (*Huiping* 73.1498).
124. The idea has deep roots in the tradition. Zichan explains in *Zuozhuan* that if a deceased person had consumed an abundance of fine things, his soul would have greater vitality and he would be more capable of returning as a ghost (*Zuo* Zhao 7.9, 3:1426–27).
125. I have modified Roy's translation here.
126. The term also refers to the penis, as in "donkey member-sized merchandise" (*lü da hanghuo* 驢大行貨) or "huge merchandise" (*da hanghuo* 大行貨) (*JPM* 3.39, 51.765, 52.780). Other vernacular novels use the terms *huo* and *hanghuo* also, but much less frequently than in *Jin Ping Mei*.
127. Both the Chongzhen edition commentator and Zhang Zhupo note the resemblance (*Huiping* 49.970–71). All the dishes in the feast for the monk are based on overt or covert sexual puns, as Zhang Zhupo implies by his repeated comments, *qu* 趣 (clever) and *xiang* 像 (look alike) (49.973–74).
128. The late Qing critic Wen Long notes Ximen Qing's lack of agency in general and enumerates the occasions when he is manipulated by Dame Wang, Auntie Xue, Pan Jinlian, Li Guijie, Ying Bojue, and Shutong (*Huiping* 35.737).
129. For allusions to these lines, see, e.g., the Yuan plays *Qujiang chi, Ti shaqi, Huolangdan*, and *Bian Huangzhou*; the Ming plays *Xiangnang ji, Lijing ji*, and *Yubei ji*; the vernacular tales "Li Shishi waizhuan," "Xihu santa ji," *Bao Longtu pan baijia gong'an, Shuihu quanzhuan* (chap. 101), *Xingshi hengyan* 31; see also Gu Qiyuan, *Kezuo zuiyu* 56.181; Feng Menglong et al., comp., *Ming Qing minge shidiao ji* (Shanghai: Shanghai guji chubanshe, 1987), 460.
130. The description in the Chongzhen edition is much briefer: "She must be depicted in both cases in bright blue and green style, with a proper headdress and robe. It should be mounted on damask with an ivory roller" (*Huiping* 63.1172).
131. This bed presumably replaces the "black lacquer bedstead, elaborately adorned with gold tracery" that Ximen Qing purchased for Pan Jinlian for sixteen taels when she entered his household (*JPM* 9.116, 1:171).
132. The description in the Chongzhen edition is shorter; there is no mention of "towers and terraces, halls and chambers" or of the comb-back-shaped backrests.
133. Chunmei is made to watch the coitus and sexual games of Pan Jinlian and Ximen Qing (*JPM* chaps. 18, 27), and she has intercourse with Chen Jingji in front of Pan Jinlian (chap. 82).
134. See, for example, Roy's reading, which construes the implied author's stringent moral critique from the perspective of Xunzi's thought (introduction to his

translation). For Andrew Plaks, the book ironically unmasks moral vacuum by drawing on sixteenth-century "learning of the heart and mind" (Plaks, *The Four Masterworks of the Ming Novel: Ssu Ta Ch'i-shu* [Princeton, N.J.: Princeton University Press, 1987]). Sophie Volpp's discussion of objects in *Jin Ping Mei* also focuses on the idea of transgression and moral collapse (Volpp, "The Gift of a Python Robe: The Circulation of Objects in *Jin Ping Mei*," *Harvard Journal of Asiatic Studies* 65, no. 1 [2005]: 133–58). In *The Substance of Fiction: Literary Objects in Ming-Qing China (1550–1750)* (New York: Columbia University Press, forthcoming), however, Volpp contextualizes that discussion and suggests that sumptuary violation also serves an "aesthetic of disjunction," "the sort of comic juxtaposition characteristic of the rhymes of drinking games."

135. Sun Shuyu sees sympathy for human weaknesses and failures as the distinct achievement of *Jin Ping Mei* (Sun, *Jin Ping Mei de yishu: jiushu xindu zhi er* [Taipei: Shibao wenhua chuban shiye youxian gongsi, 1978]); see also Tian Xiaofei, *Qiushui tang*. Among the traditional commentators, the Chongzhen commentator seems least judgmental.

136. In the extant manuscripts, chapters 17 and 18 are combined into one chapter.

137. See, e.g., Chow Tse-tsung, *Honglou meng an: Qiyuan Hongxue lunwen ji* (Hong Kong: Chinese University of Hong Kong Press, 2000), 157–67.

138. Identification of some of these exotic items relies on Qing court documents and research into the material responsibilities of imperial textile commissioners (the position held by Cao's forbears). See, e.g., Huang Yinong, "Wendulina, wangqia yangyan, yu yifona xin kao," *Cao Xueqin yanjiu*, no. 4 (2016): 33–46; "Cong huangshang Xue jia kan *Honglou meng* de wuzhi wenhua," *Zhongguo wenhua* 48, no. 2 (2018): 1–11.

139. See Li, *Enchantment and Disenchantment*, 210–16.

140. See Volpp's discussion of the plate-glass mirror in *The Substance of Fiction*, chap. 4.

141. On material culture and *Honglou meng*, see, e.g., Deng Yunxiang, *Honglou fengsu tan* (Beijing: Zhonghua shuju, 1987); Zhan Dan, *Honglou meng de wuzhi yu fei wuzhi* (Chongqing: Chongqing chubanshe, 2006).

142. See Ling-Hon Lam, "The Matriarch's Private Ear: Performance, Reading, Censorship, and the Fabrication of Interiority in *The Story of the Stone*," *Harvard Journal of Asiatic Studies* 65, no. 2 (December 2005): 357–415. Lam contrasts "the production of sentimental interiority" in reading the play with the communal experience of watching its performance.

143. *The Western Wing in All Keys and Modes* combines narration with song suites and was performed to the accompaniment of string instruments. The two versions of the play in "southern style" rewrote the play to suit southern tunes. Li Rihua here should not be confused with the late Ming scholar and collector Li Rihua (1565–1634).

144. Fan Jingzhong suggests that the prints may be part of *Huanyin* in the compendium (Dong Jie, *Ming Qing kan Xixiang ji banhua kaoxi* [Shijiazhuang: Hebei meishu chubanshe, 2006], 1–12). The album is preserved in the Museum of East Asian Art in Cologne. Wu Hung discusses these prints in *The Double Screen: Medium and*

Representation in Chinese Painting (Chicago: University of Chicago Press, 1996), 246–59. See also Dong Jie, *Ming Qing kan Xixiangji*, 107–41.
145. Yu Ying-shih interprets this as the tenuous separation of the ideal world from the real one in *Honglou meng de liangge shijie* (Taipei: Lianjing, 1978).
146. See Li, *Enchantment and Disenchantment*, 203–10.
147. At the beginning of the book, when the leftover stone asks to be taken to the human world, he is referred to as the "obtuse thing" (*chunwu* 蠢物). That term reappears as self-designation when the stone acts as the narrator of the story.
148. Wang Shifu, *Xixiang ji jijie*, comp. Fu Xiaohang (Lanzhou: Gansu renmin chubanshe, 1989), 141.
149. *Xixiang ji jijie*, 222–23.
150. *Xixiang ji jijie*, 62.
151. See Zhao Zhiqian, *Zhangke zaji*; Ping Buqing, *Xia wai qunxie*; and Futang yishi, *Xu Yuewei caotang biji* (all cited in Yishu, *Honglou meng juan*, 375–76, 393–96). Among modern scholars, Zhou Ruchang is the most insistent proponent of this theory.
152. *Taiping yulan* 82.515, 135.786. The same story is sometimes told about the femme fatale Bosi and King You of Zhou (r. 782–771 BCE). See, e.g., Zheng Qiao, *Tong zhi* (Taipei: Shangwu yinshu guan, 1987), 3B.52; Feng Menglong and Cai Yuanfang, *Dong Zhou lieguo zhi*, ed. Liu Bentong (Taipei: Sanmin shuju, 1999), 2.18.
153. The narrator's comments are deleted in the 1791 and 1792 printed editions. On the dialectics of irony and pathos in the narrative framing of the elegy, see Li, *Enchantment and Disenchantment*, 229–30.
154. John Stuart Mill, "Thoughts on Poetry and Its Varieties," *Crayon* 7, no. 4 (April 1860): 93–97.

2. ELEGANCE AND VULGARITY

1. *Jinshu* 84.2183. This is the first anecdote told about Wang Gong in the biography.
2. *Laozi jiaoshi* 98–99. Many commentators read *xing* 行 as *xing* 形, and *zhuixing* 贅形 as an unnecessary and burdensome protuberance of the body (like a sixth finger).
3. See *Shishuo xinyu* 7.26, 8.153, 31.7; *Jinshu* 84.2183–87.
4. *Cha jing*, "Wu zhi zhu," *CX* 11–12.
5. Included in *CX* 23–26. See also *Quan Tang wen* 721.7420–21; the text is also partially included in *TPGJ* 399.3201.
6. This implausible feat is disparaged by the incredulous Ouyang Xiu, but the Ming scholar-official Xu Xianzhong (1493–1569) defends it in his *Evaluations of Water* (*Shui pin*, *CX* 198). Xu believes that Nanling water, being "deep, pure, and heavy," will not mix with the muddy water by the bank.
7. One wonders whether this judgment has anything to do with the fact that the monk hails from Chu.
8. Li Jiqing is deferential in this account, but in *New Tang History* (*Xin Tang shu* 196.5612) Li is dismissive of Lu Yu, who expresses his rancor by writing the

"Disquisition on Doing Away with Tea" (Huicha lun). Cf. Wang Dang, *Tang yulin jiaozheng*, ed. Zhou Xunchu (Beijing: Zhonghua shuju, 1987), 750.

9. See *Ouyang Xiu quanji* (Beijing: Zhongguo shudian, 1986), 1:459–60. Ouyang Xiu was one of the compilers of the *New Tang History*, which condemned Zhang Youxin for being corrupt as well as "deviant and treacherous" (*Xin Tangshu* 174.5222, 175.5246–47).

10. Zhang Youxin ranks "Dragon Pond Water" tenth and does not mention water from Floating Raft Mountain at all (*CX* 25).

11. *Ouyang Xiu quanji*, 1:279–80.

12. See *Shiliu tangpin*, *CX* 27, which describes sixteen grades with the methods and implements for making tea.

13. Zhang Dafu, "Shicha," in *Meihua caotang bitan* (Shanghai: Shanghai guji chubanshe, 1986), 2.169–70.

14. *Zhongguo gudai chaxue quanshu* includes forty-six items from Ming (two of them early and mid-Ming), as compared to six from Tang, nineteen from Song, and two from Yuan. (Many Ming anecdotes on tea and discussions of tea from miscellanies and collections, including the passages from Yuan Hongdao, Zhang Dafu, and Zhang Dai discussed later, are not included in this anthology.) As noted, almost all discussions of tea encompass a section on water. Tian Yiheng's (16th c.) *Zhuquan xiaopin* and Xu Xianzhong's *Shui pin* focus almost entirely on water (*CX* 178–211). See also Zhu Guozhen, "Pinshui," *Yongchuang xiaopin* (Beijing: Zhonghua shuju, 1959), 15.340.

15. *Lüshi chunqiu jiaoshi* 18.1168, *Huainanzi* 12.379, *Liezi* 8.250. Cf. chap. 1, n. 44.

16. Feng Menglong, *Jingshi tongyan*, in *Feng Menglong quanji*, ed. Wei Tongxian (Nanjing: Fenghuang chubanshe, 2007), 2:399.

17. Ding Yonghui, *Zhitian lu*, cited in Wang Dang, *Tang yulin jiaozheng*, 7.613–14.

18. Zhang Dafu, "Shicha." Despite his disclaimer, Zhang writes about tea and water like a connoisseur. See, e.g., the entries "Pinquan," "Jiancha," "Deng Huishan," "Yunwu cha," "Xi quan," "Yunshui," "Dongshan cha," "Yixi quan," "Chaju," "Wuyi cha," "Jingjie," "cha," "Yunshui," and "Qiuye" (*Meihua caotang bitan*, 1.57–58, 1.82, 3.199–200, 3.203–4, 3.215–16, 3.230, 6.408, 8.541–42, 10,664, 13.817, 13.818–19, 14.919–20).

19. Li Rihua, *Liuyan zhai biji*, ed. Yu Zhenhong and Li Baoyang, and *Zitao xuan zazhui*, ed. Xue Weiyuan (Nanjing: Fenghuang chubanshe, 2010), 307; also included in *CX* 530–31.

20. Literally, to enjoy "the wind among pines with our jaws." The sound of boiling water for tea is sometimes compared to "wind among pines." See, e.g., Zhang Dafu, "Pinquan," in *Meihua caotang bitan*, 1.57. Here, Li Rihua is fusing the pleasure of listening to boiling water with the anticipation of drinking fine tea.

21. "Moon round" is a kind of "tea cake" made from baked tea leaves ground and reconstituted in rounds.

22. Lu Yu describes "fish eyes" (*yumu* 魚目) as the first stage of water boiling (*Cha jing*, *CX* 12), a metaphor adopted in poems on tea drinking by Bai Juyi (772–846) and Li Qunyu (808–862) (*QTS* 439.4893, 453.5126, 568.6579). See also Su Shi, "Shiyuan

jiancha": "The crab eyes are gone; the fish eyes emerge" 蟹眼已過魚眼生 (*Su Shi shiji hezhu*, annot. Feng Yingliu et al. (Shanghai: Shanghai guji chubanshe, 2001), 8.346. "Crab eyes" and "fish eyes" both refer to the size of the bubbles as water boils. Tea connoisseurs debate the state of optimal boiling for the water used to make tea.

23. When a monk criticizes Li Deyu for the toil he causes with his water transportation, he protests that his only "vice" should be excused, considering his freedom from "the desires of ordinary people." The monk eventually convinces him to give up the practice and to use instead water from a well in the capital that shares the same source as the Hui Mountain Spring (*TPGJ* 399.3208). In a poem on the Hui spring, Pi Rixiu (834–883) faults Li Deyu for his "water transportation," comparing it to the havoc caused by Consort Yang's taste for the southern fruit *lizhi* (*Quan Tang shi bubian, wai bian* 3, 9.434).

24. Zhang Dai, *Tao'an mengyi*, ed. Huai Ming (Beijing: Zhonghua shuju, 2008), 3.52–53; "Cha shi xu," *Zhang Dai shiwen ji*, ed. Xia Xianchun (Shanghai: Shanghai guji chubanshe, 1991), 117–18. Zhang's *Cha shi* (History of tea) is no longer extant.

25. These are better known as Yixing or Yangxian teapots.

26. Luojie tea is from Changxing Mountain in Zhejiang (Zhou Gaoqi, *Dongshan Jie cha xi*, *CX* 601–5). See also Chen Zhenhui's discussion of Jie tea in chap. 4; Xiong Mingyu, *Luojie cha ji*, *CX* 373–75; *MPJ* 1:547–52.

27. Having established their friendship, Zhang Dai showed Min Wenshui his *History of Tea* and discussed it with him ("Preface to the *History of Tea*").

28. See, e.g., *Cha lu*, *CX* 60, *Dou cha ji*, *CX* 91–92.

29. This story is followed by another one that presents Wang Anshi in a negative light (*Jingshi tongyan* 4). For their sources in miscellanies and drama, see Tan Zhengbi, *Sanyan Liangpai ziliao* (Shanghai: Shanghai guji chubanshe, 1980), 1:238–50. Wang's water connoisseurship recalls the story told about Li Deyu earlier.

30. Zhang Dai also pays tribute to Min's tea connoisseurship and their friendship in the poem "Min Wenshui cha," in *Langhuan wenji Shen Fucan chaoben*, ed. Lu Wei and Ma Tao (Hangzhou: Zhejiang guji chubanshe, 2016), 50.

31. Min's literati friends included Cheng Mengyang, Chen Jiru, and Dong Qichang. According to Liu Luan (1727–1756), "Min Tea of Xiuning" (Xiuning min cha) became a brand. Min Wenshui's sons, Min Zichang and Mi Jixing, continued to sell the tea profitably for decades by Peach Leaf Crossing. Liu Luan, *Wu shi hu*, "Min cha you er," in *Congshu jicheng xubian, zibu, xiaoshuo lei, zalu zhi shu* (Shanghai: Shanghai shudian, 1994), 316.

32. Zhang Dai, *Tao'an mengyi*, 8.150–51. On Wang Yuesheng (also called Wang Yue), see Mao Xiang and Yu Huai, *Plum Shadows and Plank Bridge: Two Memoirs About Courtesans*, trans. Wai-yee Li (New York: Columbia University Press, 2020), 89, 92, 142–47, 164–65. Zhang Dai compares Wang to fine tea (*Plum Shadows*, 145–47).

33. Li Yu's pointed exclusion of calligraphy and painting in *Xianqing ouji* is thus noteworthy.

34. *Shuowen jiezi zhu*, 8.23a (376a). Duan Yucai glosses "common practice" as "all cases of following each other as model."

35. Chen Jiru, *Yanqi youshi* (*Chen Meigong xiaopin*, annot. Hu Shaotang [Beijing: Wenhua yishu chubanshe, 1996], 129). Zhang Yuan (16th c.) has a comparable saying: "To sip alone is called 'spiritual,' to have two guests is called 'superior,' to have three or four is called 'enjoying the élan,' to have five or six is called 'general,' to have seven or eight is called 'offering alms'" (*Cha lu*, CX 263).
36. See Wang Yinzhi's gloss, *Xunzi jianshi* 4.38; Fu Sinian, *Fu Sinian wenji*, ed. Ouyang Zhesheng (Beijing: Zhonghua shuju, 2017), 67–69.
37. *Lunyu zhushu* 7.62b. Ruan Yuan, citing Liu Duanlin, glosses *yayan* as "following the correct speech of Zhou and not using the Lu dialect." *Yanjing shi ji*, ed. Deng Jingyuan (Beijing: Zhonghua shuju, 1993), 5.124.
38. See Yang Jing's gloss: "*Ya* means correct" (*Xunzi jianshi* 8.95). The same definition appears in *Yu pian*. Lexicographical works often have the word *ya* in their titles to indicate "proper meanings" (e.g., *Erya*, *Guangya*, *Tongya*).
39. *Maoshi zhushu* 1.18a.
40. Liu Xi, *Shiming* (Shanghai: Shangwu yinshu guan, 1939), 4.57. Liu bases his glosses on homophones or close homophones on the assumption that sounds generate meanings.
41. Yang Xiong, *Fayan yishu*, annot. Wang Rongbao, ed. Chen Zhongfu (Beijing: Zhonghua shuju, 1997), 2:23–25. Zheng music and songs (*Zheng sheng*) are said to be excessive and licentious (*Analects* 15.19, 17.18).
42. Liu Xie, *Wenxin diaolong zhu*, comp. Fan Wenlan (Hong Kong: Shangwu yinshu guan, 1986 [1960]), 27.505.
43. Wang Shizhen, "Mengxi xiangsheng ji xu," "Zhang Boqi ji xu," *xugao* 52.13b, 45.13b, in *Yanzhou sibu gao* 174 *juan*, *xugao* 207 *juan*; cf. Zheng Lihua, "Wang Shizhen yu Mingdai qizi pai shixue de tiaoxie yu bianxiang," *Wenxue yichan*, no. 6 (2016): 90–102; *Qianhou qizi yanjiu* (Shanghai: Shanghai guji chubanshe, 2015), 562–71. When it comes to song lyrics, however, Wang is willing to flout such decorum; see Xu Zhongnan, "'Fugu qiubian'—lun Wang Shizhen *Yiyuan zhiyan* shici guan zhi yitong," *Dongwu zhongwen xianshang xueshu lunwen* 6 (June 2009): 33–46.
44. Wang Shizheng, *Gu bu gu lu*, SKQS, 1041:19b–21b.
45. See, e.g., Timothy Brook, *The Confusions of Pleasure: Commerce and Culture in Ming China* (Berkeley: University of California Press, 1998); Craig Clunas, *Superfluous Things: Material Culture and Social Status in Early Modern China* (Honolulu: University of Hawai'i Press, 2004); Wu Jen-shu, *Pinwei shehua: wan Ming de xiaofei shehui yu shidafu* (Taipei: Lianjing chuban shiye youxian gongsi, 2007).
46. On the debate about its dating, see Chen Shangjun, "*Ershisi shipin* zhenwei zhi zheng yu Tangdai wenxian kaoju," in *Han Tang wenxue yu wenxian lunkao* (Shanghai: Shanghai guji chubanshe, 2008); "*Ershisi shipin* weishu shuo zai zheng—jian da Zu Baoquan, Zhang Shaokang, Wang Bugao san jiaoshou zhi zhiyi," *Shanghai daxue xuebao* 18, no. 6 (November 2011): 84–98.
47. Cf. Stephen Owen's translation and discussion of the *Twenty-four Categories* in *Readings in Chinese Literary Thought* (Cambridge, Mass.: Harvard University Asia Center, 1996), 299–357.

48. Xu's treatise discusses twenty-four moods in *qin* music and might have been influenced by the *Twenty-four Categories*, which was published in the 1630s by Mao Jin.
49. Xu Guangqi, "Yu youren lun ya su shu," in *Xu Guangqi shiwen ji*, ed. Li Tiangang (Shanghai: Shanghai guji chubanshe, 2011), 319–22. The letter was a "writing exercise" (*guanke*) for the Hanlin Academy. Xu was famous for his conversion to Christianity and for introducing Western learning to China.
50. Liu Xie, *Wenxin diaolong zhu*, 27.505.
51. For example, the famous collector Xiang Yuanbian is listed as the author of *Jiaochuang jiulu*, but the content of the section on painting is identical to the analogous section in *Kaopan yushi*, questionably attributed to Tu Long (Clunas, *Superfluous Things*, 29). The editor who included this in an 1830 collectanea opined that "half literate book merchants" fabricated this text by copying from Wu Wending's *Jiangu huibian*. *Nigu lu*, attributed to Chen Jiru, may be one other example.
52. Clunas discusses the relationship between these three texts, in *Superfluous Things*, 8–39.
53. Clunas, *Superfluous Things*, 28.
54. In Ming reprints, *Dongtian qinglu ji* 洞天清祿集 becomes *Dongtian qinglu* 洞天清錄, with the character for "records" 錄 substituting that for "emolument" 祿 (translated here as "rewards"). On its textual history, see I Lofen, "Zhao Xigu *Dongtian qinglu ji* tanxi," *Xin Song xue* 2 (2002): 410–19.
55. Zhao writes in the preface: "As for things like incense, tea, paper, and ink, if there are no mistakes in the existent treatises, I will not belabor the point with repetitions." For treatises on subjects excluded from or included in Zhao's work, see I Lofen, "Zhao Xigu."
56. See Huijun Mai, "Thinking Things: Mediated Materiality in Song Literary Culture," Ph.D. diss., Harvard University, 2020.
57. It is Zhao Xigu's wording on the same subject in *Dongtian qinglu* (50b–51a) that gets repeated, however. See Wang Zuo, *Xin zeng Gegu yaolun* (Hangzhou: Zhejiang renmin meishu chubanshe, 2011), 174, 178; *QMC* A.28a; Tu Long (attri.), *Kaopan yushi*, in *Zhangwu zhi, Kaopan yushi*, ed. Chen Jian (Hangzhou: Zhejiang renmin meishu chubanshe, 2011), 245; Tang Zhiqi, *Huishi weiyan*, ZGSHQS 4:68.
58. See Zhao Xigu, *Dongtian qinglu*, 51b; *QMC* A.7a–7b; *ZSBJ* 494; *DQC* 3:113; *ZWZ* 138; Tang Zhiqi, *Huishi weiyan*, ZGSHQS 4:66; Ruan Kuisheng, *Chayu kehua*, ed. Li Baomin (Shanghai: Shanghai guji chubanshe, 2012), 416.
59. Zhao's account of bronzes (*Dongtian qinglu*, 19b–25.b) is repeated or paraphrased in Wang Zuo, *Xin zeng Gegu yaolun*, 217–21; *QMC* A.2b–5b. His description of crack patterns on *qin* (1a–1b) also appears in *Xin zeng Gegu yaolun*, 6–7; *QMC* A.16a–16b; *ZSBJ* 562–63; Tu Long (attri.), *Kaopan yushi*, 261–62. Zhao's discussion of the color and tears in true antique paintings on silk (48b, 51a–51b) is reiterated in *Xin zeng Gegu yaolun*, 179; Tang Zhiqi, *Huishi weiyan*, ZGSHQS 4:66; *ZWZ* 5.148.
60. This means that what we now know to be erroneous, such as the notion that Xia bronze vessels are adorned with inlaid precious metals, was repeated and persisted for a long period.

61. See *Hua jian*, *ZGSHQS* 2:902; *Tuhui baojian*, *ZGSHQS* 2:849. Zhao Mengfu's scroll "Guren huagao" (dated 1317) contains the same observations (Zhao Panchao, *Yuandai huaxue yanjiu* [Beijing: Zhongyan minzu daxue chubanshe, 2014], 46–47). For Ming Qing repetitions of such injunctions, see Wang Zuo, *Xin zeng gegu yaolun*, 172; *QMC*; Tang Zhiqi, *Huishi weiyan*, *ZGSHQS* 4:66; Wu Yuxian, *Huishi beikao*, *ZGSHQS* 8:610; Mao Yixiang, *Hui miao*, *ZGSHQS* 4:819; *ZWZ* 147.
62. *Xuanhe huapu*, *ZGSHQS* 2:81–82.
63. Mi Fu, *Mi Fu ji*, ed. Huang Zhengyu and Wang Xincai (Wuhan: Hubei jiaoyu chubanshe, 2002), 148–49.
64. He Liangjun, *Siyou zhai congshuo* (Beijing: Zhonghua shuju, 1997 [1959]), 264.
65. See Wang Zuo, *Xinzeng gegu yaolun*, 178; *ZSBJ* 494; Tu Long (attr.), *Kaopan yushi*, 242; *ZWZ* 10.351. Wen Zhenheng seems to contradict himself when he criticizes the practice of hanging a long narrow scroll by itself (*dantiao* 單條) as vulgar in another chapter in *Superfluous Things* (*ZWZ* 5.151).
66. An almost identical formulation appears in Zhao Mengfu's "Guren huagao" (Zhao Panchao, *Yuandai huaxue yanjiu*, 47).
67. See, e.g., Dong Qichang, "Bingchen lunhua ce" (1616, National Palace Museum, Taipei); Mao Yixiang, *Hui miao*, *ZGSHQS* 4:819; Wang Keyu, *Shanhu wang*, *ZGSHQS* 5:1234; Wang Yuxian, *Huishi beikao*, *ZGSHQS* 8:610.
68. Clunas, *Superfluous Things*, 164.
69. Lei Huan discovers a pair of precious swords in a stone box buried underground at a prison in Fengcheng (*Jinshu* 36.1075).
70. Wang Hung-tai, "Yasu de bianzheng—Mingdai shangwan wenhua de liuxing yu shishang guanxi de jiaocuo," *Xin shixue* 17, no. 4 (December 2006): 73–143.
71. Yu Yingshi, *Zhongguo jinshi zongjiao lunli yu shangren jingshen (zeng ding ban)* (Taipei: Lianjing, 2018).
72. Wang Daokun, *Tai han ji* (Jinan: Qi Lu shushe chubanshe, 1997), 52.12a.
73. Zhou Hui, *Jinling suoshi* (Nanjing: Nanjing chubanshe, 2007), 312.
74. Wang's brother Wang Shimao, as well as well-known literati and scholar-officials such as Gui Youguang, Mao Kun, Tang Shunzhi, Jiao Hong, Chen Zilong, Feng Mengzhen, Chen Jiru, Wu Weiye, and Qian Qianyi, wrote epitaphs for merchants.
75. In *Mengzi* 4B.53, Mengzi uses the image of a filthy Xi Shi inspiring disgust as analogy for how inborn goodness can be corrupted. Sun Chengze also criticized Xiang's seals and records of prices as "extremely vulgar" (*Gengzi xiaoxia ji*, 1.16b).
76. See Feng Zhiguo, *Yu gu tong you: Xiang Yuanbian shuhua jiancang yanjiu* (Hangzhou: Zhongguo meishu xueyuan chubanshe, 2013).
77. Feng Zhiguo, *Yu gu tong you*, 422.
78. Yao Yuanzhi, *Zhuye ting zaji* (Beijing: Zhonghua shuju, 1997), 100.
79. See Lin Li-chiang, "Wan Ming Huizhou moshang," in *Huizhou: shuye yu diyu wenhua*, ed. Michaela Bussotti and Zhu Wanshu (Beijing: Zhonghua shuju, 2010), 121–97; Lin Li-chiang, "The Proliferation of Images: The Ink-stick Designs and the Printing of the *Fang-shih Mo-p'u* and *Ch'eng-shih Mo-yuan*," Ph.D. diss., Princeton University, 1998.

80. See Dong Qichang's preface to *Cheng Garden of Ink* (*DQC* 1:46); Xie Zhaozhi, *Wu zazu* (Shanghai: Shanghai shudian chubanshe, 2001), 238–39; *WL* 3:660–61; *YSZ* B.22b–23a.
81. See Wang Shixiang, *Xiushi lu jieshuo* (Beijing: Wenwu chubanshe, 1983); Craig Clunas, "Luxury Knowledge: The *Xiushilu* (*Record of Lacquering*) of 1625," *Techniques and Cultures* 29 (1997): 27–40.
82. *WL* 3:655–56; see chap. 3.
83. *ZWZ* 5.148; Tang Zhiqi, *Huishi weiyan*, *ZGSHQS* 4:66. *Jinxian guan* is a type of headgear worn by scholar-officials. Here Wen and Tang use the term to imply stodgy formalism.
84. Wang Shixing, *Wuyue youcao, Guang zhi yi*, ed. Zhou Zhenhe (Beijing: Zhonghua shuju, 2006), 219–20.
85. *WL* 3:654–55; see chap. 3, 162–63.
86. Zhang Dai is criticizing his cousin's indiscriminating acceptance of the literary judgments of Wu scholars from Incipient Society (Ji she) and names ever-changing Suzhou sartorial fashion as analogy. See Zhang Dai, "You yu Yiru baidi," *Zhang Dai shiwen ji*, 229.
87. Wu Qizhen, *Shuhua ji*, *ZGSHQS* 8:85–86. Golden Valley Garden refers to the Jin aristocrat Shi Chong's estate.
88. See, e.g., Xu Wei, "Ti *Kunlun nu zaju* hou," *Xu Wei ji* (Beijing: Zhonghua shuju, 1999), 4:1092–94; Li Kaixian (1502–1568), "*Shijing yanci* xu"; Feng Menglong's prefaces to his anthology of popular songs; prefaces to collections of vernacular stories and to *Shuihu zhuan* (Guo Shaoyu, *Zhongguo lidai wenlun xuan* [Hong Kong: Zhonghua shuju, 1979], 2:338–48, 418–30). Cf. Yasushi Ōki, *Fū Bōryū "Sanka" no kenkyū: Chūgoku Mindai no tsūzoku kayō* (Tōkyō: Keisō Shobō, 2003); Wai-yee Li, "The Rhetoric of Spontaneity in Late Ming Literature," *Ming Studies* 35 (August 1995): 35–52. Note that Li Mengyang (1473–1530), who advocated ancient models, also claimed that "true poetry is to be found among the people" (Guo Shaoyu, *Zhongguo lidai wenlun xuan*, 2:283–84).
89. See Wu Jen-shu, *Pinwei shehua*; Zhao Qiang, *"Wu" de jueqi—qian xiandai wanqi Zhongguo shenmei fengshang de bianqian* (Beijing: Shangwu yinshuguan, 2016), 93–107.
90. Wu Qizhen, *Shuhua ji*, *ZGSHQS* 8:46.
91. Wang Shizhen, *Gu bu gu lu*, 28a. In *Gudong shisan shuo*, Ming pottery from the fifteenth and early sixteenth centuries is said to rival that of earlier eras (*DQC* 3:197).
92. On the Wu School, see, e.g., Yang Xin, "The Ming Dynasty," in *Three Thousand Years of Chinese Painting* (New Haven, Conn.: Yale University Press, 1997); He Ye, *Wumen huaipai* (Changchun: Jilin meishu chubanshe, 2003); Li Weikun, *Mingdai Wumen huapai yanjiu* (Shanghai: Dongfang chuban zhongxin, 2008).
93. Wang Shizhen criticizes Ni Zan for "relying on immature and weak brushwork for his charm," which qualifies him for being "ranked as free-spirited" (*yipin* 逸品) but "not enough to be considered a great master" (*weishi dangjia* 未是當家) (*Yanzhou sibu gao*, 155.7a–7b).

94. Wang Shizhen, *Yanzhou sibu gao*, 155.12b.
95. Dong Qichang, *Huachan shi suibi*, j. 2, *DQC* 3:145; *Rongtai bieji*, j. 4, *DQC* 2:617. A similar comment appears in Shen Zhou's colophon (dated 1504) on "Pine Pavilion and Mountain Views" (Songting shanse tu) by Ni Zan. See Yu Fengqing, *Yu shi shuhua tiba ji* (1634), j. 1, *ZGSHQS* 4:582; Wu Sheng (17th c.), *Daguan lu*, *ZGSHQS* 8:506. According to Shen Zhou, only those steeped in antiquity and refinement (*guya zhi shi* 古雅之士) can appreciate Ni Zan. For Ni Zan's painting and Shen Zhou's colophon, see Richard Barnhardt, *Along the Border of Heaven: Sung and Yuan Paintings from the C.C. Wang Family Collection* (New York: Metropolitan Museum of Art, 1983), 164, 182.
96. Wang Shizhen named Zhao Mengfu, Wu Zhen, Huang Gongwang, and Wang Meng as the "four Yuan masters" (*Yanzhou sibu gao*, 155.16b–17a), a view echoed in Tu Long's *Hua jian* (*ZGSHQS* 3:995) and *Kaopan yushi* (238). Dong Qichang, following He Liangjun (*Siyou zhai congshuo*, 29.263), replaced Zhao Mengfu with Ni Zan in *Huachanshi suibi*, j. 2 (*DQC* 3:117, 125–26), and *Rongtai bieji*, j. 4 (*DQC* 2:599).
97. Dong Qichang, *Huachan shi suibi*, j. 2 (*DQC* 3:121). Dong presents the Northern and Southern Schools in Chan Buddhism, with its discussion of gradual versus sudden enlightenment, as analog of the Northern and Southern Schools in painting. On the debates surrounding Dong's invention of these genealogies, see, e.g., Xu Fuguan, *Zhongguo yishu jingshen*, 388–430; Wai-kam Ho, "Tung Ch'i-ch'ang's New Orthodoxy and the Southern School Theory," in *Artists and Traditions: Uses of the Past in Chinese Culture*, ed. Christian Murck (Princeton, N.J.: Princeton University Press, 1976), 113–29; James Cahill, "Tung Ch'i-ch'ang's 'Southern and Northern Schools' in the History and Theory of Painting: A Reconsideration," in *Sudden and Gradual: Approaches to Enlightenment in Chinese Thought*, ed. Peter Gregory (Honolulu: University of Hawaii Press, 1987), 429–46; Wang Anli, ed., *1537–1610, Nanbei zong lun de xingcheng* (Hangzhou: Zhongguo meishu xueyuan chubanshe, 2016).
98. Dong Qichang, *Huachan shi suibi*, j. 2, *DQC* 3:110, 126.
99. On the relationship and boundaries between literati and artisans, see Dorothy Ko, *The Social Life of Inkstones: Artisans and Scholars in Early Qing China* (Seattle: University of Washington Press, 2016).
100. Li Rihua, *Liuyan zhai biji, Zitao xuan zazhui*, 268.
101. Zhang Dai, "Jiuchai qi gu ji xu" (*Zhang Dai shiwen ji*, 135–36), "Pu Zhongqian diaoke," *Tao'an mengyi*, 20.
102. *WMC* 3:1059–62; Huang Zongxi, *Huang Zongxi quanji* (Hangzhou: Zhejiang guji chubanshe, 2005), 10:585–87. On Zhang Nanyuan in seventeenth-century writings, see Xie Guozhen, *Ming Qing biji tancong* (Shanghai: Shanghai shudian chubanshe, 2004), 215–23. On the relationship between rock piling and painting, see Wai-yee Li, "Gardens and Illusions from Late Ming to Early Qing," *Harvard Journal of Asiatic Studies* 72, no. 2 (December 2012): 295–336.
103. Wang Shixing, *Guang zhi yi*, 219–20. See also Wang Shizhen, *Gu bu gu lu*, 28b. On the term *wuyao* during the late Ming, see Zhao Qiang, *Wu de jueqi*, 107–15.
104. *WL* 3:660, 663. See also Xie Zhaozhi, *Wu zazu*, 241.

105. Clunas points out that in some cases signatures on vessels may work more like trademarks of a collective enterprise rather than markers of individual genius (*Superfluous Things*, 65). According to Jonathan Hay, "The signing of objects was a symptom of a trans-regional market that carried objects outside the orbit of local reputation, and by the eighteenth century that market was larger than it had ever been." Hay, *Sensuous Surfaces: The Decorative Object in Early Modern China* (Honolulu: University of Hawai'i Press, 2010), 59.
106. See chap. 1, 15.
107. *Dongtian qinglu*, 8a.
108. *WL* 3:663.
109. Qian Yong, *Lüyuan conghua*, ed. Zhang Wei (Beijing: Zhonghua shuju, 1997 [1979]), 195.
110. Mi Fu, *Huashi*, in *Mi Fu ji*, 156. Mi Fu often exchanged the ancient paintings he owned for masterpieces of calligraphy (sometimes at a ratio of ten to one).
111. Zhu Yizun also believes that Xiang recorded prices so that his sons could divide up the collection (*Pushu ting quan ji*, ed. Wang Limin [Changchun: Jilin wenshi chubanshe, 2009], 49.583). Yao Yuanzhi (early 19th c.) defended Xiang and faulted Jiang Shaoshu for his "venomous attacks" (*Zhuye ting zaji* [Beijing: Zhonghua shuju, 1997], 100). Xiang's inscriptions are found at the end of scrolls, the last page of albums, and sometimes on the axial wood. This meant that Xiang's contemporaries might not have been able to see these inscriptions, and indeed criticism about them did not arise until the dispersal of Xiang's collection in mid-seventeenth century. See Li Wankang, *Bianhao yu jiage: Xiang Yuanbian jiucang shuhua er shi* (Nanjing: Nanjing daxue chubanshe, 2012), 101–10.
112. Gao was faulted for other things, such as deliberate attempts to lend credence to forgeries.
113. Literally, "pledging to take a plum tree as wife or taking it as husband." Li Rihua, *Weishui xuan riji*, ed. Tu Youxiang (Shanghai: Shanghai Yuandong chubanshe, 1996), 6. Despite the designation of "dairy" in the title, this work has a semipublic dimension with its detailed record of Li's transactions, evaluation of artworks, and transcription of colophons. In substance and style it is not very different from Li's miscellanies, such as *Liuyan zhai biji*.
114. I have not located the source of this claim. Lin Bu did not pursue any office, nor did he have a family. He is famous for his poems on plum blossoms (Zhang Duanyi, *Gui'er ji*, in *Jin dai mishu*, ed. Mao Jin, Chongzhen era (1618–1644) Jigu ge ed., B.29a–29b). "He considered the plum tree his wife and the crane his son." Lang Ying, *Qixiu leigao* (Shanghai: Shanghai shudian, 2001), 31.3219.
115. Dong praised Wang Xiyuan's paintings and record of paintings. See *Rongtai bieji*, j. 4, *DQC* 2:618–19.
116. Tang Zhiqi, *Huishi weiyan*, *ZGSHQS* 4:67.
117. Tang Zhiqi, *ZGSHQS* 4:65.
118. It is hard to determine which version is earlier. Zhang Yingwen was a generation older than Wen Zhenheng. The dates for Zhang's son, Zhang Chou, were close to

Wen's. However, Wang Zhideng claimed in the preface to *Qing mi cang* that Zhang Chou amended his father's text, and it is possible that this passage was added later.
119. Mi Fu said that ten lines in semicursive script are not as good as one line in standard script. See Dong Qichang, *Rongtai bieji*, j. 2, *DQC* 2:537.
120. Wang Xiaoli argues that Wen Zhenheng is in effect affirming the "family brand" (i.e., Wen Zhengming's tradition) and advocating the aesthetics of literati spontaneity and self-expression (*San Wu wenren hua tiba yanjiu* [Shanghai: Shanghai renmin meishu chubanshe, 2013]). The idea that, unlike paintings, calligraphy is more amenable to pricing criterion is as old as Zhang Yanyuan: "The ways of calligraphy and paintings are different: with calligraphy one can speak about price according to the number of words; with painting there is no fixed standards for establishing worth" (*LDMHJ* 29).
121. On the uses of art in gift-giving and social networks, see Craig Clunas, *Elegant Debts: The Social Art of Wen Zhengming, 1470–1559* (Honolulu: University of Hawai'i Press, 2004).
122. Zhao Xigu, *Dongtian qinglu*, 11a–12b.
123. Tu Long (attri.), *Kaopan yushi*, 268.
124. Gao Lian does not specify that the crane should be dancing to zither music, but the passage on cranes concludes his section on zither.
125. Shih Shou-chien, "Ya su de jiaolü: Wen Zhengming, Zhong Kui yu dazhong wenhua," *Guoli Taiwan daxue meishushi yanjiu jikan* 16 (2004): 323.
126. Lu Shaoheng, *Zuigutang jian sao* (Taipei: Jinfeng chuban gongsi, 1986), 1.32.
127. Wu Congxian, "Shangxin leshi," in *Ming ren xiaopin ji*, ed. Liu Dajie (Shanghai: Beixin shuju, 1934), 17–18.
128. Dong Qichang, *Rongtai bieji*, j. 2, *DQC* 2:596.
129. Dong Qichang, *Rongtai wenji*, j. 4, *DQC* 1:123; Liu Dajie, *Mingren xiaopin ji*, 115–16.
130. Tu Long (attri.), *Kaopan yushi*, 316. A very similar passage is included in *ZWZ* 2.49–50.
131. For example, Zhang Jingyuan refers to such inscriptions as "evil karma" and fantasizes about their destruction in a conflagration. "Huxin ting xiaoji," in Zhang Dai, *Xihu mengxun*, 3.53, in *Tao'an mengyi, Xihu mengxun*, ed. Ma Xingrong (Shanghai: Shanghai guji chubanshe, 1982).
132. Wang Siren, "You Manjing ji," *Wenfan xiaopin*, ed. Jiang Jinde (Changsha: Yuelu shushe, 1989), 244.
133. Zhang Dai, *Tao'an mengyi*, 7.130–31.
134. Zhang Dai, *Tao'an mengyi*, 1.10–11.
135. Zhang Dai, *Tao'an mengyi*, 3.60–61.
136. Mi Fu, *Hua shi*, in *Mi Fu ji*, 155.
137. Hu Yinglin, *Shaoshi shanfang bicong*, ed. Liu Jun (Shanghai: Shanghai shudian, 2001), 4.46; He Liangjun, *Siyou zhai congshuo* (Beijing: Zhonghua shuju, 1997), 28.254; *ZSBJ* 493–94; Xie Zhaozhi, *Wu zazu*, 7.142–43; Tu Long, *Hua jian*, ZGSHQS 3:995; *WL* 3:653; *QMC* A.1a–3b; Zhang Chou, *Qinghe shuhua fang*, ZGSHQS 4:137, 4:366. Zhang Chou distinguishes between "true appreciation" (*zhenshang* 真賞) and "true discrimination" (*zhenjian* 真鑑) and also

criticizes the judgment of luminaries such as Chen Jiru and Dong Qichang (*ZGSHQS* 4:137, 4:226, 4:385).

138. In Zhang Yanyuan's *Lidai minghua ji*, *haoshi* means "those who are interested in (paintings)." Yuan Hongdao uses the term *haoshi* to indicate true appreciation in *Pingshi* (*YHD* 1:826), and Chen Hongshou in his colophon on Wang Meng's "Lezhi lun tujuan" uses the term *shangjian* critically, referring to "connoisseurs who mostly go by hearsay" (cited in Feng Zhiguo, *Yu gu tongyou*, 452). Li Rihua also uses the term *haoshi* without disparagement (*Weishui xuan riji*, 6.397, 6.413). Gu Qiyuan juxtaposes the two terms *shangjian* and *haoshi* without implying hierarchy (*Kezuo zuiyu*, ed. Zhang Huirong [Nanjing: Fenghuang chubanshe, 2004], 8.169).

139. Holding office did not preclude the use of these epithets. Bona fide Ming recluses are rare. *Mingshi* includes twelve in "Biographies of Recluses" (Yinyi zhuan), a far smaller number compared to other dynastic histories.

140. See Li Zhi's letter to Jiao Hong, in *Li Zhi quanji zhu*, annot. Zhang Jianye and Zhang Dai (Beijing: Shehui kexue wenxian chubanshe, 2010), 1:118–20; *WL* 2:585–87.

141. The translation of the title follows S. E. Kile, "Master Medium: Li Yu's Technologies of Culture in the Early Qing" (manuscript). Patrick Hanan translates the title as *Casual Expressions of Idle Feelings* in *The Invention of Li Yu* (Cambridge, Mass.: Harvard University Press, 1988).

142. Kile characterizes Li Yu's experimentation as "designing, renovating, and transforming human experience through his technological interventions in multiple media" ("Master Medium").

143. Kile connects the idea of "reproducible originality" in the window design to Li Yu's views on intellectual property rights and his entrepreneurial interventions in contemporary print culture ("Master Medium").

144. Hanan, *The Invention of Li Yu*, 187.

145. Li Yu wrote in a poem mourning his young concubine Qiao (who was also an actress in his troupe): "It was through you that we created the appearance of magnificence" 妝點豪華全仗汝 (*Liweng yijiayan*, in *Li Yu quanji* [Hangzhou: Zhejinag guji chubanshe, 1991], 1:208).

146. Wen's *Zhong Kui* is in National Palace Museum, Taipei. See Shih Shou-ch'ien's discussion of this painting and the genealogy of Zhong Kui paintings in "Ya su de jiaolü."

147. *Niusou* (Bovine urine) is the name of a humble herb (*cheqiancao*). *Mabo* (rotten mushrooms), also called "feces mushrooms," grows on rotten wood. Han Yu counts these two items among "the doctor's friends" in "Jin xue jie." Both are mentioned as remedies for various ailments in Li Shizhen's *Materia Medica* (*Bencao ganmu*) (Beijing: Renmin weisheng chubanshe, 1975).

148. Li Yu recounts this with mock horror—in order to avoid being linked to a meat dish (like Su Shi in the case of "Dongpo Pork") and thus metaphorically consumed, he refuses to write about meat dishes in the culinary section of his book (*XQOJ* 248).

149. Huang Guoquan notes the continuity between the sections on dramatic performance and on feminine charms, since both sections focus on women as objects

of desire. Huang Guoquan, *Ya su zhijian: Li Yu de wenhua renge yu wenxue sixiang yanjiu* (Beijing: Zhongguo shehui kexue chubanshe, 2004), 182–87.
150. Kile notes how such concerns are also reflected in the transformations of bodies in Li Yu's stories ("Master Medium").
151. See Ma Tailai, *"Zuixing shi* benshi laiyuan ji zuozhe kaozheng," in *Shizheng yu yanbian: Zhongguo wenxue shi yanjiu lunji*, ed. Fudan daxue guji zhengli yanjiu suo (Shanghai: Shanghai wenyi chubanshe, 2014), 199–211.
152. Sophie Volpp, "The Gift of a Python Robe: The Circulation of Objects in *Jin Ping Mei*," *Harvard Journal of Asiatic Studies* 65, no. 1 (2005): 158.
153. For kylin, Roy has "ch'i-lin." According to Ming sumptuary laws, the mandarin square with kylin should be worn by officials of the fourth rank. Wang Shizhen, *Yanzhou shiliao*, ed. Dong Fubiao (Fu Sinian Library, Academia Sinica, Taiwan), 69.38b; *Ming shilu* (Taipei: Zhongyang yanjiu yuan lishi yuyan yanjiu suo, 1966), 158.3028.
154. The Wang household also pawns a fur coat, which Pan Jinlian does not deign to accept, arguing instead that she must have the fur coat that belonged to Li Ping'er (*JPM* 74.1227–28), as mentioned in chap. 1, 52.
155. See *Baopu zi neipian jiaoshi*, ed. Wang Ming (Beijing: Zhonghua shuju, 1988), 17.312; Zheng Qiao, *Tongzhi* (Taipei: Shangwu yinshu guan, 1987), 76.884.
156. The locus classicus of the "Heaven penetrating rhinoceros horn" is found in *Baopu zi*; see Roy 2:528, n. 9. It is mentioned in poetry, prose, historical texts, and Song and Ming miscellanies, in addition to the sources Roy cited.
157. See Roy 4:112–13, 4:710, n. 13. Peach Blossom Cavern is in Sichuan, but Ying locates it in Wuling in order to identify it with Tao Yuanming's "Peach Blossom Spring." He also invents the story that the fisherman in "Peach Blossom Spring" meets the Hairy Maiden, a Qin palace lady who fled to the mountains and became an immortal in a story from ca. second to third century (*Liexian zhuan*, in *TPGJ* 59.365). The Hairy Maiden is said to have fled "Qin chaos," as did the inhabitants of the Peach Blossom Spring, hence the connection.
158. *Huiping* 62.1213.
159. Roy 4:698, n. 47.
160. Despite endless enumeration of dishes in the book, there are only a few discussions of taste. Aside from Ying Bojue's remarks, see also Ximen Qing's description of the "coated plums" (*JPM* 67.1079). Recipes are also uncommon—exceptions include Huilian's way of cooking pig's head (23.320) and the crabs prepared by Chang Shijie's wife (61.960).
161. I have modified Roy's translation here. Siquan is Ximen Qing's sobriquet.
162. Spotted by Ximen Qing, Wang's poem for Zheng Aiyue'er leads Zheng to downplay their liaison by deflecting attention to Wang's name change and Ximen's new and potential conquests (Wang's mother and wife). Ximen Qing's sobriquet is "Siquan" (Four Springs); those of Cai and Wang, "Yiquan" (One Spring) and "Sanquan" (Three Springs). The similarity implies a sense of affinity. Zheng Aiyue'er claims that Wang, fearful that such closely linked nomenclature may imply disrespect, has changed his sobriquet to "Xiaoxuan" (Little Studio). Ximen Qing regards Wang's deference as a significant social victory (*JPM* 77.1323).

163. Incense incorporates fragrance made from the glandular secretion of musk deer.
164. See, e.g., Mi Fu: "These days there are people who collect one thing and value it as much as life. It's truly laughable" (*Mi Fu ji*, 156). See also chap. 1, 23–28, 37–47.
165. On Yan Shifan's passion for antiques, curios, and artworks, see *Mingshi* 308.7920; *WL* 3:827; Zhao Huaiyu's preface to *Tianshui bingshan lu* (the list of items confiscated from the Yan family upon its downfall), 102.
166. The eunuch's surname, Sha 沙, is homophonous with *sha* 殺, "to kill," "to destroy." His name "Yucheng" 玉成 means "to bring about a happy union" or "to facilitate success and self-fulfillment."
167. For example, Hanan characterizes this as an example of the "extensions of comedy into new fields, such as that of homosexual love" (*The Invention of Li Yu*, 92, 98–102). Shi Ye reads the account of Yan's predatory homosexual lust as part of a broader indictment of political corruption. Shi Ye, *Zhongguo gudai wenxue zhong de tongxing lian shuxie yanjiu* (Shanghai: Shanghai renmin chubanshe, 2008), 377–79.
168. This is the standard idiom for jealousy.
169. A notable example is another Li Yu story, "The Male Mother of Mencius Thrice Moved House to Educate His Son" (Nan Mengmu jiaohe sanqian) (*Silent Opera* [*Wusheng xi*], in *Li Yu quanji* 4:1658).
170. To "drool" (*chuixian* 垂涎) is to "covet" in idiomatic usage.
171. One catty (a pound and a third) equals sixteen taels.
172. "Quan" 權, authority or expediency; "ru" 汝, you; "xiu" 修, to mend, to repair, to punish, to impose order.
173. The passage about "Hui pattern" is deleted in the 120-chapter editions from 1791 and 1792. Here the reference to earlier "Tang, Song, Yuan, and Ming masters" constitutes an explicit temporal marker, which the novel studiously avoids elsewhere.
174. Baoyu spells out this logic: "Heaven does not give someone sensibility for nothing. We always used to lament what a pity it was that a person of her qualities should be common (*su*). But here we are at last! Who could have known! It proves there is some justice in the world" (*HLM* 48.518).
175. Barbecuing surprises the visitors but seem routine to the family (*HLM* 49.530). This could be another marker of Manchu customs.
176. Zhu Xi, *Zhuzi Wengong chuandao jingshi yanxing lu*, 8.32a.
177. Shen Defu remarks on the steep rise in price of Chenghua porcelain cups by the late sixteenth century (*WL* 2:613). According to Liu Tong (1593–1637), "A pair of Chenghua cups is worth a hundred thousand strings of cash." Liu Tong and Yu Yizheng, *Dijing jingwu lue* (Beijing: Beijing guji chubanshe, 1980), 4.163.
178. Cai Xueqin and Gao E, *Bajia pingpi Honglou meng*, ed. Feng Qiyong and Chen Qixin (Beijing: Wenhua yishu chubanshe, 1991), 41.998.
179. The preface is incorporated into the first chapter in the 1791 and 1792 printed editions.
180. See Shen Congwen, *Huahua duoduo tantan guanguan* (Chongqing: Chongqing daxue chubanshe, 2014), 111–23; Meng Zhaolian, *Zhongguo hulu qi* (Tianjin: Baihua wenyi chubanshe, 2010).

181. Shen Congwen, *Huahua duoduo tantan guanguan*, 111–26. The essays by Shen Congwen and Zhou Ruchang appeared in *Guangming ribao* in 1961. They are cited in Liu Mengxi, *Honglou meng yu bainian zhongguo* (Beijing: Zhongyang bianyi chubanshe, 2005), 334–36.

182. Scholars have discussed the relationship between the décor of Baoyu's rooms and Qing visual culture. See, e.g., Volpp, *The Substance of Fiction* (New York: Columbia University Press, forthcoming), chaps. 4 and 5; Shang Wei, "Truth Becomes Fiction When Fiction Is True: *The Story of the Stone* and the Visual Culture of the Manchu Court," *Journal of Chinese Literature and Culture* 2, no. 1 (April 2015): 207–48; James Cahill, *Pictures for Use and Pleasure: Vernacular Painting in High Qing China* (Berkeley: University of California Press, 2010), 161–65; Hay, *Sensuous Surfaces*, 229–33.

183. William Hazlitt, "On Vulgarity and Affectation," in *Table-Talk; or, Original Essays on Men and Manners* (London: Printed for Henry Colburn, 1824), 1:386–87.

184. Red Inkstone remarks that Qiaojie's *youzi* 柚子 is a species of fragrant *yuan* citron 香櫞 (香橼) homophonous with *yuan* 緣 (karmic ties) and that the buddha's hand "points to the way out of the Ford of Delusion." The exchange "lays the clue a thousand miles in advance" (*ZYZ* 41.602–3).

185. In the received 120-chapter version of the novel, Qiaojie marries the scion of a rich family in Granny Liu's village.

3. THE REAL AND THE FAKE

1. *Han Feizi* 23.474. *Zuozhuan* cites an admonitory inscription on the Chan Cauldron (*Zuo* Zhao 3.3, 3:1350–51). Yue Zhengzi Chun, identified as Zengzi's disciple in *Liji*, should not be confused with Mengzi's disciple Yue Zhengzi, whose given name is Ke.

2. In *Lüshi chunqiu jiaoshi* (9.498) and *Xinxu* (7.232), the Lu man of good faith is Liu Xiahui, and the vessel is the Cen Cauldron. In both versions, Liu Xiahui refers to his good faith as his "state" and the equivalent of the Lu ruler's state: "To destroy my state in order to spare your state—that is what I balk at."

3. For example, Yu He (5th c.) in his "Lun shu biao" (dated 471) describes how forgers of ancient calligraphy use water leaked from thatched roofs to dye paper and produce the appearance of age. See Zhang Yanyuan, *Fashu yaolu*, *ZGSHQS* 1:38.

4. Shen Gua, *Mengxi bitan jiaozheng*, ed. Hu Daojing (Beijing: Zhonghua shuju, 1960), 17.540. The same passage appears in Peng Cheng, *Moke huixi*, ed. Shang Jun (Kuaiji: Banye tang, Wanli reign [1563–1620]), Fu Sinian Library, Academia Sinica, Taipei, Taiwan, 1.9.

5. Mi Fu, *Hua shi*, in *Mi Fu ji*, ed. Huang Zhengyu and Wang Xincai (Wuhan: Hubei jiaoyu chubanshe, 2002), 146.

6. Mi Fu, *Mi Fu ji*, 147. Mi Fu claims to have seen three hundred fake Li Cheng paintings (151). On the prevalence of forgeries of Li Cheng paintings, see also *Xuanhe huapu*, *ZGSHQS* 2:92.

7. Su Shi, "Ci yun Mi Fu er Wang shu bawei ershou," cited in *Mi Fu ji*, 230.

8. Zhou Hui, *Qingbo zazhi*, cited in *Mi Fu ji*, 244.
9. Mi Fu, *Shu shi*, in *Mi Fu ji*, 140. On the aesthetic thought and practice of Wang Shen and Mi Fu, see Ronald Egan, *The Problem of Beauty: Aesthetic Thought and Pursuits in Northern Song Dynasty China* (Cambridge, Mass.: Harvard University Asia Center, 2006), 162–236.
10. See Wen Jia, *Qianshan tang shuhua ji*, in *Ming Taizu ping Hu lu (wai qi zhong)* (Beijing: Beijing guji chubanshe, 2002). Wen Jia was the son of Wen Zhengming.
11. See Zhang Changhong, *Pinjian yu jingying: Ming mo Qing chu Huishang yishu zanzhu yanjiu* (Beijing: Beijing daxue chubanshe, 2010).
12. Hong Ya is said to have lived and attained immortality during the time of the legendary Yellow Emperor or King Yao. He is sometimes identified with Linglun, the Yellow Emperor's minister of music. *Zhengtong daozang*, 8:344–45.
13. Ji Ran (5th c. BCE), the Yue king Goujian's advisor and Fan Li's teacher, is said to understand "the essentials about myriad goods" (*Shiji* 129.3256). Wang Shixing also claims that Suzhou artists produce forgeries (*Wuyue youcao, Guang zhi yi*, ed. Zhou Zhenhe [Beijing: Zhonghua shuju, 2006], 219–20). On the prevalence and influence of Suzhou forgeries, see Chiu Shih-hua, Lin Li-chiang, and Lai Yu-chih, eds., *Wei haowu: 16–18 shiji Suzhou pian jiqi yingxiang* (Taipei: National Palace Museum, 2018).
14. According to Xu Fuzuo, Zhang Fengyi played Cai Bojie, the male protagonist in *The Story of the Lute* (*Pipa ji*), and his second son played Zhao Wuniang, the female protagonist, as they staged the performance in front of their house. Spectators gawked, but the Zhangs were oblivious. See "San Zhang," in *Huadang ge congtan, Xuxiu Siku quanshu, zi bu* (Shanghai: Shanghai guji chubanshe, 1995–1999), 1175:576. (Xu, himself a playwright, was the son-in-law of Zhang Fengyi's brother Zhang Xianyi.)
15. For Shen Defu's scornful depiction, see *WL* 3:676. The relationship between Wang Zhideng and Ma Xianglan is described in much more romantic terms in Qian Qianyi, *Liechao shiji xiaozhuan* (Shanghai: Shanghai guji chubanshe, 1983), 2:765–66.
16. Zhan Jingfeng, *Zhan Dongtu xuanlan bian, ZGSHQS* 4:54.
17. Zhan Jingfeng, *ZGSHQS* 4:38.
18. Zhan Jingfeng, *ZGSHQS* 4:51–52. On regional rivalries, see chapter 2, 102–3; Fu Shen, "Wang Duo ji Qing chu de beifang jiancang jia," in *Zhongguo huihua yanjiu lunwen ji*, ed. Duoyun bianji bu (Shanghai: Shanghai shuhua chubanshe, 1992). Li Rihua often expressed reservations about contemporary painters who did not hail from his native Jiaxing; see Wan Muchun, *Weishui xuan li de xianju zhe* (Hangzhou: Zhongguo meishu xueyuan chubanshe, 2008), 186.
19. Sun Kuang, *Shu hua ba ba, ZGSHQS* 3:933.
20. Zhu Guozhen, *Yongchuang xiaopin* (Beijing: Zhonghua shuju, 1959), 22.539–40.
21. Zhang Yanyuan, *Fashu yaolu, ZGSHQS* 1:32.
22. Su Shi, "Ciyun Ziyou lun shu," in *Su Shi shiji hezhu*, annot. Feng Yingliu, ed. Huang Renke and Zhu Huaichun (Shanghai: Shanghai guji chubanshe, 2001), 1:134–35. Of course, Su Shi's calligraphy came to be highly prized.

23. Zhan Jingfeng, *Zhan Dongtu xuanlan bian*, ZGSHQS 4:16. Zhan tells various anecdotes to disparage the judgments of Yunjian collectors like Mo Shilong, Gu Ruhe, and his brother Gu Ruxiu.
24. This alludes to a story in *Shishuo xinyu* 19.21: after the Jin commander Huan Wen conquered Shu, he took into his harem the younger sister of the Shu leader Li Shi. Huan's jealous wife, Princess Nankang, storms into Li's room as she is brushing her long hair. Unmoved, Li calmly states that, having lost her domain and family, she will be glad to be killed. In another source, Princess Nankang is so moved by Li's beauty and sadness that she throws down her weapon and embraces her rival.
25. Li Rihua, *Weishui xuan riji*, ed. Tu Youxiang (Shanghai: Shanghai Yuandong chubanshe, 1996), 88.
26. Zhan Jingfeng, *Zhan Dongtu xuanlan bian*, ZGSHQS 4:16.
27. Li Sixun was a famous Tang artist traditionally associated with the style dubbed "blue and green landscape."
28. Dong is referring to his skills as a painter. See Dong Qichang, *Hua Chan shi suibi*, j. 1, DQC 3:67; *Rongtai bieji*, j. 2, DQC 2:539.
29. For the colophon on the scroll *River Banks After the Snow Cleared by Wang Wei of Tang* (*Tang Wang Mojie jianggan xueji tujuan*), see DQC 8:481. The wording of this colophon is almost identical to Wang Shizhen's colophon on a landscape painting by Huang Gongwang (*Yanzhou sibu gao*, 137.19a–19b). Dong commented on this supposed Wang Wei painting in *Rongtai bieji*, j. 4, DQC 2:610–12, and also mentioned it in *Hua Chan shi suibi*, j. 2, DQC 3:118.
30. Su Shi, *Su Shi wenji biannian jianzhu*, annot. Li Zhiliang, 12 vols (Chengdu: Ba Shu shushe, 2011), 9:594. Cf. Wang Wei: "Winning undeserved praise as a poet in our era,/ I might yet have been a painter in a former life" 當代（一作宿世）謬詞客，前身應畫師 (*QTS* 125.1254).
31. Dong Qichang, *Rongtai bieji*, j. 4, DQC 2:597.
32. See chap. 2, n. 97. Dong sees Wang Wei's ink wash and the green and blue colors of Li Sixun as representative of the Southern and Northern Schools, respectively. *Hua Chan shi suibi*, j. 2 (DQC 3:121–22), *Rongtai bieji*, j. 4 (DQC 2:598).
33. J. P. Park, "Reinventing Art History: Forgery and Counterforgery in Early Modern Chinese Art," in *Archives of Asian Art* (forthcoming). See also Liu Jinku, *Nanhua beidu: Qingdai shuhua jiancang zhongxin yanjiu* (Shijiazhuang: Hebei jiaoyu chubanshe, 2008), 22–78.
34. Li Rihua, *Weishui xuan riji*, 252.
35. Ye Tingguan, *Oubo yuhua*. Ye is quoting Xiao Zhangchong's (Kangxi period) *Songnan shixiao lu*. See Zhang Xiaozhuang, *Qingdai biji riji zhong de shufa shiliao zhengli yu yanjiu* (Beijing: Zhongguo meishu xueyuan chubanshe, 2012), 2:551–52.
36. Li Rihua, *Weishui xuan riji*, 428.
37. Zhu Guozhen, *Yongchuang xiaopin*, 22.536.
38. Cheng Zhangcan, *Shike kegong yanjiu* (Shanghai: Shanghai guji chubanshe, 2009), 150–63.
39. Li Rihua, *Weishui xuan riji*, 85. Li said that he could not bear to expose Zhu because "his livelihood depends on this." Li's remark recalls similar stories about Wen

Zhengming and Shen Zhou that I will discuss later. Li and Zhu seemed to have developed a friendship. Recall that Zhu Xiaohai copied the Wang Wei painting that Dong Qichang identified as genuine (*WL* 3:658–59).

40. For these anecdotes, see *Shishuo xinyu* 21.9, 21.11–14; *LDMHJ*, 5.112–15. On Gu's remarks about making copies, see *LDMHJ* 5.117–18.
41. Quoted in Yuan Hongdao, "Xu *Zhulin ji*," *YHD* 1:700. The word *hua* 畫 (to paint, to draw) can also mean "to deliberate" or "to plan."
42. Dong Qichang is describing his interpretation qua imitation of Ni Zan's style, just as Ni Zan imitates but also transforms earlier masters. See *Hua Chan shi suibi*, j. 2, *DQC* 3:131. On how stylistic repertoires constitute "nondevelopmental sequences," see James Cahill, "Some Thoughts on the History and Post-History of Chinese Painting," *Archives of Asian Art* 55 (2005): 17–33.
43. Dong Qichang, *Hua Chan shi suibi*, j. 1, *DQC* 3:70.
44. Sun Chengze, *Yanshan zhai zaji*, 1.1a–1b, in *Qing mi cang wai liu zhong* (Shanghai: Shanghai guji chubanshe, 1993). This work contains references that postdate Sun Chengze—either these are entries added by Sun's grandson Sun Jiong (who also used the studio name Yanshan zhai) or Sun Jiong may be the author of the entire work.
45. Wang Shizhen, *Yanzhou xugao*, 164.11a–11b. Cf. Chiu Shih-hua, "Suzhou pian huajia Huang Biao yanjiu," *Gugong xueshu jikan* 37, no. 1(2020): 10.
46. Jiang Shaoshu, *Wusheng shishi*, *ZGSHQS* 4:870.
47. Huang Biao's colophon on *Jiu lao tu*, cited in Chiu Shih-hua, "Suzhou pian," 20.
48. Yang was Wang's nephew and student. According to Yu Jianwu (487–551), "he really captured Wang's style" (*Shupin*). There was a saying at the time: "To buy Wang and obtain Yang—no need to feel let down." When a friend told Wang Shizhen that the Yu Shinan calligraphy he owned was a copy made by Mi Fu, Wang said, "If it were so, then it is buying Wang and obtaining Yang, I am satisfied." See Dong Qichang, *Hua Chan shi suibi*, j. 1 (*DQC* 3:99). Wen Zhenheng used the same phrase to talk about Song imitations of earlier masters in Emperor Huizong's collection (*ZWZ* 5.150).
49. Jiang Shaoshu, *Wusheng shishi*, *ZGSHQS* 4:853–54.
50. Zhan Jingfeng, *Zhan dongtu xuanlan lu*, *ZGSHQS* 4:6.
51. Jiang Shaoshu, *Wusheng shishi*, *ZGSHQS* 4:844.
52. He Liangjun, *Siyou zhai congshuo* (Beijing: Zhonghua shuju, 1997 [1959]), 15.131. He Liangjun was Wen's friend.
53. The letter is cited in Ye Kangning, *Fengya zhi hao: Mingdai Jia Wan nianjian de shuhua xiaofei* (Beijing: Shangwu yinshu guan, 2017), 57.
54. Jiang Shaoshu, *Wusheng shishi*, *ZGSHQS* 4:849.
55. *Mingdai mingren chidu xuancui*, ed. Guojia tushu guan (Beijing: Guojia tushu guan chubanshe, 2018), 10:457. On the gift of painting and calligraphy in charting social relations, see Craig Clunas, *Elegant Debts: The Social Art of Wen Zhengming, 1470–1559* (Honolulu: University of Hawai'i Press, 2004).
56. Feng Shike, "Wen daizhao Zhengming xiaozhuan," *Feng Yuancheng wenji* (Taipei: Guolian tushu, 1964), 50.14b–15a.

57. He Liangjun, *Siyou zhai congshuo*, 15.131. Zhang Dai puts this anecdote in the chapter entitled "Great Virtue" (Shengde) in his *Kuaiyuan daogu* (Hangzhou: Zhejiang guji chubanshe, 1986), 6.
58. Wang Shizhen, *Yanzhou sibu gao*, 155.23a.
59. See, e.g., Qian Qianyi, *Liechao shiji xiaozhuan*, 2:636–37; Zhu Yizun, "Lun hua he Song zhongcheng," fifth of twelve quatrains (*Pushu ting quanji*, ed. Wang Limin et al. [Changchun: Jilin wenshi chubanshe, 2009], 16.219); Zhou Lianggong, *Duhua lu*, *ZGSHQS* 8:945–46; *YSZ* B.17a; Gu Fu, *Pingsheng zhuangguan*, *ZGSHQS* 4:1017; James Cahill, *The Painter's Practice: How Artists Lived and Worked in Traditional China* (New York: Columbia University Press, 1994), 141–42.
60. Yang Xiong's (cognomen Ziyun, 53 BCE–18 CE) contemporaries did not appreciate his writings. He said, "There will be another Yang Ziyun in a later era—he will surely love them!" Dong thus implies that those who are fooled deserve to be fooled. See Dong Qichang, *Rongtai bieji*, j. 2, *DQC* 2:538; Wai-kam Ho, ed., *The Century of Tung Ch'i-ch'ang* (Kansas City, Mo., and Seattle: Nelson Atkins Museum and University of Washington Press, 1992), 2:123.
61. See Qi Gong, *Qi Gong lun yi* (Shanghai: Shanghai shuhua chubanshe, 2010), 141–54.
62. Dong uses the line to describe the transcendent style of Dong Yuan, Ju Yuan, and Mi Fu that attains "enlightenment" through intuitive understanding, as distinct from deliberate striving toward excellence. See *Hua Chan shi suibi*, j. 2, *DQC* 3:125. Cf. Chen Zhongzhe's study of Chan aesthetics in Dong's paintings, *Yi chao zhiru rulai di* (Beijing: Zhonghua shuju, 2008), 136–39.
63. Dong Qichang, *Rongtai bieji*, j. 2, *DQC* 2:538.
64. Li Rihua praises Dong Qichang for using his "loftiness" to deal with the dangers of worldly advancement (*Weishui xuan riji*, 24). We can also consider Wang Shizhen's (1634–1711) poetics of "ineffable essence and resonance" (*shenyun* 神韻): Is it transcendence of worldly concerns or the most artful way to negotiate the perils of his era? Cf. Wai-yee Li, "Confronting History and Its Alternatives in Early Qing Poetry," in *Trauma and Transcendence in Early Qing Literature*, ed. Wilt Idema, Wai-yee Li, and Ellen Widmer (Cambridge, Mass.: Harvard University Asia Center, 2006), 73–98.
65. Qian Qianyi, *Liechao shiji xiaozhuan*, 2:637–38.
66. Chen Menglian, *Meigong fujun nianpu*, in *Beijing tushuguan cang zhenben nianpu congkan*, vol. 53 (Beijing: Beijing tushuguan chubanshe, 1999), entries for 1630 and 1634.
67. Xu Xuemo, *Shi miao shi yu lu*, published by Xu Yuangu, 1608, 18.3a–3b.
68. Zhan Jingfeng, *Zhan Dongtu xuanlan bian*, *ZGSHQS* 4:14.
69. Li is alluding to Su Shi's "Account of the Pavilion for Releasing Cranes" (Fanghe ting ji), *Su Shi wenji biannian jianzhu*, 2:137–40. Cranes symbolize purity, virtue, and transcendence, yet Lord Yi's obsession results in the destruction of his domain (see chap. 1, 25). The classics abound with warnings about indulgence in wine, yet the likes of Ruan Ji rely on it to "preserve their true nature." Su Shi concludes that political responsibility precludes obsessions while reclusion licenses them.
70. Li Rihua, *Weishui xuan riji*, 30.

71. Wen Jia dismisses the painting as being "devoid of the spirit of lofty antiquity" (*Qianshan tang shuhua ji*, 255). Cf. Dong Qichang: "Its brushwork is fine and delicate . . . unfortunately it is lacking in principled forcefulness" (*Hua Chan shi suibi*, j. 2, *DQC* 3:116).
72. On rumors about the role of Yan Song and Yan Shifan in Wang Shu's demotion and death, see also Xu Shuofang, *Xu Shuofang ji* (Hangzhou: Zhejiang guji chubanshe, 1993), 2:566–73; Wu Han, *Wu Han shixue lunzhu xuanji* (Beijing: Renmin chubanshe, 1984–1988), 37–54, 75–80. To avenge his father's persecution by Yan Song and Yan Shifan on account of the scroll, Wang Shizhen is said to have written *Jin Ping Mei*, targeting Yan Shifan through its protagonist Ximen Qing. This theory has been widely discredited.
73. See Tian Yiheng, *Liu qing rizha* (Shanghai: Shanghai guji chubanshe, 1985), 35.12a–12b (1129–30); Wen Jia, *Qianshan tang shuhua ji*, 255.
74. *Mingshi* 204.5398–99; *WL* 1:208–9.
75. Wang Shizhen, "*Qingming shanghe tu bieben* ba," *Yanzhou xugao*, 168.21b–22b; Jiang Shaoshu, *Wusheng shishi*, *ZGSHQS* 4:870. On Huang Biao, see Ye Kangning, *Fengya zhi hao*, 8–15; Chiu Shih-hua, "Suzhou pian huajia Huang Biao yanjiu."
76. Wang Shizhen, *Gu bu gu lu*, 23a–23b; *Yanzhou xugao*, 168.22b–23a.
77. Wang Shizhen, *Yanzhou sibu gao*, 51.25a. On the contrary, the tone is highly complimentary. Thus the first quatrain: "Zhong (Yao), Wang (Xizhi), Gu (Kaizhi), Lu (Tanwei), gone for almost a thousand years—/Because of you, their spirit has been passed on./Do not laugh at a lifetime's futilities:/He is, like Mi Fu, on a boat with paintings and calligraphy" 鍾王顧陸幾千年，賴汝風神次第傳。落魄此生看莫笑，一身還是書畫船。Mi Fu was famous for traveling on a boat with his collection.
78. Xu Shupi, *Shixiao lu*, in *Congshu jicheng xubian*, *zibu*, vol. 89 (Shanghai: Shanghai shudian, 1994), j. 2. Cited in Zhu Yixuan, ed., *Jin Ping Mei ziliao huibian* (Tianjin: Nankai daxue chubanshe, 2012), 81.
79. Xu is skeptical because it seems to be modeled on a story told about Su Shi's astute judgment. See Yue Ke, *Ting shi* (Beijing: Zhonghua shuju, 1997 [1981]), 2.25.
80. Gu Gongxie, *Xiaoxia xianji zhaichao*, cited in Zhu Yixuan, ed., *Jin Ping Mei ziliao huibian*, 93.
81. Versions of this story also appear in Gu Yingtai, *Mingshi jishi benmo* (Shanghai: Shanghai guji chubanshe, 1994), 54.213; Liu Tingji (b. 1653), *Zaiyuan zazhi* (this account features a Wang Wei painting instead of *Going Up the River*), cited in Zhu Yixuan, ed., *Jin Ping Mei ziliao huibian*, 82–83.
82. For Cheng Kezhong, see Qian Qianyi, *Liechao shiji xiaozhuan*, 2:631–32.
83. The scholar-official Wang Ao (sobriquet Wenzhen, 1450–1524) was not related to Wang Shu, but the author obviously intended to refer to Wang Shu's story.
84. "To be careless with hiding one's belongings is to encourage burglary," "Xici shang," in *Zhouyi zhushu* 7.152.
85. Xue Hongji and Wang Rumei eds., *Xijian zhenben Ming Qing chuanqi xiaoshuo ji* (Changchun: Jilin wenshi chubanshe, 2007), 215–17; also included in Huang Zongxi comp., *Ming wenhai*, 428.15a–18b; Cheng Kezhong, *Cheng Zhongquan xiansheng wenji*, 3.13a–16b.

86. See Feng Zhiguo, *Yu gu tong you: Xiang Yuanbian shuhua jiancang yanjiu* (Hangzhou: Zhongguo meishu xueyuan chubanshe, 2013), 101, 139–40; Liu Jinku, *Nanhua beidu*, 39; Wang Keyu, *Shanhu wang*, ZGSHQS 5:1164.
87. Liu Zhizhong, "*Yi peng xue* benshi xinzheng," *Xiju yishu*, no. 2 (1988): 79–85.
88. See Qi Biaojia's diary, *Qi Zhongmin gong riji*, cited in Cheng Huaping, *Ming Qing chuanqi biannian shigao* (Jinan: Qi Lu shushe, 2008), 240–41.
89. Four scenes from *Yi peng xue* are included in *Zui yiqing* (mid- to late 17th c.), eight in *Zui baiqiu* (18th c.), one in *Na shu ying qupu* (18th c.), and fourteen in *Jicheng qu pu* (1925). Whereas the scenes from *Yi peng xue* anthologized in *Zui yiqing* (scenes 8, 13, 14, 15) are almost identical to the version preserved in *Guben xiqu congkan*, those in *Zui baiqiu* (scenes 8, 11, 14, 15, 18, 20, 21, 30) have more colloquial titles, dialogues in the Wu dialect, and variant arias and details. *Yi peng xue* was also rewritten as *tanci* (1819) and *zidi shu*.
90. The phrase *yi peng* means "to hold with both hands [sometimes as a gesture of offering]." In his impeachment of Qian Qianyi, Zhang Hanru alleged that Qian tried to appropriate a jade cup by this name (Kang Baocheng, *Suzhou jupai yanjiu* [Guangzhou: Huacheng chubanshe, 1993], 223). Li Yù might have borrowed the name of the cup from that story.
91. See, e.g., *Zhanguo ce*, Qin 3.128; *Han Feizi* 4.239.
92. These lines are omitted in *Zui baiqiu*. What I translated as "ritual vessels" is literally "names and vessels." *Zuozhuan* (Zuo Cheng 2.3, 2:788) records Confucius's remarks: "It is precisely ritual vessels and names that cannot be lent to others, for these are the things by which a ruler governs." See also *Zuo* Zhao 32.4, 3:1724–25.
93. The historical Qi Jiguang (1528–1588) was a general famous for defending China's eastern coast against Japanese pirates and for confronting the Mongol threat along China's northern frontier. His tenure as commander in the Jizhou area lasted from 1568 to 1582, well after Yan Shifan's execution in 1564.
94. That is, he has abused his position. As noted, the jade cup is ironically juxtaposed with the ritual vessel that symbolizes state power.
95. For studies of this group, see Ariel Fox, *The Cornucopian Stage: Performing Commerce in Early Modern China* (Cambridge, Mass: Harvard University Asia Center, forthcoming); Kang Baocheng, *Suzhou jupai yanjiu*; Li Mei, *Ming Qing zhiji Suzhou zuojia qun yanji* (Beijing: Zhongguo shehui kexue chubanshe, 2000).
96. Jiao Xun, *Jushuo* (Changsha: Shangwu yinshu guan, 1939), 4.64.
97. Jiao Xun claimed that Li Yù could not take the examination because of interference from Shen Shixing's son, but Wu Weiye noted his repeated attempts (and failure) to obtain an examination degree. On the controversy around Li Yù's background, see Li Mei, *Ming Qing zhiji Suzhou zuojia qun yanjiu*, 256–60.
98. See, for example, Feng Yuanjun, "Zenyang kandai *Yipeng xue*," in *Feng Yuanjun gudian wenxue lunwen ji* (Jinan: Shandong renmin chubanshe, 1980), 257–85; Xu Mingyan, "Lun Li Yù de *Yipeng xue* chuanqi," *Nanjing Shida xuebao: shehui kexue ban*, no. 2 (1980): 35–42.
99. See the sources cited in Jiang Ruizao, *Xiaoshuo kaozheng*, ed. Jiang Yiren (Hangzhou: Zhejiang guji chubanshe, 2016), 134–36.

100. Tao Qian, *Tao Yuanming ji*, ed. Lu Qinli (Hong Kong: Zhonghua shuju, 1987), 175.
101. Li Yù's corpus includes several examples of "a play within a play"; other Suzhou playwrights also favor this trope. See Li Mei, *Ming Qing zhiji Suzhou zuojia qun yanjiu*, 216–32.
102. See Feng Yuanjun, "Zenyang kandai *Yipeng xue*"; Xu Mingyan, "Lun Li Yù de *Yipeng xue* chuanqi." For *huaben* stories about loyal servants, see *Xingshi hengyan* 35, Li Yu, *Wusheng xi*, story no. 11; for contemporaneous plays on the theme, see anon., *Weiyang tian*, *Xuanyuan jing*; Zhu Zuochao, *Jiulian deng*; Zhu Yuncong, *Longdeng zhuan*; Zou Yuqing, *Shuangchi bi*.
103. See, e.g., Ouyang Daifa, "Chongxin pingjia *Yipeng xue*: jian tan suowei 'yipu xi' de pingjia wenti," in *Zhongguo gudai wenxue lunji*, ed. Hubei daxue zhongguo gudai wenxue xueke (Beijing: Zhonghua shuju, 2002), 592–602.
104. See Sato Masayuki, *Zhongguo gudai zhong lun yanjiu* (Taipei: Taiwan daxue chuban zhongxin, 2010); Chiung-yun Liu, "Embodied Virtue: How Was Loyalty Edited and Performed in Late Imperial China?," in *Keywords in Chinese Culture*, ed. Wai-yee Li and Yuri Pines (Hong Kong: Chinese University of Hong Kong Press, 2020).
105. For the lore on the Zhao orphan and versions of the famous Yuan play on the topic, see C. T. Hsia, Wai-yee Li, and Karl Kao, *The Columbia Anthology of Yuan Drama* (New York: Columbia University Press, 2014), 17–72; Wilt Idema and Stephen West, *The Orphan of Zhao and Other Plays* (New York: Columbia University Press, 2015), 49–111.
106. That eulogy is omitted in *Zui baiqiu*, possibly because it slows down dramatic action.
107. Qi twice invokes "Changshan's tongue" as inspiration (*YPX* 17.60, 18.61): upon the fall of Changshan during the An Lushan Rebellion, Yan Gaoqing (692–756), governor of Changshan, cursed An Lushan after being captured. An Lushan cut out his tongue (*Xin Tangshu* 192.5531).
108. This aria is omitted in *Zui baiqiu*, where Mo Hao instead dramatically self-identifies as Mo Huaigu with a pause: "I, Mo—(pause) Huaigu—what a wrongful death I suffer!" There are also several additional arias (sung by the chorus) describing and lamenting the execution.
109. Huang describes the female protagonists in the play, Yang Yunyou and Lian Tiansu, as her antecedents from "thirty years ago": like them she is a "beleaguered lady" (literally, a lady rushing about with an umbrella on her back) trying to make a living by West Lake. (In the play, Yang Yunyou uses the same phrase to describe herself [*YZY* 21.387]). Since Lin and Yang were active in Hangzhou in the 1620s, it seems safe to date Huang's preface to the 1650s. According to Patrick Hanan, *The Invention of Li Yu* (Cambridge, Mass.: Harvard University Press, 1988), 16, it was written around 1655.
110. Both Dong and Chen wrote poems praising the talent and beauty of Yang and Lin; see Tsao Shu-chuan, "*Chunxing tang shiji* zhong de cainü qunxiang," in *Taiwan xueshu xin shiye*, ed. Cai Yingjun et al. (Taipei: Wunan tushu, 2007). Cf. Zhang Renquan, "Li Yu *Yizhong yuan*," in *Lidai Xihu wenxuan zhuanji*, ed. Wang Guoping et al. (Hangzhou: Hangzhou chubanshe, 2004), 14:290–305.

111. Wang Ranming was famous for, among other things, publishing Liu Rushi's poetry collection, *Hu shang cao*, and her letters. For Wang Ranming's role in bringing about the union of Liu Rushi and Qian Qianyi, see Chen Yinke, *Liu Rushi biezhuan* (Shanghai: Shanghai guji chubanshe, 1980); Mao Xiang and Yu Huai, *Plum Shadows and Plank Bridge: Two Memoirs About Courtesans*, trans. Wai-yee Li (New York: Columbia University Press, 2020), 212–15. Qian wrote a tomb inscription for Wang (*QMZ* 7:1154–56) and a poem on the catalog of Wang's collection (*QMZ* 4:58–59).
112. *Suixi an ji*, 3b–4a, in *Chunxing tang shiji*, in *Congsui Wang shi yishu* (Changsha: 1886). Huilin may be Yang Yunyou's given name. She also used the sobriquet "Spirit of the Bamboo Grove" (Lin xia feng).
113. *Tingxue an ji*, 3.12a–12b, in *Chunxing tang shiji*; *Rongtai bieji*, j. 4 (*DQC* 2:624–25). "Staunch defenders" (*jintang* 金湯) is literally "metal city walls and a deep moat" or "impregnable defense." "Grinding a brick and making it into a mirror" is a Chan paradox.
114. *Tingxue an ji*, 12b–13a.
115. In a well-known story from *Liexian zhuan*, Zheng Jiaofu receives a gift of pendants from two goddesses, but both the goddesses and the pendants soon vanish (*TPGJ* 59.365).
116. In a Tang tale by Xu Yaozuo (9th c.), Han Yi and the courtesan Liu (which means "willow") exchange poems on the hopes and fears of desire. Han Yi uses "the willows of Zhangtai" to refer to Liu (*TPGJ* 485.3995–97).
117. *Han Wudi bieguo dongmingji*, In *Han Wei Liuchao biji xiaoshuo daguan*, ed. Wang Genlin et al. (Shanghai: Shanghai guji chubanshe, 1999), 132.
118. Chen Jiru, "Ji meng ge," *Meng cao*, 8a–8b, in *Chunxing tang shiji*.
119. *Meng cao*, 6a, in *Chunxing tang shiji*.
120. The knight in yellow clothes is the heroic figure who brings the faithless Li Yi to the bedside of his lover, the pining and dying courtesan Huo Xiaoyu, in the eponymous Tang tale by Jiang Fang (*TPGJ* 487.4006–11).
121. That is, Yang Yunyou is the beautiful painter who is like "the beauty in the painting."
122. Liu Rushi, *Liu Rushi ji*, ed. Fan Jingzhong and Zhou Shutian (Hangzhou: Zhongguo meishu xueyuan chubanshe, 2002), 81.
123. See *Min you shi ji*, in *Chunxing tang shiji*, j. 4; Tsao Shu-chuan, "*Chuxing tang shiji* zhong de cainü qunxiang," 448–50.
124. For the poems Li Yu addressed to Wang Ranming, see *Liweng yijiayan*, in *Li Yu quanji*, 12 vols. (Hangzhou: Zhejiang guji chubanshe, 1991), 1:112, 170, 454.
125. See Liu Rushi's letters (Liu Rushi, *Liu Rushi ji*, 84–85, 94–97).
126. See *Min chao Dong huan shishi*, in *Ming Taizu ping Hu lu* (*wai qi zhong*), 282–322.
127. The "Preface to Orchid Pavilion" (353) by Wang Xizhi is a much sought after masterpiece of calligraphy. The true specimen is said to have been buried with the Tang emperor Taizong (r. 627–649), and various "faithful copies" circulated through the ages. See Robert Harrist, "Replication and Deception in Calligraphy of the Six

Dynasties Period," in *Chinese Aesthetics: The Ordering of Literature, the Arts, and the Universe in the Six Dynasties*, ed. Zong-qi Cai (Honolulu: University of Hawai'i Press, 2004), 31–59.

128. There are no human figures in extant landscapes by Dong Qichang. Dong acknowledged he could not paint human figures, boats, carriages, and houses, and he found consolation in the fact Ni Zan had similar limitations. See *Hua Chan shi suibi*, j. 2, *DQC* 2:126. However, he painted *Scenes from Studying at Kunshan* (*Kunshan dushu xiaojing*, no longer extant) for Chen Jiru, and the title may suggest a human figure in a study, although it is also possible that the scene represents what can be seen from the study. See *Hua Chan shi suibi*, j. 2, *DQC* 2:128–29.

129. Feng Yan (8th c.), *Feng shi wenjian ji*, *Congshu jicheng chubian* (Changsha: Shangwu yinshu guan, 1936), 10.125–26.

130. See, e.g., Xu Wei, "The Female Top Candidate Refuses One Mate and Obtains Another" (Nü zhuangyuan cifeng dehuang), in *Sisheng yuan*; Wu Weiye, *Moling chun* (see chap. 4), scene 29.

131. See, e.g., n. 14; Mao and Yu, *Plum Shadows*, 99, 170; Li Yu, *Liancheng bi* 1, *Bimu yu* (*Li Yu quanji*, 4:251–80, 2:111–211).

132. Huang Yuanjie comments: "I was also subjected to such slander when I was young. But I persisted and would not relent, and the critics could not do anything about it. In this one thing alone, I was somewhat superior to Yunyou. Those who sought my calligraphy and painting were quite capable of accommodating me" (*YZY* 21.387). The charge that women writers and painters might have relied on male "ghost artists" must have been quite common. *Ideal Matches* offers a reverse scenario of women artists painting on behalf of men.

133. This is a common trope. See Mao and Yu, *Plum Shadows*, 100–102, 124–26. Li Yu writes that a woman "only need to open a book, hold a brush in her hand, and sit under the green window" to "become a painting," but he does not particularly recommend that women learn to paint (*XQOJ* 145–16).

134. Notable examples include Feng Menglong, *Xingshi hengyan* 11 ("Su Xiaomei Sets Up Three Tests for Her Groom" [Su Xiaomei san nan xinlang]); Li Yù, *The Beauty of Meishan* (*Meishan xiu*); Wu Bing, *Green Peony* (*Lü mudan*).

135. See, for example, Zhang Dai's account of "the lean mares of Yangzhou" (*Tao'an mengyi*, ed. Huai Ming [Beijing: Zhonghua shuju, 2008], 5.102–03), when the matchmaker makes the woman "take a few steps" in front of her prospective client. See also Li Yu's excursus on the subject (*XQOJ* 114).

136. The sword imagery in Dong Qichang's colophon on one of Lin Tiansu's paintings and in his poem addressed to her suggests that the historical Lin Tiansu was known for her heroic spirit. See *Rongtai bie ji*, j. 2, j. 4, *DQC* 2:413, 495.

137. Chen Jiru, "Shou Xuanzai Dong taishi liushi xu," in *Wanxiang tang xiaopin* (Shanghai: Beiye shanfang, 1936), 259–61.

138. *Wu ge zhi yi*, cited in Wang Yongshun, ed., *Dong Qichang shiliao* (Shanghai: Huadong shifan daxue chubanshe, 1991), 337.

139. Huang Zongxi, *Si jiu lu*, in *Huang Zongxi quanji* (Hangzhou: Zhejiang guji chubanshe, 2005), 1:343–44.

140. See Wai-yee Li, "The Late Ming Courtesan: Invention of a Cultural Ideal," in *Writing Women in Late Imperial China*, ed. Ellen Widmer and Kang-I Sun Chang (Stanford, Calif.: Stanford University Press, 1997), 46–73; Li, *Women and National Trauma in Late Imperial Chinese Literature* (Cambridge, Mass.: Harvard University Asia Center, 2014), chap. 4; "Introduction," in Mao and Yu, *Plum Shadows*.
141. See, e.g., Yuan Zhen's "Poem on Encountering the Goddess" (Huizhen shi), included in his "Yingying's Story" (also called "Record of Encountering the Goddess" [Huizhen ji]).
142. This echoes Chen's aria in scene 2, cited earlier. Cf. n. 127.
143. Li Zhi, "Tong xin shuo" (*Li Zhi quanji zhu*, annot. Zhang Jianye and Zhang Dai, 14 vols. [Beijing: Shehui kexue wenxian chubanshe, 2010], 1:276–77). The last two lines adopt the metaphor of the theater: the short ones in the audience, hardly capable of seeing the stage, cannot see through the make-believe of theatrical performance.
144. Ding Yaokang, *Xu Jin Ping Mei*, in *Ding Yaokang quanji*, ed. Li Zengpo and Zhang Qingji (Zhengzhou: Zhongzhou guji chubanshe, 1999), 2:46.353–54.
145. Contemporary and later history, miscellanies, fiction, and poetry often refer to rumors regarding a man who claimed to be the Chongzhen emperor's son and one Tong shi who was supposed to have been married to the Hongguang emperor. The Hongguang court refuted these claims. See Wai-yee Li, *Women and National Trauma*, 543 n.95.
146. *Yang Yunyou Thrice Married Dong Qichang* (Yang Yunyou sanjia Dong Qichang) is in the repertoire of modern Beijing opera.
147. See Wai-yee Li, *Enchantment and Disenchantment: Love and Illusion in Chinese Literature* (Princeton, N.J.: Princeton University Press, 1993); Anthony Yu, *Rereading the Stone: Desire and the Making of Fiction in Dream of the Red Chamber* (Princeton, N.J.: Princeton University Press, 1997).
148. Shang Wei, "Truth Becomes Fiction When Fiction Is True: *The Story of the Stone* and the Visual Culture of the Manchu Court," *Journal of Chinese Literature and Culture* 2, no. 1 (April 2015): 207. See also Jonathan Hay, *Sensuous Surfaces: The Decorative Object in Early Modern China* (Honolulu: University of Hawai'i Press, 2010), 215–35; Nancy Berliner, *Juanqinzhai in the Qianlong Garden, the Forbidden City, Beijing* (London: Scala, World Monuments Fund, 2008); Berliner, *The Emperor's Private Paradise: Treasures from the Forbidden City* (Salem, Mass: Peabody Essex Museum, in association with Yale University Press, 2010); Kristina Renée Kleutghen, *Imperial Illusions: Crossing Pictorial Boundaries in the Qing Palace* (Seattle: University of Washington Press, 2015); Wu Hung, "Beyond Stereotypes: The Twelve Beauties in Qing Court Art and *The Dream of the Red Chamber*," in Widmer and Chang, *Women in Late Imperial China*, 306–65; Chih-en Chen, "Fooling the Eye: Trompe l'oeil Porcelain in High Qing China," *Les Cahiers de Framespa*, no. 31 (2019): 1-44.
149. See Wai-yee Li, "Gardens and Illusions from Late Ming to Early Qing," *Harvard Journal of Asiatic Studies* 72, no. 2 (December 2012): 295–336.

150. See Shang, "Truth Becomes Fiction;" Sophie Volpp, *The Substance of Fiction: Literary Objects in Ming-Qing China (1550–1750)* (New York: Columbia University Press, forthcoming).
151. A comment by Red Inkstone indicates that Baoyu's dream is a later addition (*ZYZ* 655). See Li, *Enchantment and Disenchantment*, 227.

4. LOST AND FOUND

1. Ankeney Weitz, trans., *Zhou Mi's Record of Clouds and Mist Passing Before One's Eyes: An Annotated Translation* (Leiden: Brill, 2002).
2. The Four Treasury Academicians claimed in their summary (1780) that *Resonant Rock* follows the model of *Record of Clouds and Mist*, with the difference that Jiang's work is organized by objects rather than by owners, and its description of objects includes provenance, loss, and ownership.
3. Jiang Shaoshu wrote *Qiongju pu*, a treatise devoted to rocks and jade.
4. See Inoue Mitsuyuki, trans. Wan Shuang and Lu Peirong, "Jiang Shaoshu yu Wang Yueshi: *Yunshi zhai bitan* suojian Ming mo Qing chu yishu shichang yu Huizhou shangren de huodong," in *Meishu shi yu guannian shi*, ed. Fan Jinzhong and Cao Yiqiang (Nanjing: Nanjing shifan daxue chubanshe, 2004), 383–411.
5. Tang Yin's painting of the gathering was still extant when Jiang was writing. In 1510 Zhu Yunming wrote "An Account of Reclusion at Southern Mountain" (Nanshan xiaoyin ji) for the Sun brothers. Jiang notes: "For Qifeng (Sun Yu) the path to immortal fame was not through metal and stone but through silk [i.e., paintings and writings on silk]" (*YSZ* A.13–14). Inoue suggests that for Jiang, local and lineage pride drives some of the narratives in his miscellany. This is evident in Jiang's discussion of a calligraphy masterpiece that his great-grandfather received from the throne and published (A.19–20).
6. For Zhou Danquan (given name Shichen), see Ajioka Yoshindo, "Shū Tansen kō—Min matsu Keitokuchin yō no ichi minshō ni tsuite," *Shūkan Tōyōgaku*, no. 39 (1978): 34–53; Cai Meifen, "Suzhou gongyijia Zhou Danquan ji qi shidai," in *Quyu yu wangluo: jin qiannian lai zhongguo meishushi yanjiu guoji xueshu yantaohui lunwen ji*, ed. Quyu yu wangluo guoji xueshu yantaohui lunwen ji bianji weiyuan hui (Taipei: Guoli Taiwan daxue yishu shi yanjiu suo, 2001), 269–98. Jiang Shaoshu praises Zhou's poetry, calligraphy, painting, pottery, and garden design in *Wusheng shishi*, j. 7, *ZGSHQS* 4:872. According to Li Rihua, for everything that passed through Zhou's hands, "what has been destroyed becomes again complete, what is vulgar turned into something elegant." Li Rihua, *Weishui xuan riji*, ed. Tu Youxiang (Shanghai: Shanghai Yuandong chubanshe, 1996), 3.164.
7. On Tang Junyu (given name Xianke) as painter and calligrapher, see Jiang Shaoshu, *Wusheng shishi*, j. 4, *ZGSHQS* 4:858.
8. In the Tang tale "The Curly Beard" (Qiuran ke), the eponymous hero (the man with a curly beard) initially strives for supremacy in the waning days of the Sui dynasty but realizes when he meets Li Shiming (later the Tang emperor Taizong) that the latter is the one mandated by heaven to become ruler. He thus gives away his

wealth to Li Jing and his wife Hongfu so that they can help Li Shimin win the empire (*TPGJ* 193.1445–48). Cf. chap. 1, n.112. Gongzi Gao of She claims to like dragons and use dragon motifs and patterns in decorations and furnishings, but when a real dragon descends to his abode, he flees in terror (*Xinxu* 5.190).

9. Jiang Shaoshu refers to Wang Yueshi by his sobriquet Tingwu. Dong Qichang, Li Rihua, and others mentioned their dealings with Wang and praised his connoisseurship in their writings. For Wang Yueshi, see Inoue, "Jiang Shaoshu yu Wang Yueshi"; Yao Yang, *Wan Ming jiangnan minjian yishu shoucang yanjiu* (Tianjin: Tianjin guji chubanshe, 2017), 281–91; Xiao Yanyi, *Gu shuhua shilun jianding wenji* (Beijing: Zijin cheng chubanshe, 2005), 303–8; Zhang Changhong, *Pinjian yu jingying: Ming mo Qing chu Huishang yishu zanzhu yanjiu* (Beijing: Beijing daxue chubanshe, 2010), 153–98.

10. Jiang Shaoshu, *Wusheng shishi*, j. 4, *ZGSHQS* 4:859. In *Zhanguo ce* (Yan, 29.1065), Guo Wei convinces King Zhao of Yan to attract talents by honoring Guo, using as analogy the king who eventually obtains an extraordinary steed by buying the bones of a fine horse and establishing a reputation for love of horses.

11. This comment echoes the judgment of Wang Shizhen (*Gu bu gu lu*, 28a) and Shen Defu (*WL* 2:653).

12. Huang Zongxi, *Hongguang shilu chao*, in *Huang Zongxi quanji* (Hangzhou: Zhejiang guji chubanshe), 2:94.

13. See Zhang Chao, *Yuchu xinzhi*, in *Shuohai*, ed. Ke Yuchun (Beijing: Renmin ribao chubanshe, 1997), 2:527–28; Ye Dehui, *Shulin qinghua* (Shanghai: Shanghai guji chubanshe, 2008), 90; Wang Shizhen, *Chibei outan* (Taipei: Shangwu yinshu guan, 1974), 19.20b; Li Zanyuan, "Lu qin xing," in Deng Hanyi, *Shiguan sanji*, in *Siku jinhui shu congkan*, vol. 3, 10.2a–2b; Lin Huiru, "Lu wang fu zhenwu," in *Mingdai yiwen* (Taipei: Zhonghua shuju, 1967), 8.10–11.

14. See, for example, the poems on a coin from the Wanli era and on a chair once owned by the artist Wen Zhengming. Wai-yee Li, "Shibian yu wanwu: luelun Qing chu wenren de shenmei fengshang," *Journal of the Institute of Literature and Philosophy*, Academia Sinica, no. 33 (September 2008): 1–40.

15. Chen Que, *Chen Que ji* (Beijing: Zhonghua shuju, 2009), 1:211–12. Chen was the disciple of the scholar, thinker, and Ming martyr Liu Zongzhou (1587–1645).

16. The length described would be the equivalent of about five feet eight inches. The famous third-century poet Ji Kang's height is said to have been seven *chi* and eight *cun*.

17. Its "shoulders" (or "neck" in an earlier passage) are injured from Chen's rubbing, and its "thigh" breaks when Chen strikes a maid with it.

18. Wang Fuzhi, *Jiangzhai wenji*, j. 9, *Chuanshan quanshu*, 15:200–204. Although translated here as "encomium," the genre of *zan*, often put at the end of a prose piece and usually quadrisyllabic, does not have to be laudatory.

19. *Xiaojing zhushu* 1.11.

20. "Zhonghui's Proclamation" (Zhonghui zhi gao, *Shangshu zhushu* 8.110–12), which contains this line, is one of the ancient script chapters in the *Documents*. The line also appears in *Zuo* Zhao 28.2, 3:1684–85, describing those who "hate the honest and vilify the right."

21. In *Lüshi chunqiu jiaoshi* (14.816), a foul-smelling man, ostracized by family and friends, lives in a place by the sea, where some "are pleased with his stench" and follow him around. See also Cao Zhi's letter to Yang Xiu, "The fragrance of orchids and angelicas is what the multitudes love, yet there are men who chase stench by the sea" (*Wenxuan* 42.1903).
22. See Lang Ying, *Qixiu leigao* (Shanghai: Shanghai shudian, 2001), 44.642; Zhang Han, *Songchuang mengyu*, ed. Xiao Guoliang (Shanghai: Shanghai guji chubanshe, 1986), 7.120. According to Jiang Shaoshu, his native Danying also produced paneled lanterns made from mineral silk (*YSZ* B.20a–20b). Wen Zhenheng claims that the Yunnan variety is superior and that the Danyang version is "not too elegant" (*ZWZ* 7.272).
23. See Gu Yanwu, *Rizhi lu jishi* (Zhengzhou: Zhongzhou guji chubanshe, 1990), 29.822. The six dimensions refer to the four directions plus above and below, thus *Shiji* 6.245: "Encompassed in the six dimensions is the emperor's land."
24. Zhang Han, *Songchuang mengyu*, 7.120.
25. According to Qu Dajun, heavenly silkworms, several times bigger than ordinary silkworms that eat mulberry leaves, feed on maple and camphor leaves (*Guangdong xinyu* [Beijing: Zhonghua shuju, 1997], 24.661).
26. According to legend, the normally muddy Yellow River clears up every thousand years, in tandem with the rise of sage kings.
27. "Changdi" 常棣: "Of all the people in the world, / none can compare to brothers" 凡今之人，莫如兄弟 (*Shijing zhuxi* 2:478–84); "Mian shui" 沔水: "I lament that among my brothers, / my compatriots and my friends, / none is willing to think of the disorder" 嗟我兄弟，邦人諸友，莫肯念亂 (2:562–65).
28. Wang Fuzhi, *Jiangzhai wenji*, j. 9, *Chuanshan quanshu*, 15:205–8. On the cultural and literary contexts of inscriptions as a genre, see Thomas Kelly, "Clawed Skin: The Literary Inscription of Things in Sixteenth Century China," Ph.D. diss., University of Chicago, 2017; "The Inscription of Remnant Things: Zhang Dai's 'Twenty-eight Friends,'" *Late Imperial China* 42, no. 1 (June 2021): 1–43.
29. Hou Fangyu, "Qiu yuan zapei xu," in *Hou Fangyu quanji jiaojian*, ed. Wang Shulin (Beijing: Renmin wenxue chubanshe, 2013), 1:41–47; Chen Zhenhui, *Qiuyuan zapei*, in *Yueya tang zongshu* 19, comp. Wu Chongyao (Taipei: Hualian chubanshe, 1965), 1a–2a. On Chen's image as a recluse, see also the poem Wu Weiye addressed to him (*WMC* 1:183).
30. See Han Tan's funereal essay on Mao Xiang (*MPJ* 2:754–56).
31. Chen Zhenhui, *Qiuyuan zapei*, 2b–3a.
32. The Tianbao reign (742–756) covered the period right before the An Lushan Rebellion.
33. Chen Zhenhui, *Qiuyuan zapei*, 4a–4b. Lu Guimeng (9th c.) describes a brocade skirt with fantastically elaborate embroidery that was at least three centuries old. See *Wenyuan yinghua*, comp. Li Fang et al. (Beijing: Zhonghua shuju, 1966) 379.1934.
34. Zhang Hua, *Bowu zhi*, in *Han Wei Liuchao biji xiaoshuo daguan*, ed. Wang Genlin et al. (Shanghai: Shanghai guji chubanshe, 1999), 217.
35. *TPGJ* 277.2192; *Nanshi* 59.1451.

36. *TPGJ* 200.1502.
37. Chen Zhenhui's son Chen Weiyue added the entry on azaleas in 1688, citing their sudden withering in 1641 as an omen for the fall of the Ming. Another son, Chen Zongshi, Hou Fangyu's son-in-law, added the entry on crabapple blossoms of Yongding in 1688.
38. On Jiang Cai's punishment, demotion, and eventual choice of Suzhou as home, as well as Jiang Gai's role in supporting him, see Jiang Cai's autobiographical annals ("Jiang Zhenyi xiansheng zizhu nianpu"), in *Jingting ji*, ed. Yin Xiaofeng (Nanjing: Huadong Shifan daxue chubanshe, 2011), 9–15.
39. The original has "silver hooks" instead of "calligraphy"; the idiom "iron strokes and silver hooks" (*tiehua yingou* 鐵畫銀鉤) refers to fine calligraphy.
40. The original has "wagtails in a row" 鶺鴒行, alluding to "Changdi" in the *Classic of Poetry* (*Shijing zhuxi*, 2:478–84): "The wagtails are on the plain; / Brothers come to each other's aid in difficulties" 脊令在原, 兄弟急難.
41. Jiang Cai adds a note here: "Formerly my younger brother sent me a letter with the line 'Pei Kai built a residence and let his older brother live there.'" The letter is also cited in Jiang Cai's elegy for Jiang Gai (*Jingting ji*, 275). On the story about Pei Kai (237–291), see *Yiwen leiju*, comp. Ouyang Xun, ed. Wang Shaoying (Shanghai: Shanghai guji chubanshe, 1999), 64.1142.
42. Su Wu is said to undertake the diplomatic mission to Xiongnu territories "in his prime" (*dingnian* 丁年). See Li Ling's letter to Su Wu (*Wenxuan* 41.1852, now widely recognized as the product of literary impersonation) and Wen Tingyun, "Su Wu miao" (*QTS* 582.6749).
43. The historian Gu Ling collected the Chongzhen emperor's calligraphy, and Du Jun described how he bowed to it in rituals of commemoration (Du Jun, "Song feng mo bao ji," *Bianya tang wenji* [Huanggang, 1894, woodblock print], 7.2a–3a. See also Wang Shizhen, *Chibei outan*, 17.1b; Wei Xi, "Chongzhen huangdi yushu ji" (*Wei Shuzi wenji*, ed. Shouren, Yao Pinwen, and Wang Nengxian [Beijing: Zhonghua shuju, 2003], 2:768–69). The first Qing emperor is said to prize the Chongzhen emperor's calligraphy and mourn his fate (Wang Hongzhuan, *Shan zhi* [Beijing: Zhonghua shuju, 1999], 13).
44. *Yi wei shilei mou*, with commentary by Zheng Xuan: "At Mount Tai we lost the golden rooster, at the Western Peak the jade ram vanished. When the rooster is lost and the ram vanishes, subjects lose all sense of restraint, rulers wander in confusion, and there is sadness all under heaven" (9a).
45. Du Fu, "Lan jing cheng Bo zhongcheng" (ca 766): "The heart's courage fails at the lair of jackals and tigers" 膽銷豺虎窟 (*QTS* 231.2539). In a poem addressed to Jiang Gai ("Songbie di Gai huan Suzhou"), Jiang Cai lauds Du Fu as poetic model: "Learning to write poetry, one must learn from Du Fu" 學詩必杜工部 (Jiang Cai, *Jingting ji*, 137). Jiang Cai mentions this also in his elegy for Jiang Gai ("Ji sandi wen," in *Jingting ji*, 275).
46. On the idea of "inner exile" and "homelessness" in early Qing poetry, see Wai-yee Li, "Introduction," in *Trauma and Transcendence in Early Qing Literature*, ed. Wilt

Idema, Wai-yee Li, and Ellen Widmer (Cambridge, Mass.: Harvard University Asia Center, 2006), 44–48.
47. Fang Zhongtong, "Zeng Liu Aoshi," cited in Deng Zhicheng, *Qingshi jishi chubian* (Hong Kong: Zhonghua shuju, 1976), 1:130.
48. Gu Yanwu, "Haishang sishou," no. 4, in *Gu Tinglin shi jianshi*, ed. Wang Jimin (Beijing: Zhonghua shuju, 1998), 1:70. Hou Ying, the knightly guardian of Yi Gate in Daliang (later Kaifeng), capital of the Warring States kingdom Wei, is remembered for his friendship with Lord Xinling (*Shiji* 77.2378–81).
49. Wu Zhaoqian, "Ji Qi Yixi," *Qiu jia ji*, ed. Ma Shouzhong (Shanghai: Shanghai guji chubanshe, 1993), 187.
50. *Xin Tangshu* 109.4097–98. Su Shi uses this allusion to imagine grandeur for his family, only to mock it as fantasy ("Guo yu hai po"), *Su Shi shiji hezhu*, annot. Feng Yingliu, ed. Huang Renke and Zhu Huaichun (Shanghai: Shanghai guji chubanshe, 2001), 42.2149–50.
51. Jingting Mountain is in Xuanzhou (Anhui), the destination of his demotion in 1644. The name thus commemorates the place Jiang Cai was sent by the Chongzhen emperor.
52. Jiang Anjie and Jiang Shijie, "Nianpu xubian" (Jiang Cai, *Jingting ji*, 18); "Yipu ji" (*Jingting ji*, 191–92); "Shuliu ting ji" (*Jingting ji*, 293–94). In both "Yipu ji" and "Shuliu ting ji," Jiang Cai implies that the Wen property was purchased through the help of his friends. Hsieh suggests that this may just be a necessary subterfuge, given the association of loyalism with poverty in early Qing. See "Qing chu zhongjun dianfan zhi suzao yu heliu: Shandong Laiyang Jiang shi xingyi kaolun," in *Ming Qing wenxue yu sixiang zhong de zhuti yishi yu shehui: xueshu sixiang pian*, ed. Yang Jinlong and Zhong Caijun (Taipei: Zhongyang yanjiu yuan wenzhesuo, 2004), 291–343. Jiang Cai's second wife was from a wealthy salt merchant family, which might have explained his economic resources. See Guo Yingde, "Xinxi shengcheng, nüxing yuedu yu yimin yishi: Zhu Suchen *Qinlou yue* chuanqi xiezuo yu kanke de qianyin houguo," *Xiju yanjiu* 7 (2011): 37–64.
53. Chen Weisong, "Yipu shi xu," in *Chen Weisong ji*, ed. Chen Zhenpeng and Li Xueying (Shanghai: Shanghai guji chubanshe, 2010), 1:293–95.
54. Mao Qiling, "Xuande yao qinghua zhifen xiang ge wei Laiyang Jiang Zhongzi fu," *Xihe wenji* (Shanghai: Shanghai guji chubanshe, 2009), 163.2736. Mao also mentions the box in *Xihe shihua*. The image of traces of cosmetics in the water of the palace moat may allude to Du Mu's poetic exposition on the Efang Palace of Qin.
55. Yu Huai, *Yu Huai quanji*, ed. Li Jintang (Shanghai: Shanghai guji chubanshe, 2011), 1:225–26. On the Xuande emperor's paintings, see *WL* 3:790; Jiang Shaoshu, *Wusheng shishi*, ZGSHQS 4:834; Liu Tiren, *Qisong tang shi xiao lu*, ZGSHQS 8:605; Wang Yuxian, *Huishi beikao*, ZGSHQS 8:687.
56. Chen Weisong, *Chen Weisong ji*, 2:1233.
57. *Quan Tang wen*, comp. Dong Gao et al. (Beijing: Zhonghua shuju, 1978), 748.7744–45.
58. Yu Huai, *Yu Huai quanji*, 1:67–69, 95–96, 203–04.

59. Li Guo, *Zaiting conggao* (1745), 9.4a–4b. Li adds that whenever Jiang reminisced about this, he showed great excitement. See also Xu Qiu, *Ciyuan congtan jiaojian*, ed. Wang Baili (Beijing: Renmin wenxue chubanshe, 1988), 567.
60. This is the only play by Zhu Suchen that survived in print instead of in manuscript form. See Guo Yingde, "Xinxi shengcheng." "Qinlou yue" is the tune title of the lyric that Chen Susu composed (ca. 1670s) on the Tang courtesan Zhenniang's grave. Chen Susu's collection, *Erfen mingyue ji*, which includes many poems addressed to Jiang Shijie, as well as poems on the Jiang-Chen romance by other women poets, are appended to the early Qing edition of the play.
61. See Guo Yingde, "Xinxi shengcheng."
62. See also Lü Bi, *Mingchao xiaoshi*; Wang Shizhen, *Guochao congji*, both cited in Wu Weiye, *Wu Meicun shiji jianshu*, comp. Wu Yifeng (Hong Kong: Guangzhi shuju, n.d.), 106. The *Liaozhai* story "Cuzhi" also uses the Xuande emperor's obsession as backdrop.
63. Feng Qiyong and Ye Junyuan, *Wu Meicun nianpu* (Beijing: Wenhua yishu chubanshe, 2007), 213. Wu and Sun both passed the *jinshi* examination in 1631.
64. Wang Renyu, *Kaiyuan Tianbo yishi*, in *Tang Wudai biji xiaoshuo daguan*, ed. Ding Ruming et al. (Shanghai: Shanghai guji chubanshe, 2000), 1723.
65. Line 16 also echoes Du Fu's line about a warhorse: "Its fierce spirit still recalls victory on the battlefield" 猛氣猶思戰場利 ("Gao duhu congma xing," *QTS* 216.2255).
66. The insurrection against Wang Mang led by Liu Xuan consisted of officers from humble origins. A contemporary ditty calls them "the menial breed under the stove" (*Hou Hanshu* 11.471). Legend has it that crickets bred in the kitchen are not good fighters.
67. "Yellow whiskers" indicates foreignness; it also describes a breed of crickets. The rebel Wang Dun refers to Emperor Ming of Jin (r. 299–325) as "the yellow-whiskered barbarian" (*Shishuo xinyu* 27.6; *Jinshu* 6.161). "The yellow-whiskered one" can suggest a valiant warrior, but that does not apply here.
68. *Baopu zi neipian jiaoshi*, Ge Hong, annot. Wang Ming (Beijing: Zhonghua shuju, 1988), 8.164, n. 92.
69. On the association of the cricket's chirping with political lamentation, see Jiang Kui's (c. 1155–c. 1221) song lyric on crickets, to the tune "Qitian le."
70. Frederic Wakeman, *The Great Enterprise: The Manchu Reconstruction of Imperial Order in Seventeenth-Century China* (Berkeley: University of California Press, 1985), 2:1129. According to Wakeman, "among the relatively prominent military officers and civilian officials whose biographies were included in the *Er chen zhuan*, exactly 100 (80 percent) came from the provinces north of the Yangtze River."
71. Fu Shen, "Wang Duo ji Qing chu beifang jiancang jia," in *Zhongguo huihua yanjiu lunwen ji*, ed. Duoyun bianji bu (Shanghai: Shanghai shuhua chubanshe, 1992); Liu Jinku, *Nanhua beidu: Qingdai shuhua jiancang zhongxin yanjiu* (Shijiazhuang: Hebei jiaoyu chubanshe, 2008).
72. Sun Chengze, *Gengzi xiaoxia ji*, 3.9b–10a.

73. This "vulgarian" (*cangfu* 傖父) does not know that the seal "Longming" 龍暝 actually refers to Li Gonglin, whose cognomen "Longmian" 龍眠 can be written as "Longming" (*Gengzi xiaoxia ji*, 3.3a)
74. Sun Chengze, *Gengzi xiaoxia ji*, 1.7a, 3.11a–b, 1.3a–b, 2.1a.
75. Liu Tiren, *Qisong tang shi xiao lu*, ZGSHQS 8:609. Liu is quoting Sun Chengze.
76. Sun Chengze, *Gengzi xiaoxia ji*, 8.1a.
77. In *Han Wu gushi*, the ghost of Emperor Wu of Han sells a jade cup (one of the items buried with him) in the marketplace (*Taiping yulan* 18.550). See also Shen Jiong's (503–561) imaginary petition to Emperor Wu of Han (*Chenshu* 19.254), the subject of Wu Weiye's short play *Tongtian tai*.
78. In his "Pan laochou" (Contra Great Sorrow), where he refutes the arguments of *Lisao*, Yang Xiong (53 BCE–18 CE) seems to understand *laochou* 牢愁 as *laosao*, meaning great sorrow or discontent. See Yang Xiong, *Yang Xiong ji jiaozhu*, annot. Zhang Zhenze (Shanghai: Shanghai guji chubanshe, 1993), 157.
79. Andrew Hsieh chronicles Sun Chengze's friendship with Gu Yanwu and Zhu Yizun in *Qing chu shi wen yu shiren jiaoyou kao* (Nanjing: Nanjing daxue chubanshe, 2001), 330–91. Zhu Yizun was active in anti-Qing resistance until the 1650s. Then he found protection as the Qing official Cao Rong's (1613–1685) secretary from 1656 to 1666. In 1679 he became a successful candidate in the examination for "Outstanding Scholars of Vast Learning."
80. Sun Chengze, *Gengzi xiaoxia ji*, 1.1a–1b.
81. WMC 1:300–02. On the dating of this poem, see Feng Qiyong and Ye Junyuan, *Wu Meicun nianpu*, 234, 242.
82. *Sanfu huangtu* records sites and landmarks of Han Chang'an, and the Blue Gate (Qingmen) was the city gate of Chang'an. Both *sanfu* (translated here as "the domain of the capital") and the Blue Gate indicate proximity to the nexus of power. The Valley of Retreat was in the Western Mountain near Beijing.
83. See Paul Pelliot, "Le prétendu album de porcelains de Hiang Yuan-pien," *T'oung Pao* 2, no. 32 (1936): 15–58; Lu Pengliang, "Xuanlu bianyi," *Wenwu*, no. 7 (2008): 64–76; Rose Kerr, *Later Chinese Bronzes* (London: Bamboo Publication in association with the Victorian and Albert Museum, 1990). Kerr dates *Xuande dingyi pu* to the seventeenth century; Lu dates it to the eighteenth century.
84. Pelliot dates *Xuanlu bolun* to the end of the seventeenth century ("Le prétendu album," 44).
85. Lu Pengliang, "Xuanlu bianyi." Lu offers convincing evidence that extant "Xuande" censers date from the late Ming.
86. Xuande censers are said to be the most noteworthy among vessels for sale at the market next to the City God Temple. See Liu Tong and Yu Yizheng, *Dijing jingwu lue* (Beijing: Beijing guji chubanshe, 1980), 130–32.
87. On Fang Gongqian and his prominent clan, see Hsieh, *Qing chu shiwen yu shiren jiaoyou kao*, 109–81.
88. Alleged corruption in the Jiangnan provincial examination in 1657 resulted in the dismissal and execution of examiners, and eight graduates from that year had their

juren degrees revoked. See Benjamin Elman, *A Cultural History of Civil Examinations in Late Imperial China* (Berkeley: University of California Press, 2000), 204.

89. Fang Gongqian, *Helou ju ji, Su'an ji* (Harbin: Helongjiang daxue chubanshe, 2010), 454–55.
90. Since Mao's father and Fang were *tongnian* (i.e., they passed their examination in the same years), Fang was Mao Xiang's *nianbo* (*tongnian* of one's father, here translated as "collegial uncle"). "Tan'an" was Fang Gongqian's sobriquet. This poem also appears in Chen Weisong's collection, where the title has *xiansheng* instead of *tongnian* (*Chen Weisong ji*, 1:591).
91. See Ōki Yasushi, *Mao Xiang he Yingmei'an yiyu*, trans. Xin Ruyi (Taipei: Liren shuju, 2013), 57–81.
92. Longmian refers to Tongcheng in Anhui.
93. According to Chen Weisong, Fang called himself "the calligraphy vendor south of the city wall" (*Chen Weisong ji*, 1:617).
94. In reality the examination scandal of 1657 was very much part of the early Qing repression of Jiangnan literati.
95. When repeating the information about the Xuande censers, Sun Chengze (*Yanshan zhai biji*, 4.12b–17b, in *Qing mi cang wai liu zhong, Siku biji xiaoshuo congshu* [Shanghai: Shanghai guji chubanshe, 1993]), Gu Yingtai (*Bowu yaolan* [Zhongguo jindai xiaoshuo shiliao xubian 25, Taipei: Guangwen shuju, n.d.], 1.10a–12b), and Wang Shizhen (*Chibei outan*, 15.11a–11b) omit the comparison with a woman's skin. Song Luo pursues similarly feminine metaphors in his poem on a Xuande censer (*Xipi leigao* [Siku quanshu, vol. 1323], 9.29b).
96. Zhang Chao, *Zhaodai congshu*, ed. Yang Fuji and Shen Maode (Shanghai: Shanghai guji chubanshe, 1990), 1:80–81. Cf. Son Suyoung, *Writing for Print: Publishing and the Making of Textual Authority in Late Imperial China* (Cambridge, Mass.: Harvard University Asia Center, 2018).
97. Du Jun, *Bianya tang wenji*, 4.3a–4b.
98. Ōki, *Mao Xiang he Yingmei'an yiyu*, 57–81.
99. Mao Xiang and Yu Huai, *Plum Shadows and Plank Bridge: Two Memoirs About Courtesans*, trans. Wai-yee Li (New York: Columbia University Press, 2020), 36.
100. Mao and Yu, *Plum Shadows*, 35–37, 57.
101. See Mao and Yu, *Plum Shadows*; Ōki, *Mao Xiang*, "Romantic Loyalists"; Wai-yee Li, *Women and National Trauma in Late Imperial Chinese Literature* (Cambridge, Mass.: Harvard University Asia Center, 2014), 307–14.
102. Wu probably also wrote his preface in 1653. See Feng Qiyong and Ye Junyuan, *Wu Meicun nianpu*, 214.
103. Feng Qiyong and Ye Junyuan, *Wu Meicun nianpu*, 181, 185; Guo Yingde, "Wu Weiye Moling chun chuanqi zuoqi xinkao," *Qinghua daxue xuebao* 27, no. 6 (2012): 67–74.
104. See Chen Pao-chen, *Li Houzhu he ta de shidai: Nan Tang yishu yu lishi lunwen ji* (Taipei: Shitou chuban gufen youxian gongsi, 2007).
105. "Baoyi" refers to the rank of a palace lady. The historical Huang Baoyi's father served Ma Xi'e, ruler of Southern Chu (907–951), and was killed when Southern Tang eliminated Southern Chu. Huang Baoyi was taken into the Southern Tang

palace as a young child, and the historical sources do not mention any brother (Ma Ling, *Nan Tang shu*, 58; Lu You, *Nan Tang shu*, 336).

106. The Daoist priestess Geng was known for her magical arts during the reign of Yuanzong (Houzhu's father, r. 943–61). She is said to have borne Yuanzong's child, although no one saw it, and she left the palace after Yuanzong's death (Ma Ling, *Nan Tang shu*, 168–69). According to Lu You, her departure is linked to the mysterious disappearance and restoration of Yuanzong's mother (Lu You, *Nan Tang shu*, 347–48). Geng's history is told when she is introduced in the play (*MLC* 8.1255).

107. Master Yiguan was active during the reign of Emperor Ling of Han, another last ruler enamored of calligraphy (Pei Songzhi's commentary in *Sanguo zhi* 1.30; *TPGJ* 206.1576).

108. Ouyang Xiu, *Xin Wudai shi*, 74.917–19.

109. See Sun Chengjuan, "Jiushi fengliu shuo Nan Tang: Wu Meicun *Moling chun* de lishi yinyu yu guwan huaijiu," *Zhongzheng daxue zhongwen xueshu niankan*, 2011 no. 2 (December), 75-92.

110. In Jianjian jushi's "Xiaoqing's Story" (Xiaoqing zhuan), Xiaoqing writes in one of her poems: "Coming to the spring pond, I look at the slender reflection: / You have to cherish me, as I do you" 瘦影自臨春水照, 卿當憐我我憐卿. "Xiaoqing zhuan" (1612), in Xue Hongji and Wang Rumei eds., *Xijian zhenben Ming Qing chuanqi xiaoshuo ji* (Changchun: Jilin wenshi chubanshe, 2007), 233–37.

111. "The Exhortation to Learning" (Quanxue pian) by Emperor Zhenzong of Song (r. 997–1022) contains this line: "In books there is naturally jade-like beauty" 書中自有顏如玉. Here Xu Shi is playing on the double meaning of *shu* as "books" and "writing." He is giving up the jade cup, but he is also gaining proximity to the jade-like beauty Zhanniang because the calligraphy scroll contains her colophon.

112. "Casting into darkness" here refers to the lack of recognition. Zou Yang compares unrecognized talent to pearls on the road that arouse suspicion and would not be picked up because they were left there during the hours of darkness (*Shiji* 83.2476).

113. Xu Shi's friend Cai You comments: "General Huang is a military man and does not understand connoisseurship, but his daughter seems to be someone who can recognize the value of things" (*MLC* 3.1253). On seeing an image of Zhanniang holding his cup in a later scene, Xu Shi says, "Recently Suzhou dealers have been saying that men don't understand anything, fortunately there are a few ladies in distinguished families who have discernment and are willing to pay. Just look at my cup: the glaze and the feel of the jade is ever more lustrous (from fond caressing): she is a true collector" (17.1282).

114. Tao Yuanming, *Tao Yuanming ji*, ed. Lu Qinli (Hong Kong: Zhonghua shuju, 1987), 152–59.

115. The idea of "human as antique vessel," comic and parodic here, becomes earnest self-representation as the embodiment of historical memory in *Peach Blossom Fan*, where the ninety-seven-year-old Master of Ritual introduces himself thus in the

prologue: "An antique gentleman nonpareil: who can compare to me? / This vessel, neither jade nor bronze, / is wrapped in the luster of appreciation."
116. On the representation of female spirits and ghosts on stage, see Judith Zeitlin, *The Phantom Heroine: Ghosts and Gender in Seventeenth-Century Chinese Literature* (Honolulu: University of Hawai'i Press, 2007).
117. Sun Chengjuan, "Jiushi fengliu shuo Nan Tang," 87.
118. See Ma Ling, *Nan Tang shu*, 58; Lu You, *Nan Tang shu*, 336; Chen Pao-chen, *Li Houzhu*, 172–87.
119. See Ma Ling, *Nan Tang shu*, 54–56.
120. See Ma Ling, *Nan Tang shu*, 57; Lu You, *Nan Tang shu*, 336.
121. Ma Ling, *Nan Tang shu*, 58. The wording is slightly different in Lu You's account: "These are all treasured by the former ruler. If the city cannot hold out, you should just burn them, do not let them fall into the hands of others" (*Nan Tang shu*, 337).
122. See Li Houzhu's colophon on *Jin lüzi*, cited in Xia Chengtao, *Nan Tang erzhu nianpu*, 78–79; Chen Pao-chen, *Li Houzhu*, 203.
123. See Shao Bo, *Wenjian houlu*, 27.348; cited in Chen Pao-chen, *Li Houzhu*, 206.
124. See Gu Qiyuan, *Kezuo zuiyu*, ed. Zhang Huirong (Nanjing: Fenghuang chubanshe, 2005), 5.159.
125. The word for seeking an audience (*ye* 謁) (*MLC* 12.1267) is associated with seeking office (*ganye* 干謁), and Xu Shi's friend Cai You refers to Xu Shi's journey as "becoming a hanger-on" (*da choufeng* 打抽豐, *MLC* 7.1254).
126. Zhang Duan'er, *Gui'er ji*, B.22b–23a.
127. Ma Ling, *Nan Tang shu*, 53.
128. Lu You, *Nan Tang shu*, 336.
129. Ma Ling, *Nan Tang shu*, 53.
130. Besides Bai Juyi's famous "Changhen ge" (*QTS* 435.4820), other poems by Bai (*QTS* 426.4690, 444.4971), Yuan Zhen (*QTS* 419.4617, 421.4630), Liu Yuxi (*QTS* 356.3999), and the historical Xu Xuan (*QTS* 756.8605) reprise these themes.
131. Ma Ling, *Nan Tang shu*, 53. On the association of rapid hand movements with dangerously exciting music, see *Zuo* Zhao 1.2, 3:1328–29.
132. *Faqu* (translated here as "stately tunes") is literally "dharma tunes," a term suggesting its original use in Buddhist ritual. Formal music for court feasts during Sui and Tang dynasties came to be called *faqu*.
133. Ma Ling, *Nan Tang shu*, 53. See also Lu You, *Nan Tang shu*, 335.
134. See *Liji zhushu* 19.663, 19.679.
135. Lu You, *Nan Tang shu*, 335–36.
136. Ma Ling, *Nan Tang shu*, 49.
137. Wu Weiye wrote poems and prose about all four (*WMC* 1:55–60, 1:246–48, 283–85, 2:646–48, 3:1055–59, 3:1078–79).
138. See Wai-yee Li, "History and Memory in the Poetry of Wu Weiye," in Idema, Li, and Widmer, *Trauma and Transcendence in Early Qing Literature*, 99–148; Li, "Early Qing to 1723," in *Cambridge Literary History of China*, ed. Kang-i Sun Chang and Stephen Owen (Cambridge: Cambridge University Press, 2010), 152–244.

139. Li Houzhu had his own reign titles from 961 to 968, but in the eleventh month of 968 Southern Tang adopted the reign title of the first Song emperor (Kaibao) to mark its total submission.
140. See Lu Qinli, *Xian Qin Han Wei Jin Nanbei Chao shi* (Beijing: Zhonghua shuju, 1983), 1:100. The poem conveys amorous longing through the image of the phoenix seeking its mate. Sima Qian tells how Sima Xiangru seduces Zhuo Wenjun with *qin* music without giving any titles of songs or tunes (*Shiji* 117.3000).
141. *Hainai shizhou ji*, in *Han Wei Liuchao biji xiaoshuo daguan*, 66.
142. On sloping shoulders as a trait of feminine beauty, see Cao Zhi (192–232), "Luoshen fu" (*Wenxuan* 19.879). The pipa cannot bear the weight of the strings, just as the beauty cannot bear the weight of her clothes and is too ethereal for this world.
143. Ma Ling, *Nan Tang shu*, 56; *QTS* 8.73.
144. See Dietrich Tschanz, "Wu Weiye's Dramatic Works and His Aesthetics of Dynastic Transition," in Idema, Li, and Widmer, *Trauma and Transcendence in Early Qing Literature*, 427–87; Wai-yee Li, *Women and National Trauma*, 526–53; Xiaoqiao Ling, *Feeling the Past in Seventeenth-Century China* (Cambridge: Mass.: Harvard University Asian Center), 248–96.
145. Lu You, *Nan Tang shu*, 240.
146. Dou Yi (914–966) was an official under the Later Jin, Later Han, Later Zhou, and Song; Lu Duoxun (934–985) served Later Tang and then the Song.
147. In the tomb inscription, Xu Xuan faults Houzhu for having been "rash in trusting his own judgment and lax in defensive preparations" but attributes the fall of Southern Tang to predestined dynastic cycles (*Qi xing ji*, 29.1a–4b). The two poems are cited in Chen Pao-chen, *Li Houzhu*, 112, n.2.
148. Qing rulers understood this very well. The Kangxi emperor, for example, offered sacrifices at the Ming imperial tombs (Wang Shizhen, *Chibei outan*, 4.1a).
149. Wang Zhi, *Mo ji*, cited in *Song caizi zhuan jianzheng*, ed. Fu Xuanzong (Shenyang: Liaoyang chubanshe, 2011), 13.
150. On Jie tea, see Mao Xiang, *MPJ* 1:545–52; Mao and Yu, *Plum Shadows*, 34–35. On the "*jie* tea behind the temple," see Chen Zhenhui's *Miscellaneous Accouterments* (chap. 4, 229).
151. Wu Weiye pays tribute to Mao Jin's "Jigu ge" publications. It was in Mao Jin's studio that Wu read the Song loyalist Xie Ao's "Wailing at the Western Terrace" (Xitai tongku ji), copied by the early Ming calligrapher and scholar-official Wu Kuan (*WMC* 1:10–12, 68–69).
152. Li Qing and Wu Weiye passed the *jinshi* examination in the same year (1631).
153. Mao Xianshu was the disciple of Wu Weiye's friend Chen Zilong.
154. For Wu Yan, see Sun Chengjuan, "Jiushi fengliu shuo Nan Tang," 81–82.
155. See Yang Chung-wei, "Wanwu he yimin yishi de xingsu: lun Wu Weiye de *Moling chun*," *Xiju yanjiu*, no. 16 (July 2015): 51–82.
154. Cf. Philip Alexander Kafalis, *In Limpid Dream: Nostalgia and Zhang Dai's Reminiscences of the Ming* (Norwalk, Conn.: EastBridge, 2007); Wai-yee Li, "The Collector, the Connoisseur, and Late-Ming Sensibility," *T'oung Pao* 81 (1995): 269–302; Kelly,

"The Inscription of Remnant Things." On the comparison between "the culture of things" in Zhang Dai and Wu Weiye, see Yang Chung-wei, "Wanwu he yimin yishi de xingsu."

EPILOGUE

1. Dieter Tschanz notes the parallel function of the Terrace Reaching Heaven in *Tongtian tai* and the Yue King Terrace in *Facing Spring Pavilion*, the two other plays by Wu Weiye. The site of commemoration "enables people to enter a liminal state" and promise escape and enlightenment. See Tschanz, "Wu Weiye's Dramatic Works and His Aesthetics of Dynastic Transition," in *Trauma and Transcendence in Early Qing Literature*, ed. Wilt Idema, Wai-yee Li, and Ellen Widmer (Cambridge, Mass: Harvard University Asia Center, 2006), 427–53.
2. On Yushan, see Cao Shujuan, *Liubian zhong de shuxie: Qi Biaojia yu Yushan yuanlin lunshu* (Taipei: Liren shuju, 2006); Wai-yee Li, "Gardens and Illusions from Late Ming to Early Qing," *Harvard Journal of Asiatic Studies* 72, no. 2 (December 2012): 295–336.
3. Yushan was also the site of the activities of a female literary community headed by Qi Biaojia's wife Shang Jinglan (1604–ca. 1680). See Dorothy Ko, *Teachers of the Inner Chamber: Women and Culture in Seventeenth-Century China* (Stanford, Calif.: Stanford University Press, 1994); Cao Shujuan, *Liubian Zhong de shuxie*.

Bibliography

Works cited by their titles first in the notes are listed by their titles here.

Ajioka Yoshindo 味岡義人. "Shū Tansen kō—Min matsu Keitokuchin yō no ichi minshō ni tsuite" 周丹泉攷—明末景德鎮窯の一民匠について. *Shūkan Tōyōgaku* 集刊東洋學, no. 39 (1978): 34–53.

Baopu zi neipian jiaoshi 抱扑子內篇校釋. Ge Hong 葛洪, annot. Wang Ming 王明. Beijing: Zhonghua shuju, 1988.

Barnhardt, Richard. *Along the Border of Heaven: Sung and Yuan Paintings from the C. C. Wang Family Collection*. New York: Metropolitan Museum of Art, 1983.

Berliner, Nancy. *The Emperor's Private Paradise: Treasures from the Forbidden City*. Salem, Mass: Peabody Essex Museum, in association with Yale University Press, 2010.

———. *Juanqinzhai in the Qianlong Garden, the Forbidden City, Beijing*. London: Scala, World Monuments Fund, 2008.

Brook, Timothy. *The Confusions of Pleasure: Commerce and Culture in Ming China*. Berkeley: University of California Press, 1998.

Cahill, James. *The Painter's Practice: How Artists Lived and Worked in Traditional China*. New York: Columbia University Press, 1994.

———. *Pictures for Use and Pleasure: Vernacular Painting in High Qing China*. Berkeley: University of California Press, 2010.

———. "Some Thoughts on the History and Post-History of Chinese Painting." *Archives of Asian Art* 55 (2005): 17–33.

———. "Tung Ch'i-ch'ang's 'Southern and Northern Schools' in the History and Theory of Painting: A Reconsideration." In *Sudden and Gradual: Approaches to*

Enlightenment in Chinese Thought, ed. Peter Gregory, 429–46. Honolulu: University of Hawai'i Press, 1987.

Cai Meifen 蔡玫芬. "Suzhou gongyijia Zhou Danquan ji qi shidai" 蘇州工藝家周丹泉及其時代. In *Quyu yu wangluo: jin qiannian lai zhongguo meishushi yanjiu guoji xueshu yantaohui lunwen ji* 區域與網絡：近千年來中國美術史研究國際學術研討會論文集, ed. Quyu yu wangluo guoji xueshu yantaohui lunwen ji bianji weiyuan hui 區域與網絡國際學術研討會論文集編輯委員會, 269–98. Taipei: Guoli Taiwan daxue yishu shi yanjiu suo, 2001.

Cao Huajie 曹花杰. "*Taiping guangji* jingguai gushi muti yanjiu" 《太平廣記》精怪故事母題研究. M.A. thesis, Jimei University, 2013.

Cao Xueqin 曹雪芹 and Gao E 高鶚. *Honglou meng bashi hui jiaoben* 紅樓夢八十回校本, ed. Yu Pingbo 俞平伯 and Wang Xishi 王惜時. Hong Kong: Zhonghua shuju, 1985.

———. *Bajia pingpi Honglou meng* 八家評批紅樓夢, ed. Feng Qiyong 馮其庸 and Chen Qixin 陳其欣. Beijing: Wenhua yishu chubanshe, 1991.

Cha jing 茶經. Lu Yu 陸羽. In *Zhongguo gudai chaxue quanshu*.

Cha lu 茶錄. Cai Xiang 蔡襄. In *Zhongguo gudai chaxue quanshu*.

Chao Yuanfang yixue quanshu 巢元方醫學全書. Cao Yuanfang 巢元方, comp. Wang Xudong 王旭東. Beijing: Zhongguo zhongyiyao chubanshe, 2018.

Chen Chih-en. "Fooling the Eye: *Trompe l'oeil* Porcelain in High Qing China." *Les Cahiers de Framespa*, no. 31 (2019): 1–44.

Chen Dengyuan 陳登原. *Guoshi jiuwen* 國史舊聞. 3 vols. Beijing: Zhonghua shuju, 1958.

Chen Jiru 陳繼儒. *Chen Meigong xiaopin* 陳眉公小品, annot. Hu Shaotang 胡紹棠. Beijing: Wenhua yishu chubanshe, 1996.

———. *Wanxiang tang xiaopin* 晚香堂小品. Shanghai: Beiye shanfang, 1936.

Chen Menglian 陳夢蓮. *Meijun fujun nianpu* 眉公府君年譜. In *Beijing tushuguan cang zhenben nianpu congkan* 北京圖書館藏珍本年譜叢刊, vol. 53, 377–498. Beijing: Beijing tushuguan chubanshe, 1999.

Chen Pao-chen 陳葆真. *Li Houzhu he ta de shidai: Nan Tang yishu yu lishi lunwen ji* 李後主和他的時代：南唐藝術與歷史論文集. Taipei: Shitou chuban gufen youxian gongsi, 2007.

Chen Qinghao 陳慶浩, ed. *Xinbian Shitou ji Zhiyan zhai pingyu jijiao* 新編石頭記脂硯齋評語輯校. Taipei: Lianjing chuban gongsi, 1986.

Chen Que 陳確. *Chen Que ji* 陳確集. 2 vols. Beijing: Zhonghua shuju, 2009 (1979).

Chen Shangjun 陳尚君. "*Ershisi shipin* weishu shuo zai zheng—jian da Zu Baoquan, Zhang Shaokang, Wang Bugao san jiaoshou zhi zhiyi"《二十四詩品》偽書說再證—兼答祖保泉、張少康、王步高三教授之質疑. *Shanghai daxue xuebao* 上海大學學報 18, no. 6 (November 2011): 84–98.

———. "*Ershisi shipin* zhenwai zhi zheng yu Tangdai wenxian kaoju fangfa"《二十四詩品》真偽之證與唐代文獻考據方法. In *Han Tang wenxue yu wenxian lunkao* 漢唐文學與文獻論考. Shanghai: Shanghai guji chubanshe, 2008.

Chen Weisong 陳維崧. *Chen Weisong ji* 陳維崧集, ed. Chen Zhenpeng 陳振鵬 and Li Xueying 李學穎. Shanghai: Shanghai guji chubanshe, 2010.

Chen Yinke 陳寅恪. *Liu Rushi biezhuan* 柳如是別傳. 3 vols. Shanghai: Shanghai guji chubanshe, 1980.

Chen Zhenhui 陳貞慧. *Qiuyuan zapei* 秋園雜佩. In *Yueya tang congshu* 粵雅堂叢書 19, comp. Wu Chongyao 伍崇曜. Taipei: Hualian chubanshe, 1965.

Chen Zhongzhe 陳中浙. *Yi chao zhiru rulai di: Dong Qichang shuhua zhong de Chan yi* 一超直入如來地: 董其昌書畫中的禪意. Beijing: Zhonghua shuju, 2008.

Cheng Huaping 程華平. *Ming Qing chuanqi biannian shigao* 明清傳奇編年史稿. Jinan: Qi Lu shushe, 2008.

Cheng Yu-yu 鄭毓瑜. *Yinpi lianlei: wenxue yanjiu de guanjian ci*. 引譬連類: 文學研究的關鍵詞. Taipei: Lianjing chuban gongsi, 2012.

Cheng Zhangcan 程章燦. *Shike kegong yanjiu* 石刻刻工研究. Shanghai: Shanghai guji chubanshe, 2009.

Chenshu 陳書. Yao Silian 姚思廉. Beijing: Zhonghua shuju, 1972.

Chiu Shih-hua 邱士華. "Suzhou pian huajia Huang Biao yanjiu" 蘇州片畫家黃彪研究. *Gugong xueshu jikan* 故宮學術季刊 37, no. 1 (2020): 1–37.

Chiu Shih-hua, Lin Li-chiang 林麗江, and Lai Yu-chih 賴毓芝, eds. *Wei haowu: 16–18 shiji Suzhou pian jiqi yingxiang* 偽好物: 16–18 世紀蘇州片及其影響. Exhibition catalog and essays. Taipei: National Palace Museum, 2018.

Chongkan Songben Shisan jing zhushu fu jiaokan ji 重刊宋本十三經注疏附校勘記, ed. Ruan Yuan 阮元. Taipei: Yiwen yinshu guan, 1965.

Chow Tse-tsung 周策縱. *Honglou meng an: Qiyuan Hongxue lunwen ji* 紅樓夢案: 棄園紅學論文集. Hong Kong: Chinese University of Hong Kong Press, 2000.

Chunqiu fanlu 春秋繁露, annot. Lai Yanyuan 賴炎元. Taipei: Shangwu yinshu guan, 1987.

Clunas, Craig. *Elegant Debts: The Social Art of Wen Zhengming, 1470–1559*. Honolulu: University of Hawai'i Press, 2004.

———. "Luxury Knowledge: The *Xiushilu (Record of Lacquering)* of 1625." *Techniques and Cultures*, no. 29 (1997): 27–40.

———. *Superfluous Things: Material Culture and Social Status in Early Modern China*. Honolulu: University of Hawai'i Press, 2004.

Daxue zhangju 大學章句. In *Dianjiao sishu zhangju jizhu*.

De Bary, Wm. Theodore. *Sources of Chinese Tradition*. 2 vols. New York: Columbia University Press, 2000.

Deng Hanyi 鄧漢儀. *Shiguan sanji* 詩觀三集. In *Siku jinhui shu congkan* 四庫禁燬書叢刊, vol. 3. Beijing: Beijing chubanshe, 1997.

Deng Yunxiang 鄧雲鄉. *Honglou fengsu tan* 紅樓風俗譚. Beijing: Zhonghua shuju, 1987.

Deng Zhicheng 鄧之誠. *Qingshi jishi chubian* 清詩紀事初編. 2 vols. Hong Kong: Zhonghua shuju, 1976.

Dianjiao sishu zhangju jizhu 點校四書章句集注, comp. Zhu Xi 朱熹. Beijing: Zhonghua shuju, 2003 (1983).

Ding Yaokang 丁耀亢. *Xu Jin Ping Mei* 續金瓶梅. In *Ding Yaokang quanji* 丁耀亢全集, ed. Li Zengpo 李增坡 and Zhang Qingji 張清吉, vol. 2. Zhengzhou: Zhongzhou guji chubanshe, 1999.

Dong Jie 董捷. *Ming Qing kan Xixiang ji banhua kaoxi* 明清刊《西廂記》版畫考析. Shijiazhuang: Hebei meishu chubanshe, 2006.

Dong Qichang 董其昌. *Dong Qichang quanji* 董其昌全集, ed. Li Shanqiang 李善強. 8 vols. Shanghai: Shanghai shuhua chubanshe, 2013.

Dongtian qinglu wai wu zhong 洞天清錄外五種. In *Siku biji xiaoshuo congshu* 四庫筆記小說叢書. Shanghai: Shanghai guji chubanshe, 1993.

Dou cha ji 鬬茶記. Tang Geng 唐庚. In *Zhongguo gudai chaxue quanshu*.
Du Jun 杜濬. *Bianya tang wenji* 變雅堂文集. Woodblock print. Huanggang, 1894.
Ebrey, Patricia. *Accumulating Culture: The Collections of Emperor Huizong*. Seattle: University of Washington Press, 2008.
Egan, Ronald. *The Literary Works of Ou-yang Hsiu*. Cambridge: Cambridge University Press, 1984.
———. *The Problem of Beauty: Aesthetic Thought and Pursuits in Northern Song Dynasty China*. Cambridge, Mass.: Harvard University Asia Center, 2006.
Elman, Benjamin. *A Cultural History of Civil Examinations in Late Imperial China*. Berkeley: University of California Press, 2000.
Er Cheng wenji 二程文集. Cheng Hao 程顥, Cheng Yi 程頤. In *Yingyin wenyuan ge Siku quanshu*, vol. 1345.
Er Cheng yulu 二程語錄. Cheng Hao, Cheng Yi. Comp. Zhang Boxing 張伯行. Reprinted by Zuo Zongtang 左宗棠. Fuzhou: Zhengyi shuyuan, 1866–1870.
Ershi si shipin 二十四詩品. Attributed to Sikong tu 司空圖. In *Lidai shihua* 歷代詩話, comp. He Wenhuan 何文煥. Beijing: Beijing tushuguan chubanshe, 2003.
Fang Gongqian 方拱乾. *Helou ju ji, Su'an ji* 何陋居集, 甦庵集. Harbin: Helongjiang daxue chubanshe, 2010.
Fang Shao 方勺. *Bozhai bian* 泊宅編. In *Congshu jicheng chubian* 叢書集成初編. Beijing: Zhonghua shuju, 1991.
Fei Yuanlu 費元祿. *Zhaocai guan qingke* 鼂采館清課. In *Siku quanshu cunmu congshu* 四庫全書存目叢書, *zi bu* 子部, vol. 118. Jinan: Qi Lu chubanshe, 1997.
Feng Menglong 馮夢龍. *Feng Menglong quanji* 馮夢龍全集, ed. Wei Tongxian 魏同賢. 18 vols. Nanjing: Fenghuang chubanshe, 2007.
——— et al., comps. *Ming Qing minge shidiao ji* 明清民歌時調集. Shanghai: Shanghai guji chubanshe, 1987.
Feng Menglong and Cai Yuanfang 蔡元放. *Dong Zhou lieguo zhi* 東周列國志, ed. Liu Bendong 劉本棟. Taipei: Sanmin shuju, 1999.
Feng Qiyong 馮其庸 and Ye Junyuan 葉君遠. *Wu Meicun nianpu* 吳梅村年譜. Beijing: Wenhua yishu chubanshe, 2007.
Feng Shike 馮時可. *Feng Yuancheng wenji* 馮元成文集. Taipei: Guolian tushu, 1964.
Feng Yan 封演. *Feng shi wenjian ji* 封氏聞見記. *Congshu jicheng chubian*. Changsha: Shangwu yinshu guan, 1936.
Feng Yuanjun 馮沅君. "Zenyang kandai *Yipeng xue*" 怎樣看待一捧雪. In *Feng Yuanjun gudian wenxue lunwen ji* 馮沅君古典文學論文集, 257–85. Jinan: Shandong renmin chubanshe, 1980.
Feng Zhiguo 封治國, *Yu gu tong you: Xiang Yuanbian shuhua jiancang yanjiu* 與古同游：項元汴書畫鑒藏研究. Hangzhou: Zhongguo meishu xueyuan chubanshe, 2013.
Fox, Ariel. *The Cornucopian Stage: Performing Commerce in Early Modern China*. Cambridge, Mass: Harvard University Asia Center, forthcoming.
Fu Shen 傅申. "Wang Duo ji Qing chu beifang jiancang jia" 王鐸及清初北方鑒藏家. In *Zhongguo huihua yanjiu lunwen ji* 中國繪畫研究論文集, ed. *Duoyun* bianji bu 《朵雲》編輯部. Shanghai: Shanghai shuhua chubanshe, 1992.

Fu Sinian 傅斯年. *Fu Sinian wenji* 傅斯年文集, ed. Ouyang Zhesheng 歐陽哲生. 7 vols. Beijing: Zhonghua shuju, 2017.
Gao Lian 高濂. *Zunsheng bajian* 遵生八箋. Chengdu: Ba Shu shushe, 1988.
Gu Fu 顧復. *Pingsheng zhuangguan* 平生壯觀. In *Zhongguo shuhua quanshu*, vol. 4.
Gu Gongxie 顧公燮. *Xiaoxia xianji zhaichao* 消夏閑記摘抄. Taipei: Shangwu yinshuguan, 1967.
Gu Qiyuan 顧起元. *Kezuo zhui yu* 客座贅語, ed. Zhang Huirong 張惠榮. Nanjing: Fenghuang chubanshe, 2005.
Gu Yanwu 顧炎武. *Gu Tinglin shi jianshi* 顧亭林詩箋釋, ed. Wang Jimin 王冀民. 2 vols. Beijing: Zhonghua shuju, 1998.
——. *Rizhi lu jishi* 日知錄集釋. Annot. and commentaries by Huang Rucheng 黃汝成. Zhengzhou: Zhongzhou guji chubanshe, 1990.
Gu Yingtai 谷應泰. *Bowu yaolan* 博物要覽 (*Zhongguo jindai xiaoshuo shiliao xubian* 中國近代小說史料續編 25). Taipei: Guangwen shuju, n.d.
——. *Mingshi jishi benmo* 明史紀事本末. Shanghai: Shanghai guji chubanshe, 1994.
Guanzi 管子, annot. Li Mian 李勉. Taipei: Shangwu yinshu guan, 1990.
Guo Shaoyu 郭紹虞 et al., comps. *Zhongguo Lidai wenlun xuan* 中國歷代文論選. 3 vols. Hong Kong: Zhonghua shuju, 1979.
Guo Yingde 郭英德. "Wu Weiye *Moling chun* chuanqi zuoqi xinkao" 吳偉業《秣陵春》傳奇作期新考. *Qinghua daxue xuebao* 清華大學學報 27, no. 6 (2012): 67–74.
——. "Xinxi shengcheng, nüxing yuedu yu yimin yishi: Zhu Suchen *Qinlou yue* chuanqi xiezuo yu kanke de qianyin houguo" 新戲生成、女性閱讀與遺民意識：朱素臣《秦樓月》傳奇寫作與刊刻的前因後果. *Xiju yanjiu* 戲劇研究, no. 7 (2011): 37–64.
Guoyu 國語, ed. Shanghai Shifan daxue guji zhengli zu 上海師範大學古籍整理組. Shanghai: Shanghai guji chubanshe, 1978.
Hainai shizhou ji 海內十洲記. In *Han Wei Liuchao biji xiaoshuo daguan*, 61–71.
Han Feizi 韓非子, annot. Chen Qiyou 陳奇猷. Beijing: Zhonghua shuju, 1958.
Han Shi waizhuan 韓詩外傳, annot. Lai Yanyuan 賴炎元. Taipei: Shangwu yinshu guan, 1986.
Han Wei Liuchao biji xiaoshuo daguan 漢魏六朝筆記小說大觀, ed. Wang Genlin 王根林, Huang Yiyuan 黃益元, and Cao Guangfu 曹光甫. Shanghai: Shanghai guji chubanshe, 1999.
Han Wudi bieguo dongming ji 漢武帝別國洞冥記. In *Han Wei Liuchao biji xiaoshuo daguan*, 119–36.
Hanan, Patrick. *The Invention of Li Yu*. Cambridge, Mass.: Harvard University Press, 1988.
Harrist, Robert. "Replication and Deception in Calligraphy of the Six Dynasties Period." In *Chinese Aesthetics: The Ordering of Literature, the Arts, and the Universe in the Six Dynasties*, ed. Zong-qi Cai, 31–59. Honolulu: University of Hawai'i Press, 2004.
Hay, Jonathan. *Sensuous Surfaces: The Decorative Object in Early Modern China*. Honolulu: University of Hawai'i Press, 2010.
Hazlitt, William. "On Vulgarity and Affectation." In *Table-Talk; or, Original Essays on Men and Manners*, vol. 1, 375–400. London: Printed for Henry Colburn, 1824.

He Liangjun 何良俊. *Siyou zhai congshuo* 四友齋叢說. Beijing: Zhonghua shuju, 1997 (1959).
He Ye 賀野. *Wumen huapai* 吳門畫派. Changchun: Jilin meishu chubanshe, 2003.
Ho Wai-kam, ed. *The Century of Tung Ch'i-ch'ang*. Kansas City, Mo., and Seattle: Nelson Atkins Museum and University of Washington Press, 1992.
——. "Tung Ch'i-ch'ang's New Orthodoxy and the Southern School Theory." In *Artists and Traditions: Uses of the Past in Chinese Culture*, ed. Christian Murck, 113–29. Princeton, N.J.: Princeton University Press, 1976.
Hou Fangyu 侯方域. *Hou Fangyu quanji jiaojian* 侯方域全集校箋, ed. Wang Shulin 王樹林. 3 vols. Beijing: Renmin wenxue chubanshe, 2013.
Hou Hanshu 後漢書. Fan Ye 范曄. Beijing: Zhonghua shuju, 1973 (1965).
Hsia, C. T., Wai-yee Li, and Karl Kao. *The Columbia Anthology of Yuan Drama*. New York: Columbia University Press, 2014.
Hsieh, Andrew C. 謝正光. *Qing chu shi wen yu shiren jiaoyou kao* 清初詩文與士人交遊考. Nanjing: Nanjing daxue chubanshe, 2001.
——. "Qing chu zhongjun dianfan zhi suzao yu heliu: Shandong Laiyang Jiang shi xingyi kaolun." 清初忠君典範之塑造與合流：山東萊陽姜氏行誼考論. In *Ming Qing wenxue yu sixiang zhong de zhuti yishi yu shehui: xueshu sixiang pian* 明清文學與思想中的主體意識與社會：學術思想篇, ed. Yang Jinlong 楊晉龍 and Zhong Caijun 鍾采均, 291–343. Taipei: Zhongyang yanjiu yuan wenzhesuo, 2004.
Hu Yinglin 胡應麟. *Shaoshi shanfang bicong* 少室山房筆叢, ed. Liu Jun 劉駿. Shanghai: Shanghai shudian chubanshe, 2001.
Huacun kangxing shizhe 花村看行使者. *Huacun tan wang* 花村談往, ed. Zhang Junheng 張鈞衡. *Congshu jicheng xubian* 叢書集成續編. Shanghai: Shanghai shudian, 1994.
Huainanzi 淮南子, annot. Liu Wendian 劉文典. Beijing: Zhonghua shuju, 1989.
Huang Guoquan 黃果泉. *Ya su zhijian: Li Yu de wenhua renge yu wenxue sixiang yanjiu* 雅俗之間：李漁的文化人格與文學思想研究. Beijing: Zhongguo shehui kexue chubanshe, 2004.
Huang Yinong 黃一農. "Cong huangshang Xue jia kan *Honglou meng* de wuzhi wenhua" 從皇商薛家看紅樓夢的物質文化. *Zhongguo wenhua* 中國文化 48, no. 2 (2018): 1–11.
——. "Wendulina, wangqia yangyan, yu yifuna xinkao" "溫都里納" "汪怡洋煙" 與 "依弗哪" 新考. *Cao Xueqin yanjiu* 曹雪芹研究, no. 4 (2016): 33–46.
Huang Zongxi 黃宗羲. *Huang Zongxi quanji* 黃宗羲全集. 16 vols. Hangzhou: Zhejiang guji chubanshe, 2005.
——. *Si jiu lu* 思舊錄. In *Huang Zongxi quanji*, vol. 1, 340–99.
——. *Song Yuan xue'an* 宋元學案. In *Huang Zongxi quanji*, vols. 3–5.
——. *Hongguang shilu chao* 弘光實錄鈔. In *Huang Zongxi quanji*, vol. 2.
Huangdi suwen lingshu jing 黃帝素問靈樞經. Beijing: Zhongyi she, 1923.
Huiping huijiao Jin Ping Mei 會評會校金瓶梅. Lanling xiaoxiaosheng 蘭陵笑笑生, ed. Liu Hui 劉輝 and Wu Gan 吳敢. 5 vols. Hong Kong: Tiandi tushu gongsi, 1998.
I Lofen 衣若芬. "Zhao Xigu *Dongtian qinglu ji* tanxi" 趙希鵠《洞天清祿集》探析. *Xin Song xue* 新宋學 2 (2002): 410–19.
Idema, Wilt, Wai-yee Li, and Ellen Widmer, eds. *Trauma and Transcendence in Early Qing Literature*. Cambridge, Mass.: Harvard University Asia Center, 2006.

Idema, Wilt, and Stephen West. *The Orphan of Zhao and Other Plays*. New York: Columbia University Press, 2015.
Inoue Mitsuyuki 井上充幸, trans. Wan Shuang 萬爽 and Lu Peirong 陸蓓容. "Jiang Shaoshu yu Wang Yueshi: Yunshi zhai bitan suojian Ming mo Qing chu yishu shichang yu Huizhou shangren de huodong" 姜紹書與王越石—《韻石齋筆談》所見明末清初藝術市場與徽州商人的活動. In *Meishu shi yu guannian shi* 美術史與觀念史, ed. Fan Jinzhong 范景中 and Cao Yiqiang 曹意強, 383–411. Nanjing: Nanjing shifan daxue chubanshe, 2004.
Jiang Cai 姜埰. *Jingting ji* 敬亭集, ed. Yin Xiaofeng 印曉峰. Nanjing: Huadong Shifan daxue chubanshe, 2011.
Jiang Ruizao 蔣瑞藻. *Xiaoshuo kaozheng* 小說考證, ed. Jiang Yiren 蔣逸人. Hangzhou: Zhejiang guji chubanshe, 2016.
Jiang Shaoshu 姜紹書. *Wusheng shishi* 無聲詩史. In *Zhongguo shuhua quanshu*, vol. 4.
——. *Yunshi zhai bitan* 韻石齋筆談. In *Zhibuzhu zhai congshu* 知不足齋叢書, first series, comp. Bao Tingbo. 1872.
Jiao Hong 焦竑. *Danyuan ji* 澹園集, ed. Li Jianxiong 李劍雄. Beijing: Zhonghua shuju, 1999.
Jiao Xun 焦循. *Ju shuo* 劇說. Changsha: Shangwu yinshu guan, 1939.
Jijiao Cheng Xuanying Daode jing yishu 輯校成玄英《道德經義疏》. Cheng Xuanying 成玄英, ed. Meng Wentong 蒙文通. In *Meng Wentong wenji* 蒙文通文集, vol. 6, *Dao shu jijiao shi zhong* 道書輯校十種, 342–543. Chengdu: Ba Shu shushe, 2001.
Jin Ping Mei cihua (Mengmei guan jiaoben) 金瓶梅詞話（夢梅館校本）. Lanling xiaoxiaosheng, ed. Mei Jie 梅節. 3 vols. Taipei: Liren shuju, 2007
Jinshu 晉書. Fang Xuanling 房玄齡 et al. Taipei: Dingwen shuju, 1980.
Kafalis, Philip Alexander. *In Limpid Dream: Nostalgia and Zhang Dai's Reminiscences of the Ming*. Norwalk, Conn.: EastBridge, 2007.
Kang Baocheng 康保成. *Suzhou jupai yanjiu* 蘇州劇派研究. Guangzhou: Huacheng chubanshe, 1993.
Kelly, Thomas. "Clawed Skin: The Literary Inscriptions of Things in Sixteenth Century China." Ph.D. diss., Chicago University, 2017.
——. "The Inscription of Remnant Things: Zhang Dai's 'Twenty-eight Friends.'" *Late Imperial China* 42, no. 1 (June 2021): 1-43.
Kerr, Rose. *Later Chinese Bronzes*. London: Bamboo Publication in association with the Victorian and Albert Museum, 1990.
Kile, S. E. "Master Medium: Li Yu's Technologies of Culture in the Early Qing" (manuscript).
Kleutghen, Kristina Renée. *Imperial Illusions: Crossing Pictorial Boundaries in the Qing Palace*. Seattle: University of Washington Press, 2015.
Ko, Dorothy. *The Social Life of Inkstones: Artisans and Scholars in Early Qing China*. Seattle: University of Washington Press, 2016.
——. *Teachers of the Inner Chamber: Women and Culture in Seventeenth-Century China*. Stanford, Calif.: Stanford University Press, 1994.
Lam Ling-Hon. "The Matriarch's Private Ear: Performance, Reading, Censorship, and the Fabrication of Interiority in *The Story of the Stone*." *Harvard Journal of Asiatic Studies* 65, no. 2 (December 2005): 357–415.

Lang Ying 郎瑛. *Qixiu leigao* 七修類稿. Shanghai: Shanghai shudian, 2001.

Laozi Heshang gong zhangju 老子河上公章句. In *Zhengtong daozang* 正統道藏, comp. Zhang Yuchu 張宇初, Shao Yizheng 邵以正, and Zhang Guoxiang 張國祥. Taipei: Xinwenfeng, 1985. Facsimile reproduction of the Shanghai Hanfenlou ed.

Laozi jiaoshi 老子校釋, ed. Zhu Qianzhi 朱謙之. Beijing: Zhonghua shuju, 1984.

Li Congqin 李从芹. "*Gudong shisan shuo* zuozhe xianyi ji qi sheji sixiang" 《骨董十三說》作者獻疑及其設計思想. *Anhui Shifan daxue xuebao (renwen shehui kexue ban)* 安徽師範大學學報（人文社會科學版）41, no. 6 (2013): 779–86.

Li Guo 李果. *Zaiting conggao* 在亭叢稿. 1745. Harvard Yenching Library rare book.

Li Kaixian 李開先. *Li Kaixian quanji* 李開先全集, ed. Bu Jian 卜鍵. 3 vols. Beijing: Wenhua yishu chubanshe, 2004.

Li Mei 李玫. *Ming Qing zhiji Suzhou zuojia qun yanji* 明清之際蘇州作家群研究. Beijing: Zhongguo shehui kexue chubanshe, 2000.

Li Rihua 李日華. *Liuyan zhai biji* 六研齋筆記, ed. Yu Zhenhong 郁震宏, and Li Baoyang 李保陽, *Zitao xuan zazhui* 紫桃軒雜綴, ed. Xue Weiyuan 薛維源. Nanjing: Fenghuang chubanshe, 2010.

———. *Weishui xuan riji* 味水軒日記, ed. Tu Youxiang 屠友祥. Shanghai: Shanghai Yuandong chubanshe, 1996.

Li Shizhen 李時珍. *Bencao gangmu* 本草綱目. Beijing: Renmin weisheng chubanshe, 1975.

Li Wai-yee. "The Collector, the Connoisseur, and Late-Ming Sensibility." *T'oung Pao* 81 (1995): 269–302.

———. "Confronting History and Its Alternatives in Early Qing Poetry." In Idema, Li, and Widmer, *Trauma and Transcendence in Early Qing Literature*, 73–98.

———. "Early Qing to 1723." In *Cambridge Literary History of China*, ed. Kang-i Sun Chang and Stephen Owen, 152–244. Cambridge: Cambridge University Press, 2010.

———. *Enchantment and Disenchantment: Love and Illusion in Chinese Literature*. Princeton, N.J.: Princeton University Press, 1993.

———. "Gardens and Illusions from Late Ming to Early Qing." *Harvard Journal of Asiatic Studies* 72, no. 2 (December 2012): 295–336.

———. "History and Memory in the Poetry of Wu Weiye." In Idema, Li, and Widmer, *Trauma and Transcendence in Early Qing Literature*, 99–148.

———. "Introduction." In Idema, Li, and Widmer, *Trauma and Transcendence in Early Qing Literature*, 1–72.

———. "The Late Ming Courtesan: Invention of a Cultural Ideal." In *Writing Women in Late Imperial China*, ed. Ellen Widmer and Kang-I Sun Chang, 46–73. Stanford, Calif.: Stanford University Press, 1997.

———. "The Rhetoric of Spontaneity in Late Ming Literature." *Ming Studies* 35 (August 1995): 35–52.

——— 李惠儀. "Shibian yu wanwu: luelun Qing chu wenren de shenmei fengshang" 世變與玩物：略論清初文人的審美風尚. *Journal of the Institute of Literature and Philosophy* 中國文哲研究集刊, Academia Sinica, no. 33 (September 2008): 1–40.

———. *Women and National Trauma in Late Imperial Chinese Literature*. Cambridge, Mass.: Harvard University Asia Center, 2014.

Li Wankang 李萬康. *Bianhao yu jiage: Xiang Yuanbian jiucang shuhua er shi* 編號與價格: 項元汴舊藏書畫二釋. Nanjing: Nanjing daxue chubanshe, 2012.
Li Weikun 李維琨. *Mingdai Wumen huapai yanjiu* 明代吳門畫派研究. Shanghai: Dongfang chuban zhongxin, 2008.
Li Yu 李漁. *Li Yu quan ji* 李漁全集. 12 vols. Hangzhou: Zhejiang guji chubanshe, 1991.
Li Yù李玉. *Li Yù xiqu ji* 李玉戲曲集, ed. Chen Guyu 陳鼓虞, Chen Duo 陳多, and Ma Shenggui 馬聖貴. 3 vols. Shanghai: Shanghai guji chubanshe, 2004.
Li Zhi 李贄. *Li Zhi quanji zhu* 李贄全集注, annot. Zhang Jianye 張建業 and Zhang Dai 張岱. 14 vols. Beijing: Shehui kexue wenxian chubanshe, 2010.
Liezi jishi 列子集釋, annot. Yang Bojun 楊伯峻. Beijing: Zhonghua shuju, 1979.
Liji zhushu 禮記注疏. Commentary by Zheng Xuan 鄭玄 and subcommentary by Kong Yingda 孔穎達. In *Chongkan Songben Shisan jing zhushu fu jiaokan ji*.
Lin Huiru 林慧如. *Mingdai yiwen* 明代軼聞. Taipei: Zhonghua shuju, 1967.
Lin Li-chiang 林麗江. "Wan Ming Huizhou moshang Cheng Junfang yu Fang Yulu moye de zhankai yu jingzheng" 晚明徽州墨商程君房與方于魯墨業的展開與競爭. In *Huizhou: shuye yu diyu wenhua* 徽州: 書業與地域文化, ed. Michaela Bussotti and Zhu Wanshu 朱萬曙, 121–97. Beijing: Zhonghua shuju, 2010.
——. "The Proliferation of Images: The Ink-stick Designs and the Printing of the *Fang-shih Mo-p'u* and *Ch'eng-shih Mo-yuan*." Ph.D. diss., Princeton University, 1998.
Ling Xiaoqiao. *Feeling the Past in Seventeenth-Century China*. Cambridge: Mass.: Harvard University Asia Center, 2019.
Liu Chiung-yun Evelyn. "Embodied Virtue: How Was Loyalty Edited and Performed in Late Imperial China?" In *Keywords in Chinese Culture*, ed. Wai-yee Li and Yuri Pines, 219-67. Hong Kong: Chinese University of Hong Kong Press, 2020.
Liu Dajie 劉大杰, ed. *Mingren xiaopin ji* 明人小品集. Shanghai: Beixin shuju, 1934.
Liu Jinku 劉金庫. *Nanhua beidu: Qingdai shuhua jiancang zhongxin yanjiu* 南畫北渡: 清代書畫鑒藏中心研究. Shijiazhuang: Hebei jiaoyu chubanshe, 2008.
Liu Luan 劉鑾. *Wu shi hu* 五石瓠. In *Congshu jicheng xubian, zi bu, xiaoshuo lei, zalu zhi shu* 叢書集成續編。子部。小說類、雜錄之屬 96, 307–42. Shanghai: Shanghai shudian, 1994.
Liu Mengxi 劉夢溪. *Honglou meng yu bainian zhongguo* 紅樓夢與百年中國. Beijing: Zhongyang bianyi chubanshe, 2005.
Liu Rushi 柳如是. *Liu Rushi ji* 柳如是集, ed. Fan Jingzhong 范景中 and Zhou Shutian 周書田. Hangzhou: Zhongguo meishu xueyuan chubanshe, 2002.
Liu Shilin 劉士鏻, comp. *Wen zhi* 文致. Changsha: Yuelu shushe, 1998.
Liu Tiren 劉體仁. *Qisong tang shi xiao lu* 七頌堂識小錄. In *Zhongguo shuhua quanshu*, vol. 8.
Liu Tong 劉侗 and Yu Yizheng 于奕正. *Dijing jingwu lue* 帝京景物略. Beijing: Beijing guji chubanshe, 1980.
Liu Xie 劉勰. *Wenxin diaolong zhu* 文心雕龍註, comp. Fan Wenlan 范文瀾. Hong Kong: Shangwu yinshu guan, 1986 (1960).
Liu Zhizhong 劉致中. "*Yi peng xue* benshi xinzheng" 《一捧雪》本事新證. *Xiju yishu* 戲劇藝術, no. 2 (1988): 79–85.
Lü Dalin 呂大臨. *Kaogu tu (wai wu zhong)* 考古圖 (外五種). Shanghai: Shanghai shudian chubanshe, 2016.

Lu Pengliang 陸鵬亮. "Xuanlu bianyi" 宣爐辯疑. *Wenwu* 文物, no. 7 (2008): 64–76.
Lu Qinli 逯欽立. *Xian Qin Han Wei Jin Nanbei Chao shi* 先秦漢魏晉南北朝詩. 3 vols. Beijing: Zhonghua shuju, 1983.
Lu Shaoheng 陸紹珩. *Zuigutang jiansao* 醉古堂劍掃. Introduction by Zheng Zhiming 鄭志明. Taipei: Jinfeng chuban gongsi, 1986.
Lu, Tina. *The Coin and the Severed Head: Ownership and Fungibility in the Seventeenth Century*. Cambridge, Mass.: Harvard University Asia Center, forthcoming.
Lu Yitian 陸以湉, ed. Cui Fanzhi 崔凡芝. *Lenglu zashi* 冷廬雜識. Beijing: Zhonghua shuju, 1984.
Lu You 陸游. *Nan Tang shu* 南唐書. In *Nan Tang shu: liangzhong*.
Lunyu jizhu 論語集注, comp. Zhu Xi. In *Dianjiao sishu zhangju jizhu*.
Lüshi chunqiu jiaoshi 呂氏春秋校釋, annot. Chen Qiyou 陳奇猷. 2 vols. Shanghai: Shanghai guji chubanshe, 2002.
Lynn, Richard John, trans. *The Classic of Changes: A New Translation of the I Ching as Interpreted by Wang Bi*. New York: Columbia University Press, 2004.
Ma Ling 馬令. *Nan Tang shu* 南唐書. In *Nan Tang shu: liangzhong*.
Ma Tailai 馬泰來. "*Zuixing shi* benshi laiyuan ji zuozhe kaozheng" 《醉醒石》本事來源及作者考證. In *Shizheng yu yanbian: Zhongguo wenxue shi yanjiu lunji* 實證與演變：中國文學史研究論集, ed. Fudan daxue guji zhengli yanjiu suo 復旦大學古籍整理研究所, 199–211. Shanghai: Shanghai wenyi chubanshe, 2014.
Mai Huijun. "Thinking Things: Mediated Materiality in Song Literary Culture." Ph.D. diss., Harvard University, 2020.
Mao Qiling 毛奇齡. *Xihe shihua* 西河詩話. Shanghai: Shanghai shudian, 1994.
——. *Xihe wenji* 西河文集. Shanghai: Shanghai guji chubanshe, 2009.
Mao Xiang 冒襄. *Mao Pijiang quanji* 冒辟疆全集, ed. Wan Jiufu 萬久富 and Ding Fusheng 丁富生. 2 vols. Nanjing: Fenghuang chubanshe, 2014.
Mao Xiang and Yu Huai. *Plum Shadows and Plank Bridge: Two Memoirs About Courtesans*, trans. Wai-yee Li. New York: Columbia University Press, 2020.
Mao Yixiang 茅一相. *Hui miao* 繪妙. In *Zhongguo shuhua quanshu*, vol. 4.
Meng Zhaolian 孟昭連. *Zhongguo hulu qi* 中國葫蘆器. Tianjin: Baihua wenyi chubanshe, 2010.
Mengzi jizhu 孟子集注. In *Dianjiao sishu zhangju jizhu*.
Mengzi zhushu 孟子注疏. Commentary by Zhao Qi 趙岐 and subcommentary attributed to Sun Shi 孫奭. In *Chongkan Songben Shisan jing zhushu fu jiaokan ji*.
Mi Fu. *Mi Fu ji* 米芾集, ed. Huang Zhengyu 黃正雨 and Wang Xincai 王心裁. Wuhan: Hubei jiaoyu chubanshe, 2002.
Min chao Dong huan shishi 民抄董宦事實. In *Ming Taizu ping Hu lu (wai qi zhong)*, 282–322.
Ming shilu 明實錄, ed. Zhongyang yanjiu yuan lishi yuyan yanjiu suo 中央研究院歷史語言研究所. Taipei: Zhongyang yanjiu yuan lishi yuyan yanjiu suo, 1966.
Ming Taizu ping hu lu (wai qi hong) 明太祖平胡錄（外七種）. Beijing: Beijing guji chubanshe, 2002.
Mingdai mingren chidu xuancui 明代名人尺牘選萃, ed. Guojia tushu guan 國家圖書館. 12 vols. Beijing: Guojia tushu guan chubanshe, 2018.

Mingshi 明史. Zhang Tingyu 張廷玉 et al. 28 vols. Beijing: Zhonghua shuju, 1974.

Moser, Jeffrey. "The Ethics of Immutable Things: Interpreting Lü Dalin's 'Illustrated Investigations of Antiquity.'" *Harvard Journal of Asiatic Studies* 72, no. 2 (December 2012): 259–93.

Nan Tang shu: liang hong 南唐書：兩種. Ma Ling, Lu You, ed. Pu Xiaonan 濮小南 and Hu Axiang 胡阿祥. Nanjing: Nanjing chubanshe, 2010.

Nie Tao 聶濤. "Lü Dalin *Liji jie* zhong de 'Qu li' quanshi ji xueshu tese fenxi" 呂大臨《禮記解》中的「曲禮」詮釋及學術特色分析. *Jingxue yanjiu luncong* 經學研究論叢, no. 25 (June 2020): 67–93.

Ōki Yasushi 大木康. *Bō Jō to "Eibaian okugo" no kenkyū*. 冒襄と「影梅庵憶語」の研究. Tokyo: Kyūko Shoin, 2010.

——. *Fū Bōryū "Sanka" no kenkyū: Chūgoku Mindai no tsūzoku kayō* 馮夢龍「山歌」の研究：中国明代の通俗歌謠. Tōkyō: Keisō Shobō, 2003.

——. "Mao Xiang and Yu Huai: Early Qing Romantic yimin." In Idema, Li, and Widmer, *Trauma and Transcendence in Early Qing Literature*, 231–48.

——. *Mao Xiang he Yingmei'an yiyu* 冒襄和影梅庵憶語, trans. Xin Ruyi 辛如意. Taipei: Liren shuju, 2013.

Ouyang Daifa 歐陽代發. "Chongxin pingjia *Yipeng xue*: jian tan suowei 'yipu xi' de pingjia wenti" 重新評價《一捧雪》：兼談所謂「義僕戲」的評價問題. In *Zhongguo gudai wenxue lunji* 中國古代文學論集, ed. Hubei daxue zhongguo gudai wenxue xueke 湖北大學中國古代文學學科, 592–602. Beijing: Zhonghua shuju, 2002.

Ouyang Xiu 歐陽修. *Ouyan Xiu quanji* 歐陽修全集. 2 vols. Beijing: Zhongguo shudian, 1986. Facsimile reproduction of the 1936 Shijie shuju ed.

Owen, Stephen. *Readings in Chinese Literary Thought*. Cambridge, Mass.: Harvard University Asia Center, 1996.

Park, J. P. "Reinventing Art History: Forgery and Counterforgery in Early Modern Chinese Art." In *Archives of Asian Art* (forthcoming).

Pelliot, Paul. "Le prétendu album de porcelains de Hiang Yuan-pien." *T'oung Pao* 2, no. 32 (1936): 15–58.

Peng Cheng 彭乘. *Moke huixi* 墨客揮犀, ed. Shang Jun 商濬. Kuaiji: Banye tang, Wanli reign (1563–1620). Fu Sinian Library. Academia Sinica, Taipei, Taiwan.

Plaks, Andrew. *The Four Masterworks of the Ming Novel: Ssu Ta Ch'i-shu*. Princeton, N.J.: Princeton University Press, 1987.

——. *Ta Hsüeh and Chung Yung (the Highest Order of Cultivation and on the Practice of the Mean)*. London: Penguin Books, 2003.

Pu Songling 蒲松齡. *Liaozhai zhiyi huijiao huizhu huiping ben* 聊齋誌異會校會註會評本, ed. Zhang Youhe 張友鶴. Shanghai: Shanghai guji chubanshe, 1983.

Qi Gong 啟功. *Qi Gong lun yi* 啟功論藝. Shanghai: Shanghai shuhua chubanshe, 2010.

Qian Qianyi 錢謙益. *Liechao shiji xiaozhuan* 列朝詩集小傳. 2 vols. Shanghai: Shanghai guji chubanshe, 1983.

——. *Qian Muzhai quanji* 錢牧齋全集, annot. Qian Zeng 錢曾, ed. Qian Zhonglian 錢仲聯. 8 vols. Shanghai: Shanghai guji chubanshe, 2003.

Qian Yong 錢泳. *Lüyuan conghua* 履園叢話, ed. Zhang Wei 張偉. Beijing: Zhonghua shuju, 1997 (1979).

Qiu Xigui 裘錫圭. *Gu wenzi lunji* 古文字論集. Beijing: Zhonghua shuju, 1992.
Qu Dajun 屈大均. *Guangdong xinyu* 廣東新語. 2 vols. Beijing: Zhonghua shuju, 1997.
Quan Tang shi 全唐詩, comp. Peng Dingqiu 彭定求 et al. 25 vols. Beijing: Zhonghua shuju, 1960.
Quan Tang shi bubian 全唐詩補編, comp. Chen Shangjun 陳尚君. Beijing: Zhonghua shuju, 1992.
Quan Tang wen 全唐文, comp. Dong Gao 董誥 et al. Beijing: Zhonghua shuju, 1978.
Roy, David Tod, trans. *The Plum in the Golden Vase, or Chin P'ing Mei*. 5 vols. Princeton, N.J.: Princeton University Press, 1993–2013.
Ruan Kuisheng 阮葵生. *Chayu kehua* 茶餘客話, ed. Li Baomin 李保民. Shanghai: Shanghai guji chubanshe, 2012.
Ruan Yuan 阮元. *Yanjing shi ji* 揅經室集, ed. Deng Jingyuan 鄧經元. Beijing: Zhonghua shuju, 1993.
Sanguo zhi 三國志. Chen Shou 陳壽. Commentary by Pei Songzhi 裴松之. Beijing: Zhonghua shuju, 1982 (1959).
Sato Masayuki 佐藤將之. *Zhongguo gudai zhong lun yanjiu* 中國古代忠論研究. Taipei: Taiwan daxue chuban zhongxin, 2010.
Shang Wei. "Truth Becomes Fiction When Fiction Is True: *The Story of the Stone* and the Visual Culture of the Manchu Court." *Journal of Chinese Literature and Culture* 2, no. 1 (April 2015): 207–48.
Shangshu zhushu 尚書注疏. Commentaries by Kong Yingda 孔穎達 et al. In *Chongkan Songben Shisan jing zhushu fu jiaokan ji*.
Shao Yong 邵雍. *Shao Yong ji* 邵雍集, ed. Guo Yu 郭彧. Beijing: Zhonghua shuju, 2010.
Shen Congwen 沈從文. *Huahua duoduo tantan guanguan* 花花朵朵坛坛罐罐. Chongqing: Chongqing daxue chubanshe, 2014.
Shen Defu 沈德符. *Wanli yehuo bian* 萬曆野獲編. 3 vols. Beijing: Zhonghua shuju, 1997 (1959).
Shen Gua 沈括. *Mengxi bitan jiaozheng* 夢溪筆談校證, ed. Hu Daojing 胡道靜. Beijing: Zhonghua shuju, 1960.
Shi Ye 施曄. *Zhongguo gudai wenxue zhong de tongxing lian shuxie yanjiu* 中國古代文學中的同性戀書寫研究. Shanghai: Shanghai renmin chubanshe, 2008.
Shi Zhecun 施蟄存 ed. *Wan Ming ershi jia xiaopin* 晚明二十家小品. Shanghai: Shanghai shudian, 1984. Facsimile reproduction of the 1935 Guangming shuju ed.
Shi Zhenghao 史正浩. *Songdai jinshi tupu yanjiu* 宋代金石圖譜研究. Zhengzhou: Henan daxue chubanshe, 2017.
Shih Shou-chien 石守謙. "Ya su de jiaolü: Wen Zhengming, Zhong Kui yu dazhong wenhua" 雅俗的焦慮: 文徵明、鍾馗與大眾文化. *Guoli Taiwan daxue meishushi yanjiu jikan* 國立台灣大學美術史研究集刊 16 (2004): 307–42.
Shiji 史記. Sima Qian 司馬遷, annot. Pei Yin 裴駰, Sima Zhen 司馬貞, and Zhang Shoujie 張守節. Beijing: Zhonghua shuju, 1985 (1959).
Shiliu tang pin 十六湯品. Su Yi 蘇廙 (attributed). In *Zhongguo gudai chaxue quanshu*.
Shiming (Congshu jicheng chubian) 釋名(叢書集成初編). Liu Xi 劉熙. Shanghai: Shangwu yinshu guan, 1939.

Shishuo xinyu jianshu 世說新語箋疏. Liu Yiqing 劉義慶 et al. Commentary by Liu Xiaobiao 劉孝標, comp. Yu Jiaxi 余嘉錫, ed. Zhou Zumo 周祖謨 et al. Taipei: Huazheng shuju, 1984.

Shuowen jiezi zhu 說文解字注. Xu Shen 許慎. Annot. with commentaries by Duan Yucai 段玉裁. Shanghai: Shanghai guji chubanshe, 1981.

Son Suyoung. *Writing for Print: Publishing and the Making of Textual Authority in Late Imperial China.* Cambridge, Mass.: Harvard University Asia Center, 2018.

Song ben Yu pian biaodian zhengli ben: fu fenlei jiansuo 宋本玉篇標點整理本：附分類檢索. Gu Yewang 顧野王, ed. Wang Ping 王平, Li Jianting 李建廷, and Liu Yuanchun 劉元春. Shanghai: Shanghai shudian chubanshe, 2017.

Song Caizi zhuan jianzheng 宋才子傳箋證, ed. Fu Xuancong 傅璇琮. Shenyang: Liaoyang chubanshe, 2011.

Song Luo 宋犖. *Xipi leigao* 西陂類稿. In *Yingyin wenyuan ge Siku quanshu*, vol. 1323.

Songshi 宋史. Tuo Tuo 脫脫 et al. Taipei: Dingwen shuju, 1980.

Su Shi 蘇軾. *Dongpo zhilin* 東坡志林, ed. Wang Yufen. Hohhot: Yuanfang chubanshe, 2006.

——. *Su Shi shiji hezhu* 蘇軾詩集合注, annot. Feng Yingliu 馮應榴, ed. Huang Renke 黃任軻 and Zhu Huaichun 朱懷春. 3 vols. Shanghai: Shanghai guji chubanshe, 2001.

——. *Su Shi wenji biannian jianzhu* 蘇軾文集編年箋注, annot. Li Zhiliang 李之亮. 12 vols. Chengdu: Ba Shu shushe, 2011.

Su Shufen 蘇淑芬. "Su Shi yu Wang Shen jiaoyou kaoshu" 蘇軾與王詵交遊考述. *Furen guowen xuebao* 輔仁國文學報 37 (October 2013): 75–106.

Sun Chengjuan 孫承娟. "Jiushi fengliu shuo Nan Tang: Wu Meicun *Moling chun* de lishi yinyu yu guwan huaijiu" 舊事風流說南唐：吳梅村《秣陵春》的歷史隱喻與古玩懷舊. *Zhongzheng daxue zhongwen xueshu niankan* 中正大學中文學術年刊 18 (December 2011): 75–92.

Sun Chengze 孫承澤. *Gengzi xiaoxia ji* 庚子銷夏記. In *Yingyin wenyuan ge Siku quanshu*, vol. 1826.

—— (attributed). *Yanshan zhai zaji* 硯山齋雜記. In *Qing mi cang wai liu zhong* 清秘藏外六種. *Siku biji xiaoshuo congshu* 四庫筆記小說叢書. Shanghai: Shanghai guji chubanshe, 1993.

Sun Kuang 孫鑛. *Shu hua ba ba* 書畫跋跋. In *Zhongguo shuhua quanshu*, vol. 3.

Sun Shuyu 孫述宇. *Jin Ping Mei de yishu: jiushu xindu zhi er* 金瓶梅的藝術：舊書新讀之二. Taipei: Shibao wenhua chuban shiye youxian gongsi, 1978.

Taiping guangji 太平廣記, comp. Li Fang 李昉 et al. Taipei: Shangwu yinshu guan, 1975.

Taiping yulan 太平御覽, comp. Li Fang et al. Taipei: Shangwu yinshu guan, 1975.

Tan Zhengbi 譚正璧. *Sanyan liangpai ziliao* 三言兩拍資料. 2 vols. Shanghai: Shanghai guji chubanshe, 1980.

Tang Hou 湯垕. *Huajian* 畫鑑. In *Zhongguo shuhua quanshu*, vol. 2.

Tang Wudai biji xiaoshu daguan 唐五代筆記小說大觀, ed. Ding Ruming 丁如明, Li Zongwei 李宗為, Li Xueying 李學穎, et al. 2 vols. Shanghai: Shanghai guji chubanshe, 2000.

Tang Zhen 唐甄. *Qian shu jiaoshi* 潛書校釋, annot. Huang Dunbing 黃敦兵. Changsha: Yuelu shushe, 2011.

Tang Zhiqi 唐志契. *Huishi weiyan* 繪事微言. In *Zhongguo shuhua quanshu*, vol. 4.

Tao Qian 陶潛. *Tao Yuanming ji* 陶淵明集, ed. Lu Qinli 逯欽立. Hong Kong: Zhonghua shuju, 1987.

Tian Xiaofei. "A Preliminary Comparison of the Two Recensions of Jin Ping Mei." *Harvard Journal of Asiatic Studies* 62, no. 2 (December 2002): 347–88.

—— 田曉菲. *Qiushui tang lun Jin Ping Mei* 秋水堂論金瓶梅. Tianjin: Tianjin renmin chubanshe, 2003.

Tian Yiheng 田藝蘅. *Liu qing rizha* 留青日札. 3 vols. Shanghai: Shanghai guji chubanshe, 1985.

——. *Zhu quan xiaopin* 煮泉小品. In *Zhongguo gudai chaxue quanshu*.

Tianshui bingshan lu 天水冰山錄. In *Ming Taizu ping Hu lu (wai qi zhong)*, 99–241.

Tsao Shu-chuan 曹淑娟. "*Chunxing tang shiji* zhong de cainü qunxiang" 春星堂詩集中的才女群像, in *Taiwan xueshu xin shiye* 台灣學術新視野, ed. Cai Yingjun 蔡英俊 et al. Taipei: Wunan tushu, 2007.

——. *Liubian zhong de shuxie: Qi Biaojia yu Yushan yuanlin lunshu* 流變中的書寫：祈彪佳與寓山園林論述. Taipei: Liren shuju, 2006.

Tschanz, Dieter. "Wu Weiye's Dramatic Works and His Aesthetics of Dynastic Transition." In Idema, Li, and Widmer, *Trauma and Transcendence in Early Qing Literature*, 427–53.

Tu Long 屠隆. Hua jian 畫箋. In *Zhongguo shuhua quanshu*, vol. 3.

—— (attributed). *Kaopan yushi* 考槃餘事. In *Zhangwu zhi, Kaopan yushi* 長物志、考槃餘事, ed. Chen Jian 陳劍. Hangzhou: Zhejiang renmin meishu chubanshe, 2011.

Volpp, Sophie. "The Gift of a Python Robe: The Circulation of Objects in *Jin Ping Mei*." *Harvard Journal of Asiatic Studies* 65, no. 1 (2005): 133–58.

——. *The Substance of Fiction: Literary Objects in Ming-Qing China (1550–1750)*. New York: Columbia University Press, forthcoming.

Wakeman, Frederic. *The Great Enterprise: The Manchu Reconstruction of Imperial Order in Seventeenth-Century China*. 2 vols. Berkeley: University of California Press, 1985.

Wan Muchun 萬木春. *Weishui xuan li de xianju zhe* 味水軒裏的閒居者. Hangzhou: Zhongguo meishu xueyuan chubanshe, 2008.

Wang Anli 王安莉. *Nanbei zong lun de xingcheng* 南北宗論的形成. Hangzhou: Zhongguo meishu xueyuan chubanshe, 2016.

Wang Dang 王讜. *Tang Yulin jiaozheng* 唐語林校證, ed. Zhou Xunchu 周勛初. Beijing: Zhonghua shuju, 1987.

Wang Daokun 汪道昆. *Tai han ji* 太函集. *Siku quanshu cunmu congshu, ji bu* 集部, vols. 117–18.

Wang Fuzhi 王夫之. *Chuanshan quanshu* 船山全書, ed. Chuanshan quanshu bianji weiyuan hui 船山全書編輯委員會. 16 vols. Changsha: Yuelu shushe, 1988.

Wang Guowei 王國維. *Guantang jilin* 觀堂集林. 4 vols. Beijing: Zhonghua shuju, 1991 (1959).

Wang Hongzhuan 王宏撰. *Shan zhi* 山志. Beijing: Zhonghua shuju, 1999.

Wang Hung-tai 王鴻泰. "Yasu de bianzheng—Mingdai shangwan wenhua de liuxing yu shishang guanxi de jiaocuo" 雅俗的辯證—明代賞玩文化的流行與士商關係的交錯. *Xin shixue* 新史學 17, no. 4 (December 2006): 73–143.

Wang Keyu 汪珂玉. *Shanhu wang* 珊瑚網. In *Zhongguo shuhua quanshu*, vol. 5.

Wang Niansun 王念孫. *Jingyi shuwen* 經義述聞. Nanjing: Jiangsu guji chubanshe, 1985.
Wang Renyu 王仁裕. *Kaiyuan Tianbao yishu* 開元天寶遺事. In *Tang Wudai biji xiaoshuo daguan*.
Wang Ruqian 汪汝謙 et al. *Chunxing tang shiji* 春星堂詩集. In *Congsui Wang shi yishu* 叢睢汪氏遺書. Changsha, 1886.
Wang Shixiang 王世襄. *Xiushi lu jieshuo* 髹飾錄解說. Beijing: Wenwu chubanshe, 1983.
Wang Shixing 王士性. *Wuyue youcao, Guang zhi yi* 五岳游草、廣志繹, ed. Zhou Zhenhe 周振鶴. Beijing: Zhonghua shuju, 2006.
Wang Shifu 王實甫. *Xixiang ji jijie* 西廂記集解, comp. Fu Xiaohang 傅曉航. Lanzhou: Gansu renmin chubanshe, 1989.
Wang Shizhen 王世貞. *Gu bu gu lu* 觚不觚錄. In *Yingyin wenyuan ge Siku quanshu*, vol. 1041.
———. *Yanzhou shiliao* 弇州史料, ed. Dong Fubiao 董復表. Wanli (1573–1619) ed. Taiwan: Fu Sinian Library, Academia Sinica.
———. *Yanzhou sibu gao 174 juan, xugao 207 juan* 弇州四部稿 174 卷, 續稿207卷. In *Yingyin wenyuan ge Siku quanshu*, vols. 1279–81.
Wang Shizhen 王士禎. *Chibei outan* 池北偶談. Taipei: Shangwu yinshu guan, 1974.
Wang Shouren 王守仁. *Wang Yangming quanji* 王陽明全集, ed. Wu Guang 吳光, Qian Ming 錢明, Dong Ping 董平, and Yao Yanfu 姚延福. Shanghai: Shanghai guji chubanshe, 1992.
Wang Siren 王思任. *Wenfan xiaopin* 文飯小品, ed. Jiang Jinde 蔣金德. Changsha: Yuelu shushe, 1989.
Wang Xiaoli 王曉驪. *San Wu wenren hua tiba yanjiu* 三吳文人畫題跋研究. Shanghai: Shanghai renmin meishu chubanshe, 2013.
Wang Yongshun 王永順, ed. *Dong Qichang shiliao* 董其昌史料. Shanghai: Huadong shifan daxue chubanshe, 1991.
Wang Yuxian 王毓賢. *Huishi beikao* 繪事備考. In *Zhongguo shuhua quanshu*, vol. 8.
Wang Zuo 王佐. *Xin zeng Gegu yaolun* 新增格古要論. Based on *Gegu yaolun* 格古要論 by Cao Zhao 曹昭. Hangzhou: Zhejiang renmin meishu chubanshe, 2011.
Wei Xi 魏禧. *Wei Shuzi wenji* 魏叔子文集, ed. Hu Shouren 胡守仁, Yao Pinwen 姚品文, and Wang Nengxian 王能憲. 3 vols. Beijing: Zhonghua shuju, 2003.
Wei Yong 衛泳. *Zhen zhong mi* 枕中秘. In *Siku quanshu cunmu congshu, zi bu*, vol. 152.
Weitz, Ankeney, trans. *Zhou Mi's Record of Clouds and Mist Passing Before One's Eyes: An Annotated Translation*. Leiden: Brill, 2002.
Wen Jia 文嘉. *Qianshan tang shuhua ji* 鈐山堂書畫記. In *Ming Taizu ping Hu lu (wai qi zhong)*.
Wen Zhenheng 文震亨. *Zhangwu zhi* 長物志, annot. Chen Zhi 陳植, ed. Yang Chaobo 楊超伯. Nanjing: Jiangsu kexue jishu chubanshe, 1984.
Wenxuan 文選, comp. Xiao Tong 蕭統 et al. Commentaries by Li Shan 李善 et al. Shanghai: Shanghai guji chubanshe, 1986.
Wenyuan yinghua 文苑英華, comp. Li Fang et al. Beijing: Zhonghua shuju, 1966.
Wu Congxian 吳從先. *Xiaochuang ziji* 小窗自紀, annot. Guo Zhengfan 郭征帆. Beijing: Zhonghua shuju, 2008.
Wu Han 吳晗. *Wu Han shixue lunzhu xuanji* 吳晗史學論著選集. Beijing: Renmin chubanshe, 1984–1988.

Wu Hung. "Beyond Stereotypes: The Twelve Beauties in Qing Court Art and *The Dream of the Red Chamber*." In *Writing Women in Late Imperial China*, ed. Ellen Widmer and Kang-i Sun Chang, 306–65. Stanford, Calif.: Stanford University Press, 1997.

——. *The Double Screen: Medium and Representation in Chinese Painting*. Chicago: University of Chicago Press, 1996.

Wu Qizhen 吳其貞. *Shuhua ji* 書畫記. In *Zhongguo shuhua quanshu*, vol. 8.

Wu Jen-shu 巫仁恕. *Pin wei shehua: wan Ming de xiaofei shehui yu shidafu* 品味奢華：晚明的消費社會與士大夫. Taipei: Lianjing chuban shiye youxian gongsi, 2007.

Wu Sheng 吳升. *Daguan lu* 大觀錄. In *Zhongguo shuhua quanshu*, vol. 8.

Wu Weiye 吳偉業. *Wu Meicun quanji* 吳梅村全集, ed. Li Xueying 李學穎. 3 vols. Shanghai: Shanghai guji chubanshe, 1990.

——. *Wu Meicun shiji jianzhu* 吳梅村詩集箋注, comp. Wu Yifeng 吳翌鳳. Hong Kong: Guangzhi shuju, n.d.

Wu Zhaoqian 吳兆騫. *Qiu jia ji* 秋笳集, ed. Ma Shouzhong 麻守中. Shanghai: Shanghai guji chubanshe, 1993.

Xia Chengtao 夏承燾. *Nan Tang erzhu nianpu* 南唐二主年譜. Taipei: Shijie shuju, 1962.

Xia Wenyan 夏文彥. *Tuhui baojian* 圖繪寶鑑. In *Zhongguo shuhua quanshu*, vol. 2.

Xiang Yannan 向燕南. *Cong lishi dao shixue* 從歷史到史學. Beijing: Beijing Shifan daxue chubanshe, 2010.

Xiao Yanyi 蕭燕翼. *Gu shuhua shilun jianding wenji* 古書畫史論鑑定文集. Beijing: Zijin cheng chubanshe, 2005.

Xiaojing zhushu 孝經注疏. With commentaries by Zheng Xuan and Xing Bing 邢昺. In *Chongkan Songben Shisan jing zhushu fu jiaokan ji*.

Xie Guozhen 謝國楨. *Jiang Zhe fangshu ji* 江浙訪書記. In *Xie Guozhen quanji* 謝國楨全集, vol. 5, ed. Xie Xiaobin 謝小彬 and Yang Lu 楊璐. Beijing: Beijing chubanshe, 2013.

——. *Ming Qing biji tancong* 明清筆記談叢. Shanghai: Shanghai shudian chubanshe, 2004.

Xie Zhaozhi 謝肇淛. *Wu zazu* 五雜俎. Shanghai: Shanghai shudian chubanshe, 2001.

Xin Tangshu 新唐書, comp. Ouyang Xiu 歐陽修 et al. Taipei: Dingwen shuju, 1981.

Xin wudai shi 新五代史. Ouyang Xiu, annot. Xu Wudang 徐無黨. Taipei: Dingwen shuju, 1980.

Yingyin wenyuan ge Siku quanshu 景印文淵閣四庫全書. Taipei: Shangwu yinshuguan, 1986.

Xinshu 新書. Jia Yi 賈誼. Taipei: Zhonghua shuju, 1981.

Xinxu 新序. Lu Jia 陸賈, annot. Lu Yuanjun 盧元駿. Taipei: Shangwu yinshu guan, 1991.

Xiong Mingyu 熊明遇. *Luojie cha ji* 羅岕茶記. In *Zhongguo gudai chaxue quanshu*.

Xu Fuguan 徐復觀. *Zhongguo yishu jingshen* 中國藝術精神. Taipei: Xuesheng shuju, 1981 (1966).

Xu Fuzuo 徐復祚. *Huadang ge congtan* 花當閣叢談. In *Xuxiu Siku quanshu* 續修四庫全書, *zi bu* 子部, vol. 1175. Shanghai: Shanghai guji chubanshe, 1995–1999.

Xu Guangqi 徐光啟. *Xu Guangqi shiwen ji* 徐光啟詩文集, ed. Li Tiangang 李天綱. Shanghai: Shanghai guji chubanshe, 2011.

Xu Mingyan 徐銘延. "Lun Li Yù de *Yipeng xue* chuanqi" 論李玉的《一捧雪》傳奇. *Nanjing Shida xuebao: shehui kexue ban* 南京師大學報：社會科學版, no. 2 (1980): 35–42.

Xu Qiu 徐釚. *Ciyuan congtan jiaojian* 詞苑叢談校箋, ed. Wang Baili 王百里. Beijing: Renmin wenxue chubanshe, 1988.

Xu Shangying 徐上瀛. *Xi shan qin kuang* 谿山琴況. *Siku quanshu cunmu congshu, zi bu,* vol. 74.

Xu Shuofang 徐朔方, *Xu Shuofang ji* 徐朔方集. 5 vols. Hangzhou: Zhejiang guji chubanshe, 1993.

Xu Shupi 徐樹丕. *Shi xiao lu* 識小錄. In *Congshu jicheng xubian* 叢書集成續編, *zi bu* 子部, vol. 89. Shanghai: Shanghai shudian, 1994.

Xu Wei 徐渭. *Xu Wei ji* 徐渭集. 4 vols. Beijing: Zhonghua shuju, 1999.

Xu Xianzhong 徐獻忠. *Shui pin* 水品. In *Zhongguo gudai chaxue quanshu*.

Xu Xuan 徐鉉. *Qi xing ji* 騎省集. In *Yingyin wenyuan ge Siku quanshu*, vol. 1085.

Xu Xuemo 徐學謨. *Shi miao shi yu lu* 世廟識餘錄. Published by Xu Yuangu 徐元嘏, 1608. Harvard Yenching Library Rare Book.

Xu Youzhen 徐有貞. *Xu Youzhen ji* 徐有貞集, ed. Sun Bao 孫寶. Hangzhou: Zhejiang renmin meishu chubanshe, 2015.

Xu Zhongnan 許仲南. "'Fugu qiubian' yu 'da ya zuiren'—lun Wang Shizhen *Yiyuan zhiyan* shici guan zhi yitong." 「復古求變」與「大雅罪人」——論王世貞《藝苑卮言》詩詞觀之異同. *Dongwu zhongwen xianshang xueshu lunwen* 東吳中文線上學術論文 6 (June 2009): 33–46.

Xuanhe huapu 宣和畫譜. In *Zhongguo shuhua quanshu*, vol. 2.

Xue Hongji 薛洪勣 and Wang Rumei 王汝梅, eds. *Xijian zhenben Ming Qing chuanqi xiaoshuo ji* 稀見珍本明清傳奇小說集. Changchun: Jilin wenshi chubanshe, 2007.

Xunzi jianshi 荀子柬釋, comp. Liang Qixiong 梁啟雄. Taipei: Shangwu yinshu guan, 1993 (1965).

Xunzi jijie 荀子集解, comp. Wang Xianqian 王先謙. Beijing: Zhonghua shuju, 1988.

Yang Chung-wei 楊中薇. "Wanwu he yimin yishi de xingsu: lun Wu Weiye de *Moling chun*" 玩物和遺民意識的形塑：論吳偉業的《秣陵春》. *Xiju yanjiu* 戲劇研究, no. 16 (July 2015): 51–82.

Yang Xiaoshan. *Metamorphosis of the Private Sphere: Gardens and Objects in Tang-Song Poetry.* Cambridge, Mass.: Harvard University Asia Center, 2003.

Yang Xiong 揚雄. *Fayan yishu* 法言義疏, annot. Wang Rongbao 汪榮寶, ed. Chen Zhongfu 陳仲夫. 2 vols. Beijing: Zhonghua shuju, 1997.

——. *Yang Xiong ji jiaozhu* 揚雄集校注, annot. Zhang Zhenze. Shanghai: Shanghai guji chubanshe, 1993.

Yang Xin. "The Ming Dynasty." In *Three Thousand Years of Chinese Painting.* New Haven, Conn.: Yale University Press, 1997.

Yang Zhishui 揚之水. *Gu shiwen mingwu xinzheng hebian* 古詩文名物新證合編. Tianjin: Tianjin jiaoyu chubanshe, 2012.

——. *Shijing mingwu xinzheng* 詩經名物新證. Beijing: Beijing guji chubanshe, 2000.

——. *Wu se: Jin Ping Mei du "wu" ji* 物色：金瓶梅讀「物」記. Beijing: Zhunghua shuju, 2018.

Yao Hua 姚華. "Su Shi shige de 'Qiuchi shi' yixiang tanxi" 蘇軾詩歌的「仇池石」意象探析. *Wenxue yichan* 文學遺產, no. 3 (2016): 155–65.

Yao Jiheng 姚際恆. *Haogu tang jiacang shuhua ji* 好古堂家藏書畫集. In *Zhongguo shuhua quanshu*, vol. 8.

Yao Xiaosui 姚孝遂 et al., eds. *Yin xu jiagu keci leizuan* 殷墟甲骨刻辭類纂. Beijing: Zhonghua shuju, 1989.

Yao Yang 姚暘. *Wan Ming jiangnan minjian yishu shoucang yanjiu* 晚明江南民間藝術收藏研究. Tianjin: Tianjin guji chubanshe, 2017.

Yao Yuanzhi 姚元之. *Zhuye ting zaji* 竹葉亭雜記. Beijing: Zhonghua shuju, 1997.

Ye Dehui 葉德輝. *Shulin qinghua* 書林清話. Shanghai: Shanghai guji chubanshe, 2008.

Ye Junyuan 葉君遠. *Wu Weiye pingzhuan* 吳偉業評傳. Beijing: Shoudu shifan daxue chubanshe, 1999.

Ye Kangning 葉康寧. *Fengya zhi hao: Mingdai Jia Wan nianjian de shuhua xiaofei* 風雅之好：明代嘉萬年間的書畫消費. Beijing: Shangwu yinshu guan, 2017.

Ye Mengde 葉夢得. *Shilin yanyu* 石林燕語. Beijing: Zhonghua shuju, 1984.

Yi Su 一粟. *Hong lou meng juan* 紅樓夢卷. Taipei: Liren shuju, 1981.

Yi wei shilei mou 易緯是類謀. In *Yingyin wenyuan ge Siku quanshu*, vol. 53.

Yingyin wenyuan ge Siku quanshu 景印文淵閣四庫全書. Taipei: Shangwu yinshuguan, 1986.

Yiwen leiju 藝文類聚, comp. Ouyang Xun 歐陽詢, ed. Wang Shaoying 汪紹楹. Shanghai: Shanghai guji chubanshe, 1999.

Yu, Anthony C. *Rereading the Stone: Desire and the Making of Fiction in Dream of the Red Chamber*. Princeton, N.J.: Princeton University Press, 1997.

Yu Fengqing 郁逢慶. *Yu shi shuhua tiba ji* 郁氏書畫題跋記. In *Zhongguo shuhua quanshu*, vol. 4.

Yu Huai 余懷. *Yu Huai quanji* 余懷全集, ed. Li Jintang 李金堂. 2 vols. Shanghai: Shanghai guji chubanshe, 2011.

Yu Ying-shih 余英時. *Honglou meng de liangge shijie* 紅樓夢的兩個世界. Taipei: Lianjing, 1978.

——. *Zhongguo jinshi zongjiao lunli yu shangren jingshen (zeng ding ban)* 中國近世宗教倫理與商人精神（增訂版）. Taipei: Lianjing, 2018.

Yuan Haowen 元好問. *Yuan Haowen quan ji* 元好問全集, ed. Yao Dianzhong 姚奠中 and Li Zhengmin 李正民. Taiyuan: Shanxi guji chubanshe, 2004.

Yuan Hongdao 袁宏道. *Yuan Hongdao ji jianjiao* 袁宏道集箋校, ed. Qian Bocheng 錢伯城. 2 vols. Shanghai: Shanghai guji chubanshe, 1981.

Yue jue shu 越絕書. Yuan Kang 袁康, ed. Li Bujia 李步嘉. Wuchang: Wuhan daxue chubanshe, 1992.

Yue Ke 岳珂. *Ting shi* 桯史. Beijing: Zhonghua shuju, 1997 (1981).

Zeitlin, Judith. "The Cultural Biography of a Musical Instrument: Little Hulei as Sounding Object, Antique, Prop, and Relic." *Harvard Journal of Asiatic Studies* 69, no. 2 (December 2009): 395–441.

——. *Historian of the Strange: Pu Songling and the Chinese Classical Tale*. Stanford, Calif.: Stanford University Press, 1993.

——. *The Phantom Heroine: Ghosts and Gender in Seventeenth-Century Chinese Literature*. Honolulu: University of Hawai'i Press, 2007.

Zhai Qinian 翟耆年. *Zhou shi* 籀史. In *Congshu jicheng chubian* 叢書集成初編. Shanghai: Shangwu yinshu guan, 1935.

Zhan Dan 詹丹. *Honglou meng de wuzhi yu fei wuzhi* 紅樓夢的物質與非物質. Chongqing: Chongqing chubanshe, 2006.

Zhan Jingfeng 詹景鳳. *Zhan Dongtu xuanlan bian* 詹東圖玄覽編. In *Zhongguo shuhua quanshu*, vol. 4.

Zhang Changhong 張長虹. *Pinjian yu jingying: Ming mo Qing chu Huishang yishu zanzhu yanjiu* 品鑑與經營：明末清初徽商藝術贊助研究. Beijing: Beijing daxue chubanshe, 2010.

Zhang Chao 張潮. *Youmeng ying* 幽夢影, ed. Duangan Muming 段干木明. Hefei: Huangshan shushe, 2011.

———. *Yuchu xinzhi* 虞初新志. In *Shuohai* 說海, ed. Ke Yuchun 柯愈春 et al., vols. 1:251–2:715. Beijing: Renmin ribao chubanshe, 1997.

———. *Zhaodai congshu* 昭代叢書, ed. Yang Fuji 楊復吉 and Shen Maode 沈楙德. 4 vols. Shanghai: Shanghai guji chubanshe, 1990.

Zhang Chou 張丑. *Qinghe shuhua fang* 清河書畫舫. In *Zhongguo shuhua quanshu*, vol. 4.

Zhang Dafu 張大復. *Meihua caotang bitan* 梅花草堂筆談. 3 vols. Shanghai: Shanghai guji chubanshe, 1986.

Zhang Dai 張岱. *Kuaiyuan daogu* 快園道古. Hangzhou: Zhejiang guji chubanshe, 1986.

———. *Langhuan wenji Shen Fucan chaoben* 瑯嬛文集沈復燦鈔本, ed. Lu Wei 路偉 and Ma Tao 馬濤. Hangzhou: Zhejiang guji chubanshe, 2016.

———. *Tao'an mengyi* 陶庵夢憶, ed. Huai Ming 淮茗. Beijing: Zhonghua shuju, 2008.

———. *Tao'an mengyi, Xihu mengxun* 陶庵夢憶、西湖夢尋, ed. Ma Xingrong 馬興榮. Shanghai: Shanghai guji chubanshe, 1982.

———. *Zhang Dai shiwen ji* 張岱詩文集, ed. Xia Xianchun 夏咸淳. Shanghai: Shanghai guji chubanshe, 1991.

Zhang Duanyi 張端義. *Gui'er ji* 貴耳集. In *Jin dai mishu* 津逮秘書, ed. Mao Jin 毛晉. Chongzhen era (1618–1644), Jigu ge ed.

Zhang Han 張瀚. *Songchuang mengyu* 松窗夢語, ed. Xiao Guoliang 蕭國亮. Shanghai: Shanghai guji chubanshe, 1986.

Zhang Hua 張華. *Bowu zhi* 博物志. In *Han Wei Liuchao biji xiaoshuo daguan*, 179–226.

Zhang Pu 張溥. *Qilu zhai heji* 七錄齋合集, ed. Zeng Xiao 曾肖. Jinan: Qi Lu shushe, 2015.

Zhang Renquan 張人權. "Li Yu *Yizhong yuan* zhong liang nü huashi" 李漁《意中緣》中兩女畫師. In *Lidai Xihu wenxuan zhuanji* 歷代西湖文選專輯, ed. Wang Guoping 王國平 et al., vol. 14, 290–305. Hangzhou: Hangzhou chubanshe, 2004.

Zhang Xiaozhuang 張小莊. *Qingdai biji riji zhong de shufa shiliao zhengli yu yanjiu* 清代筆記日記中的書法史料整理與研究. 2 vols. Beijing: Zhongguo meishu xueyuan chubanshe, 2012.

Zhang Yanyuan 張彥遠. *Fashu yaolu* 法書要錄. In *Zhongguo shuhua quanshu*, vol. 1.

———. *Lidia minghua ji* 歷代名畫記, ed. Qin Zhongwen 秦仲文 and Huang Miaozi 黃苗子. Beijing: Renmin meishu chubanshe, 1983 [1963].

Zhang Yingwen 張應文. *Qing mi cang* 清秘藏. In *Qing mi cang wai liu zhong* 清秘藏外六種. Shanghai: Shanghai guji chubanshe, 1993.

Zhang Zai 張載. *Zhang Zai ji* 張載集, ed. Zhang Xichen 章錫琛. Beijing: Zhonghua shuju, 1985 (1978).

Zhanguo ce 戰國策, ed. Liu Xiang 劉向. 3 vols. Shanghai: Shanghai guji chubanshe. 1978.

Zhao Panchao 趙盼超. *Yuandai huaxue yanjiu* 元代畫學研究. Beijing: Zhongyan minzu daxue chubanshe, 2014.

Zhao Qiang. "*Wu*" *de jueqi—qian xiandai wanqi Zhongguo shenmei fengshang de bianqian*. "物"的崛起—前現代晚期中國審美風尚的變遷. Beijing: Shangwu yinshuguan, 2016.

Zhao Xigu 趙希鵠. *Dongtian qinglu* 洞天清錄. In *Dongtian qinglu (wai wu zhong)*.

Zhao Yuan 趙園. "Shuo 'wanwu sangzhi': dui Ming Qing zhiji shiren de yizhong yanlun de fenxi" 說「玩物喪志」: 對明清之際士人的一種言論的分析. *Zhongguo wenhua* 中國文化, no. 2 (2009): 114–31.

Zheng Lihua 鄭利華. *Qian hou qizi yanjiu* 前後七子研究. Shanghai: Shanghai guji chubanshe, 2015.

——. "Wang Shizhen yu Mingdai qizi pai shixue de tiaoxie yu bianxiang" 王世貞與明代七子派詩學的調協與變向. *Wenxue yichan* 文學遺產, no. 6 (2016): 90–102.

Zheng Qiao 鄭樵. *Tong zhi* 通志. Taipei: Shangwu yinshu guan, 1987.

Zhengtong daozang 正統道藏, comp. Zhang Yichu 張宇初, Shao Yizheng 邵以正, and Zheng Guoxiang 張國祥. 512 vols. Taipei: Xin wenfeng, 1985. Facsimile reproduction of the Shanghai Hanfenlou ed.

Zhong Rong 鍾嶸. *Zhong Rong Shipin jianzheng gao* 鍾嶸詩品箋證稿. Annot. Wang Shumin 王叔岷. Taipei: Zhongyan yuan Zhongguo wenzhe yanjiu suo, 1991.

Zhongguo gudai chaxue quanshu 中國古代茶學全書, comp. Yang Dongfu 楊東甫. Guilin: Guangxi shifan daxue chubanshe, 2011.

Zhongguo shuhua quanshu (zhen cang ben) 中國書畫全書, ed. Lu Fusheng 盧輔聖, Cui Erping 崔爾平, and Jiang Hong 江宏. 14 vols. Shanghai: Shanghai shuhua chubanshe, 1993–2000.

Zhou Gaoqi 周高起. *Dongshan jiecha xi* 洞山岕茶系. In *Zhongguo gudai chaxue quanshu*.

Zhou Hui 周暉. *Jinling suoshi* 金陵瑣事. Nanjing: Nanjing chubanshe, 2007.

Zhou Lianggong 周亮工. *Duhua lu* 讀畫錄. In *Zhongguo shuhua quanshu*, vol. 8.

Zhou Mi 周密. *Yunyan guoyan lu* 雲煙過眼錄. In *Dongtian qinglu (wai wu zhong)*.

Zhouli zhushu 周禮注疏. With commentary by Zheng Xuan 鄭玄 and subcommentary by Jia Gongyan 賈公彥. In *Chongkan Songben Shisan jing zhushu fu jiaokan ji*.

Zhouyi zhushu 周易注疏. With commentaries by Wang Bi 王弼 and Han Kangbo 韓康伯 and subcommentary by Kong Yingda 孔穎達. In *Chongkan Songben Shisan jing zhushu fu jiaokan ji*.

Zhu Guozhen 朱國禎. *Yongchuang xiaopin* 湧幢小品. 2 vols. Beijing: Zhonghua shuju, 1959.

Zhu Jianxin 朱劍心, ed. *Wan Ming xiaopin wen xuan* 晚明小品文選. 4 vols. Shanghai: Shangwu yinshu guan, 1937.

Zhu Suchen 朱素臣. *Qinlou yue* 秦樓月. In *Congshu jicheng xubian*, *jibu*, no. 163. Shanghai: Shanghai shudian, 1994.

Zhu Xi 朱熹. *Jin si lu* 近思錄. Hong Kong: Tianyuan shuwu, 1987.

——. *Zhuzi Wengong chuandao jingshi yanxing lu* 朱子文公傳道經世言行錄. In *Siku quanshu cunmu congshu, zhuanji lei* 傳記類, *shi bu* 史部, vol. 87.

Zhu Yixuan 朱一玄, ed. *Jin Ping Mei ziliao huibian* 金瓶梅資料匯編. Tianjin: Nankai daxue chubanshe, 2012.

Zhu Yizun 朱彝尊. *Pushu ting quan ji* 曝書亭全集, ed. Wang Limin 王利民 et al. Changchun: Jilin wenshi chubanshe, 2009.

Zhuangzi jiaoquan 莊子校詮, annot. Wang Shumin 王叔岷. 3 vols. Taipei: Zhongyang yanjiu yuan lishi yuyan yanjiusuo, 1988.

Zhuangzi jishi 莊子集釋, comp. Guo Qingfan 郭慶藩, ed. Wang Xiaoyu 王孝魚. 4 vols. Beijing: Zhonghua shuju, 1961.

Zhuangzi zuanjian 莊子纂箋, comp. Qian Mu 錢穆. Taipei: Dongda tushu gongsi, 1985.

Zhuzi yulei 朱子語類, comp. Li Jingde 黎靖德, ed. Wang Xingxian 王星賢. Beijing: Zhonghua shuju, 1986.

Zuo Tradition/Zuozhuan: Commentary on the "Spring and Autumn Annals," trans. and annot. Stephen Durrant, Wai-yee Li, and David Schaberg. 3 vols. Seattle: University of Washington Press, 2016.

Index

aesthetic contemplation, 113–14
aficionado, 116, 126, 305n138
agency, 36; and commodification, 206; and discourses on things, 8, 14, 20, 22; loss of, 54; political, 143; of servants, 190–91
antiques, 1–5, 34–35, 104, 124, 159–65, 170, 183
artisans, 101–2, 106–7, 124, 170; and literati, 182; perspectives of, 177
artworks, 162, 246–47, appreciation for, 160, 165, 247, 307n165; attribution of, 160, 167; authenticity of, 161–62, 174, 176; in a boat, 26, 313n77; loss of, 212; market of, 162, 246; prices of, 123
authenticity: and aesthetic appeal; 6, of aesthetic objects and artworks, 10, 12, 158–59, 161–62, 164, 174, 176; debates of, 163–64; judgment of, 9, 12, 161–62, 166; and genuineness or sincerity, 9, 158; stamp of, 172; test of, 169; and value, 16, 158, 161, 168; of Xuande censer, 255

Ban Gu, 61
Bao Zhao, 94
branding, 91, 107, 124, 173, 207, 297n31, 304n120
bronze vessels, 83, 98, 220, 254; imitation antique, 170; mid-Ming, 104; Shang-Zhou, 30–31
Burnt Groove Pipa, 257, 266–69, 275, 278–79

calligraphy, 26, 30, 32–33, 99–100, 108–9, 171, 257–59, 262–63, 265, 275
Cao Xueqin, 62–63, 145, 150; see also *Honglou meng*
Cao Zhao, 98–99
Cao Zhi, 94
Chen Jiru, 92, 102, 106, 119, 162, 173, 191, 194–95, as character in *Ideal Matches*, 197–98, 200–1, 205
Chen Que, 220–21; "The Account of the Dragon Staff" (Longzhang ji), 220; "Inscription on the Dragon Staff" (Longzhang ming), 221
Chen Susu, 239

Chen Weisong, 230, 236–38; to the tune "Manting fang," "On the Xuande Porcelain Cosmetic Box, Painted in Cobalt Blue" (Manting fang yong Xuande yao qinghua zhifen xiang), 237–39
Chen Yidian, 101
Chen Zhenhui, 228–30, 231–32, 279; *Miscellaneous Accountrements for the Autumn Garden* (*Qiuyuan zapei*), 228–32
Cheng Dayue, 102
Cheng Hao, 22, 28–29
Cheng Jibai, 2–3
Cheng Kezhong, 177, 183, 208; "Tang Biaobei," 177–81
Cheng Yi, 28–29
Chongzhen emperor, 233–35, 262, 279; calligraphy of, 264, 322n43
Classic of Changes (*Yijing*), 14, 29
Classic of Poetry (*Shijing*), 29, 93, 225
collecting, 4, 30; art, 33; antiques, 35; culture of, 276; Dingware, 217; Mao Xiang and, 279; memories, 277; and misrule, 127; Shen Defu and, 161; and sociocultural space, 248–49; Sun Chengze and, 246
collector, 1, 3–4, 11, 32, 46, 160, 216; Emperor Huizong as, 27; Gao Shiqi as, 108; Gu Ruhe as, 165; Huan Xuan as, 26; Huizhou, 46, 100; Jia Sidao as, 25; late Ming, 259; Li Houzhu as, 266; Mi Fu as, 33; rapacious, 139, 183; the obsessive, 3; as purveyor of memories, 212; Sun Chengze as, 171, 244–48; Tang Hou as, 99; undiscerning, 160; Xiang Yuanbian as, 101, 108, 163, 214
commodification, 50, 206
commodity, 9, 108
connoisseur, 116, 138, 174, 177, 212; as antagonist, 183; Chen Jiru as, 162; the demotic, 122; Emperor Huizong as, 27; the discerning, 159–60; the ideal, 170; the fake, 100, 129, 143; Jia Sidao as, 25; as hero, 165; the perfidious, 174; suspicion of, 24; the true, 34, 37; the vulgar, 9, 117, 126–36; Wang Zhideng as, 162
connoisseurship, 2–4, 10–11, 25, 41, 83, 85, 89, 91–92, 140, 247, 258, 279; of Chen Jiru, 102; and the contradiction between service and withdrawal, 249; and corruption and deception, 182; discourse of, 174, 208, 259; in early Qing, 246; of the ears, 159; as equalizing force, 162; and excessive devotion, 39; and homosexual romance, 137–43; and late Ming sensibility, 212; literature of, 9, 25, 34, 83, 96–98, 101, 106–7, 114, 120, 123, 165–66, 213, 273; and loyalism, 295; meanings of, 116; and misrule, 4, 127; Mi Fu's definition, 116; and moral failure, 143; moral significance of, 34–36; of tea, 41; pleasures of, 170, 214, 254; and psychological escape, 216; and social consensus, 91; as social practice, 10; socioeconomic contexts of, 89, 160, 245–49, 254; true, 119; of water, 83–92; and withdrawal from politics, 248–49; of Xiang Xuanbian, 101; of the zither, 36
courtesans, 52, 91, 93, 136, 161, 191, 195–96, 205–7; *see also* Wang Yuesheng, Lin Tiansu, Yang Yunyou, Wang Wei, Chen Susu
cricket fights: and Jia Sidao, 25, and the Xuande emperor (Emperor Xuan of Ming), 25, 239–45
cricket pan, 240, 244–45, 279
cultural continuity, 265–66, 276, 279

delusion, 8, 78–79, 155, 245
desire, 60–61, 77, 94; for acquisition, 160, carnal, 67, 70–71; common, 93–94; contradictions of, 71, 196; inchoate, 73; and illusion, 66, 209; ineffability and pathos of, 70–71; and inner

354 *Index*

vacuity, 52; insinuations of, 195; material, 49; mediator of, 196; mimetic, 71; multiple dimensions of, 70; for things, 53, 61; objects of, 47, 56, 125, 143, 193, 202, 259, 269; renouncing, 210–11; triangular, 57; vagaries of, 128
detachment, 33–34, 119–20, 248, 251, in *An Offering of Snow*, 173, 186; contemplative, 133; Buddhist, 153; Daoist, 82, 243; plum tree as symbol of, 108
Ding Yaokang, 208
Dingware, 1–4, 170, 216–20, 230
Dong Qichang, 2–3, 100, 102, 114, 162–63, 167–68, 171–73, 205, 317n128; and the 1616 riots, 196; and authorized delegates, 173; as character in *Ideal Matches*, 191, 197–99, 200–1, 203, 207; and the discourse of imitation, 171; forgeries of his works, 168–69, 205; and Ni Zan, 105; *Thirteen Points About Antiques and Objets d'art* (*Gudong shisan shuo*), 34; and the Southern School, 105, 302n97; and Yang Yunyou, 193–96
Doupeng xianhua (*Stories Under the Bean Arbor*), 126
Du Fu, 88, 234, 267
Du Jiuru, 217, 219
Du Jun, 253, 255
Du Mu, 238–39
Du Shengzhi, 217
dynastic transition, 228, 230, 244–46, 249, 251–52, 256–57, 265; Ming-Qing, 5–7, 11, 185, 208, 212, 214, 220, 229, 233, 254, 276, 280; Southern Tang to Song, 11, 256

early Qing, 5, 120, 246; literature of remembrance, 11–12, 267, 277; accounts of the fate of things, 212–13; theme of exile, 235
eccentricity, 38

economic transactions, 59, 107, 137, 205–6
elegance, 7, 9, 83, 92, 100, 139, 143, 145–46, 148, 156–57; and abstraction, 104–5; as aesthetic category, 94–95; classical, 94–96, contradictions of, 144; defying norms, 103; demotic, 120; and economic realities, 157; equivocal paean to, 152; formulations of, 96; literati standards of, 151; moral and political associations of, 94; normative, 93, 96, 102, 107, 120, 136–37, 208; personal brand of, 89, 144; and poverty, 107; in *qin* (zither) music, 95–96; and the quotidian, 98; redefining, 143; self-conscious, 110, 120, 127; and social consensus, 102–3, 144, 146; vulgarized, 133–34; in vulgarity, 139
empathy, 8, 24, 40, 47, 67, 77–78, 80, 192, 204, 251, 253
Emperor Huizong of Song, 4, 27, 31, 133
Emperor Wu of Liang, 26
Emperor Yang of Sui, 26
Emperor Yuan of Liang, 26

fake, 9–10, 207–9; and characterization, 154–55; distinction between the real and the, 9–10, 158–60, 166–70, 174, 199–200, 245, 252–53; Dingware, 217–19; Dong Qichang works, 173; *Going Up the River at Qingming Fesetival*, 176–77; the value of the, 164, 218; Wen Zhengming works, 172; Xuande vessels, 252–53
fallen blossoms, 64–68, 71–72
Fan Yulan, 46
Fang Gongqian, 249–50, 251, 255; "Seeing the Xuande Censer Again, Three Poems" (Zaijian Xuande lu san shou), 250–51
Fang Wen, 188
Fang Yizhi, 229
Fang Yulu, 102

Index 355

Fang Zhongtong, 235
Fang Ziqian, 42
fans: anomalous, 106; as elegant things, 107; folding, 232; tearing, 75–76
fashion, 103–7
fasting of the mind, 15, 21
Fei Yuanlu, 35; *Unworldly Routine of the Morning Pickings House* (*Zhaocai guan qingke*), 35–36
Feng Menglong, 38; *Jingshi tongyan*, 86–87, 91; *Past and Present Aid to Conversation* (*Gujin tan'gai*), 87–88
flowers, burying, 68–69, 153; comparisons with women, 44; passion for, 37, 45; as refined thing, 137–38
forgery, 10, 162, 164, 168, 174–75, 253; authorized, 173; in *Ideal Matches*, 197, 199, 200–201; of Xuande censers, 253
fragrant *yuan* citron, 157, 230
friendship, 82; and connoisseurship, 89–91, 248, 251; and homosexual romance, 141–42; between literati and artisans, 170; between literati and courtesans, 161, 193, 195, 205; and social boundaries, 89, 91–92; with objects, 45, 221
fu, 61–62

Gao Lian, 97–99, 110, 111–13, 116, 170, 250; *Eight Treatises on the Art of Living* (*Zunsheng bajian*), 97–99, 110–11, 121, 250
Gao Shiqi, 108
garden, 209; Garden of the Arts (*Yipu*), 235; Genyue Garden, 27; Grand View Garden, 64, 66–68, 143–57, 209–10; and illusions, 209–10; Painted-in-Water Garden, 256, 279; and paintings, 114–15; Yushan, 279–80
Ge Hong, 38, 243
genuineness: of a person, 9–10, 39, 103, 120, 158; of artworks, 161; of character, 253; *see also* authenticity

Gong Chun, 107
Gu Gongxie, 177
Gu Kaizhi, 171
Gu Ruhe, 165
Gu Tinglin, 1, 3
Gu Yanwu, 235
Guan Tong, 104–5

Han Siwei, 215
He Liangjun, 99, 116
He Rixian, 215
Hongguang: court, 208, 214, 215, 219, 270, 279; reign, 256; *see also* Zhu Yousong
Honglou meng, 7–12, 61–80, 143–57, 209–11, 277, 280–81, *see also* Cao Xueqin
Hou Fangyu, 228–32
Hu Yinglin, 116
Hua Shu, 38
Huaisu, 164
Huan Xuan, 25–26, 32
Huang Biao, 171–72, 176
Huang Cheng, 102
Huang Gongwang, 166, 302n96
Huang Jingxing, 171
Huang Jishui, 172
Huang Tingjian, 97
Huang Yuanjie, 191–92, 206, 317n132
Huang Zhengbin, 215, 218–19
Huang Zongxi, 106
Huizhou, 100, 103–4, 163; collector, 46, 292n114; ink makers, 106; merchants, 100, 102, 105, 160, 168–69; and regional rivalry, 102, 163

illusion, 112, 155–56; and aesthetic pleasure, 121, 209–11; and desire, 70–71; of depth and receding distance, 156; dialectics of reality and, 11, 64, 121, 156, 209–10; mediation and, 65–66
imitation, 170–71
impermanence, 72, 214

indulgence, 86, 266–67; self-indulgence, 7, 11; sensual, 24, 134, 137, 237–38
ink stick, 106, 226–27
inkstone, 33, 42, 44, 214, 227
innovation, 121
inscriptions: rubbings of, 30; by Chen Que, 221–22; by Wang Fuzhi, 226–28; by Xu Wei, 42–43
interiority, 8, 14–5, 20
intuitive reasoning, 167–68

jade: Baoyu's 63, 74, 211; seal of mandate, 214; box, 215; ram-shaped paper weight, 233–35, 279
jade cup: in *An Offering of Snow*, 10, 183–90; in *Honglou meng*, 152–53; with proper names, 4–5; in "Tang Biaobei," 178–82; Yutian, 257–62, 269, 274–75, 278
Ji Kang, 32–34, 39–41, 94, 231, 291, 322
Ji Yuyong, 103, 215
Jia Sidao, 25, 240
Jiang Cai, 233–36, 239; "The Jade Ram on My Desk," 233–36
Jiang Gai, 233–34, 236, 239
Jiang Qing, 214–15, 219
Jiang Shaoshu, 101, 108, 171–72, 213–16, 219, 319n5; *Notes from Resonant Rock Studio* (*Yunshi zhai bitan*), 101, 213–20
Jiang Shijie, 236, 239
Jiao Xun, 185
Jin Junming, 45; four short accounts on orchids, 45–46
Jin Ping Mei, 8–9, 47–61, 126–36, 207–8, 281
Jin Shengtan, 65–66
Jin Yunpeng, 168
Jing Hao, 104, 105, 246–47
Ju Jie, 172
judgment, 159–66, 206; aesthetic, 10, 38, 99, 104, 116, 119, 145, 160, 162–65, 175, 204, 208, 246, 262; consensus in, 85; historical, 238, 245; moral, 10, 38, 86, 174, 236; scenes of, 200

King Wu of Zhou, 24

Laozi, 14–15, 32, 82, 95, 285n6
late Ming, 48; art market, 3; commercial boom, 7; discourse on elegance, 110–11; discourse on objects, 83–85; discourse on obsessions, 37–47; early Qing reflections on the, 205, 212, 228, 264, 276, 280; literati merchants, 100–101; refinements, 279; sensibility, 7, 8, 10–11, 191, 212, 277, 280
Li Binzhai, 215
Li Deyu, 86–88, 297n23
Li Duanyuan, 84–85
Li Gonglin, 30, 99
Li Houzhu, 27, 46; as character in *Spring in Moling*, 257–58, 261–69, 275, 278
Li Jiqing, 84
Li Qing, 274
Li Qingzhao, 213
Li Rihua, 83, 87–88, 92, 103, 106, 108, 166, 170, 174; "Contract on Transporting Spring Water from the Pine Rain Studio" (*Songyu zhai yun quan yue*), 87–89
Li Sixun, 104, 167
Li Weizhen, 42; "Postscript to Poems from Half-Stone Studio" (*Banshi zhai shi ba*), 42
Li Weizhu, 46
Li Yu, 10, 106, 120–26, 137–39, 140–43, 191, 196–9, 206–9, 280; "House of Elegant Ensemble" (*Cuiya lou*), 9, 137–43; *Ideal Matches* (*Yi zhong yuan*), 10, 191–207, 209, 280, 317n132; *Leisure Notes* (*Xianqing ouji*), 120–26
Li Yù, 10, 183, 185–90; *An Offering of Snow* (*Yipeng xue*), 10, 183–91, 314n89, 314n90
Li Zhi, 207
Liji, 18, 20, 21, 24; "Record of Music" (*Yueji*), 18, 24, 28; "Great Learning" (*Daxue*), 21; "Doctrine of the Mean" (*Zhongyong*), 21–22
liminality, 119, 139

Lin Bu, 108
Lin Hong, 98
Lin Tiansu, 191, 193–96, 317n136; as charcter in *Ideal Matches*, 197–207
literary creation, 18–19
literati, 3; and artisans, 106–7; and courtesans, 195–96, 205–6; identity, 91–92; and merchants, 100–2, 139, 163; painting, 105, 168, 176, 193; and performers, 103; pretensions, 208; self-definition, 92, 119; as trendsetters, 105
literati culture, 83, 100, 103, 127, 132, 136, 146, 160, 246, 264
Liu Songnian, 165
Liu Tong, 250, 252
Liu Xi, 93; *Shiming (Elucidation of Names)*, 93–94
Liu Xie, 94, 96; *Literary Mind and the Carvings of Dragons (Wenxin diaolong)*, 18–19, 94, 96
Lord Huan of Qi, 24
loss, 11, 12, 46, 213–14, 220, 230, 234, 254, 276, 279
love, in *Honglou meng*, 66–80; in *Ideal Matches*, 191, 199, 209; in *Spring in Moling*, 256, 259–60, 263, 265
love tokens, 55, 57, 72–74, 239
loyalism, 228, 233, 239, 257, 279
loyalty: in master-servant relationship, 188–90; to the Ming, 234, 236, 253; to the Southern Tang, 274
Lü Dalin, 31
Lu Ji, 18, 62, 275; "Poetic Exposition on Literature" (Wen fu), 18
Lu Shaoheng, 43, 113
Lu Shusheng, 42
Lu Wan, 175
Lu You, 273–74
Lu Yu, 39, 41, 83–84, 86, 88; *Classic of Tea (Cha jing)*, 41

Mao Jin, 274
Mao Qiling, 236

Mao Xiang, 229, 249–55, 279, "The Song of the Xuande Bronze Censer" (Xuande lu ge), 251–54; "Notes on 'The Song of the Xuande Bronze Censer'" (Xuan tonglu ge zhu), 252–53
Mao Xianshu, 274
market, 6, 10, 108, 127, 137, 160–65; demands, 104–5; forces, 165, 173; value, 8, 48–49, 144, 167, 205
marketplace, 61, 108, 123, 133, 145, 150, 233, 237–38, 246–47
memory, 6, 12, 212, 242, 267, 269, 276; historical, 11, 239, 245, 254–55, 256, 265, 273, 278; personal, 12, 235, 254
Mengzi, 20, 23
merchants, 99–101, 105, 138, 168–69
Mi Fu, 33, 38–41, 45, 97–99, 105, 108–9, 114, 116, 160, 290–91, 301, 304–5, 309–15, 342
Min Qiji, 65–66
Min Wenshui, 89–91
mirror: in *Honglou meng*, 63–64, 156, 210; in *Spring in Moling* (Yiguan Mirror), 257–61
moral authority, 93, 143, 159
moral meaning, 8, 11, 36, 61
moralization, 10, 174, 208, 210, 281
music, 16, 18, 24, 28–29, 43, 93–95, 110, 226, 230–31; in *Spring in Moling*, 262–63, 266–67; *see also* zither

Ni Zan, 104–5
nostalgia, 91, 239, 257, 267

objects: anthropomorphized, 56, 44–45, 62, 221, 242, 252, 269; Ming imperial, 233, 237; objets d'art, 34, 258, 273
objectification, 54–5, 61, 140, 142, 203
obsession, 9, 10, 25, 32, 36–47, 54, 143, 152–53, 175, 217, 239, 243, 259, 279
Ouyang Xiu, 30–2, 44, 84–85, 87, 98; "Ling Stream Rock" (Ling xi shi ji),

31–32; "Account of the Water from Great Brightness Temple" (Daming shui ji), 84, "Account of the Water from Floating Raft Mountain" (Fucha shan shui ji), 84–85
ownership, 5, 6, 10, 11, 33, 47, 118, 213, 215–16, 258, 276

paintings, 26, 32, 99, 108–9, 114, 171, 247; literati, 105, 168, 176, 193; viewing, 103; the Wu School, 104
Pan Zhiheng, 38
paradox, 47, 55, 83, 88, 107, 120, 137, 156, 173, 198, 203, 206, 211, 280–81; of humanizing things, 63; of *Jin Ping Mei*, 61; of obsession, 39; of self-conscious elegance, 127; of self-observation, 113–14; in *Zhuangzi*, 15, 36
pleasure, 6, 8, 24–32, 35–36, 76, 87–89, 96, 103, 121–22, 124–25, 143; aesthetic, 30, 111, 143, 209–10, 279–80
political accommodation, 273–74
political allegory, 22
political meaning: of early Qing writings on things, 212, 221, 223, 229, 265, 275; of the jade cup, 183; of ritual vessels, 31; of water connoisseurship, 85
portraits, 58–59
pottery: Chenghua, 89, 104, 106, 151, 219, 230, 307n177; Song, 104; Xuande, 89, 104, 106, 219, 230, 236–40
price, 49, 92, 104–5, 107–9, 123–24, 162–63, 168
Pu Songling, 47; *Liaozhai zhiyi*, 47
Pu Zhongqian, 106

Qi Biaojia, 183, 279
Qian Gu, 172
Qian Qianyi, 36, 46, 100, 106, 173, 292n115; "Postscript to Dong Qichang's Letter to Feng Mengzhen" (Ba Dong Xuanzai yu Feng Kaizhi chidu), 100

Qian Yong, 107
Qiu Tan, 85–86

recluse, 88, 118, 123, 147, 186, 248–49; social, 119, 160–63, 191, 208
reclusion, 9, 85–87, 120, 223, 229, 272, 275
Red Inkstone, 63, 67–68, 73, 77
regional rivalry, 102, 161–63
remembrance, 263, 266, 278
roaming, 17–18, 30
rock: at Amber Creek, 232; The Ling Stream Rock, 31–32; Mi Fu's obsession with, 38–39, 41; Nine Blossoms in a Gourd, 33–34; Qiu Pool Rock, 33
romance, 257; homosexual, 140, 141

seal of mandate, 214
self-consciousness, 255, 276; in elegance, 9, 110, 113, 116, 119–20; in mental attitudes, 36, 39; and the view from below, 126; and theatricality, 205
self-cultivation, 21–22, 27–30, 34, 111
self-observation, 41, 68, 112–16, 276
sensibility, 38, 76, 119, 124–25, 148–49, 259; aristocracy of, 91, 116, 118; late Ming, 7, 10, 191, 205, 212, 277; and obsession, 38, 40
Shangshu (*Documents*), 18, 24, 43
Shao Yong, 22
Shen Chunze, 117–18
Shen Defu, 100, 102, 104–7, 116, 161–68, 175, 208, 239; *Gleanings from the Wanli Reign* (*Wanli yehuo bian*), 161
Shen Gua, 159
Shen Zhou, 104–5, 109, 172, 302n95
Shi Chong, 45
Shi Dabin, 106
Shishuo xinyu (*New Accounts of Tales of the World*), 38, 40, 81, 83, 310n24
Shu Min, 35
Sikong Tu, 95; *Twenty-four Categories of Poetic Styles* (*Ershisi shipin*), 95
Sima Qian, 94

Index 359

Sima Xiangru, 61
Su Shi, 32–34, 44, 97, 105, 168, 213–14, 289n78; "Account of the Hall of Treasured Paintings" (Baohui tang ji), 32–34, 41, 213–14
Sun Chengze, 171, 244, 246–48
Sun Kuang, 163–64
Sun Xiaowei, 259
Sun Zhen, 216
Suzhou: dealers, 126; forgery, 172; literati, 101–2, 161; trend setting, 106, 163
symbolism, 11, 236; private, 74–75, 77, 220, 229, 232; public, 220, 229, 232

Tang Biaobei, 174–77, 182–83; as character in *An Offering of Snow* (also called Tang Qin), 183–91; as character in "Tang Biaobei," 177–81
Tang Hezheng, 216
Tang Hou, 98–99, 103
Tang Junyu, 217
Tang Xianzu, 70; *The Peony Pavilion* (*Mudan ting*), 70–72, 259, 263
Tang Yin, 87, 101, 105, 172
Tang Zhiqi, 102, 109
Tao Yuanming, 41, 249, 260, 290, 308, 317, 329, 346
taste, 6, 9, 83, 96–97, 99, 104–5, 118
tea: and the discourse on water, 85; Luojie, 89; Jie tea behind the temple, 229, 273; competition, 91
the Way, 34–35, 107
theatricality, 205
things, 7, 285n7, 285n10; affective, 64, 72, 125; anomalous, 106; anthropomorphized, 43–45; being moved by, 28–29; dangers of, 23, 24; discourses on, 6–7, 14, 80, 212, 281; exotic, 24, 63; investigation of, 21–23, 35, 286n33; myriad, 8, 13–15, 21, 285n13; people and, 14, 20, 28; people as, 49; recalcitrant, 55, 61; references to, 8, 19; superfluous, 8, 81–82, 117–18;

taking pleasure in, 8; transformation of, 17, 28
Tian Yiheng, 44
Tu Long, 97, 99; *Remaining Concerns of the Recluse* (*Kaopan yushi*), 97, 98, 99, 110, 115

value, 1, 3, 85, 104, 108–9, 158, 202; aesthetic, 6–7, 124, 127, 280; market, 8, 48–49, 144, 167
Verses of Chu (*Chuci*), 79, 223, 229
vessels, 5–6, 30–31, 87, 104–6, 152–55, 184, 216–17, 219, 273, 327n115
vulgarity, 9, 92, 95, 126, 131, 145–46, 150, 156

Wang Ao, 101
Wang Chen, 81, 82
Wang Daokun, 101
Wang Fuzhi, 221–28; "Encomia on Miscellaneous Things" (Zawu zan), 221–26; inscriptions on eleven things, 226–28
Wang Gong, 81–82
Wang Guxiang, 109
Wang Ji, 40
Wang Ranming (Wang Ruqian), 101, 192–96, 206; "Ascending the Convent of Karmic Joy" (Deng Suixi An), 192–93; "Account of a Dream by the Secluded Window" (Youchuang jimeng), 194
Wang Shifu, 65; *The Western Wing* (*Xixiang ji*), 64–65, 69–72
Wang Shimao, 163, 170
Wang Shixing, 102, 106
Wang Shizhen, 46, 94, 101–2, 104, 163–64, 170–72, 176, 259
Wang Shu, 174–82
Wang Siren, 115
Wang Wei (Tang poet and painter), 167–68
Wang Wei (Ming courtesan), 195
Wang Xiyuan, 109, 259
Wang Xizhi, 134, 159, 165, 172, 200, 255, 257–58, 263

Wang Yangming, 22–23
Wang Yong, 216
Wang Yuesheng, 91
Wang Yueshi, 217–19
Wang Zhenqi, 175
Wang Zhideng, 119, 161–63
Wang Zuo, 99
water, 83; Central Cold Spring, 86–87; Floating Raft Mountain, 84–85; Hui Mountain Spring, 85–87, 90; Nanling, 84; post stations, 87; Zhongling River, 86
Water Margin (*Shuihu zhuan*), 50–51
Wei Zhongxian, 2–3, 189
Wen Jia, 172
Wen Peng, 101, 172
Wen Zhengming, 105, 122, 165, 170, 172
Wen Zhenheng, 97–99, 102–3, 109, 115, 117–18; *Superfluous Things* (*Zhangwu zhi*), 97–99, 109, 115, 117
Wen Zhenmeng, 5, 230–31, 236
Wu Congxian, 113
Wu Daozi, 104
Wu Kuan, 101, 161
Wu Qizhen, 103
Wu Weiye, 11, 106, 240–43, 245, 248, 256, 263–67, 271, 274–75; "The Song of the Valley of Retreat" (Tuigu ge), 249; "The Song of the Xuande Emperor's Gold Inlaid Lacquer Cricket Pan" (Xuanzong yuyong qiangjin xishuai pen ge), 240–45; *Spring in Moling* (*Moling chun*), 11, 256–76, 278
Wu Yingji, 230
Wu Zhaoqian, 235

Xia Wenyan, 98
Xiang Yuanbian, 2–3, 101, 108, 163, 214, 299n51, 303n111
Xie An, 134
Xie Liangzuo, 28
Xie Zhaozhi, 116
Xu Guangqi, 96
Xu Kai, 272, 274

Xu Shangying, 95; *Moods of the Zither by Streams and Mountains* (*Xi shan qin kuang*), 95
Xu Shen, 13, 38
Xu Shi; historical, 271; as character in *Spring in Moling*, 256–76
Xu Shilang, 272–73
Xu Shupi, 177
Xu Wei, 42–43; "Inscription on the Broken Pear-Shaped Vase Chime Stone, with Preface" (Podan qing ming bing xu), 42–43
Xu Xuan, 265, 273
Xu Xuemo, 174
Xu Youzhen, 35
Xuande censer, 249–55, 279
Xuande emperor (Emperor Xuan of Ming), 239–40, 242–43, 245
Xunzi, 13, 19–21, 23–24, 93, 285n10, 286n28

Yan Liben, 162
Yan Shifan, 177–81, 183–85
Yan Song, 174–76
Yan Tiaoyu, 36
Yang Ming, 102
Yang Xiong, 94; *Model Sayings* (*Fayan*), 94
Yang Yunyou, 191–93, 195–96; as character in *Ideal Matches*, 197–207
Yao Yuanzhi, 101
Yiya, 24, 86, 287n44
Yu Huai, 120, 236
Yu Yizheng, 250
Yuan Haowen, 213
Yuan Hongdao, 37–41, 44, 85–86, 106–7, 113–14, 118–19, 291, 297, 307, 313, 350; *History of the Vase* (*Ping shi*), 39, 44; *Rules on Drinking* (*Shangzheng*), 113
Yuan Zhen, 65
Yuan Zhongdao, 86
Yushan, 279–80

Zhai Qinian, 30
Zhan Jingfeng, 101–2, 163, 165–66, 174

Index 361

Zhang Chao, 39, 253, 291, 322, 328, 351; Secret Dream Shadows (You meng ying), 39
Zhang Chou, 116, 158
Zhang Dafu, 85, 87, 91
Zhang Dai, 39, 46, 89–93, 102–3, 106, 115–16, 277, 283, 287, 291, 293, 297–98, 302–3, 305, 307, 314, 319–20, 323, 331–32, 339, 341, 351; Dream Memories of Tao'an (Tao'an mengyi), 89, 91, 115–16, 277
Zhang Fengyi, 161
Zhang Nanyuan, 106
Zhang Taijie, 168
Zhang Yanyuan, 25, 97, 99, 108, 213; Famous Paintings Through the Ages (Lidai minghua ji), 25, 98, 99, 213
Zhang Yingwen, 97, 106, 109, 116
Zhang Youxin, 83–84, 88; "An Account of Boiling Water for Tea" (Jian chashui ji), 83–84
Zhang Zai, 22
Zhang Zeduan, 174, 176; Going up the River at Qingming Festival (Qingming shanghe tu), 174, 176, 177, 183
Zhang Zhupo, 129–30
Zhao Mengfu, 46, 170–71, 240
Zhao Qian, 170
Zhao Xigu, 97, 99, 107, 110; Pure Rewards of the Cavern Heaven (Dongtian qinglu), 97–99
Zhao Zuo, 172
Zheng Xuan, 93
Zhong Rong, 18, 94; Classification of Poetry (Shipin), 18, 94
Zhong Yao, 32, 159, 257–58, 263, 290n90
Zhou Chen, 172
Zhou Danquan, 170, 216–17, 219
Zhou Lianggong, 246, 274
Zhou Mi, 213
Zhou Youxin, 89–90
Zhou Zaijun, 274
Zhu Changfang (Prince of Lu), 219–20
Zhu Dashao, 4
Zhu Guozhen, 164
Zhu Jingxun, 163
Zhu Lang, 172
Zhu Suchen, 239
Zhu Xi, 21–22, 29, 149
Zhu Xiaohai, 170
Zhu Yousong (Prince of Fu, Hongguang emperor), 218, 219; see also Hongguang
Zhu Yunming, 105
Zhuangzi, 13, 15–21, 23, 28, 36, 95, 107, 121, 243
zither, 36, 43, 95–98, 107, 110, 114, 131–32, 136, 220, 231
Zou Zhilin, 254
Zuixing shi (Sobering Stone), 126–27
Zuo Si, 61
Zuozhuan (Zuo Tradition), 14, 18, 25

GPSR Authorized Representative: Easy Access System Europe, Mustamäe tee
50, 10621 Tallinn, Estonia, gpsr.requests@easproject.com

www.ingramcontent.com/pod-product-compliance
Lightning Source LLC
Chambersburg PA
CBHW022026290426
44109CB00014B/769